Of Powers

and Their Politics

PRENTICE-HALL CONTEMPORARY POLITICAL THEORY SERIES

David Easton, *Editor*

ARTHUR LEE BURNS

Of Powers and Their Politics: A Critique of Theoretical Approaches

PRENTICE-HALL, INC., ENGLEWOOD CLIFFS, N.J.

PRENTICE-HALL INTERNATIONAL, INC., *London*
PRENTICE-HALL OF AUSTRALIA, PTY. LTD., *Sydney*
PRENTICE-HALL OF CANADA, LTD., *Toronto*
PRENTICE-HALL OF INDIA PRIVATE LTD., *New Delhi*
PRENTICE-HALL OF JAPAN, INC., *Tokyo*

Library of Congress Catalog Card Number: 69-10414

Printed in the United States of America

Current printing (last digit):
10 9 8 7 6 5 4 3 2 1

In memory of
CRAYTON BURNS
(*May 26, 1898–September 18, 1952*)
a political journalist

Acknowledgments

Parts of Chapters 2, 3, 4, 8, 9, 11 and 12 are adapted, with permission, as follows:

CHAPTER 2, SECTION II, from "International Consequences of Expecting Surprise," *World Politics,* X (July 1958), 512–36.

CHAPTER 3, SECTIONS I THROUGH III, from "International Theory and Historical Explanation," *History and Theory* (The Hague) I, No. 1 (December 1960), 55–74. Copyright © by Wesleyan University.

CHAPTER 4, SECTION I, from "Some Biblical Sources of Concepts in International Theory," *Australian Biblical Review,* XI (December 1963), 24–32.

CHAPTER 8 AND CHAPTER 11, SECTION II, from "Quantitative Approaches to International Politics," in *New Approaches to International Relations,* ed. Morton A. Kaplan (New York: St. Martin's Press, 1968).

CHAPTER 9, PP. 189–99, from "Must Strategy and Conscience be Disjoined?," *World Politics,* XVIII (July 1965), 687–702.

CHAPTER 12, PP. 257–64, from "Prospects for a General Theory of International Relations," *World Politics* XIV (October 1961), 25–46, and simultaneously in *The International System,* eds. K. Knorr and S. Verba (Princeton, N.J.: Princeton University Press, 1961). Copyright © by Princeton University Press.

Preface to Contemporary Political Theory Series

This volume is part of a new series in political science that is devoted to empirically oriented theory. Nothing testifies more eloquently to the growing strength of empirical political theory than the conviction that now, after more than twenty-five hundred years of development, it is for the first time possible to think of building a publication series out of volumes devoted exclusively to the construction of such theory. The series is itself a sign of the times; we hope it will also provide a means for vigorously and creatively reinforcing the present tendencies.

This series will contribute to the development of contemporary political theory in several distinctive ways. First and foremost, our primary objective is to gather together brief but exciting monographs that will explore alternative approaches to empirical theory. Some of these may be concerned with general, overarching theories that seek to bring order and coherence to the whole field of political science. Others may devote themselves to less comprehensive, partial theories that help to integrate selected aspects of political life, intranational, international, and cross-national. Still others may seek to explore the theoretical assumptions of existing empirical research and to systematize and assess their findings in the hope of bringing added clarity to a subfield, enhancing its theoretical relevance, and giving it a new sense of purpose and direction. Although the main emphasis will be on stimulating the production of critical and creative works that deal with the substance of theories in such areas, on occasion it will be appropriate to include volumes that direct their attention to the methodological tasks of theory construction itself.

We expect the series to leave its impact on the development of theory in a second way. It will provide a single medium through which original monographs in empirical or descriptive theory can be assembled. We would hope thereby to stimulate and reinforce the broadest range of experimentation with respect to alternative approaches to theory. Underlying the whole series is the basic premise that only through innovative and courageous efforts in a multitude of divergent and conflicting directions will it be possible for a gradual and meaningful consensus to arise in the course of time with regard to the outlines of a useful general theory or set of partial theories. It is the very essence of the theoretical enterprise that, if and when it seems appropriate, it should feel free to sever itself from the bonds of traditional ways of looking at political life. By providing an established publishing outlet, we would hope to lend encouragement in this direction at a time when it is most needed.

Third, we would hope that the availability in a single series of a growing assemblage of volumes on empirical theory will have a decisive influence on teaching and training in this field. We are in a process of transition in political science toward a more rigorous science and the series may be seen as another small effort to aid the change.

With regard to teaching and training in the function, tasks, and substance of empirical theory, a strong desire to improve the facilities in political science has not been wanting. But a major barrier has blocked the way. We have lacked a sufficient number of serious monographs to provide enough scope and depth to make formal courses in this area feasible as well as desirable. We would expect that in due time this series would offer a core around which courses on empirical theory might be initially developed, or where they already exist, enriched. In themselves such courses would contribute immeasurably to attracting the best minds in each generation of students to the field of theory or in sensitizing them to the actual function of theory in empirical research. By testifying to the challenge that theory presents and to the opportunities for empirical research, the series should, in its long range effect, reinforce empirical theory as an appropriate and adventuresome area for teaching and research.

Preface

Can we form cogent theories of the politics of the Powers? If so, could we test them?

This volume is a critique of theorizing, specifically of quantitative and formal theorizing; it is not a compendious review of the recent literature on international relations. The few theories critically analyzed below were selected not only for their intrinsic merits but also to help expound my outlook and theory; indeed, contributions to my own exposition have been levied from many of them. Many leading theorists pass unmentioned, certainly not from my lacking admiration for their work, but merely because, in the present study, I have not been able to cannibalize them.

Readers will notice on another page that earlier articles and studies, between two and ten years old, account in revised form for rather more than a quarter of the book. Most of these articles have been adapted to its structure and argument during the past fifteen months, in a drastic revision of the whole. I must thank the editor of the series and the publishers for the opportunity, afforded by the composing of this volume, to bring together former themes in a synoptic view of the theory of world politics. It would be invidious to thank by name only some of the many friends and mentors, on three continents, whose writings and conversation have enriched the exposition that follows; one can only hope that they will be not displeased at the traces of their own thought which they find in it.

A. L. B.

The Australian National University, Canberra

Table of Contents

SECTION THREE: THEORY OF DYNAMICS

SECTION FOUR: THEORY OF STATICS

SECTION FIVE: THE HUMANIZING OF POWER POLITICS

Of Powers

and Their Politics

SECTION I

SCOPE AND ASSUMPTIONS

ONE

The Nature of World Politics

Statesmen cannot tell what will or even what may happen. Research can do little to amend ignorance in either form, for it is in large part logically necessitated. Thus, a positive science of world politics or, more generally, of international relations seems impossible.

This very unpredictability, however, entails a universal proposition: that men always have acted and always will act in ignorance of the future. Sometimes they are aware, sometimes unaware of that truth. To many kinds of political action, it has little logical relevance, e.g., to the conduct of an election campaign in an established democracy. A settled institution, such as the holding of elections, is a fiat: internal politics shall go forward only within the following limits, only by the following calendar. External is distinguished from internal politics, firstly, by the scarcity or ineffectiveness of fiats meant to bind its agents jointly; so that, on the whole, action in (external) statecraft must be taken in even darker ignorance than action in internal politics. Furthermore, the conduct of relations between states requires of the statesman a longer temporal perspective than does the management of internal affairs, e.g., party conflict; and this also tends to broaden and deepen the shadow of his ignorance. So world politics is an incalculable process.

Armed force, secondly, pertains much more to external than to internal politics, especially for established polities. That is enough to make statesmanly action momentous; but even short of submission or conquest, such processes as secession and the unification of states usually set in train more internal change than does internal politics itself.

Statesmanly action, then, is often momentous; and, as we have seen, always more or less in the dark. Those in a position to take such action must be in any age much fewer than those taking action in internal politics. For with notable exceptions, they have been recruited from already select groups: internal political leaders, or the military, or the established civil ruling class.

Other vocations sometimes involve the taking of lonely, momentous, incalculable, and representative or responsible decisions: the field officer's, the ship's captain's. But those deal with what confronts them, which in any case are often mainly physical states of affairs. That is rarely the statesman's case—except, for instance, when starting a war or despatching material aid. The issuing of commands is only incidentally a part of statecraft, which is essentially an art of communicating with one's peers, the statesmen of other nations.

The world-political situation usually has some institutional context, but no single institution is peculiar or necessary to it. From the days of the medieval kingdom, the relevant institution was often a royal court; in the nineteenth century, it was often a chancellery; now, in an era of "personal diplomacy," it has been deliberately informalized—even the green baize table seems too official—and has become simply a "meeting." As an epitomy for world-political activity, the word that has suggested itself is "conversation."

"Conversation" may be too inconsequential: a power-balance is at issue in summit conversations; material and social resources are the substance of power; and, by them, physical force can in the last resort take effect. But it rarely does. Indeed, one is often hard put to it to indicate significant physical consequences issuing from many a significant world-political denouement. Consider, by contrast, high finance. A contemporary meeting of financiers is likely to be as little institutionalized as the statesmen's. (To represent either would defeat poet and painter alike.) No check books are produced, no banknotes change hands. But from most financiers' conversations there issue definite changes in the process of production of goods. Now, though that kind and even more momentous kinds of physical consequence sometimes result from summit meetings—and always *might* result—mostly they do not.

Nevertheless, commentators and historians seem compelled to write as though pseudo-physical consequences always followed: "tension," we are told, has "decreased" as a result of the meeting, or it has "built up." I used to be puzzled, as a schoolboy, by historians of eighteenth-century wars who would end their accounts of peace treaties, ". . . and thus the balance of power was restored." What mysterious scales tilted level, what transcendent chandelier burned down to an equipoise? What observations could possibly check the truth of these portentous opinions?

To attempt serious answers to the latter question is to undertake the theory of international politics. If the balance of power has indeed been restored, one expects troops to have been posted back to routine duties, and orders for armaments to have stopped increasing; or, if not necessarily that, then at least one does not expect the contrary. If tension has decreased, one expects the same kind of thing, and that the stockmarket will recover. If tension is building up, one is not surprised that parliament should be called together, or that more letters on the international situation should appear in the papers.

No single one of these signs, however, is entailed in that change in "tension" which it helps to indicate, and which therefore cannot consist in a change of *material* states of affairs. This recognition that the change is not a physical one has misleadingly suggested that "tension" (likewise "stability" of the balance, "increase of power," and such terms of world-political discourse) must refer to *psychological* conditions: states of feeling and so forth. No doubt behavior associated with states of feeling does supervene upon world-political changes—there may well be people who sigh with relief when tension is reported "decreasing," or bite their nails when it is "building up." But political terminology does not connote such feelings or their expressions: its reference is not affective, but cognitive and conative.

Since, then, international "tension" does not refer either to physical or to psychological states, what is the journalist reporting when he says that as a result of the summit meeting, tension has decreased?—given he is not thereby merely reiterating that those who met at the summit declared they had reached an understanding, nor merely predicting that troop movements, armament increases, stock-exchange panics, and so on will soon diminish.

The journalist's report would be substantiated if, for example, he had information that the summit understanding had been taken notice of by the people whose actions might bring about those more-or-less predictable effects. "Changes in tension" thus refer to the communication or, better, to the diffusion of what Kenneth Boulding has called an "image" of the international situation; but not to a merely general dissemination. Diffusion of the new image is relevant to the state of tension only when it is diffusion to men of affairs directing those organizations and institutions which would have been immediately affected by a different—say, a warlike—outcome of the statesmen's select "conversations."

The journalist's "increase" or "decrease" of tension thus properly refers to the sense of the information or impression which issues from the informal political interchanges of world statesmen and passes to the directing echelons of military, economic, and political organizations—primarily, national organizations, though supranational organizations and groups, e.g., the diplomatic corps, are to be included. When, for instance, men of affairs in these directing echelons are on the *qui vive* for information, and fearful of what they are receiving, tension may be said to be increasing.

Sometimes, for example, after the breakdown of an attempt at conciliation, the information itself takes the form of commands to the military and similar directives. But it need not take those forms; it need not be deliberately transmitted by the statesmen; its channels can be the mass media, or private chat, from which men of affairs on the relevant periphery take their cues. And in the last case the information diffused will probably have no single official definition or clear-cut interpretation, so that the various world-outlooks of the persons receiving it may largely determine the nature of the response each makes to it.

The foregoing analysis of world-political terms is intended to illustrate how any thoughtful reader of newspapers could construct a theory (build a model) of the development and transmission of foreign policy—part of the more general theory or model of international relations. He could do so by reflecting upon the kinds of observation he would try to make as a check upon journalists' or historians' assertions about international "tension," "stability," and so forth. Whereas in meditating on the meaning of assertions about tension he would discover his implicit model of the communications infrastructure within the typical Western nation-state, in reflecting on "stability" he would be piecing together his picture of the whole competitive-cooperative system of nation-states. The thought of academic political theorists is not different in kind. Indeed, this volume will occasionally suggest brief and incomplete but direct descriptions of how, in the writer's view, international relations are carried on.

But that is not my principle intention here. In any adequate description of world-political processes, one has to include an account of the several actors' models (or theories or pictures) of the whole: much of the process is inexplicable without reference to these models—their geneses, developments, and contradictions of each other. When their role in the world-political process is understood, the long-debated methodological dilemma—"Are the systems and subsystems, as modeled by theorists, actual and objective features of the historical process of international affairs; or are they merely subjective though convenient devices for characterizing the otherwise unordered flux of objective international events?"—begins to resolve itself. Thus, those whose actions constitute the historical process—statesmen, and their retinues of subordinates and collaborators—themselves are bound to have models or pictures of the political world they are acting in, and to conform their actions to the lineaments of their picture (most obviously, a body of citizenry behaves as a nation only by virtue of each citizen's having the "picture" of his nation and of himself and the others as citizens of it). Most of the leading features are common to the models of the actors in the international process and to those of the commentators upon the process (journalists, historians, theorists)—that is to say, the commentators rarely impose ideas upon the process which were not already in the minds of the actors and embodied in their actions. All of these models, however, are conceptual constructions; they are not perceptions: one does not perceive the system of nation-states just by opening one's eyes. Therefore, each of them can be internally contradictory and incoherent; or false (e.g., in its view of how foreign policy in a particular nation is normally determined); or, most often, shallow, crude, jejune. Political theorists are mainly concerned to test, to refine, and generally to improve upon such models, which invariably have much in common, whether or not set out in technical terms, with popular and traditional views of world affairs. This volume, then, chiefly attempts an analysis and critique of models, particularly certain important examples developed by leading political theorists during the last twenty years. From that critique, the author's own conception of international order should emerge.

It should already have emerged, for example, that I see within the total process of international relations a central and strongly determining process of pure politics: personalized and informal politics carried on by a necessarily small company of public figures. The "conversation" of these personages differs from the free relationships of film stars and stage players in that the statesman's is under constraint. The more obvious of these constraints are institutional: each nation's statesmen fill particular roles within their respective states' internal political institutions, or, in the case of Secretaries-General of the UN and suchlike, of inter- or supranational organizations. There, the man is greatly delimited by the organizational role. The statesman, contrarywise, not only is an official of a particular kind, but in some states there have been vigorous attempts to make him so —e.g., Venice with her Doges, Bolshevik Russia with its delegates to Brest-Litovsk. Such attempts are rarely long persisted in; for there are ranges of nationally useful action open to a freewheeling statesman that are closed to officials and delegates.

In face of the much increased bureaucratization of internal politics and government, and of the multiplication of intergovernmental organizations, to insist upon the informality and personalism of contemporary statecraft has seemed to other political scientists mistaken and even perverse. The emphasis may seem less paradoxical when we take account of the following features of bureaucratization: though it consists in the devolving of lower-level decision-making, from another aspect it amounts to an increased flow upward of information, primarily within each governmental structure; and this, taken together with ever-swifter global communication and with the consequent need for quick decision, has made high-level policy- and decision-making *more difficult* to devolve. At least in the quarter-century since World War II broke out, internal and external political leadership have thus changed in opposite ways, the former becoming more impersonal and regulation-bound, the latter less so.

Yet even the statesman least constrained by the official role that would bind him to the mechanism of his nation's political and administrative institutions is constrained by something else—by his own envisaging of the current distribution of power between nations with varying interests. I am concerned to emphasize this kind of constraint by one's world-vision, for it is all too easy to misunderstand the world-political conversation as though it were a contest of the leading players from various national teams in some kind of world sport. But teams competing in the same sport have very similar internal constitutions, and of course, their leading players' conceptions of the nature of the contest are almost identical. The internal constitutions of nations, on the other hand, differ as much as do those of a gridiron football team, a debating club, and a nation's group of tennis players at Wimbledon. Sometimes, too, their respective statesmen's views of the nature of the international "game" are almost as much at variance with each other.

The latter differences are partly to be explained by cultural differences between the several nations' conventional wisdom about history and society; but more, by radical differences in valuation. I shall contend that it is impossible to develop a model or view of international affairs which is value-free, taking it as obvious that one cannot transvalue one's valuations at will. Certainly, national and international institutions constrain, and to that degree determine the actions of statesmen. But in the international anarchy, it is rare that the media of institutional constraint are themselves institutions: the constraining is done for institutions by their statesmen's own conceptions.

Power politics has not always been so informal: what was sketched above is the style of conducting world affairs at the mid-twentieth century. European dynastic politics of the sixteenth to eighteenth centuries involved a far more homogeneous group of state institutions. The roles of monarchs and their ministers had been highly elaborated through tradition and the arts, but not so as to forbid those who filled them from taking diplomatic initiatives, which were effectively as personal as today's. Yet along with tradition, the general acknowledgment of a common legitimist interest—

against popular insurgence such as had arisen with the religious "total" wars of the preceding centuries—constrained most of the monarchs to limit their ambitions. Would agreement—as advocated by jurists since early in the sixteen-hundreds—upon a body of international law have constrained them more effectively? Again, the audience of seventeenth- and eighteenth-century European politics was numerically restricted, class-bound, and, because of the period's methods of communication, more measured in its responses than the huge, quickly excited publics of today.

Our current unformalized and personal style of world politics need not, on the other hand, turn out to be the final, completely evolved form of the statesman's art. Even without the emergence of universal government at a single world-center of power and authority, other developments of the system of nation-states could in considerable degree institutionalize and regularize the statesmen's now freewheeling "conversation." Growth of and increasing recourse to international organizations could be one of the tendencies in that direction. Such regularizing has already gone far in economic international relations—e.g., through GATT, the EEC, the Montevideo Treaty's arrangements for Latin America. In world-political affairs, however, even the proliferating of such an organization as the UN has occurred along with further informalizing of statesmanly contacts. Consider, as against that, a nonorganizational arrangement like the "hot phone." While that has the effect of a "conversation," it nevertheless prevents either Superpower's leader from breaking contact with the other, in order to embark upon dangerous adventures—e.g., Khrushchev's deployment of missiles in Cuba. Communication can become continuous, each regular message less momentous and less potentially surprising. The "conversation" turns into a perpetual conference, and egregious statesmen at the summit are once again shouldered by a bureaucracy of diplomats.

Some such change of style could come over world politics even though the system of nation-states remained: the growth of their powers of destruction might do much to bring it about. But it is not to be expected that the international conversation will ever be wholly institutionalized. Indeed, the residual element of true politics in even the most bureaucratized of *internal* systems of government ensures that a necessarily larger political element will persist in external affairs. For if we contemplate as a system the external relations maintained between nations by their several statesmen, then amongst that system's inputs we shall have to include resultants from each nation's internal politics—e.g., changes in foreign policy, weapon development, tariff arrangements, and so on—instituted after a change of government. (If, on the other hand, we consider the system of party politics within a given democratic nation-state, we shall have to regard as part of its input the "signals" arriving from the world-political conversation. These will be taken up by the internal political parties as "issues." The internal system is usually well equipped to interpret and to cope with those inputs from the international situation; whereas the international order is as yet ill equipped, so that its interpretation of much of its input is in terms of "crisis.") We shall return later to these contrasts between the international and the various national systems. Much can be understood about the nature of international politics by reflecting upon it as a system receiving inputs from its ingredient national systems' polities.

Firstly, international politics moves in a pattern of complex rhythms. One is reminded here of analyses of the business cycle provided by economists of the '30s and '40s, who distinguished several subcycles, short-term and long-term. The analogy is imperfect, insofar as only a few of the international rhythms (e.g., war conclusively ended; postwar disarmament; break up of wartime alliances and the emergence of new challengers; rearmament) are genuinely cyclical; but it is helpful in indicating the contrast of short-term and long-run rhythms. The most apparent rhythm is short-term and episodic: it consists of the succession of international crises that comprise the history of a given *era* of world politics.

The "crisis" or "episode," then, may be considered as the briefest historical unit within which the international system as a whole can possibly be perceived to be undergoing a shift or change. The "episode," however, is not all of a piece, but consists of a sequence of actions—usually, statesmen's actions—made in response to one another, as well as to the expectations entertained by statesmen as to how the situation will develop.

When the several actions are examined *seriatim,* the system as a whole appears only through the agent-statesman's eyes—that is, only insofar as he considers it in forming his expectations. This is why systems analysis provides a background to the study of the particular actions of statesmen. The latter study has traditionally sought *historical* explanations; the *theoretical* structure most relevant to it is that recently developed in behavioral science—i.e., that concerned with decision-making.

Like systems analysis, the study of decision-making appears to have been the issue of a marriage between operations research and management science, which takes in the bureaucratic elements of economics, strategic planning, and some other manipulative investigations that have eliminated politics and anything like politics from their purviews. Not only have such abstractions proved quite fruitful in explaining and in prescribing for more rational means-ends activity within the partly closed spheres of business and administration; but negatively they help also to reveal the nature of the nonroutine aspects of political activity to which they do *not* apply. The typical Power's response to a crisis comprises both routine behavior and uncalculated spur-of-the-moment action. The former aspect is to be explained with the aid of theory such as that of decision-making, the latter through nontheoretic historical reconstruction. The methodologist need not suppose that the use of either of those types of explanation invalidates the hypothesis of a system of Powers. Systems, as we have said, are not directly visible during the usually short interval required for action in a crisis; while in the longer perspective of an era, the fine detail of historical or decision-theory analysis is apt to have much less explanatory power than has the hypothesis of a system (though occasionally, the action of an hour can affect events for many years). Later in this volume I shall be concerned with a more precise analysis of the proper combination of short-run and long-run hypotheses (not that the precision of physical science, e.g., in the Law of Combination of Forces, is to be expected), and at that point the question will be raised again whether, despite its "invisibility" during so short a duration, the world-political system does not impinge in various deducible ways upon the conduct of the crisis.

Within limits, the extent of an "era" is a matter of the historian's personal selection; but one most readily thinks of it as the *duration of a clear constellation of major Powers.* Between the Wars, for example, we might define either a single era or two eras, with the second beginning 1930–33 between the China Incident and Hitler's accession to power.

On a longer time-scale, we may notice more comprehensive "periods," such as 1814–1914, in which there may well be a succession of eras and changes of Power-constellation, but in which various *regions* of the world *maintain,* despite gradual change, *a certain relative order of importance*—e.g. Western Europe was dominant, Austria-Hungary and Turkey receding, and Russia and America emerging in the nineteenth century. The tempo of successive historic periods seems to have been quickening, whereas the rhythm of crises and incidents within each era, and of the succession of eras themselves, seem rather more constant, in part because crises at least are mainly dependent upon random inputs from the several nation-states; whereas the changes throughout and between historical "periods" seem to owe more to long-run but quickening developments such as industrial revolution and increases of population.

Yet another long-run rhythm is established by the *persistence of a particular type of relationship between states,* which seems determined in large measure by persistence of some great military mode. The European age of shifting alliances, from its first beginnings in the defeat of mailed horsemen by archers or crossbowmen, through the gunpowder and the naval revolutions, to the first explosion of a thermonuclear weapon in an era of long-range bomber forces, reveals a reasonably continuous system of relations between sovereign national states, the earlier form of which—competition for sole hegemony over Western Christendom—gave way, after Louis XIV's reign, to "the balance of power." Later we argue that the changes of the 1950s inaugurated an altogether new type of relationship between states, depending upon command of thermonuclear instruments of destruction.

Military technology in the narrow sense, however, need not be the only agent of change for this type of international relationship. The age of the Mediterranean city-state, from the seventh to the second century BC, was brought to an end through the superiority of Rome's political, social, and military organization, of which the legion, a more technically military achievement, was merely a resulting implement. In that case, the type of relationship was changed by the abolition of all the related autonomous units of the international system, and the superimposing of a single imperium upon the whole region. Not only a period and an age but a whole dispensation ended. I shall call that kind of change, and also the changes in types of relationship that nevertheless leave the former units more-or-less intact, a *systemic* revolution. The world at present is undergoing the latter kind of systemic change, though there has as yet been no determination whether most of the currently significant nation-state units will survive; or whether the effective units will in future be Powers (blocs) of continental dimensions; or whether the whole system will be so formalized and institutionalized as to create a world-political order for which there are no previous analogies.

It would be theoretically neater if all periods were made up of numbers of entire eras of which none overlapped into other periods; all ages, similarly, of complete periods; and all dispensations, of unitary ages; but of course overlapping and untidiness is characteristic of the world-political process. We are concerned here to notice that during any quarter-century or so, at least for the last few hundred years, the process of world politics has moved to a complex pattern of at least three distinctively generated rhythms, two being long-term but of recently quickening tempo. The distinctions are worth making for practical reasons: many a mere change of era, sometimes just an incident within an era, has been greeted as a transition of ages—e.g., the temporary eclipse of Western Europe 1945–56—and vice versa. It is for theoretical reasons, however, that we here draw attention to the varieties of rhythm: the different rhythmic sequences require each a distinct model for their theoretical explanation. For the events of an "era," we need the model of a constellation of Powers, each represented in the "conversation" by its statesmen; for the "period," we need a much-enlarged version of the era-model, together with the structure of population changes, economic developments, and so on; for the "age," it may be possible to dispense with the detail of competing Powers (models of which in the two prior cases must be quite specific to be useful), and instead to refer generally to large-scale, long-term economic, social, and political development and of course to the state of military art. (The significance of generality in this third case is brought out by the reflection that in 1939 there were possibly five distinct national candidates for inventor of the atomic bomb—the UK, Germany, France, the USA, and the USSR—and the actual time and place of invention and development was decided by the concurrent "accidents" of scientific research and of the wars. The fusion bomb—together with intercontinental strike forces, the true agent of our epoch's systemic change—might have waited one or two decades had Germany not been defeated, or had the Japanese not attacked at Pearl Harbor. Similarly, the firepower revolution of the later Middle Ages could have been led by many of the provinces on the outer borders of Christendom. North Africa rather than Italy might have engendered the imperium that unified the Mediterranean world.) It should be apparent that the three kinds of model are not independent but continuous one with another, the second embracing the first, and the third partly comprehending the second.

Granted, our selection of just those three "rhythms," and not of other *prima facie* equally interesting may seem arbitrary: may there not be more, or fewer, distinct trends in the historical process? That topic will be dealt with in the theoretical parts of this volume. Our subject, however, is not the course of world history in its entirety, but the abstracted sequence of external relationships, chiefly in their political aspect. ("External" rather than "international" or "interstate," since nation-states are not the sole possible units in external relations; and "external" rather than "*world*-political," since the present international order is the first to have been worldwide.) Reflection upon the historical sequence of external relationships suggests a mingling of processes with various time scales and tempos. That, in turn, suggests hypotheses (propounded later in this book) about the distinct determinants of external political affairs.[1] But, as was contended above, the political behavior of a statesman can be understood only through an understanding of *his* hypotheses about those determinants and *his* interpretation of the international incident or crises that confronts him. (Is it, in our words, a crisis resulting from some short-term and probably reversible change in the power constellation of his era, to which, therefore,

[1] The phrase "determinants of external political affairs" does not imply causal determinism, even in those cases where, after the event, the most powerful combination of statesmanship and expertise is helpless to reverse or even to control the situation. Before the event, the characteristic future situation is not merely unknown: it is, usually, in principle undetermined. The most one can assume is a negative determinism—that certain powerful long-run developments have ruled out some possibilities. Nor is the case any more determined in the short run. Even in a narrow and confined struggle for power, the number of distinct strategems open to a statesman is usually incomputable, though none, perhaps, will be at all satisfactory to him, so that he will feel driven into a corner. What has been said concerning the complex rhythmic pattern of world politics cannot, and has not been intended to, afford predictive extrapolations of the pattern.

he may hope to make an adjustment favorable to his own country? Or has it been precipitated by some development that nobody planned and nobody can hope to reverse, such as the discovery of thermonuclear explosives?) The political theorist has not, in fact, the option of leaving questions about the tempo and time scale of international events out of consideration: the most empirical, down-to-earth investigation of world-political behavior requires him at least to match in range of vision the more imaginative of the statesmen he is studying.

We have now filled out the picture of world politics as proceeding in a subtle episodic tempo, partly constant but mainly rising, partly repetitive but mainly once-for-all, and in any case difficult to decipher; as being incalculable, momentous, and carried on by a very small number of variously but distinctively selected representatives, informally and through the medium of ordinary speech.

The picture is meant to exhibit the *qualities* of the phenomena as human action, and it is no accident that, in this depiction, the features of power, force, and violence are masked—principally behind the concealment of the word "representatives." For most of the statesmen represent Powers, though a few—the Secretary-General of the United Nations, the Pope and other religious leaders, and perhaps some great industrialists—who participate occasionally in the international conversation are not primarily national representatives. Obviously, the part taken by each statesman in the international conversation depends much less upon his individual character than upon the weight that can be carried by the Power he represents. That weight is produced by the Power's relative armed strength; its economic resources; its potential for extending or terminating alliances, military or commercial; its degree of social and political cohesion; and by some other factors which vary in importance with the times—e.g., scientific and higher technological manpower is quickly becoming an element in national power that cannot be wholly construed as a mere aspect of military or economic potential.

Now, it is decisive for the theme of this volume to make the point that even if, through barely imaginable technological changes, the means of destruction and conquest were universally debilitated or restricted, or had come to cancel themselves out, there would still remain a deal of substance to Powerhood and to power politics. The sovereign societies could still use their economic and other resources, alone or in alliance, to help or to hinder each other; there could be major changes of internal regimes affecting the interests of external Powers; and all this would be sufficient to sustain the statesmen's conversations and the rest of the expression of power politics, which would be otherwise only some degrees less momentous, but still incalculable.

If incalculable, however, then not directable. A favorite theme of the secular sermon—that Man has learnt to direct and control Nature, but not himself—makes a pointless lament. Short of abolishing world politics altogether, and with it the capacity for reasoned action in concert, there is no way of directing it along a specific path; and only a dictatorial world-state would have even a chance of abolishing it. World politics is thus, like economic choice, an inescapable mode of historical existence. This is not to say that the more disastrous consequences of uncontrolled struggle for world power (*viz.*, major war; the subjugation of free peoples) could not be guarded against by institutional and other methods. That is a hope more credible than ever, though to prescribe for its fulfillment is daunting work. Nor are we maintaining that sovereign independence, whether of nation-states or continental blocs, is likewise a permanent feature of the world system. We contend only that whatever the unit of external relationships, and however great the systemic revolutions, an activity recognizably continuous with current world politics will be carried on.

Suppose, then, that world politics is, short of world dictatorship, ineradicable and indirigible: so is internal politics, short of internal dictatorship. But there is an important difference. The fact that a man belongs to some organization of internal politics in a free society—for example, to one of several competing parties—cannot in most cases establish the degree of loyalty that sheer accident of birth generates within a nation-state, a feudality, an imperium, a city-state, a tribe. One is not, typically, bound to one's party by birthright.[2] The "native land," and "the people" like the family and unlike the political party, are elemental groups, from whose spirit and outlook voluntary detachment is ordinarily an emotional impossibility.

From this cause alone a detached, objective study of world politics is almost too much for the human frailties of the political scientist. Yet the kind of political theory contended for in this study requires as a matter of method imaginatively entering into those patterns of loyalty and evaluation that identify another people e.g., to discern through imagination others' comparative evaluations (or, preference-schedules) is a necessary condition for the *applying* of game-theoretical models to the real world of power politics (though it may well turn out that, for reasons other than the

[2] Perhaps one is bound to social class and to religious creed, but can these allegiances establish a political entity equivalent with the blood-and-soil union of the state? That is a vast subject in itself. A short way with it is to point to the four hundred years of history since the Reformation, and the mere forty since the Russian Revolution, in practical demonstration that, as for the mass, creed and class cannot stand out indefinitely against country and state as claimants for loyalty. Even states founded upon religious or revolutionary allegiance survive from the second generation by birthright patriotism. But creed and to a lesser extent class sometimes give individuals and small contractual groups a standpoint for criticism of patriotic loyalties. In this sense, the world society is better and freer for its religious and social distinctions.

difficulty of imaginative discernment, such an application of game theory is not possible). Parochialism can be mitigated by a broader and deeper sympathy with alien value systems—an approach contrary to those who hope to make political science cogent and objective through insisting upon its being value-free. Even so, it would be rash to expect anyone entirely to escape parochialism.

That is not all. In the last half-century or so the human race has come to have *some* common interest against the present workings of the world-political system, at least against the latter's unimpeded and extreme destructive manifestations. Philosophic objections to there being a truly "common" interest are overcome in this case by the prospect of universal devastation; though "common interest" must not be taken here to mean that the preference schedule of every human being is dominated by avoidance of universal nuclear destruction, yet those who rate other outcomes as worse, rate only one or two so. On the other side, as contended immediately above, only a few people are genuinely denationalized and emancipated from the *mores* or interests of some particular Power—interests which will often include the maintenance of an uncontrolled world system of sovereign Powers. The chances are, then, that the politically concerned will be divided in his mind and in his heart toward the world order (as indeed he may be toward his own nation, since nationality, though a birthright affair, is learned later than, say, kinship, and at a stage of growth already intellectualized). Thus, the theory of the subject, far from being value-free, is likely to be confused by powerfully contradictory evaluations—of one's own nation, of others, and of the world system. Such, in fact, is the impression which the literature of the subject makes upon one coming to it for the first time.

If contradictory evaluations confuse theorists of international politics, they are likely also to affect its practitioners. These confusions should be depicted in our account of the world-political conversation. Statesmen in their conversations are not always single-minded—they are not quite like learned counsel, each pertinaciously representing his own client's interests in some forensic debate. As a person, each is more likely than not to feel the pull of rival evaluations—primarily those of his country, but also of other groups, from his own family, his class, his communion, to the whole alliance, or to mankind at large. A reader has called my attention to the phenomenon in internal politics of "identification with opponents." One sometimes sees the leader of an alliance of Powers turning with some distaste from an ally, and "identifying" with the leader of the opposed alliance. Indeed, there appear to have been evanescent occasions when a common group loyalty has emerged among the statesmen participating in an international conference.

Even if he manages to be a single-minded contender for his nation's interest, a statesman can easily fall into confusion in ranking the possible outcomes before him as furtherances of that interest: he may not be wholly clear about the course of action which, as his nation's representative, he should favor. Sometimes international meetings are held mainly to exchange the information needed for those and other clarifications. For all these reasons the "rationality" of world-political processes, which on a few favored occasions permit of the application to them of simplified rationalistic theories and models, such as those of game and bargaining theory, is nevertheless a frequently impaired rationality.

A consequence for political theory follows immediately. In any rationalistic theoretical structure, the more "impaired" the assumed rationality, the less specific and determined the derivations and the less point, therefore, in bothering with any theoretical structure at all. Why not then try a nonrationalistic, a naturalistic structure? Because impaired reason is reason all the same: we know quite definitely in what direction to look for explanations, even though we must also expect that when we have unraveled them, they will be inelegant and particularistic sections of minute history or biography.

From that, in turn, by a much less direct route, another conclusion seems to follow. Given that the various agents realize, more or less, that by virtue of the impairment of its participants' rationality, their situation is not very specifically determined: then each of them will concentrate his attention upon the larger and overriding considerations and decide his policy accordingly, even if it should appear that a cleverer, finer-grained policy offers the possibility of much more favorable results.

Ingenuity is not, indeed, commonly displayed in international policies —one feels that it is even less common than profundity or wisdom. To report a mere personal impression: most of the moves in world politics look quite crude; yet one recognizes that World Affairs is among the few subjects of study in which the persons investigated are for the most part much more gifted and intelligent than those investigating their behavior. The impaired rationality of statesmen is fairly widely understood to characterize world politics.

Impaired or not, the rationality we have been referring to is that of persons, either individual or cohesively grouped in a governing set. All such rationality, however, has a limited range: it applies only to the span of action for which the agents are capable of envisaging the possible alternative consequences. Because of this limitation, resultants of any long-lived system of interaction (for our purposes, the power-political system) become at some stage in the future unforeseeable, and the system as such possibly "irrational," even when all its constituent members are, within their limits, "rational."

"Systemic irrationality" is an appropriate label, in the first place, for cases where some result of interaction, having not been foreseen, is contrary to the purposes of those who interacted: the occurrence of depression when all entrepreneurs want a boom might be thought a "paradoxical" result, sufficient for labeling the economic system "irrational." When a system works so as to confront each of its constituent members with inescapable alternatives neither of which he would accept, we also speak of the system as irrational, since it engenders "dilemma." The present international system is styled irrational by some because it seems to compel high expenditure upon armaments (and worse, upon dangerous thermonuclear armaments) even though most governments would wish to spend very little. To attack a system upon such grounds is to presuppose that its constituents, if they understood its unwanted propensities, could change its appropriate determinants so as to eliminate the irrationality. Thus the rationality or irrationality of a system is related to that of its constituent members in several ways. A system is said to be irrational if and only if (1) its resultants conflict with what was intended by the several (rational) policies which, jointly or competitively implemented, produce those resultants; and (2) there is at least the theoretical possibility of a reform of the system by some or all of its constituent policy-makers, which would remove that conflict. (Whether we characterize a system as rational or irrational thus depends upon the relations between its resultants and some human intention. So far as the resultant is unintended and is contradictory to some intention, the attribution of the adjective "irrational" can be an objective judgment about the real world; but it must always have a subjective aspect also, since one term of the relation in question is someone's intention.)

Secondly, constituents who might reform a system but make no attempt to do so, whether from shortsightedness, indecision, or divided intentions, are sometimes considered irrational on that ground alone—so that even systemic irrationality is apt in the last analysis to be laid at some individual door. Thirdly, a *system* is sometimes called irrational (though to do so would conflict with the definition of systemic irrationality already set out in the previous paragraph), not merely because its constituents have limited foresight, but primarily because even within those limits they are "irrational" in some formal sense, e.g., their several preference schedules are intransitive. (Notice that a system is *not* called irrational when, though some of its resultants are paradoxical and highly disliked by all, its reform or abandonment are known or believed to be impossible both by its constituents and by external analysts.)

Chiefly because of the momentousness of its resultants, some diffuse and often conflicting movements for reform and rationalization of the world-political system have been supported in Western societies since the Enlightenment. Leaders of most parties in the Cold War prefer that the world shall not be devastated merely because they are at cross purposes with themselves and with each other. Even those who would prefer universal destruction to surrender do not want destruction prematurely foreclosing the search for other, cheerful alternatives. Some recognize the possibility that, unimpeded, the world system may work itself into dilemma and paradox, and that that possibility is founded, though in part only, upon individual statesmen's own propensities toward irrationality; so from time to time the international conversation is directed toward agenda which, primarily concerned with practical advantages, incidentally help to rationalize the system. Considered as a whole, the world-political system has now some slight self-reforming propensity.

Notice how slight, how episodic. Stronger and more immediate interests claim the attention of national statesmen. Neither separately nor in concert, as we have seen, could they in any event make over the whole system as though its structure were the rules for a game of cards: many of its determinants, especially the processes of fundamental scientific discovery and consequent technological innovation, in principle cannot be directed or programmed. And supposing it did turn out that a concert of the Powers could eliminate the practical possibility of world devastation by reforming the system along one of various alternative lines: how severally do they choose and how jointly agree upon one line rather than another? That it avoids such a device is one reason for adopting a really short-term perspective upon world affairs. The effect of statesmen's short-term perspective is to produce conservative reactions, even though those who so react are often ostensibly liberal. On the other hand, anyone genuinely wishing to have the present system conserved should consequentially wish to have it reformed and controlled. But no one, it is safe to say, has as yet devised any plausible scheme for adequate reform, so that we simply do not know whether or not any variety of reformed world would appeal to the genuinely conserving frame of mind. The system and its members have engendered as yet even less motivation than opportunity for self-correction. Nevertheless, so slight a propensity is decisive for the political theorist attempting to characterize the present international system, which, in virtue of that propensity, he can regard as containing in embryo some of the elements of a *polity,* though as we contend in the concluding chapter of this volume, a single world-wide polity may prove impossible.

Lacking an aptitude for self-correction, the system could quite properly be regarded as an anarchy, even though the relationships which interconnect it look in themselves like political relations and may indeed be called so without much extension of ordinary usage. Amongst political philosophers, the common assumption seems to be that an anarchic system of power relationships is convertible into a political system when and only when a single center of rule or government has been set up over it.

We here contend that established central rule is neither sufficient nor necessary to make a system into a rudimentary polity: a sacred kinship can be virtually nonpolitical; while a frontier society in which there is no effective central rule but yet a general recognition of *law* as a criterion for relationship is already a political system. Not the lack of an Austinian sovereign, but the want of motive and opportunity for amendment from within their structure of relationships, was what justified "anarchy" as a designation of most earlier power-political systems.

The current state of the world system is thus more rational in one sense of that term, and in another, less rational than its earlier states: more rational, in the sense of having a slight propensity to self-correction; less in the sense of "rationality" as "self-consistency in purpose and action." In the latter sense, a struggle for power, measurable in quantities of land, guardsmen, and gold, between sovereign monarchs each enlightened in his self-interest, is amenable to study by rationalistic methods like those of the economist. (It will turn out, later in this study, that the calculations required are in fact still beyond human or mechanical capacity; but so they are also in chess, contract bridge, or solo, where we think of strategies as being selected by "rational intuition," there being no question of the contestants' preferences and evaluations departing from self-consistency because of anything in the game situation.) We may suppose the sovereigns of the *ancien régime* to have been rational in a more-or-less economic sense. Already in the eighteenth century, however, the *philosophes* had called in question the European State system: was the balance-of-power a game that human beings should play at all? But the motivations they offered to princes for reforming the system were never as strong as were those for continuing the power struggle, given opportunities such as the opening-up of the New World and the weaknesses of states in Central and Northeastern Europe. The politics of European kings and their ministers, then, could be rational in the limited sense of "self-consistent for each individual," even though, considering the perennial incalculability and the increasing momentousness of human affairs, the notion of an applied (or applicable) science of power politics already conveyed some impression of that obsessive craziness later clearly exemplified in the Comtean and other positivist philosophies of history.

The two senses of "rationality" and their logical interrelations are examined at length in later chapters. The primary reference of both senses is to individuals or to cohesive governing groups—a derivative reference to social systems as wholes has just been employed. The first sense—*viz.*, openness to information and a propensity to adjust one's opinions and plans to it—is frequently incompatible in practice with the second sense—*viz.*, internal self-consistency—since consistency amongst one's evaluations may not be maintainable if one keeps adding to one's list of valued and disvalued states of affairs. Nevertheless the person open to novelty is probably one who will also work at getting his constantly-disordered preferences rearranged consistently—a subject discussed below.

There is much in the current situation continuous with the pre-1914 world, yet discontinuity also appears with the emergence in the international system of the propensity of self-correction. If indeed a worldwide political community is to develop around the international "conversation" —and there is absolutely no guarantee that it will—then its form, the very idea of it, will have to be *invented*. To take from internal politics the accepted idea of the sovereign state and to inflate it to global dimensions will not serve: that structure, which evolved under pressure as much from the demand for external security as from that for internal peace and order, cannot, however transformed, provide the institutional skeleton of a world community. The changes called for will be much greater than the synthesizing of Rome's institutions that made it over from a republic into an imperium, or than the inventions of federalism and of the separation of powers—greater, because those had so much less to accommodate.

In principle, the second kind of rationality can be programmed into a cybernetic machine, provided there exists an algorithm for doing so; the first cannot. Explanation, therefore, of processes in which the first kind is an ingredient will not be much advanced by the type of rationalistic theory or model based upon the second kind. Indeed, it is generally true that world politics of the last fifty years has acquired so many new features that the theory of it (or rather, the scraps of theory, since a complete theory is, as we shall contend, unobtainable) will probably need to be logically very much richer than that of any other political subject.

A critic has suggested to me that in the last resort such a comparison cannot be sustained since "political thought as such is impure"—i.e., even internal politics is so little an isolable system that one cannot say anything definite about its logical richness. That view has considerable attractions: the whole is often less than the sum of its parts; so that it would not be surprising if sometimes one could not tell which was the richer. My argument depended upon the simple notion that in the twentieth century there is a process called "world politics" which comprehends the external politics of virtually all internal polities; and that though there is a nodal distinction, marked by the concept of sovereignty, between internal and external affairs, the latter somehow include the former, and just for that reason have to be logically the richer. From the other side, one might consider the number of individuals politically active in either field: it has been a burden of the present chapter that the number of persons effectively active in world politics is very small; while in a well-developed polity, the numbers could be larger. Information, in a logically significant sense, occurs only in the heads of individuals. Who is to say that an account of some civilized internal polity may not be logically richer than the account of the world-political situation as it now obtains? At the present stage I cannot resolve this problem, but perhaps it may be possible to do so after a more detailed examination of the politics of the Powers.

To summarize the novel features of world politics in the last fifty years: forces of destruction have increased in vastly greater proportion than any other element, and are only a little offset by the greater powers of recuperation from war developed by advanced nations. Both of these increases result from the "second industrial revolution," which has had many other consequences for world politics.

Firstly, it has provided a prime example for the quickening of tempo (mentioned above) in changes of the nature of relationship between Powers and in the nature of the Powers themselves. Secondly, it has opened up a great and widening gap between technologically advanced societies and traditional societies. That distinction between Powers is now generally more significant than the distinction in potential previously caused by disparity of population, land, and physical resources. Thirdly, in combination with this earlier kind of distinction based upon population and resources, the technological revolution has established certain sharp gradations of military power, the most obvious of which is that marking off more-or-less independent thermonuclear states from the rest. Fourthly, it has made possible a worldwide network of communications having at least two mutually opposed effects upon world politics: on the one hand, news of crises has since 1914 spread around the world instantaneously; on the other hand, it is now possible for statesmen to be in both continuous and immediate communication with each other, thereby reducing the chances of crisis by inadvertance. Fifthly, the possibility of universal benefit from technological advance is now obvious, and leads to general appreciation of the positive common advantages thus available to the world community. Sixthly, the disadvantages of international anarchy are accentuated by the dangers of universal destruction.

Most of these changes have occurred during the prevalence of no more than two or three constellations of Powers (no more than two or three "eras") and in a period when the balance of importance was shifting only in degree from Western Europe to North America and Russia. This of course is a reversal of that relation *between* the rate of change of a whole system *and* that of its constituent groupings which has prevailed throughout history; usually, systemic changes have taken at least several eras to become apparent. But changes within a constellation of Powers have usually been either direct and intended consequences of policy, or at least the outcome of interaction of policy even though unintended. The second industrial revolution and its consequences, by contrast, have not been intended in any direct way. As has been maintained in the last few pages, it has introduced a new motif into the process of world politics: statesmen acting within the world system must now attend to the operation of the system as a whole, as much as to the machinations of their fellow statesmen. Thus, while the traditional forms of diplomacy are being outmoded by personalized and informal conversation, the subject matter of the conversation now has to do much more with impersonal workings, everywhere evident, of the world system. The First World War seems to have provided the earliest indication of this changed tenor in world affairs —having been a conflict that no Power planned or wanted but which resulted from the operations of the system.

A concomitant change, long recognized in political theory, has been the "nationalization" of several spheres of conduct previously beyond the competence of the State—a process which was well under way half a century before 1914. We are concerned here only with its consequences for international politics. First amongst these is the increased inclusiveness and complexity of the international system: a model of one of its component Powers must now be an economic and internal-political model as well as a bare construct of power politics. Though, as already contended, this does not mean that the study of world politics is now coextensive with the study of history as a whole, it does—like the consequences of the second industrial revolution mentioned above—imply that an adequate theory of the current world system cannot be developed merely by reapplying the models which were more or less adequate for the world politics of the balance of power. (For example, a model of alliance based on European history up to 1914 will have little predictive power for the relations of Superpowers in the 1970s.) Conversely no analysis of international *economic* affairs is nowadays adequate unless set in the context of world *politics*. Admittedly scientific and intellectual development is both an autonomous process in itself and also an independent source of inputs into the world-political system, while from the other side the military programs of the Superpowers have powerfully advanced the technological application of autonomous discoveries in fundamental science. These inputs from the fundamental scientific process are to be distinguished from all others by their propensity for "perspective-dissolving surprise"—a topic examined at some length later in this volume. It will be found that they affect the theory of international relations as radically as phenomena of innovation have affected economic theory—for example, by making inappropriate the traditional system of cardinal probabilities and suggesting its replacement by a matrix of ordinal possibilities.

An adequate picture of the current international system must be political, military, economic, demographic, and geographic at once. Thus, a serious methodological problem arises in handling so complex a model. The obvious solution would be to make a distinct model of each of the separate ingredients, and then to try to combine them in some more or less mechanical fashion. Leading theorists of international relations have attempted this—e.g., by the synthesizing of factor analyses. But a merely mechanical combination is in danger of ignoring the cross-effects of each of these realms on the other, whereas one can see intuitively that the cross-effects often have more explanatory power than does the sum of the ingredients when each is taken in isolation.

Another approach—to construct a model of all the realms in their interconnection—sets a practically impossible task. One might have some idea of how to go about it; one might even be able to guess at the general range of the effects that such a model would yield: but such notions do not by themselves add up to a properly constructed theory. Yet if this practical restriction upon theorizing were somehow overcome, for instance with cybernetic and mechanical aid, it could easily turn out that the result produced by machines would not advance theoretical understanding very much.

Theoretical exploration can, however, make some slight contribution to policy. Firstly, it can indicate what kinds of prediction are beyond anybody's power, and why—whether for reasons of principle or because of the practical difficulties just mentioned. Secondly, it can distinguish between those processes which may come within, and those which must occur beyond human control, and thus ascertain which matters may be subjects of policy. Thirdly, it can indicate in a general way what persons, groups, and roles in the various internal-political systems can be expected to effect reforms of the international political order. We may already guess that they will comprise those very few statesmen whom we have seen conducting the international conversation. With them the responsibility must rest, since it already appears that the international systems' propensity for self-correction is not an automatic or an involuntary one, but will depend upon personal initiative. There seems to be no hidden hand, either liberal or Marxist, that will solve the greatest of world-political problems for us.

The Powers are even fewer than the statesmen who represent them. We owe to Morton Kaplan a distinction between types of multisystemic system analogous to that in economics between perfect competition and oligopoly: in one type (like perfect competition) the agents in the system are so numerous that the structure of the system as a whole dominates its behavior—no single agent needs to be considered as a separate center of causation in the process. Kaplan calls this the "system-dominant" type. But where, as in international politics and oligopoly, the number of agents (or subsystems) is small, the subsystems are said to be "dominant," and explanations of the behavior of the system as a whole can be found only by tracing the behavior of each of the agents. Under system dominance, the agents are anonymous; under subsystem dominance, as in international politics, they must normally be referred to by name. Analyses of the former's impersonal operation often permit one to judge that *the system* tends to have harmful (or beneficial) effects, but short of the possibility of reforming the whole system from without, there can be no question of considering any agent or person responsible for those consequences. Given subsystem dominance, however, at least when the subsystems are represented by individuals, it becomes possible to trace responsibilities for the workings of the system, in those cases where the individual might have been expected to have had some foresight of his policy's consequences. But subsystems predominate in international affairs, so it is likely that analyses of international processes though they do not compel us to draw inferences about responsibility, will point to specific individuals as responsible, at least on the short time scales of incident and era.

For these reasons the theory of international relations at any rate contributes to the literature of "political criticism," i.e., to writing that judges political action in the various ways that artistic criticism judges works of art. Artists' performances can be judged simply as exhibitions of their craft: so can politicians', but only after one has discovered the ends that the politician is seeking to further. An instrument of political analysis such as game theory, since it presupposes that the agent holds certain systems of preference, may provide a criterion to show whether he has been skilful or not in maximizing his return. Thus, international theory enters into political criticism, first of all by providing a measure for skilfulness. But the most difficult questions in politics involve discovering just what ends the characteristic politician is trying to promote. (Such questions must be asked; and they presuppose that politics is not merely a skill.) A strictly neutral political theory, supposed to have no admixture of ethics in it, does nothing to help the critic's judgment about ends. It may bring him to the point of deciding that the statesman under study had conflicting loyalties, but can say nothing about which allegiance the statesman should have maintained. The problem now arises whether any international theory is adequate *as a theory,* unless it has already incorporated a critical theory of ethics within it.

Leicester Webb maintained that "political science . . . has, and has always had, a commitment to the polity." If the contemporary international political order is the external equivalent for the polity in internal politics, can it require a similar commitment from international theory? It has been pointed out that, since the international order has by its inputs a direct effect upon the polity, political theorists committed to the polity cannot be wholly neutral about the international order. But this does not answer our question, which suggests that the commitment of international theory can only be made to the possibly emerging world polity directly. One obvious reason against the necessity of such a commitment is that, for all we know, the best available international theory may show that a world polity is after all not possible. A counter-argument is that nontheoretical criticism of the world-political order is in fact always designed to reveal the defects in it that militate against the emergence of world polity, or at least against stability, including the avoidance of total destruction. Even the use of international theory to develop a military policy takes for granted that at least one State should survive. In practice no one wants to use theory to promote annihilation. It seems then that, in application, international theory is directed either to world conquest by one Power, or to the promotion of some kind of international stability.

Such a conclusion can be challenged from at least two directions. One comes from those who adhere to the belief that political science, like any science, *should* be value-free. Such scholars might argue that there are many other possible alternatives than one-Power hegemony *or* general stability (in practice, a self-balancing *status quo*), and that the only questions scientifically significant concern (1) what has actually happened in the history of Power politics, and why; (2) what might happen, and, if anything can be said about the matter, what alternatives are likely to arise; (3) whether any general principles are discernible as a result of investigating the subject. In this volume such an approach is alleged to be both misconceived and impractical.

A contrary challenge comes from religious conviction. If one conceives of the Powers as "spiritual" yet dubious entities; if one supposes that the least of persons is infinitely more significant that the greatest of Powers, however strong its influence as a "spiritual" entity, then one will be committed to seeking the establishment of a situation in which Powers rise and decline with no more than political acclaim or political lament; and in which no individual is ever destroyed (though he may be elevated or cast down) as a foreseeable concomitant of the rise or decline of any Power. This religiously motivated approach, which has been explicitly promoted at least since the early seventeenth century, resembles the "world-government" ideal in seeking to eliminate or reduce the employment of armed force, but differs from it in accepting the indefinite continuation of *political* activity amongst the Powers. Indeed, it intends an increasing politicization of the relations between Powers. In this, it is both the equivalent and the complement—in respect of external politics—of the kind of "commitment to the polity" that Webb maintained the science of internal politics was involved in.

The question whether a science of Power politics (external politics) is or could be value-free would thus boil down to the question whether all classes of problem about Power politics could be posed in such a way as to involve no ethical or evaluating presuppositions about how the Power system should be allowed to develop. Can the theorist of Power politics mention, *without*—in his capacity as theorist—*embracing any of them,* the differing and opposed values that the statesmen whom he studies act to promote? Or must the scientific questions that he asks be elicited by and somehow presuppose his interest in the developing state of the world-political conversation? Perhaps at the conclusion of this volume, after a closer examination of power-political theory, we may have found an answer.

As a whole, the present work attempts to discover the scope and limits of world-political theory by examining a selected few amongst recent approaches, and by attempting to develop these and other approaches as far as logic and testability will allow them to be taken. In many directions the limits are discoverable only by such exploration, not by *a priori* reasoning or by the construction of a general conceptual framework for all possible international theory. While the scope for theorizing turns out to be quite circumscribed in most directions, in others no limit has yet been discovered by our exploratory probing.

The second and third chapters of Section I expound a philosophy of the theory of world politics. The second develops a set of expressions for the discussion of real, nonstatistical uncertainty—a condition of deliberate and nonroutine action in general, but approached here particularly insofar as it concerns the actions of statesmen. The third chapter proceeds from a philosophic theory of historical explanation (in which several logical skeletons explicating different kinds of historical explanation are constructed) to a discussion of possible uses for a theory of external politics. Not until Section II, Chapter 4, do we begin, by a definition, the critical examination and construction of such a theory.

TWO

Real Uncertainty and Surprise: Their Consequences in Politics

Since, as asserted above (p. 3), statesmen have never been able to tell exactly what would happen, nor even to make an exhaustive list of all the developments that *might* occur; and since what does occur in power politics is often momentous: then an adequate formal model has to make allowance for these two facts of power-political life. If such radical ignorance of the future were confined to its unmomentous aspects, model-builders could disregard the matter. In fact, except for a few relatively stable periods, it has been precisely the momentous which has most often been liable to radical uncertainty. As suggested in our introductory chapter, since about the First World War, radical uncertainty about the power-political future has increased.

I

Some degree of radical uncertainty, however, has and will always be comprised within the expectations of any rational creature: though we are here expounding the concept as background to a political theory it is, if valid at all, of universal import. Underlying our exposition in the present chapter is the epistemological doctrine that knowledge is a category inapplicable to our expectations of future events (contrasted with "our apprehension of past events"), and thus, that the degrees of probability expressed colloquially as (nonradical) uncertainties or even "certainties," with which we expect some events are necessarily qualified by and set in a context of radical uncertainty.

Moderate skepticism of that kind does not by itself much advance understanding of the problems of expectation. If radical (or "real") uncertainty could be safely relegated to the background of our expectations, which otherwise could all be characterized as *either* certain *or* uncertain (upon some such ground as an epistemology of degrees of belief, in which all discussable future events somehow had probabilities ranging from almost zero to almost unity), it would hardly present a practical difficulty to political theorists. But it does present a difficulty when it obtrudes into an array of nonradically uncertain expectations. Consider a political journalist's expectations, two or more years before the election, about the identity of contenders for the Presidency: he may be able to name several "possibles" and assign subjective numerical probabilities to their chances; but he should not allow those probabilities to sum to unity, since he is bound to consider that possibly a name he has not even thought of as yet will be advanced two years later. He can formally complete his array of expectations only by assigning a numerical probability to *that* possibility. It is upon expectations of just such a logical character that political action has to be undertaken. Therefore a critique of power-political theory requires a prior framework for the analysis and evaluation of expectations, and especially expectations of radical uncertainty.

We shall now attempt to illustrate the differences between what is here intended by "radical uncertainty" and what are otherwise ordinarily understood as the different kinds of uncertainty. Consider first a game in which the uncertainty is that of *pure chance*—i.e., it is in no sense a game of skill or strategy. The two players simultaneously toss coins, once and then again. One player wins a coin from the other if and only if he tosses two heads and the other does not. That game involves neither strategic uncertainty or radical uncertainty. We need know nothing about either of the players in order to calculate exactly the probabilities of each possible distinct outcome.

Our next game involves *strategic uncertainty* as well as pure chance or risk. Again two players move simultaneously, if necessary twice. At each move, each player either clenches his fist (C) or holds it palm-open (P). If on the first move both clench, then the toss of a coin decides which player pays the other a penny. If on either the first or the second move one plays C and the other P, the C player calls heads or tails on the toss of a coin: if he wins, he gains one "life"; if he loses, the other gains one life and he loses one. If on either the first or the second move both play P, a coin is tossed twice. Suppose one player calls "heads" for both tosses: if he wins twice, he gains a life; if he loses twice, the other gains a life; if he does neither, then neither player wins or loses anything. If there is a second move and both players play C, then the toss of a coin decides which player pays the other a penny. If on the second move either plays P, the player with one or more extra lives is paid a penny by the other. If neither has more lives than the other, neither gains or loses a penny.

The outcomes of this second game are determinable partly by chance and partly by choice. We can list exhaustively all the possible strategies and, *given* each possible mix of strategies, we can calculate as in the first game of pure chance what the probabilities of each of the possible final outcomes will be. But if we know absolutely nothing about either of the players we can say nothing informative about the probabilities of the specific outcomes. (The "principle of insufficient reason" is discounted, at least at this stage of our exposition.) Only if we know how "rational," "insightful," "risk-preferring," etc., is each player, can we calculate the probabilities of every possible outcome, and even then only on the assumption that such propensities of the players will not change without cause, or be gratuitously changed by the players, during the course of the game. (Such knowledge on our part can itself be probabilistic—e.g., we may have some evidence of an objective nonzero probability that at each move a particular player will allow pure chance to determine his strategy, rather than calculate advantages through to the end. The "proportions" of rational choice and pure chance in each player's contribution to the possible range of outcomes can be determined, though not precisely. We are not, however, concerned in this chapter with the admittedly troublesome question about the cogency of evidence for people's future propensities.) If one believes that gratuitous and unpredictable changes of purpose are always possible among human beings, then to that extent one has to admit even in this case the possibility of radical and not merely strategic uncertainty. But unless, for the sake of the argument, *that* particular source of radical uncertainty is assumed away, one cannot make out a case, as we have tried to do here, for a distinct category of strategic uncertainty. Analyzing a strategic system from without (i.e., *not* as one of the contenders who, whatever he supposes about the others, presupposes that his own dealings in the strategic situation need to be based upon calculations of possible advantage), we can limit the range of strategic uncertainty —at one end, by the case of strategic certainty as in the game of pure skill where there are no chance elements; at the other by the game of pure chance from which the last residual element of skill—e.g., the possibility of bluffing—has been removed. Though "strategic certainty" is a quite clear concept it does not, as the phrase might suggest, imply either determinism or statistical certainty (i.e., a probability equal to unity) in respect of the outcome of the strategic situation, which is dependent (as we have argued) upon all the relevant contenders' being "rational" as that term is defined by the formal "Postulates of Rationality."

We are now ready to introduce into the strategic game a source of *radical uncertainty,* which we shall provisionally define as "ignorance of possible qualitative changes that might well produce quantitative changes in at least limited fields." Any such qualitative change is precluded by the fundamental rules of our second game. (It is here assumed that "change of one's intention" is one source of qualitative change: this enables us to make allowance for the human capacity to change one's course; and, because of the attractive power of a genuinely optimal course, we can also discount in part the likelihood of a change from a course that is demonstrably so.) The essential feature of qualitative change in a game is that it can alter (1) at least some of the fundamental rules; (2) the number of strategies available to players; (3) the number of players. Thus suppose some third person (N for "Nature") compiles a pack of cards, some of which announce qualitative changes that produce, in the strategic game described in the last two pages, alterations of one or more of the three kinds just mentioned. The number of cards and the sense of what is written on them is kept concealed from the players but the latter are told that either of them, by spending one of his accumulated "lives," can buy one card and, should the consequent change of rules appear to favor him, may have it introduced into the game.

Notice that the prospect of an opponent's buying a card that actually turns out favorable to him in some specific fashion cannot be given a probability. (We have already indicated, that, for all the outcomes of the game in its first form—i.e., without the card pack—there were straightforward probabilities calculable upon the assumption and *only* upon the assumption that a game theory solution was available in principle which would prescribe optimum strategies for each player *and* that each would play it.) Each player in this second version of the game is radically uncertain about the eventual outcomes of the game—except (as we shall suppose) that he knows that he cannot lose more than a penny. (If next we wish to introduce the idea of momentousness as well as that of radical uncertainty, we might now introduce the rule that neither player can avoid playing the game for a stake of not less than half his annual income.) But each player can in this case discern the *limited* situations in which alone the possibility of radical uncertainty might arise.

For example, it cannot arise if both play C on the first move. The possibility *must* arise for the disfavored player (though the favored player need not avail himself of his opportunity, and can thus prevent the possibility arising for himself) if one plays C and the other P. But in the mere *strategic*-uncertainty game, assume it to be the case that optimal strategy for both the (symmetrical) players enjoins that both play P on the first move. If in the *radical*-uncertainty game each assumes that the other does so, then before Move One each can calculate exactly: "The probability that my opponent will gain an opportunity to confront me with radical uncertainty is just .25. So is the probability that instead I shall gain such an opportunity. The probability that neither one gains it, and therefore that the game will produce *no* possibility of radical uncertainty, is .5." Thus we have introduced the concept of a numerical strategic uncertainty (or "subjective probability") of radical uncertainty.

It is contended in this study that all adequate formal models of any given constellation of Powers must begin with a first requirement: that no Power's government knows what will or even what may happen. We can then decide how many of them, in any particular model under design, know that they are in fact ignorant. Only then, within the general premise of universal uncertainty, do we introduce the conception of a government's array of assessed likelihoods or subjective probabilities, amongst which will be the assessed likelihood of uncertainty or of surprise. Suppose then that at some given stage of the international process we imagine the government of a Power to envisage no more than the following three equally likely alternatives: (1) specified alternative A; (2) specified alternative B; (3) uncertain and unknown alternative X.

For every stage from this initial stage onward, one's assessment of later possibilities must, if rational, take account of there being no known resultants for alternative X. One's perspective could therefore be represented in summary as follows (P = objective probability, and assigning one-third as the subjective probabilities for these equally likely alternatives):

P.3· — X = unknowable;
P.6· — A *or* B

Suppose now that A's resultants are known to be just the following equiprobable alternatives: (1) α^1; (2) α^2; (3) α^3; and B's also equiprobable: (1) β^1; (2) β^2; (3) an unknown and uncertain alternative, γ. Then for this second stage it *seems* (but see NOTE, p. 46) we should write:

P.4· — $(X + \gamma)$ = unknowable;
P.1· — α^1;
P.1· — α^2;
P.1· — α^3;
P.1· — β^1;
P.1· — β^2;

Thus, if one knows that surprising innovation is possible at all, then the later stages of one's picture of future probabilities and possibilities are more and more eaten away by the prospect of the likely unknowable. But then why not accept these broadening reaches of the unknowable as the theme of our picture, and why not regard any preliminary sketching of probabilities as a quite subordinate foreground? If we do so accept uncertainty, important consequences immediately follow for any theory of the world-political system.

Firstly, to abandon the zero-sum condition for world-political models is not to go nearly far enough; we have no means of telling whether future innovations will not eliminate most of the motives for military—even, perhaps, for economic—competition between Powers; nor, if so, what other motivations might replace those, and generate other systemic relations. Thus, game theory has useful application, if at all, chiefly to historical cases and to those few sharply defined present situations in which we know that the possibility of radical surprise was—correctly as it has turned out—discounted. (Unfortunately, as we shall find, the most useful of the latter applications—*viz.,* to changes in alliance—is in practice impossible because of the order of numbers required for calculation.)

Secondly, a government's determining of its national policy cannot be represented, without gross self-deception, as its choosing that which, within an exhaustive set of alternative future goals or possible states of affairs, is believed to maximize something, such as security, power, or even GNP. A more sensible way to envisage the choice would be as between the employment of national capacities and resources to store up reserves against possible surprise and uncertainty, and on the other hand their more immediate use to produce a favorable change or continuity which is directly within the government's power and control. This rather cautious appreciation we might style the "Augustan" approach to uncertainty, as it reminds us of eighteenth-century statecraft. The "Romantic" approach would be to initiate something calculated to break up the existing constellation, being then alert to exploit surprise and to restructure the new situation. Both the last-mentioned attitudes are appropriate to the later twentieth-century expectation of uncertainty, whereas probability-calculating and optimizing is absurd. International theory, of course, must reckon with the possibility that all three, and more, will be adopted in practice.

Theorists try to stand their construction upon the "rational" response. They are right to do so, since *if available to the ordinary person,* it is also the likeliest response. But they have a better reason: it is on such a basis that the simplest models, most suitable for elaboration, can be constructed. Furthermore, irrational or stupid responses can be understood in terms of the rational response; but not the other way round. Thus the next step in our argument must be to examine the "rational" responses to innovation and surprise.

II

Expectation of surprise, as a subproblem within the general problem of uncertainty, has until now interested few besides economists.[1] Our approach is therefore nearer to the economic and political than to the psychological, and set, for sharp definition, in a strategic context.

The surprising, for our purposes, is not the unlikely or hardly expected—i.e., not the subject of a very long-odds bet; it is the totally unexpected—i.e., something which, as a distinct prospect, you have not considered at all for any odds whatsoever, or having considered, have ruled out as impossible. Nevertheless, recognition (1) of an enemy's technological and scientific parity with oneself, and (2) of the innovation-producing propensities evinced by technological and scientific enterprise, should tend sooner or later to cause one to *expect surprise:* to expect not something of a kind one can specify but something that until it actually occurs will have had no place at all in one's scheme of considerations. But if someone confidently expects surprise, and if the grounds of his expectation have more than a little explanatory and predictive power, then at that stage where he expects the surprise to impinge, his sequence of alternative pictures of the future must dissolve.

"Technological" and "scientific" surprise, as we have called them, are to be distinguished by the different fashions in which they change the "information" of the surprised party. ("Information" is here used in something like the technical sense of the information theorist: a *new* item of information is information which for logical reasons could not have been extracted by any method whatsoever from the surprised party's current stock of information.) The bases in information of different kinds of surprise can be dichotomized: (1) *All* the information conveyed by the surprise to the surprised party was implicit in information *already available* to him before the event, but it had not been extracted or put together by him—not even conjecturally. Technological surprise—i.e., the production of some device (e.g., a weapon) pertinent to economic, military, or world-political relations, has this kind of information basis; but so do certain social and political innovations—e.g., the synthesizing of the Augustan principate from several previously separate offices and roles. (2) Some item(s) of information conveyed by the surprise had been in no way available to the surprised party before the event—i.e., it was a "new

[1] E.g., G. L. S. Shackle, "The Logic of Surprise," *Economica,* XX (May 1953), 112–17; reprinted in his *Uncertainty in Economics* (Cambridge, Eng., 1955), pp. 56–62.

item of information" (see above), and could not be adequately described using only the concepts then in his vocabulary: given that the surprised party is a scientifically advanced Power, the weapon-system or other device constituting the surprise must be a technological development of some recent discovery in fundamental science—one which has necessarily involved some new concept, unpredictable in principle. The idea of anti-matter when first developed had the kind of novelty referred to. By contrast, a weapon-system depending upon controlled thermonuclear fusion, though a great technological surprise, would nowadays presumably not be an instance of scientific surprise since controlled fusion, though at present unobtainable, is a generally received idea.[2] Technological surprise has occurred quite often: scientific surprise, by its nature, has been much less likely, for it must also involve some technological innovation; and, more importantly, scientists disseminate their basic discoveries quickly except when major warfare enables their governments to restrict freedom of publication. Scientific surprise may never yet have been anything but a logical possibility for the most scientifically advanced of Powers.

Why, then, distinguish between the information bases of surprise, if our interest lies in the theory of current world politics? Later in this chapter the relevance of our surprise dichotomy to the preparing and to the forefending of surprise, both of which have sometimes been objectives of policy, will be indicated. For quite general reasons, however, the distinction has been drawn at this stage: contemplation of the possibility of one's being surprised on account of one's information basis approximating type (1) should dissolve only a segment of our future perspective; whereas contemplation of the possibility of scientific surprise—*viz.*, surprise arising from one's having an absolutely inferior information basis of the (2) type—seems apt, if it is not discountably unlikely, to blur our whole range of pictured alternative futures. That is, we can schematize by means of probability-arrays like those on p. 32 the rational consequences that expectation of technological surprise should have upon our prospect of alternative future histories, noticing that such surprise, though possible, is rather unlikely—after all, an advanced society does a great deal of positive forecasting upon the basis of generally available information, and this should in consistency tend step by step to reduce expectation of technological surprise. Probably something like technological surprise has been a perennial possibility since the first cities.

Scientific surprise is to be expected, on the other hand, only when scientific investigation is pursued by the leading Powers at least—and that

[2] This topic is related to the deterrent situation in *From Balance to Deterrence,* Social Science Monograph No. 9 (Australian National University, December 1956), pp. 16 ff.; published in a revised form in *World Politics,* IX, No. 4 (July 1957), especially pp. 509–29.

began to obtain only in the nineteenth century. Indeed, it would not be overconservative to suppose that the matter has become serious for advanced societies only since 1940, though the Australian aborigine, for example, suffered scientific and technological surprise from the firearms of Europeans. But it is now understood in advanced societies that basic discoveries, now unforeseeable for logical reasons, are a possibility, and that these in turn might enable technological and other material innovations which in turn might alter the way in which even those perennial features of world politics not directly affected by the innovation impinge upon the future. Such an understanding presumably has some more-or-less rational effect upon the structure of our expectations: how can the theorist schematize them and it? As a preliminary to answering that question, we need now to mark out some of the relations between expectation and planning.

We must imagine at least two major advanced Powers, each of which can induce some scientists to work in military secrecy on fundamental theoretical problems—admittedly, a state of affairs unlikely to be long maintained, since basic science flourishes even less than technology under security restrictions. Nevertheless, military planners upon either side should allow for the possibility that the others will make a fundamental discovery—in principle unpredictable—which might be technically applied by embodiment in some unheard-of device that *ex hypothesi* one cannot plan against. After the fashion of the schedule on p. 32, one would wish to assign a cardinal though subjective probability to that possibility. But how? Certainly, the number that one assigns must be in the nature of the case be greater than zero and less than unity. Further, if one knows, of two possible enemy countries, that whereas both can support a major research effort in some particular field such as low-temperature physics, only one of the two has the resources for work in some other, quite disconnected field, then one must suppose that the latter is more likely to achieve scientific surprise than is the former. Again, several kinds of technological capacity might be necessary for the production of the material vehicle or device intended to "carry" the surprise (assuming, of course, that the fundamental discovery is such as to require a technological auxiliary); this again would affect a nation's surprise-producing propensity. But even when combined, these three factors provide no adequate basis for the assigning of a meaningful *cardinal* number to one's judgments of comparative (i.e., ordinal) probability of one's being scientifically surprised. Are there other kinds of information that might justify cardinality for that subjective probability judgment?

To anticipate our later discussion of the topic: a major Power's intelligence organizations, dealing in both scientific and technological information, might report the presence (or absence) of *inexplicable* installations and activities. Such evidence, being cumulative with the three kinds of general consideration mentioned in the previous paragraph, might be sufficient in some cases to narrow the maximum range of subjective probability—"greater than zero, less than unity"—to a vague but cardinal quantity—e.g., "more than" or "less than .5".

That conclusion reverses the writer's 1957 opinion[3] on this question of cardinality. It had then seemed to me that either one discounted altogether the possibility of scientific surprise, or one took account of it, in which case one's inability to assign to it a probability even in a subjective schedule provided an *additional* reason why it must wholly dissolve one's perspectives. This supplementary reason no longer appears to me to hold; therefore the perspective-dissolving properties of the expectation of scientific surprise must depend upon other effects.

The first of these that we shall now consider follows from the likelihood that a discovery in fundamental science, if it is technologically and thereby strategically applicable, will have drastic consequences for many other technological and practical fields. A merely technological innovation, by contrast, though its implications in its own area may be quite as dire, is likely to have a more confined effect. If, for instance, we contrast, with the generally understood projects for anti-ballistic-missile defense, the idea of constructing a dome of force that would repel objects and explosive energy outward (something, one assumes, conceivable only if we are given a discovery in basic science indescribable at the time this passage was being composed), then we can imagine many more decisive military technologies being affected than that of the ballistic missile alone: indeed the political consequences, including great changes in the nature of the balance of power, would destroy the foundations of most current military planning.

Again, the situation when given only technological surprise is radically different: a brilliant combination of the anti-ballistic-missile devices already contemplated might yet do nothing against manned bombers or against unmanned craft that could sneak in at tree-top level. A probability of technological surprise, when confined to a particular field, need not cast in doubt many other expectations. A probability of scientific surprise renders one unable to decide whether or not any particular area of technology will be affected. Hence the epithet "perspective-dissolving" surprise.

The other principal effect of one's expecting scientific surprise and of attaching a roughly cardinal probability to it (*viz.*, after receiving intelligence of some large-scale inexplicable activity) has to do with the sort of intellectual effort needed to explain the inexplicable. Whereas for the

[3] In "The International Consequences of Expecting Surprise," *World Politics*, X, No. 4 (July 1958), 512–36, from which Sections II and III of this chapter are considerably adapted.

Power expecting technological surprise, recourse to technological experts could be reasonably supposed to offer a prospect of deciphering the indications discovered by the Power's intelligence organizations, this is not so with expectation of scientific surprise: for in that case, it would be the failure of technological experts to decipher the indications which created the presumption in favor of the expectation. Not experts alone, but creative scientists, who would have to discover independently the same novel and basic principle, might just conceivably invent a means to interpret the puzzling evidence. Clearly there can be no question of there being a method or expertise in discovering such basic principles. Thus at the very first stage of a Power's responding rationally to expectation of scientific surprise, the information basis for the making of a plan to respond is, by our definition above, irremediably deficient for logical reasons.

The possibility of basic scientific surprise, then, undermines the expectations of planners and politicians much less often but more seriously than does that of technological surprise. Can we determine a point at which such undermining sets in?

To begin, we may consider the *long-term* expectations of any ordinary adult in a contemporary advanced society. He should understand that new discoveries in fundamental science are always possible, which may radically alter the conditions of human existence everywhere. The interval between scientific innovation and such consequent changes, even when the urgencies of major war are not hastening the implementation of discovery, is now shortening to a matter of years rather than decades, so that processes once thought quite ineluctable—e.g., those of demography and economic geography—may for all we know be modified out of recognition by the end of the century. Thus the prospect of unforeseeable scientific advance tends to dissolve all other social perspectives thirty or more years on. Though we may be confident that essentially human activities will persist (and amongst those, it is contended below, politics is to be included), the scientific forecasting of specific social events becomes logically impossible. This condition determines when, in the long run and for all of us irrespective of power-political divisions, perspective-dissolving surprise sets in.

The dissolving effect is very different for the *immediate* future, especially from the viewpoint of some particular State expecting scientific surprise. The restrictions of security inhibit discovery in fundamental science, which is in itself so interesting that the most disguised forms of publication quickly attract the attention and perhaps the understanding of other scientists. Even if they are successfully diverted, technological development of the basic discovery conceivably may provoke an attack by the potential enemy, just because he cannot understand what the technical activity is all about. Since these considerations make scientific surprise difficult to achieve, the potentially surprised Power has reason to discount its possibility. But when, as supposed above, his intelligence organization supplies him with presumptive evidence that scientific surprise is already prepared against him, then the perspective and context of his planning dissolves abruptly—he may well lose all sight of the future further ahead than a few months. So while the long-term perspective-dissolving effect of our apprehending possible basic discovery is ever-present but directly alters expectations some decades away, the short-term effect is likely to be very uncommon, but, when it does set in, affects particular Powers—some, but necessarily *not* all—by quite obliterating their immediate view.

By contrast, technological surprise is quite common. Though the scientific kind is so little to be expected, it has seemed important to discuss it at considerable length, because of the significant and newly emerged limitations that awareness of possible innovation in basic science imposes upon all political and social theory; but even more because the nature of rational response to expectation of the unforeseeable is of itself a theme calling at present for scientific investigation.

We shall now consider how the statesmen of some particular advanced Power might respond to an expectation of novelty, whether scientific or merely technological. Such expectations, as we have seen, can be general and long-term: scientific and technological innovation should be expected, within the next few decades, by all of us. On the other hand there are particular circumstances, notably when advanced Powers fear and oppose each other, where the other's security arrangements are so effective that it is reasonable to expect him to be capable even within a few years of producing technological surprise and, much less probably, scientific surprise.

In preparing for both long-term and short-term exigencies, an obvious measure in response would be to invest in the *gathering* of intelligence about the other's activities. Next, one would need to invest in the scientific *interpreting* of that intelligence, which would involve the recruitment of technologists and of fundamental scientists into one's own security establishments. Now, the second of these measures, especially, is apt to increase the potential of one's own security establishment for surprising an opposed Power. Further, considerations of security may reinforce a government's concern to promote general scientific advance—since the enterprise of scientific discovery may produce disturbing innovations, it is better to have a community of scientists who can keep abreast of the enterprise, or even innovate on their own account.

One rational response to expectation of unforeseeable scientific advance in circumstances of inter-Power rivalry thus has the effects of (1) giving the opposed Power firmer ground for expecting surprise from the other(s); (2) somewhat increasing the human race's collective propensity to innovate in technology and fundamental science; and, therefore, of (3) somewhat increasing any rational observer's expectation of innovation and thus in general of *his* being surprised. However, the latter increase of expectation of surprise is not necessarily uniform for all rational observers, irrespective of nationality—identical-twin scientists, one in the service of the United States and the other in that of Sweden, are likely to have access to different ranges of scientific and technological enterprise. The Swede's prospects for scientific insight very well may be quite as deep as the American's in fields accessible to both; but the American, because of his nation's greater population and resources, is apt to have more fields open to him, supposing always that there are some developments in science and technology which such an advanced Power as the United States can and will for a while keep secret from other advanced but less populous and less well-equipped Powers.

Evidence at the time of writing suggests that the United States will continue to do this—e.g., American attempts to stop thermonuclear proliferation. Potential enemies of the United States, and to a lesser extent neutrals and even allies excluded from American secrets, might therefore rationally expect surprises of some kind from that quarter. The question is whether Americans should expect to be surprised by any other Power (and reciprocally, whether any other Power might feasibly attempt to surprise the USA). The stronger the evidence that they should do so, the more powerful the tendency for our system of potentially rival Powers to increase our *common* expectation of unforeseeable developments at a greater rate than would be the case if no Power kept scientific or technological secrets from any other. Mutually increasing expectation of surprise between any two Powers is possible upon conditions which are perhaps best classified in terms of our concept outlined above of the difference between the information bases of technological and of scientific surprise.

The case of potential for reciprocal scientific surprise can be understood through the idea of the comparison of "dictionaries." Let us call the set of concepts known to the statesmen and militarily relevant scientists of a given Power its "dictionary." (The word "concept" is here used in a way probably unsatisfactory to the semanticist—that is, not only to designate universals but also to refer to hypotheses and other statements, e.g., the "concept" of anti-matter.) Considering for a moment the relationship of just *two* Powers' information bases, and supposing that one of them, here called the "sender," is giving evidence of preparing some kind of surprise, while the other, called the "receiver," has acquired that evidence, then four possibilities will obtain: (1) the receiver has a larger dictionary than the sender—i.e., has the logical power to interpret correctly more than every signal put out by the sender—while the latter cannot reciprocate, though it might at any moment make for itself the theoretical scientific discoveries necessary for doing so; (2) *vice versa,* the sender has a larger dictionary than the receiver; (3) each dictionary contains some concepts not contained in the other; (4) the dictionaries are identical.

If the fourth, or even more the first condition prevails, the sender cannot for logical reasons achieve scientific surprise, though he might manage a technological surprise. If the second, he might achieve both. The Power with the smaller dictionary could not know but might guess that it had the smaller. The Power with the larger might infer that superiority from its own completely successful deciphering and interpreting of every "signal" put out by the other. But either might instead suppose the other's signals to be accidental, or deliberate gibberish, or from one cause or another incomplete. Every Power has a motive for getting itself the larger dictionary. This is one aspect of the broader case for basic research as a defensive measure.

The interesting situation is that under (3): for logical reasons, neither side could ever be sure whether or not the surprises the other was preparing were scientific surprises; but each might well have strong reasons for supposing so. Moreover, advantage in any one branch of fundamental research need not by itself increase the probability of interpreting correctly the signs of advance by an enemy in any other distinct branch. Suppose an intensification of secrecy and of a "cold war in science": then on general grounds each of the two Powers should increase its expectation of scientific surprise, since a limit to the rate at which it can enlarge its dictionary is set by the scarcity of creative scientists and perhaps also by the restrictions upon their art which security imposes.

Another source of limitation upon the innovatory process in science is the increasing economic cost of further discoveries along already-developed lines—as O. H. K. Spate has versified. "The micro-microcosmos takes the macro-macro-money." Projects relevant to strategy, such as weather control and satellite surveillance, also tend often toward increasing expense. This feature ought generally to limit or reduce any particular Power's hopes of achieving surprise, but also its fears of being surprised.

Ordinary scientific publicity provides the greatest limitation, given our idea of separate national dictionaries, since it reunites them. Our definitions of the information bases necessitates that scientific surprise between Powers is possible only if concepts are available to one Power's scientists that are not to the others'. We may reasonably conclude there would remain only a universal and long-term expectation of scientific surprise if no basic scientific work were ever classified for security purposes by any Power.

This conclusion is not true of technological surprise, in regard to which the Superpowers and other populous advanced States enjoy a considerable advantage. Technological processes are much more readily kept under security classification. Even though Swedish scientists, for example, are aware of all current developments in fundamental science, Sweden's technological intelligence may not be able to keep abreast of every new technological development in United States weaponry. Technological surprise, which may be strategically as upsetting as some scientific surprise, should be much more expected by all Powers—including the greatest, but especially the middling kind of advanced Powers. The likelihood of technological innovation demands consideration in all contemporary policy, and not merely in strategic affairs: a middle Power may nowadays set itself back as seriously by premature investment in, say, hydroelectric works or nuclear reactors as by buying early-generation ICBMs. Here the Superpower with a rapid rate of obsolescence has every chance of predominating.

III

In the previous section, it emerged that while features of technological innovation may tend to act as a brake upon expectation of surprise, features of scientific innovation should further accelerate it.

In developing our argument for the latter contrast, we introduced the notion of a "dictionary" of scientific and other concepts—a notion that seemed to be involved in our initial definition of scientific surprise. A further way of looking at expectation of surprise now suggests itself: to expect scientific surprise is to expect some unforeseen addition to one's dictionary. The greater the ratio between the expected dimensions of the expected addition and the known dimensions of one's present dictionary, the greater the surprise to be expected. The greater one's estimate of the dimensions of an opponent's dictionary, and the greater one's estimate of the difference in dimension between his and one's own, the greater one's expectation of surprise.

Moreover, insofar as it is considered as being based on a "dictionary," *merely* technological development is to be regarded for most practical purposes as a figment of our analysis. Further, our distinction between scientific and technological surprise, being formal, would not often be apparent in practice—surprises are likely to seem to the victim technological and scientific at once. Again, we have recognized throughout this chapter that the most important subset of limitations upon achievement of surprise are ordinary economic limitations, and that most problems concerned with the effects of innovation can be subsumed as problems in the theory of economic growth. It becomes clear, then, that we are dealing with a subject matter requiring not only military and international-relations theory, but also economics and the theory of information. Together with the theoretical aspects of those four disciplines, a realistic approach, which of course is not here attempted, would also require factual data of the sort characteristically annexed to each of them and to the basic natural sciences. The problem of expectation of surprise in a scientific age remains, nevertheless, one problem, in the sense that in principle it could be analyzed by means of a single coherent model. Even this would not give a completely realistic picture: for, within the boundaries fixed by technical conditions, the "human element" will always blur the outlines of our nicest calculations. Indeed, quantification of the evidence remains an unsolved, maybe insoluble problem. Nevertheless, the predicting of unpredictability, despite its suggestion of paradox, is not precluded by logic.

In the foregoing sections, the question of surprise has been discussed within the framework of an extremely abstract model of relationships between contemporary nuclear Powers, which have been represented as almost mechanical receivers and transmitters of "information." Of course, in the real world they are no such thing. The point of using such a framework was to provide a refutation of the most generally favored hypotheses about the nature of uncertainty and how to deal with it: essentially probabilistic hypotheses well-adapted to cybernetic instruments for dealing with information considered as a physical signal. Nevertheless, such hypotheses —though, I think, in error—are not *wholly* irrelevant to power-political action, in which statesmen consider certain outcomes as "likely," "unlikely," "so unlikely at to be discountable," and so forth, and are, moreover, sometimes at a loss, because they expect surprise, to know what *specific* outcomes to expect for any but the immediate future. I have here tried to show that in a scientific age the possibility of such radical ignorance of the arising political situation is an ineluctable fact which any philosophy of Power politics must take into account.

So indeed must the philosophy of any human action: though the concepts of creativity, novelty, emergence, and intuition have been suspect as the stock-in-trade of obscurantist philosophers, their hardheaded critics seem now more willing to agree that these concepts themselves cannot be reductively analyzed, but when employed with logical rigor are necessary terms in an account of human nature. The person is not only a wellspring of creativity, though himself a created and conditioned one: he is also capable on occasion of responding positively to surprise and to novelty which for logical reasons must defeat any mechanical device.

In the real world, only the individual man can suffer surprise, expect surprise, or indeed expect or be informed of anything. Systems of cybernetic devices can be set up so that their behavior exhibits analogies to these human experiences, but of course they cannot be programmed to extemporize the profounder human responses to them. Nor is it always the case that a group of individuals (e.g., a cabinet or an administration) must produce a creative response to the impact of startling new information, for the innovation may fail to "come home" to any of the administration's individual members, or at least to the decisive ones. In such circumstances the human group "responds" to novel events rather as would a cybernetic system—i.e., by construing (or misconstruing) the unfamiliar and strange as something familiar. But men are not fated to respond in that way: sometimes a decisive individual may apprehend the novel information and interpret it to the rest; sometimes a few individuals in *rapport* will together discover the novelty, so that it could not be said that just one of them had made the discovery. However it is done, such apprehending of and responding creatively to novelty is a genuine and non-negligible, though of course infrequent, feature of statesmanly political action, which a theory of the subject must take into account (as is done later in this study). Since surprise is a leading element in the philosophy of world politics advanced in the first chapter above, I have in the present chapter discussed it within a more complex abstract framework.

Models of the politics of the Powers, insofar as they are built within a context of real uncertainty and embody ranges of response to real uncertainty, must be models of discrete but interacting agencies whose several actions require for their explanation an account of each particular agency's range of expectations. It has been contended in this chapter that among the outcomes which an agent will expect as more-or-less likely there may well be one item which is nonspecific and indescribable and which can only be labeled "surprise."

We have also seen that what is surprise for one agent may or may not feature as surprise in other agents' ranges of expectation. Some of the conditions under which one Power may expect to be able to produce a specific outcome that would feature as a surprise to some other opposed Power and might therefore have been expected *as* surprise by the latter were discussed above—in terms of "dictionaries" for scientific surprise and "signals" for merely technological surprise. From those discussions it emerged as neither necessary nor impossible that a soundly erected uncertainty model of world politics should include a representation of at least one Power which in its range of expectations mentions, as specific and concrete outcomes, certain items that in the ranges of another Power or Powers are mentioned as surprises. The variety of possible models, that is, is *increased* when we relativize the concept of real uncertainty by developing from it the idea that one Power can cause another to expect surprise—can, in other words, increase the second Power's real uncertainty.

We may nevertheless eliminate one family of models as unrealistic: we have seen that no one and therefore no ruler can fail, if fairly well informed and minimally rational, to expect surprise at least in the long term; and that that expectation ought at some stage in the long term to dissolve all specific prospects. Thus in models of the politics of the

Powers, *perfect information should never be supposed.* Model-builders therefore require a methodology that enables them to represent those occasions upon which some Power is to some degree accurately informed (and furthermore knows that it is—i.e., is in possession of evidence that rationally warrants its conviction that in this respect it is accurately informed) as limiting cases of that general and pervasive situation in which every Power constructs or guesses at the prospects before it.

Because guessing need not be sheer fantasy, but may be made self-consistent and also open to correction by evidence, the limiting case of someone's being—and knowing himself to be—accurately informed *can* be provided for in models of which the primary assumption is that of real uncertainty, even though on first thoughts the natural and perhaps the sole rational method apparently would be to begin from assumptions of perfect information and then to weaken those assumptions so as to make room for imperfect information and eventually for guess work—e.g., for a progression of tasks: from solving chess-problems, to developing strategies for chess, to developing them for Kreigspiel. Political information is of a different species from information about games, for the latter depends upon rules which have been established by fiat.

Beginning from perfect information is precluded also because liability to surprise and to the dissolution of distant prospects afflicts the model-builder himself in this field. He has no reason to suppose himself perfectly informed; indeed, along some lines he is certain to be worse informed than the rulers of Powers he is studying. But while that probability casts some doubt on the usefulness of his models, it need not weaken their formal structure. A related fact must however condition them: in order for models of Powers to have explanatory force, they must specify what happens when any agent in the model interacts with any other agent, or acts upon whatever in the model corresponds to the natural or social environment of political interaction. This means that any would-be explanatory model must contain descriptions and projections of the environment and of the possible consequences of interactions with it and, within it, amongst the agents. Now, from the viewpoint of internal consistency, the model-builder must accept the consequence that some of his agents as he has modeled them will have expectations that differ from or even contradict the descriptions and projections which he himself included in the model. These agents also are his creatures, whom sometimes he will have created "uninformed" or "misinformed"—relative, however, to his own "information." Clearly, those complexities add to the difficulty of applying such models, whether in retrospective explanation or in forecasting.

The philosophic analysis of the nature of retrospective explanation in power-political history that comprises the next chapter has been designed to take account of such complexities, and of the effects upon historical agents of that radical uncertainty about their picture of the world which they could no more overcome than can contemporary statesmen. Before discussing general and theoretical explanations of the politics of the Powers, we need a clear view of the structure of particular and historical explanation.

NOTE: The argument of this chapter implies that one's rational expectations cannot be completely and validly expressed as they are on p. 32—i.e. as an array of probability-assignments—because:

1. The ideally comprehensive array of probability-assignments (*Lp*) at some near future time *t* would be that derived by assigning a fraction between zero and unity to each outcome *logically* possible at *t*, the most adequate list of these outcomes being those derivable from all the "concepts" in the best currently-available "dictionary" (see above), together with the list of initial conditions ascertained and explained in the currently best available "contemporary history."

2. But it is rational to expect that, by time *t*, some novel outcomes (*o, n*), by definition unmentioned in *Lp*, will have been produced by innovating agencies not all of which need have been mentioned in the list of initial conditions, and to which therefore no probability-fraction can be cogently assigned at the present time—i.e. before *t*.

3. Therefore, the totality (*e,t*), of one's rational expectations of outcomes at *t*, cannot be completely expressed by *Lp* alone, since one also expects some novel outcomes, *o,n*.

4. Further, no-one's *actual* array (*Pp*) of "personal" (i.e., subjective) probabilities can in practice embrace *Lp*. The strength of one's necessarily vague impression of the extent to which *Pp* falls short of *Lp*—($Lp > Pp$)—is an index of one's expectation of "technological" and similar surprise (see above). So in practice,

$$e,t = Pp + (Lp > Pp) + o,n$$

5. Moreover, *e,t* includes the expectation that an unpredictable list of the novel outcomes occurring before *t* will have been, by that time, *t*, conceptualized in the then-best "dictionary," while certain items in both the best dictionary and the best contemporary history "now" current will inevitably have been lost. Therefore the (Lp^t) theoretically available at *t* can in no way be derived from the current *Lp*, let alone from *Pp*. Thus the idea adumbrated on p. 32, of a tree-like succession of probability-arrays in principle extendable indefinitely despite the rapidly increasing probability of "unknowable" outcomes, is not finally tenable, even as an ideal construct.

Instead, consider expectations as fundamentally negative: we may hope to know, not what might, but what *cannot* happen, e.g., a basic scientific discovery could not be applied in a few hours. The personal estimating of the "probability" of future outcomes can then be understood as the consistent ordering of concepts in one's "dictionary" and "contemporary history"—not, i.e., as knowledge. *Retrospective* assessments of probability, on the other hand, being corrigible by evidence, are resistant to the erosion caused by expectation of novelty.

THREE

Explanations in Theory and History

I

Theoretical inquiry in the broadest sense can be concerned with general theories, or with models, or with both. The enterprise in any case involves, firstly, the formulating of propositions in which the key terms are characteristically abstract (i.e., the terms refer to interconnected abstractions from concrete reality, and do not name singular individuals except at the limit when a whole model is said to be the model of some particular historic system—say, that of eighteenth-century Europe); and secondly, the testing of those propositions—internally, for logical consistency; and externally, against evidence searched out either previously by historians with other interests, or on the spot for the particular purposes of testing.

Many of the distinctions made between the model and the general theory are verbal—indeed, some of the nonverbal distinctions seem to be almost a matter of aesthetic preference. In this volume, however, we shall try to confine our usages as follows.

The set of propositions designated as a general theory we take to be *all* universal propositions, the weakest and most restricted of them logically stronger (and therefore more vulnerable) than the most extensive conjunction of all those empirical generalizations which it helps to explain, and also of a higher order of abstraction. (The last condition is added in order to exclude propositions which are trivially more general—e.g., the conjunction of a set of conjoined empirical generalizations with another empirical generalization already strongly confirmed. The present writer holds the philosophic view that a proposition or propositions in a general theory do *not* stand simply as the major premise in a syllogism of which the conclusion is the empirical generalization which it or they, together with some propositions about initial conditions, purport to explain.) The crux of this approach to general theory is the exclusion from it of all singular or existential propositions, all propositions about initial conditions, and of course all first-level empirical generalizations. Thus in order to explain any empirical generalization, the most powerful of surviving general theories must be combined with some appropriate and thoroughly attested statement of initial conditions.

A model, on the other hand, we take to be a complex *singular* proposition or conjunction of them, including enough conjoined propositions—amongst them, if necessary, universal propositions—to warrant the inferring of descriptions of later states from the description of the earlier state propounded by the singular proposition specified by the model. A model thus embodies in itself descriptions of initial conditions, but abstracted rather than concrete descriptions. If the latter are well attested, and if some of the later states which can be inferred from them by means of the model square satisfactorily with an appropriate abstract description of the case to be explained, the model has explanatory power—provided of course that the *explicandum* could not have been inferred directly from a description of the embodied initial conditions alone, or from them when embodied in some logically simpler model.

It is not unreasonable to think of the model as a logically more primitive (less evolved) species of explanatory device than would be the combination of entirely singular or particular propositions about initial conditions with entirely universal propositions of high generality (i.e., with theoretical propositions). In the latter case, the universal propositions presumably will be generalizations of some model's universal ingredient, which has been enucleated from the model and developed or tested in other contexts. The advanced among the natural sciences are supposed constantly to pass in this way from "model" explanations to "general law" explanations. The present writer has long maintained[1] that for a number of reasons this progress from singularistic or "model" explanations to those mediated by "universal laws" is not possible in political and historical studies—for which the model of the ordinary singularistic explanation remains adequate.

Nevertheless, in the present chapter the purposes and some of the

[1] See "Ascertainment, Probability and Evidence in History," *Historical Studies—Australia and New Zealand,* IV, No. 16 (May 1951), 328–39.

conditions necessary for a general theory of world politics are explored. The emphasis here is thus less on models than on theories.

General theories in such fields as international relations have an intrinsic interest; but they are also sought as aids for the making of predictions, which in turn are needed to guide the making of policies for the future. Some theorists have suggested that they may help the historian by providing him with laws (generalizations, universal premises) which will enable him to construct historical explanations of past international events. In his *Generalized Foreign Politics,*[2] for example, Lewis F. Richardson was hoping to assist both the statesman and the historian. He himself needed help from the historian. His mathematical theories concerning the arms race and the conditions of outbreak of war were informed by a methodology similar to that then commonly attributed to Newtonian physics; and the factors he wished to use in explanation included, for instance, expenditure on armaments and (something he regarded as the contrary of that) involvement in international trade. His hypotheses thus needed testing against historical cases, and would have been available for use in prediction only insofar as they survived such historical tests. If the hypotheses had then survived *further* testing through their successful use in prediction, Richardson might have claimed that they had been in some degree confirmed; and he could thereupon offer them back to the historians for use in historical explanation—e.g., in explaining the outbreak of wars.

These particular hypotheses of Richardson's were not in fact successful (see pp. 183–186 for an assessment). Their failure is partly to be attributed to his having envisaged physical science as his exemplar. In the present study, a methodology is adopted that owes much to the economists. It is not easy to show, in the study of world politics—where we lack a ready-made index such as money, where the operators can be counted in tens, and where the closed systems which we know to have existed are less than a dozen—that any general theory which follows the example of the economists can have more than an intellectual interest. It is not easy to show that a theory can do anything for the statesman and the military strategist on one side, or for the historian on the other, that they could not do perfectly well without theoretical assistance.

Later in this chapter, I hope to point to some few ways in which nevertheless such theories might be of interest to policy-makers and even to historians. Here, I shall try to set out what I think historians look for in a good historical explanation—in particular, an historical explanation of the kind of event that a theorist of international relations might also be interested in.

[2] *British Journal of Psychology,* Monograph Supplement XXII (Cambridge, 1939).

To such a theorist, the most interesting of all are the events that happened though nobody contrived or planned or even wanted them—for example, arms races and the outbreak of wars on one hand; and on the other, long periods free of major wars in which the balance of power did not change. Modern thought has divided, on the whole, between two ways of looking at the world in which such unintended things happen. One way in Tolstoy's, in the Epilogue to *War and Peace*. On that view, a great event or process such as Napoleon's invasion of Russia and its repulse actually *causes* the lesser events that go to make it up. The analogy is with a wave, conceived as causing the movement of the molecules of water that from instant to instant make up the wave.

On the other view, such historic events are comprised of or result from the more or less rational actions of persons who—being necessarily incapable of knowing what each other person involved with them intends, and therefore of grasping any but the more immediate implications of their own intended action—jointly give rise to a process itself unintended or even counter-intended as a whole. One instance: a number of people hurrying for various reasons to get out of a room, and finding themselves jammed together in the doorway.

In general those who, like Tolstoy, are committed to the holistic point of view have looked forward to developments in social science that might do something for the historian, with his intuitive judgments, his qualitative reasoning, his literary approach; whereas individualistic analysts are inclined to say that the historian already understands his own business, and has managed to provide explanations which really explain and which do so without mentioning or using those general laws or law-like propositions looked for by orthodox methodologists of social theory:

> If by historical thinking we already understand how and why Napoleon established his ascendancy in revolutionary France, nothing is added to our understanding of that process by the statement (however true) that similar things have happened elsewhere.[3]

Though that aphorism leaves obscure the nature of the understanding which Collingwood supposes to arise from historical investigation, its point is well taken against the deductive theory of historical explanation: that an historical event is explained if and only if the statement that it took place can be deduced from a statement about initial conditions together with a previously established law (or "law-like statement") to the effect that initial conditions of that class are always followed by instances of the class of event to be explained.

The deductive theory has been propounded in its modern version by

[3] R. G. Collingwood, *The Idea of History* (Oxford, 1946), p. 223.

Karl R. Popper and Carl G. Hempel.[4] They adopted the practice (which is followed in the remainder of this chapter) of constructing a logical skeleton of their hypothecated form of explanation. Figure 3.1 is the skeleton of a *deductive explanation.*

Figure 3.1

Explicans:	(i):	c^1 occurred at time t.
	(ii):	whenever an instance of C occurs, an instance of E follows at interval n.
Explicandum:		e^1 occurred at time $t + n$.

Hempel's and Popper's skeletons, similar to the above, purport to display the necessary and sufficient *explication* of the plain-English concept of "historical explanation," i.e., their hypothesis is that *anything* properly considered to be an historical explanation is such by virtue of conformity to a deductive skeleton, though in practice the major or universal premise may not be made explicit, being too trite, or may be taken for granted.

Two amongst several lines of test for that kind of explicatory hypothesis are (1) to derive logical consequences from it and see whether they agree with what we assume on other grounds; and (2) to confront it with examples of historical explanation that may or may not conform with it. In hypothecating below three other explicatory skeletons (motivational, constitutive, and compositive) I follow the second line. The constitutive and compositive forms should be searching tests of the Popper-Hempel hypothesis, since at first sight they appear to conform to it.

Objections to the deductive theory of historical explanation are now well known. Collingwood's implies that reference to a law or law-like proposition is not necessary. Others question the explication's sufficiency: explicit deductions are found rarely in historical writing; what is more, when one tries to make explicit the general law alleged to be implicit in a good historical explanation, one usually educes something either false or *ad hoc.* Consider the accepted explanation of Charles I's summoning the Long Parliament in October 1640: he did so in order to buy the Scots out of the northern counties of England where (by the Treaty of Ripon

[4] K. R. Popper, *The Open Society and Its Enemies* (London, 1945), II, 248–49; and 342–44 n. 7. C. G. Hempel, "The Function of General Laws in History," *Journal of Philosophy,* XXXIX (1942), 40 ff.

with which their Commissioners had forced Charles to conclude the Second Bishops' War) their soldiers were to stay until the high indemnity they had secured by the Treaty was paid in full. Other circumstances pertinent to the explanation would be that the King's own resources were insufficient to pay the indemnity, and that English parliamentarians, who had colluded with the Scots, organized petitions for the calling of parliament. But if *Explicans* (i) were made to include along with c^1 such circumstances, *Explicans* (ii)—the major premise—would need generalizations of those circumstances included along with *C*. Clearly, there is no known causal law corresponding to such an expanded major premise. Thus the deductionist theory of explanation is not to be rescued by an otherwise proper request to the historian for fuller explanation.

That last-mentioned difficulty is avoided in some *natural*-historical explanations by reference to known second-order laws—laws of Composition of Forces. These would allow us to calculate the combined causal power of distinct "factors" (as they are called) in human behavior. Though social psychologists and others have been trying to find these second-order laws in human affairs, none has yet been discovered—indeed, some of us believe that they cannot obtain: statesmen and similar human actors are rarely doing or being one thing at a time. Thus, no account of the structure of historical explanation will be satisfactory if it cannot leave room for the explanatory features of mixed motives, of different but convergent and cumulative motives, and, when motives conflict, of why one consideration overrode another. It must also take account of a peculiarity of human etiology: a man may have more than one quite sufficient and compelling reason for doing something, and yet his manner of doing it may be just as if he had only one (cf. in physics the implications of the Law of the Composition of Forces).

Those objections question the sufficiency of the deductive theory. A further difficulty is that all deductive explanation employing previously established "law" involves a parallel in prediction, of the strictest sort: if, at time *t,* the law in *Explicans* (ii) were already known, the *Explicandum* could have been predicted with certainty; if not it could not have been explained. Any theory of explanation must take account of the logical parallel between prediction and explanation while avoiding the consequences of determinism and "prophecy"—as we hope to do in the following skeleton of *motivational* explanation, which also takes account of the features of human etiology mentioned in the previous paragraph.

The skeleton of motivational explanation in Figure 3.2 is in fact a dressing-up of Aristotle's "practical syllogism."[5] Aristotle showed that the conclusion of a certain type of syllogism was not a proposition but an

[5] E.g., Aristotle, in *Nic. Eth.,* trans. F. H. Peters (Kegan Paul, 1894), vii. 3.

Figure 3.2

Explicans:

(i): Before time t^0,
A intended to take any opportunity O to do Y.

(ii): At time t^0,
(a) A believed an opportunity o^1 to be arising;
(b) A resolved, by time t^1, to do y^1.

Explicandum: At time t^1, A did y^1.

---

action.[6] In my version, the *explicans* consists of the agent's having argued with himself and come as a conclusion to a resolution or determination which, if he had expressed it, would have corresponded logically with the *explicandum*—that is, with the thing that in fact he did. Though within the *explicans* itself there is a syllogistic argument, actual or virtual (which could be couched in the first person throughout, with minor premise in present indicative, but major premise and conclusion in jussive mood), attributed on conclusive evidence to the agent, and though that argument should make the auditor both understand the action and also, understanding it, acquire rational confidence in the force and cogency of the explanation, yet the *explicans* does not entail the *explicandum* as is the case with the deductive skeleton. It seems that we all know—if only from our own experience—that a person may, until the very moment of action, have the strongest intention to do something, and yet not do it. (Earlier chapters refer to an irreducible uncertainty about human behavior at this point which the most exhaustive analysis of motivation cannot eliminate.)

[6] "You may have (1) a universal judgment, (2) a judgment about particular facts which fall at once within the province of sense or perception; but when the two are joined together, the conclusion must in matters of speculation be assented to by the mind, in matters of practice be carried out at once into act; for instance if you judge (1) 'all sweet things are to be tasted,' (2) 'this thing before me is sweet'—a particular fact—then, if you have the power and are not hindered, you cannot but at once put the conclusion into practice." *Loc. cit.* In my version of motivational explanation (see the skeleton in Fig. 3.2 above), the conclusion of the syllogism is retained within the *explicans.* This is meant to diminish the quasi-logical force with which, according to Aristotle's doctrine, the act emerges from union of the universal and particular judgments. I allow a share of the power of this kind of explanation to reside in the coincidence (given appropriate changes of person, mood, and tense) between the statement of the conclusion and the statement of the *explicandum.* What the agent (called "*A*" in Fig. 3.2) intended, believed, and resolved can all be put into direct speech, which better brings out the syllogistic quality of his purposive reasoning, and the gap between its conclusion and his action.

Nevertheless, we can and do put value on the power of motivational explanations (we assign degrees of plausibility, persuasiveness, clarification), and these values vary with the depth to which we feel we understand the agent's reasons and motives for action.

One may elicit from oneself these valuations of explanatory power by means of the following mental trick. Ask yourself "What would I have considered a fair offer of odds for a bet on the agent's doing what he did before he actually came to do it, given that I knew nothing of his reasons or intentions? Secondly, and by contrast, what would I have considered a fair offer of odds, given that I had this evidence concerning his reasons and intentions?"

Now put each set of odds into the form of a probability fraction (remembering that they are not objective probabilities but only expressions of your valuations, arranged for consistency in accordance with rules equivalent with those of the Calculus of Probabilities plus an additional strengthening requirement[7]). Then lastly, divide your second valuation by your first. You will be judging that your information about the agent's intentions has logical power to explain his act only if and to the extent that the resulting quotient exceeds unity.

This device for expressing one's estimate of explanatory power is not proposed as a method of assessing explanations. Its use is as a model in my general analysis of historical explanation. A conflict of intentions could be expressed as follows. Suppose we have evidence that the agent had indeed formed these intentions, but had also formed others which, taken alone, would have been a sufficient reason for his *not* doing what in fact he did. Now if we go through the motions of putting betting values on the explanatory power of these countervailing intentions, we should find that the odds on the actual deed *sans phrase* are shorter than those we assigned it after discovering the countervailing intention. If the product of such an expression (indicating, say, "counter-predictiveness," and written with the latter odds over the former) and of an expression, similarly structured, indicating our valuation of the positive intention's explanatory power, should exceed unity, we still have, in our information about the

[7] Viz. $P(x,y) = 1$ only if x entails y; and $P(a,b) = 0$ only if a entails *not-b*. See A. Shimony, "Coherence and the Axiom of Confirmation," *Journal of Symbolic Logic,* XX (March 1955), 1–28; R. Sherman Lehman, "On Confirmation and Rational Betting," *ibid.* XX (September 1955), 263–73.

Reading $P(e)$ as "the quotient for the odds which I would accept as a fair bet on the *explicandum e,* without other information" and $P(c,e)$ as a comparable quotient for a bet on e, "given the fact of c, as an *explicans,*" theorists will recognize the ratio $P(c,e)/P(e)$ as common in confirmation theory; e.g., when scaled as $[P(c,e)/P(e) - 1] / [P(c,e)/P(e) + 1]$, it is equivalent to Popper's measure E for explanatory power, as originally expounded in the *British Journal for the Philosophy of Science,* and republished in *The Logic of Scientific Discovery* (London: Hutchinson, 1959), pp. 399–400.

positive intentions, an adequate explanation, though not as strong a one as we might at first have thought.[8] If the product is less than unity, our explanation is not adequate by itself, and we will usually wish to look for evidence of other intentions and reasons which would be cumulative with the original positive ones—or we may conclude that this is one of those cases of final uncertainty that the previous chapter referred to, in which at the last moment a person fails to do what he had determined to do.

I do not, of course, suppose that any historian has ever set himself little sums like these in thinking about his explanations. But I do suggest that historians in fact allow weight to the purpose and intentions which, so they have evidence, were entertained by their subjects; that these estimates of weight vary when the reasons vary; and that each historian would be inclined to somehow compare and collate the various estimates which he makes. Insofar as the whole process of weighting and comparing is consistent with itself, it must have a formal equivalent in the fair-bets procedure sketched above.

[8] The requirement is: $\frac{P(d,e)}{P(e)} < 1 < \frac{P(c,e)}{P(e)}; \frac{P(c,e)}{P(e)} \times \frac{P(d,e)}{P(e)} > 1.$

II

So far I have been dealing with the explanation of intended consequences only—that is, with actions, or "deeds," and their explanation. I now need another type of explanation—one which, combined with the previous motivational type, may serve as a form of explanation of some kinds of unintended consequences. I call the required type *"constitutive* explanation."

This form has a peculiar feature—somehow, it involves in the *explicans* a logical or semantic or definitional metalinguistic proposition. In other words, we would be committed, by offering such an explanation, to maintaining that *A*'s doing x^1 at *time* t^1 and *B*'s doing y^1 at the same time together *constitute* or *amount* to or *aggregate* into the occurrence of e^1 at t^1. Clearly "to constitute, amount to, or aggregate to" does not there mean any physical or actual unification—item (iii) signifies no more than the semantic proposition: "the denotation of the conjunction, '*A* did x^1 at t^1, and *B* did y^1 at t^1,' is identical with one of the legitimate denotations of the *explicandum,* 'Event e^1 occurred at t^1.'" It would be a matter for logicians to decide whether or not this proposition is a third *premise* in the *explicans* along with the explicitly factual pair of premises—items (i) and (ii). Notice, however, that we now have a form of explanation which might apply to some of the simpler types of unintended resultants from intentional acts. In this form, for example, agent *A* might dislike the prospect of e^1's occurring at t^1, and the possibility of it may not have entered

*Figure 3.3**

	(i):	*A* did x^1 at time t^1.
	(ii):	*B* did y^1 at time t^1.
Explicans:		
	(iii):	(i) + (ii) constitute e^1 at t^1 or, in formal terms, (i) + (ii) $\equiv$ (e^1 at t^1).
Explicandum:		Event e^1 occurred at time t^1.

* In item (iii) of the constitutive *explicans,* the alternative formulation used an identity symbol ($\equiv$) which may mislead without further explanation. The point is that items (i) and (ii) together would comprise only one of indefinitely many possible denotations of the *explicandum.* If they comprised the sole possible denotation, an identity sign would be completely in order; but then, no explanation of the "*explicandum*" would have been required. As it is, item (iii) can be "meta-linguistic" without being factually vacuous.

One further point: explanations involving reference to some sort of physical conjunction or unification of actual processes are *not* what I mean by "constitutive explanation," and can, in my opinion, be re-stated so as to fit the deductive model of Hempel and Popper.

B's head. But if, before his act, each were ignorant of the fact that the other was intending to do what later he did, then we ought to be in a position to offer an explanation in which is comprehended the *necessitation* of an unintended or counter-intended consequence by the fully intentional acts that together amount to it.

Next let us suppose that these two premises which make up the *explicans* of the constitutive explanation are each of them the *explicandum* of some satisfactory motivational explanation (i.e., suppose we know why *A* did x^1 at t^1, and why *B* did y^1 at that time); unless both of those conditions are fulfilled, the *explicans* of the constitutive skeleton conveys no new factual information, and therefore has zero explanatory power: premise (iii) is a purely formal necessary condition for the transmitting of the explanatory power which the other premises provide. Then in the conjunction of these motivational explanations with the consequent constitutive explanation, we would have a characteristically "transparent" historical account of unintended consequences, analyzed into its elements of individual action and intention, but with no mention of a general law or universal proposition, nor with the use or mention of any general theory.

Let me put some color on the model. Suppose an historian wishes to explain the disappearance of some undervalued specie from amongst the metal coinage previously circulating in a small town of the early nineteenth century; and suppose that he knows with reasonable accuracy how much disappeared in a given year. The historian now finds sets of records of the town's two banks. From one set he discovers that one banker had exchanged overvalued specie in his private possession for undervalued specie from time to time deposited in the bank he operated on his shareholders' behalf, and had melted down and sold the undervalued specie which he had thus acquired, in order to make a profit for himself. From the other set of records he learns that the other banker, with his shareholders' concurrence, was collecting all undervalued specie deposited, and was using it as bullion to pay off the bank's overseas debts at a discount. Suppose finally that he adds up what the one melted down and the other exported, and finds that the sum amounts, with a margin of error, to the quantity that disappeared in the year in which he was interested. I have chosen this example because it could be the kind of thing which a diligent amateur historian *who had never heard of Gresham's Law,* even as an empirical generalization, might work out for himself.

Now an imaginary international example. Two otherwise friendly nations, rather isolated from the rest of the world, have each a quantity and a disposition of arms just sufficient to afford to each a strong probability of being able to withstand a surprise attack by the other. Each knows, however, that in every year for the next three years, either side—if that side alone were to add to the quantity of its arms—could achieve a position of high security from the other's surprise attack, but *ipso facto* would also have become able to destroy the other's forces by surprise attack. Each also knows that if both arm to their full annual capacities, each will have reached, at the end of the third year, an absolute and a relative level of armaments which, though now very unlikely to enable it to withstand a surprise attack by the other at its current level of forces, is for that very reason equally likely to guarantee it success in overwhelming the other by surprise attack. Now let us suppose that certain later events are known—e.g., that at each of the two earlier year's-ends, the two nations held desperate but unsuccessful conferences on arms control; and that just before the end of the third year they launched simultaneous surprise attacks against each other. An imaginative historian should now be able to explain the reciprocal increases of armaments, and the eventual war that broke out, entirely as the unintended consequence of actions that were in their own way rational and intended. He may well be able to trace out the development of policies on either side, the imputation of divers policies by each to the other at the several critical stages, and the effects of such imputations in maintaining the arms race and provoking the preemptive attacks—and all without having so much as to mention any such general concepts as "arms race" or "preemption."

Each of these imaginary historical cases *could* be regarded as instances of an empirical generalization—the first as an instance of Gresham's Law, the second as an instance of part of a multiplier theory of the arms race. What is more, we supposed the respective historians to be working through, in their concrete historical reconstruction, the equivalents of part of the abstract arguments one could use to demonstrate, respectively, Gresham's Law or the arms-race theory.

But we saw, even so, that neither historian needed to employ, or "apply," the abstract theoretical laws in order to complete his explanation. Though the imaginary economic case, for instance, was in some sense an instance of Gresham's Law, and though Gresham's Law is certainly a general proposition, it was not required to be used as such, or indeed at all, within the explanation that appeared to instantiate it. At first sight deductive in form, that explanation changes its shape under further examination. My first conclusion, therefore, is that in these nondeterministic studies, the relation between theoretical laws and historical explanations is not necessarily that prescribed either by positivistic methodology, or by Popper and Hempel.

There is an obvious objection to the conclusion just drawn. It is that laws and theories in the natural and the social sciences are concerned with large numbers, and that nobody bothers with invoking laws in cases of the nearly unique or the nearly singular, such as those I have been instancing. For example, one can say that Gresham's Law is concerned with the effects *throughout a whole nation or economy* of autonomous variations in the metallic value of specie against some second type of currency—i.e., that Gresham's Law has its application in situations where there are so many operators that no historian could ever tell just who exported or melted down or hoarded how much of the undervalued specie. Instead, the historian literally "applying" Gresham's Law (restated, not as an empirical generalization, but as a "compositive" law) would have to work upon a relation between the degree of imbalance of payments with other countries and the nature of the market for bullion on the one hand, and on the other hand the speed and completeness with which the bad currency drove out the good. And if he were to follow that line—the objection might continue—the historian would be applying economic theory in a direct and obvious fashion.

I think that objection is valid for the most part; but before I enter into qualifications, I should point out that economics is almost the only field of nondeterminist social theory in which the operators are as numerous and anonymous as the objection requires them to be (psephology, demography, and some of the study of party politics may also have this numerosity). Students of international affairs in particular rarely have to deal simultaneously with the relations of more than a dozen or so nations. In Chapter 1 (pp. 24–25), I mentioned Morton A. Kaplan's invention of the convenient phrases "system-dominant" and "subsystem-dominant" to make this distinction.[9] One might add to the above explication that if an operator in a system-dominant situation is to respond with sensitivity to the whole system's behavior, there must be some public quantitative medium, such as money or votes or seats in the House, through which the behavior of the system is reflected. In international affairs, apart from the dubious and ambiguous comparison of military budgets, there is characteristically no universal quantitative medium.

Between clear system dominance and clear subsystem dominance there are mixed situations, in which one can neither distinguish and name specific subsystems nor be certain that independent but anonymous agents are so many that system dominance might well obtain. With such mixed situations, historians have often to do the best they can. Some of them cast about for laws or at least well-confirmed generalizations to carry their explanation sketches across these unknown areas. Others combine commonsense motivational explanation which is informative but not easily set out as valid inference (see the comments above on motivational explanation) with the inferentially valid but partly verbal constitutive argument. I refer to this combination as "compositive" explanation, borrowing the adjective from F. A. Hayek,[10] though, as is implied in his "Communication"[11] concerning an earlier publication of the material in the present chapter, the compositive structure which he had shown to inform much sound social theory is proper to a higher level of abstraction and of cogency than to the more concrete and merely empirical level of historical investigation which we are now discussing. Nevertheless, formal resemblances in the modes of reasoning employed at the two levels perhaps warrant the borrowing.

To explain certain kinds of effect which are *generalized* throughout a cluster of systematic relationships, a compositive argument is often needed; the constitutive argument already discussed can explain only particularized effects, and deals furthermore with specific and nameable agents. In contrast, a disjunctive array of anonymous agents are referred to in compositive explanation. Historical inquiry strives to reduce anonymity and disjunctiveness to specific and particularized narrative, but in the range of situations between system and sub-system dominance such reduction is rarely possible. The following skeleton is intended to indicate that nevertheless *compositive explanation* can be adequate.

[9] Morton A. Kaplan, *System and Process in International Politics* (New York, 1957), Chapter 1 *passim*.

[10] F. A. Hayek, *Individualism and Economic Order* (London, 1949), pp. 73 ff.

[11] F. A. Hayek, "Communication: The Uses of 'Gresham's Law' as an Illustration in Historical Theory," *History and Theory* II, No. 1 (1962), 101–2.

Figure 3.4

Explicans:

(i): At time (t minus i)
where i is an interval long enough for the performance of actions (d^1 or d^2... or d^n)
there occurs in or to a system S
comprising a number, perhaps not known exactly, of agents (a^1 ... a^m)
a cue or causally initiating event c^1.

(ii): For at least some of (a^1... a^m), c^1 could have afforded opportunity for the actions (d^1... or d^n).

(iii): The disjunction (d^1... or d^n) during i constitutively explains or entails or amounts to the occurrence of the *explicandum* e^1 not later than time t.

(iv): In S, e^1 occurs at or by time t.

(v): In S, given c^1 at (t minus i), e^1 at t is conclusive evidence for d^1... or d^n) during i,

(vi): Therefore (d^1 ... or d^n) are enacted during i.

Explicandum: Event e^1 occurred at time t.

Some comment is required:

1. Compositive argumentation is pertinent only where human agents, individual or corporate, are systematically interrelated: hence the systematic context *S*. It need not be a closed social system—what we require is a certain intensity and complexity of interrelationship, in matters that are more or less calculable, even utilitarian (that is, the agents in the case are not as such a community of scientists, artists, or saints). So far as the outcomes of those interrelationships are calculable, historians are in a position to judge concerning the entailments of the disjoined possible actions and interactions by the anonymous interrelated agents.
2. Compositive explanation combines motivational—see items (i) and (ii)[12]—and constitutive—see item (iii)—arguments, but in anonymous and unspecific forms. It is at the limit of sound historical and scientific method, on the one hand liable to be reduced to the named specifics of historical narrative; on the other

[12] In the conditional mood, these first two premises carry us through the "practical syllogism" which I have spelt out in my formalizing of the "motivational" type of explanation.

hand, if only the situation were nearer system dominance, liable to be turned into the general and quantitative argument of compositive social science.

3. The "cue or causally initiating event, c^1" may, but need not, be consciously perceived by the agents as an "opportunity": provided it is the kind of event they might be expected to act on, that is enough.
4. The disjunction of possible actions (d^1 . . . or d^n) can be of the same or of different kinds from each other; or, indeed, from the agent's precedent course of action: as Professor Hayek points out in the above-mentioned "Communication," the agents may report doing only the same *kind* of things as they were doing before—e.g., exporting full-weight gold coins, though more of them. The employment of a disjunction of actions in an explanation, though it must appear to historians as imperfect—perhaps unavoidably so—is in logical terms valid; disjunctive explanation turns up in natural science.
5. The work of compositive explanation is to fill a gap in narrative between the causally initiating event (c^1) and the *explicandum* e^1. The gap in such a case can be filled only by actions of the kinds which would constitutively explain—i.e., entail—e^1, and only if conclusive evidence is available that one or another action of those kinds was performed. The form of the required inference-from-evidence has been much discussed in confirmation theory, but item (v) presents no special or unfamiliar difficulties to the formalizer. However, it may appear something of a formal curiosity to introduce in that item the *explicandum* as evidence for an essential step in our *explicans*. Historians, on the other hand, may recognize how usual is such a step in historical reconstruction. A consequent and rather more otiose feature of the *explicans* is item (iv), which we need in order to warrant item (v) and which simply states the *explicandum*. If we then consider the whole explanation skeleton of Figure 3.4 simply as an inference, it is trivially valid (being an identity) on account of item (v) alone. But when all six items are taken together as premises, the whole skeleton is a nontrivially valid inference (formally like that of the constitutive argument), and on that account the explication of one kind of adequate historical explanation.
6. In filling the gap, i.e., in demonstrating the truth of item (iii), the historian would need to argue, in part, statistically. He would need, for instance, in explaining the disappearance of new or unworn gold coins from circulation, to consider the size of population, the degree of devaluation and of the adverse balance of

payments, the size of the outlets for bullion and of payments abroad, and to make some sort of model in order to get a result which could be tested against the statistics in the *explicandum* for goodness of fit. Therefore he would be forced into investigations that were basically abstract provided that he had the evidence in a form that warranted statistical handling, and provided he required such a degree of precision. But he could still get by without actually invoking Gresham's Law or any other abstract theory in the form of a universal proposition.

In any case it may be misleading to say of even the most theoretically informed historical explanation that it actually "invokes" an economic law—i.e., imports a universal proposition, elsewhere derived or assumed or put to the test, into a collection of premises that without it would fail adequately to explain the *explicandum*. Rather, the historical explanation (*viz.*, a compositive explanation of an economic change) may share with the theoretical economist's exposition of an economic law both certain theoretical concepts and certain formal structures of argument, of the kind set out in the logical skeleton of Figure 3.4.

At this stage, then, my conclusions are to be summarized as follows: when the subsystems are dominant, historical explanation of unintended consequences will be isomorphic with some features of theory construction in the equivalent theoretical field. The historical explanation will not, however, use or employ or apply the theory; and it is not strictly necessary for the historian to be trained in theory.

But where the system is dominant, the historian's explanatory work will be more precise and cogent the nearer his methods approach an analytic and quantitative type of argument virtually indistinguishable from the theoretician's. Preeminently this will be so whenever the historian has need to construct a mathematical model. Thus in some types of historical explanation, the historical and the theoretical approaches are forced to meet.

III

In the previous sections of this chapter we have examined certain kinds of historical explanation, in order to show which kinds are, and which are not, necessarily dependent upon universal theoretical laws. The notion of a "theory" has remained undefined. While not here offering a formal definition, we shall now turn again to the matter of a theoretical approach to international relations.

The theoretical may be contrasted with the historical and journalistic approaches to world politics. Journalists and historians concern themselves, the one with present and the other with past concrete relations between nation-states, with policies espoused by national leaders, with the economic and other potentials of nations, and with what has resulted or might result from concatenations of such circumstances.

A theoretical approach need not be more directed toward the actual world than toward any of the other possible "worlds" comprising related sovereign states (for example, Morton Kaplan considers six possible international systems, only two of which have actually existed).[13] Whereas journalists and historians are concerned with exhibiting the actual relations between states in all their apparent contingency, the theoretician will wish to identify certain elements of necessary connection within a relationship. (I am here following the view that the connections which theorists try to discover are either necessary connections or demonstrable necessities that certain types of actual connection cannot be necessary.) From such a view the ideal—certainly unattainable in practice, and open, as we shall see, to theoretical objections as well—is the development of a general theory of international affairs having the completeness and the rigor of economic theory. It would deal exhaustively with every type of systematic relationship between sovereign states, from situations in which they were barely emergent to some such unitary systems as world government. But not all kinds of relation between states are our concern (for example, cultural relations which happen not to bear upon more systematic relations); nor are we directly concerned with the economic connections between states which we may nevertheless need to be aware of in our more specific studies; our interest is in the systems formed by states when interrelated as Powers.

I shall suppose that such a system exists if, when one of the ingredient states changes its posture toward another, at least the relation of the latter with a third or more will change concomitantly (e.g., if the European countries of NATO lose confidence in the United States' capacity to retaliate massively on their behalf, and begin devoting their resources less to joint NATO defense than to the development of individual strategic nuclear forces, then the USSR-US relationship changes necessarily in the Russians' favor, at least in the short run. The long-run analysis is not easy to forecast—it may even show that eventually the Europeans' move favors the United States).[14]

Marshall's well-known marbles-in-a-bowl analogy for the economic system seems suitable, with certain modifications, to illustrate the international system as well.[15] Think of the agents in an economy as a number of frictionless marbles in a hemispherical bowl. Take out one marble, or put

[13] *Op. cit.*, Chapters I and II.

[14] This example was invented in its present form in May 1959. On reflection, I am prepared to let it stand as a whole.

[15] Alfred Marshall, *Principles of Economics* (London, 1890).

a new one in, or shift the position or change the size of an old one—and the position of every other marble changes to some extent. As an analogy for the international system, we should think of relatively few marbles, several of them ten or a hundred times larger than the smallest, all perhaps more or less brittle, moving in a shallower bowl with an uneven surface. Many of the effects of large numbers, apparent in the economic system, cannot occur in international affairs.

The general theory we should like to develop if we could would thus be a theory of those systems which consist of sovereign Powers or alliances of Powers capable of exercising armed force, and in competitive, cooperative, or mixed relationship with each other. In that description three concepts are mentioned which connect international studies with three other disciplines: "sovereign Power" with political science; "armed forces" with military studies; "capability" or "potential" with economics.[16]

At one time or another each of these fields of study has claimed international affairs as one of its own provinces. Political science has of course a traditional claim—international affairs are external politics (world- or power-politics), while the term "politics" is commonly restricted to internal politics. The traditional claim has been expressed in the doctrine of "the primacy of politics." Provided that this does not mean the primacy of internal politics—i.e., does not mean that a sovereign state's relations with its fellows are wholly determined by the stresses and strains of its internal politics—I believe the doctrine to be sound. It has at least a healthy corollary—that the critical decisions in world politics cannot be completely made over to experts, but must be the decisions of the national leadership, or of some larger group of citizens which includes leaders, or of the nation as a whole in its decisive capacity. Such decisions will always depend upon some exercise of judgment; and judgments cannot be read off even from the most exhaustive collection of economic or military data. They characteristically involve the concomitant evaluation of objectives from distinct realms (e.g., military, economic, and political at once). They are thus beyond the scope of technicalities, and they typically incorporate an element of moral judgment.

During the late '50s there was a trend, not then explicitly formulated, toward what might be called "military determinism"—that is, toward the belief that international relations are in part identical with or, for the rest, caused by military relations, when the latter are considered in a long perspective and as including more than merely two-sided relationships. For a time this proved a fruitful trend. The nature of the new weapons, which

[16] I discuss these connections more fully in *From Balance to Deterrence,* Australian National University Social Science Monograph No. 20 (Canberra, 1956), pp. 2–3; revised and republished in *World Politics,* IX (1957), 494–529; see pp. 496–97.

certainly put remarkable constraints upon future world politics, also suggested to us that the nature of former weapons might have been an important constraining element which was obscured in the earlier part of this century by the dominance of a kindred doctrine—economic determinism.

Even so, extreme military determinism is clearly false when considered as a factual hypothesis, while as an interpretation of history it embodies a "category-mistake," and so does not require falsification by evidence. The argument against it is well known, and is at least as old as the works of Clausewitz.

Amongst the other claims to academic dominion the most interesting is that which asserts international politics to be a branch of economics. R. G. Hawtrey stated the case for this in his *Economic Aspects of Sovereignty*.[17] The international system is—to state the claim another way—an unintended consequence of each nation's endeavor to preserve its national integrity, by the use if necessary of military force or the threat of force, which is as it were a producer-good itself, produced from scarce resources having alternative uses. The struggle for national security could thus be treated as an economic struggle carried on without benefit of political order.

These and similar varieties of economic interpretation subsume the more plausible features of military determinism. By the same token, however, they are logically dependent upon a prior assessment—that international affairs are no more than power politics, and that military force is (not only the final arbiter, but also) the one substantial nexus for relations between states. If there should be, beside force and sharply distinct from it, other instruments of relationship between states, the unqualified economic interpretation ceases to be tenable. In any case, both that interpretation and military determinism take the politics out of Power politics. But to do that is a mistake, since the international anarchy, however considerable, does not amount to a sheer Hobbesian state of nature. The political art of persuasion is from day to day more important in diplomacy than are the rare threats and promises backed by force. Rudiments of an international ethics and law mitigate both the asperities of power and the duplicities of world politics. Even the keystone of the economic interpretation—*viz.,* haggling over the military budget—is now recognized as being in substance as much politics as economics.[18]

Yet even if all the foregoing are admitted, much of the subject matter of international studies remains economic, and much of its methodology and terminology derives from economics. There could be worse fates for it

[17] London, 1930.

[18] See Charles E. Lindblom, *Bargaining: The Hidden Hand in Government,* Rand Corporation Research Monograph RM–1434–RC (Santa Monica, Calif., February 1955), *passim.*

than the present degree of its dependence upon the most sophisticated of the social sciences.

But such dependence has never been quite one-sided, and it is becoming less so. The resemblances between political and internation-trade theory would seem to suggest this. It is also evident that international politics and the theory of economic growth must nowadays have two-way connections. Perhaps economics, military studies, politics internal and external, and the study of scientific and technological development will come to be thought of as forming a single constellation concerned with the investigation of rational decision and its implications under conditions of radical uncertainty.

Many interesting economic theories are concerned with system-dominant situations, i.e., those in which there are so many independent agents (marbles in the bowl) that the effects of a change of position by any one of them, though quite real, may not be distinguishable in the mass, or even if distinguishable, not traceable in detail. The significant changes under system dominance are those resulting from similar coincident action by large numbers of the agents.

Since in the politics of the Powers *sub*system dominance is the rule (e.g., a single Power's change of alliance often has noticeable effects throughout the system), students of international affairs are more likely to learn from the theory of oligopolistic competition than from theories of the market. Further, the scope and practical usefulness of general international theory is necessarily more limited than is that of economic theory. All in all, the historian of international affairs needs international theory less than the economic historian needs theoretical economics. But theory of either kind may also help by raising problems for explanation that might well escape the notice of the nontheoretical historian.

We have noticed above that the ideal general theory is as much concerned with the many possible histories as with the one actual history of any given international system. We have also implied that not all of the possible outcomes of a characteristic political situation are to be equally expected—statesmen, soldiers, journalists devote their resources unequally between the various plans for responding to the several alternative outcomes that each envisages for an emergent situation. The minute historian, investigating some incident or crisis in the long history of an international system (before the nuclear age, they lasted for at least a century or two) will be able to assign *a priori* some sort of likelihood to the alternative possible resolutions of the particular crises he studies. The subjective likelihoods which he assigns must, so far as they are sound, be compatible with those to be derived from a valid general theory pertinent to the system as a whole. But the general theory, by virtue of its larger compass, can also provide the criteria of likelihood for judging whether the last stages of the system were surprising or to be expected. A surprising final outcome should suggest problems both to the minute and to the general historian. Did the course of events take an unexpected turn at some particular point? Or was there some standing condition, not allowed for in the theory and unrecognized by the historians, which gradually diverted the political process from its otherwise likely direction?

Sometimes, of course, it is the likely that happens. Hundreds of warring states formed the international system in China of the eighth century B.C. These gradually reduced in number (the survivors expanding by submission of their neighbors) to a dozen, then to half a dozen. At the last—

> The totalitarian Power to the west, Ch'in, eventually absorbed one by one all the other six states whose ambitions prevented them from uniting for common defence. The Ch'in leader proclaimed himself the First Emperor of all China in 221 B.C.[19]

Among the few late survivors were some relatively new states on the extreme eastern coast, and also an older strong Power to the south. Early in the struggle, most of the strong Powers had been nearer the geographical center of the system.

From such international theory as we have at present, reasons can be brought for supposing that, given the weapons and communications of ancient continental systems, the states fringing an area of balance of power have the best chance of emerging eventual victors and acquiring imperial authority. No one could have predicted that, amongst the half dozen outlying city-states, it was Ch'in that would be the victor. But the theorist, transported to the eighth century B.C. and deprived of his twentieth-century A.D. hindsight, would have put his money on one of the outliers rather than one of the inliers. So the actual outcome, though not to be certainly predicted, nor even warranting an even-money bet, should not have been counter-expected. Theory here does not add to the narrative historian's explanation. All it does is to show that the final outcome had in any case a certain *a priori* plausibility—or, conversely, that what called for historical explanation was *not* startling.

If, on the other hand, it had turned out that the very ancient and inlying state of Chou had emerged as eventual victor, and if an historian had been able to give us an illuminating narrative explanation of Chou's victory, then looking at it through the spectrum of theory, we should be bound to congratulate him on providing and validating an *a priori* *im*plausible explanation of untoward and unlikely events.

To sum up this discussion of the limits and scope of a theoretical approach to the history of international affairs, or more generally, of the

[19] R. L. Walker, *The Multi-State System of Ancient China* (Hamden, Conn., 1953), p. 7.

external relationships of societies: to supplement an account of what *did* happen with a number of sketches of what *might* have happened is certainly not to provide additional explanations. But it does allow one to say whether what happened was to be expected or not upon the basis of theory. And this gives us a means of assessing both the likelihood of developments in matters which are of the essence of the subject, and also the importance of certain factors that impinge upon international affairs but are neither of the essence of them, nor peculiar to the discipline in which they are studied—the forces of tradition, morale, genius, and so on. Historians must always think of some of the alternatives that might have occurred, merely in the course of finding out what did occur. One use of international theory, then, is to do more thoroughly what they do already, and thereby to deepen our understanding of the historical process.

IV

The approach to international affairs as essentially Power politics, though first renewed (by Reinhold Niebuhr and Hans Morgenthau amongst others) in philosophic and ideological terms, was greatly accelerated by the development of game theory. The latter's presuppositions, and the conditions necessary for its application, suggest that a complete general theory of international competition and conflict cannot be devised. Game theory enables one to determine the limits of a competition's possible results, given that each competitor uses his "best" strategy. But his "best" strategy is itself discoverable only in those situations where he can list, before the game at least, all its significant possible outcomes. In actual politics, this of course can rarely be done. Furthermore, the game theorist must suppose that his competitors are engaged in only one species of game at a time, or that, in any case, if they are playing several distinct games with one and the same set of "pieces," all these contests can be integrated into a single grand game to which each contest contributes. Again, it is by no means evident that the statesman whose single maneuver may be designed to further several disparate ends—economic, political, ideological, collective, individual—can be considered as engaged in a single supercontest. Below (pp. 200–213), we return to a discussion of the scope of game theory in the study of Power politics, and also (pp. 245–247) to the limits of any possible theory.

Notice that so far we have been considering the influence upon an *historian's* expectations exercised by a theory of international relations (specifically, a theory of Powers and their politics). But what of the expectations of the statesmen whose actions this historian seeks to explain? Must there not be some correspondence between their expectations then, and his now?—between his more or less explicit model or theory, and their several—perhaps implicit—pictures of their worlds? The correspondence might be reasonably close between the expectations of an eighteenth-century European monarch and those of a somewhat later historian who assumes the general trustworthiness of the balance-of-power model. But sometimes such an historian will suppose a somewhat different model from those of his subjects: he may, for instance, consider the balance of power a much more precarious and chancy mechanism than they do. He will then expect them to have been misled from time to time about the *a priori* likelihood of responses from their fellows, or of other kinds of event or concatenation of circumstances within the European system. The historian's theory may in this case still guide him, even though its correspondence with the thought of the time he is studying is by no means exact.

There can be, however, a more radical failure to correspond: the historian's model may consist of elements quite of another kind from those that made up his subjects' world-views: he would have to hold that they had quite misconceived their situation. A plausible illustration is hard to imagine; but suppose an historian of late-sixteenth-century Spain whose own interpretation is that several countries including Spain itself had already evolved into nation-states of which the economies were more and more mercantilized, and which were acquiring colonial empires, yet who holds that the politically effective among the Spaniards all suffered from Don Quixote's illusion, believing themselves to be knightly feudal rulers of a Christendom owing allegiance to the Holy Roman Empire under Papal primacy.

Such interpretations can hardly dispense with something like the Marxist concept of "false consciousness": they must always be able to show how the subjects, acting out of a misconception of their situation, nevertheless brought about those events which now are differently and more correctly characterized by the historian, and are thought by him to be explicable upon conceptions different from theirs. But the fact of the subjects' false consciousness *must* enter into his explanations—*viz.,* by the difference it made to the history of Spain throughout the period, which otherwise would have been more consistently mercantilist, nationalistic, and so on. We may concede that so to interpret a period is, though difficult, methodologically possible: the difficulty or strain arises from the effect that historical agents' preconceptions always have upon the outcome of their interactions; the strain becomes so great as to produce a contradiction when the effect is pronounced enough to have made the outcomes foreseeable by the agents upon the basis of their own preconceptions—i.e., preconceptions about their own motivations and places in society. We can then imagine that the agents' explanation of their own history would formally contradict that of our twentieth-century historian, but would yet have accounted, pretty much as well as his does, for the broad facts of sixteenth-century Spanish history.

Such contradictions do occasionally break out in historiography; sometimes, however, the *appearance* of a contradiction between rival explanations can be eliminated if we notice that they are not truly rivals, but are designed to explain different levels of event, or events in different time scales. In Chapter 1, we considered types of explanations on greatly differing time scales: the age, which has been measurable in millennia; the period, of a century or so; the era, of twenty or thirty years; and the crisis or incident, which may last for anything from a few years to a few days. J. W. Burton, recently arguing that a decision-making model is superior to a power-balancing model, considers it a virtue of the former that it is

> . . . necessarily a national one. Whereas the traditional "(scil. balance-of-power)" model demonstrates the resultant of all national pressures which operate and lead to changes in balances, a decision-making model focuses attention on the nature of each national pressure.[20]

Notice, Burton does not suggest that the power-balance model and the decision-making model engender logically alternative and rival explanations of exactly the same *explicandum:* he rather implies that since, as a model of the international system, the power-balance model is more general than and somehow includes the nationally oriented decision-making model, the former calls for and would be incomplete without the latter (incomplete, perhaps, without as many different varieties of the latter as there are different systems of national decision-making amongst the nations that comprise the international system); but not vice versa. A decision-making model would be designed, presumably, to help explain those of a nation's actions and responses that are relevant to or call forth responses from other nations. The model would need also to explain any *failure* by the nation to respond to external changes in the international system; and this in turn requires some assumptions about what constitutes a *relevant* stimulus—assumptions based on historical experience gathered independently of the decision-making model.

The family of "traditional" power-balancing models, as Burton has pointed out,[21] prejudges in one way or another this issue of the relevant stimulus: when power over other nations, and security from their attacks and attempts to establish predominance, are supposed to be the chief objectives of any nation's action, an *a priori* standard of relevance is entailed that may or may not square with historical experience. Burton is quite right to contend that any proponent of the security-power approach

[20] J. W. Burton: *International Relations: A General Theory* (London: Cambridge University Press, 1965), p. 144.

[21] *Ibid.*, pp. 143–44 and elsewhere.

denies himself a means of testing his model if—though only if—he insists that *it* shall dictate the principle of selection for a national decision-making model. For the standard of relevance which a national leader applies to his taking of decisions obviously shapes their course, so that when they are interpreted on the assumption that he thought that only considerations of power or security were relevant, that interpretation is apt to overlook much actual evidence about his actions.

Considerations of security (if not of power) can never, on the other hand, appear totally irrelevant in any sensible model of national decision-making. So long as a model of the international system, being more general than that of any particular national system, sets up some canon of relevance for national decision-making, it will be logically strong enough to come to grips with the explaining of changes affecting the international system as a whole—i.e., to serve the prime explanatory purpose of such a model, and also to explain at least something about the behavior of the nation-states constituting it. On the other hand, no mere refinements or proliferation of national decision-making models can serve that purpose: to do so, they need to be combined within a multinational model. Of narrower scope, less likely to be refuted, and therefore logically weaker than models of the international system as a whole, models of national structure can by themselves explain nothing but the behavior of particular nations.

V

We have been contending in the last few paragraphs that considerations of security or power will always carry some weight in the policy-forming and decision-making of sovereign nations (or, as they are more generally called in this volume, Powers). We shall now argue that that is true whether or not the words "security" and "power" are ever specifically used by the policy- and decision-makers of any Power. In other words, historians could, after the event, characterize as "security-maintaining action" the kinds of decision that statesmen have taken "simply on the merits of the case," having discussed it in wholly concrete terms. Even though one's model of the international system included the strong proposition that the Powers making up the system always give first consideration to the maximizing of security, one would not be logically obliged to include the same strong proposition in any *intra*national model of decision-making. The intranational model might not, indeed, make use at all of so general a concept as maximization of power or security, especially if the scope of the model is limited narrowly (as in practice it is likely to be) in space and time. Instead of a general security-maximizing rule, the model would be directed by a list prescribing the modeled nation's responses to particular kinds of stimuli provided by the specific challenging or disturbing actions of its neighbors. On the whole, short and specific lists are often sufficient for the modeling of a short-run crisis or incident.

Let us look a little more carefully at this idea. May it not be that the short-run incident is the minimum and irreducible reality of world politics? The issues that governments, statesmen, and officials can cope with are, in most instances, few and brief. Not many statesmen hold office for more than a decade, and some of those who do (e.g., the dictators of Spain and Portugal) have been ineffectual. The notion that states, as distinct from their leaders, are swayed by long-term considerations of security or power, can get substance and support only from the generalization of the outcomes of particular incidents. If, through changes of government, some state exhibits a continuous interest and direction, we do not ascribe the continuity to any mental process or firmly held purpose of the state itself: we assume that, to successive governments coping with different situations, the same important list of situational pressures has occurred.

Continuity of tradition about foreign politics, which sometimes helps explain continuity of interest and direction in policy, itself requires to be explained by the historical facts of continuing situational pressures during several generations, and by a habit—at least in the governing class—of reflection upon past politics. In subsequent chapters of this volume, we shall give some account of these interesting historical processes, which go to provide the empirical sense of the ideas of "nationhood" and "Powerhood." Here, it may be enough to notice that the skeletons of historical explanation set out above foreshadow an ultimately individualistic approach to the analysis of tradition and, indeed, to all the phenomena of collective action. But the skeleton of compositive explanation, in particular, is meant to explicate the formal means for deriving explanatory accounts of the interaction of collective entities, such as Powers, from prior accounts which employ essentially individualistic categories of analysis.

Thus to the question whether "the short-run incident" is not the minimum and irreducible constituent for the study of world politics, we answer at this stage that indeed it is an irreducible minimum, but that the longer-run processes, notably the evolving of a group of rulers who preserve through several generations some continuity of purpose and understanding, are not less real than the shortest-run processes, though the natural order of understanding them proceeds from the shorter to the longer run.

On certain levels and time scales, from a year or two to several centuries, the Powers and their politics are explanatory themes necessary though not sufficient for historical understanding. The attempt to rewrite universal history to the exclusion of the history of the Powers and upon some a-political principle—social, economic, or religious—has proved as unsatisfying as the Hegelian program in which the actors in world history were "peoples that are States." In the present chapter we have reviewed some of the functions in historical explanation of theories, or rather, since a truly general theory seems unavailable, of theoretical approaches to the subject matter we have variously styled "international relations," "world politics," or "Power politics." From the other side, the skeletons of historical explanation were set out to show how particular explanations might be connected with the kinds of general theorizing and model-building that seem to hold out most promise for world politics. Later, we considered the question of levels and time scales at which the concepts of power-balancing and of systems of Powers have their most direct application. Clearly, the most appropriate timescale is that which in Chapter 1 above we styled "the era"—the duration of some particular "constellation of powers."

That duration cannot be less than a few years, for we use the expression to include, potentially, such changes as upsets in and returns to the balance of power, wars, changes of alliance, the rise to or decline from preeminence of various particular constituent Powers. By observation, constellations have usually persisted for something between a decade and a generation, and perhaps never as long as a century, though often some of the constituent Powers have survived from one constellation to another. Evidently, "duration" is partly in the eye of the observer, but not altogether: when in 1917 the United States involved itself in a European war, the most obstinate "European" theorist could hardly contend that the constellation of 1816 still persisted.

For another general reason, the duration of about ten to twenty-five years is salient: it is the span of an eminent statesman's reasonable purpose: the range of a motivational explanation, as sketched above, can be no more, in the context of politics, than twenty or thirty years. Though, as we have argued, a developing tradition of interest and policy can perhaps stretch the duration of collective purpose to several times that range, even the longest-lived traditions of statecraft (e.g., the Byzantine and the Venetian) suffer change and declension.

Has power-political theory a peculiar subject matter, e.g., alliances; opposition and confrontation between nations; arms races and disarmament; the initiating, the political conduct, and the concluding of warfare; the politics of major international organizations; certain large-scale economic transactions; and so forth? The term "statecraft" suits rather well the art of conducting such affairs. The objectives of promoting security and/or power once seemed to me to afford common and sufficient grounds for national engagement in Power politics.

That characterization no longer seems adequate: political action when most thoroughly political is undertaken from a conspectus of ends that includes the picture of a valued possible world—not inevitably an "ideal" or a utopia—along with the ends of security and power. One need not, like the idealists, rationalize away the objectives of security and power as mere means toward attainment of the valued possible world. Nor should one assume that the picturing of a valued world order necessarily ennobles external policy—sometimes it has been a more evil end than that of mere security. But the objectives of power and/or security alone yield an activity better described as "strategics" than as "politics" which, even when conducted by and amongst states, is by no means a purely instrumental activity.

So now we call our subject "the politics of the Powers," remembering that power and security are not characteristically the *sole* objectives promoted on behalf of a Power by its leaders. In the next chapter we shall discuss the concept of Powerhood, as a point of departure for examining various theories and models of the relations between Powers.

SECTION II

DEFINITION

FOUR

Powerhood

I

We have introduced the notion that a world-political "conversation" is carried on by "representative persons," and that this conversation is what unifies and gives continuity to the world-political process (just as, before the involvement of the whole globe in the European state system, earlier political interchanges had integrated, for example, the Latin American and the Islamic international processes). What or whom do the "representative persons" represent?

To answer that question in a human context, the term we require should be capable of denoting any persisting "agent" or "actor" or "player," in any historical age. We know that "the state" and, much more, "the nation-state," are historically limited concepts. We need a name that includes them, and with them tribes, agricultural empires, city-states, feudalities, armed and embattled parties in civil strife, the supranational communities which may one day emerge, and so on. But the fact that we can make such a list suggests that we have already, in ordinary discourse, the very universal that the list instantiates. That universal is the Hebraic, Hellenistic, and Christian concept—"the Power."

Our notions of internal politics come for the most part from the Greeks and the Stoic philosophers. But our conceptions of the relationship between nations, and of nations as World Powers, are more Biblical and theological than classical or philosophic. It is here contended (1) that the dominant tradition in the study of international politics conceives of the nations whose interactions it studies as "Powers," and assumes that these Powers form some sort of order or system; (2) that such preconceptions are not directly verifiable—either one sees the world in those terms or not; and (3) that from the Biblical source of our notions about international politics there have also emanated judgments which, if sound, would imply the impossibility of the dream that political science should be "value-free" and impersonal—that one should be able to study this subject without commitment.

No classical author broke quite free from the beautiful typology of the city-state. Even the Stoics' *cosmopolis*—"dear city of Zeus"—is simply the *polis* universalized. On the other hand, the Old Testament (partly because of Hebrew history before the Exile, but mainly from an early apprehension of the Covenant relationship) juxtaposes the ideas of "a peculiar people" and "the Gentiles," i.e., the (other) nations. The latter throughout the Scriptures are conceived of as spiritual entities, or as having a spiritual aspect, and as such are "Powers."

The "Powers," as Biblically portrayed, are deeply ambiguous: "ordained by God" and therefore, within their little realms, to be obeyed; subject to the forces of evil and at least in part demonic; not to be worshiped. They are, in the Old Testament, at God's disposal to fulfil His purposes of judgment and mercy. These purposes are considered for the most part to have been wholly in pursuit of His covenant with Israel; but there are significant exceptions—e.g., "Did I not bring up Israel from the land of Egypt, and the Philistines from Caphtor and the Syrians from Kir?" (Amos, 9:7.) What befalls them is thus "providential" but not altogether orderly. Again the Stoics are contrasted, whose *cosmos* is ordered, but without ambiguity.

The New Testament presupposes *cosmos* in the Stoic sense, so that the nations form an order, or "system" as we should say; yet the impression of ambiguity is deepened: the world order is at God's disposal—e.g., ". . . you know what is restraining him [the lawless one] now so that he may be revealed in his time. For the mystery of lawlessness is already at work; only He who now restrains it will do so until he [the other one] is out of the way" (II Thess. 2: 6–7); but its constituent Powers have characteristically failed to acknowledge His authority. The order is spiritual but nonetheless wicked, and "subject to vanity" because it is associated with the "present dark age" which is passing away. Christians do not know how the divine control operates, nor can they by natural reason foretell its operations, even though sometimes—confronted with the facts—they can "read the signs of the times." The effects of the world order are not wholly malign; nevertheless the main contest of believers is against it and not against "flesh and blood" (Eph. 6: 10–12). The contest is a spiritual one, and requires all the contender's Divinely bestowed inner resources. Finally the Powers, insofar as they are now rebellious, are in process of being subjected to the authority of the exalted Christ. At the last they shall all submit to him because—though they do not at present acknowledge the fact —Christ has overcome them. They did their worst, but he has "made a show of them" (Col. 2: 15).

That passage may be construed as implying that under the Old Testamentary dispensation there had been a decree binding both Jew and Gentile to obey the Powers, and embracing both the Torah (the Law of the Old Testament) and the laws and morality of the Gentiles, which Jesus, by obeying it to the point of death, spiked on a nail of the Cross as a cancelled bill or contract. So the Powers lost their authority, which had been a necessary condition for their perpetuating their spiritual effectiveness (Col. 2: 13–14).

Amongst present-day thinkers about international politics, redemption from the Powers is dismissed as metaphor and myth, even while the myth of the Powers themselves is presupposed. Few recognize that the latter is *myth,* not mere factual classification. Fewer still recognize how far each one's incorporation in his nation-state has fixed his perspective for him. Thus for many the question how to be freed from domination by "principalities and powers" does not arise. But once it is allowed to, evidently no answers that do not go as deep as the question itself will seem relevant. For the faith of the Old Testament, the relevant answer had been given in the Divine election of Israel from amongst the nations; for that of the New, it was given in a fulfilment which was also a cancellation of those obligations that the Powers had had authority to impose. At their lowest, the Powers include the "weak and beggarly" elemental spirits who had enslaved the Galatians (Gal. 4: 9): how these could have exercised authority requires considerable explanation. But at their most potent and also most ambiguous, amongst the chief of the Powers was the Torah—the Mosaic Law—of the Old Covenant.

This conception, developed in the Pauline epistles, and in the Paulinizing letter to the Colossians, is instructively examined in G. B. Caird's *Principalities and Powers,*[1] on which the present chapter much relies. Few instances better illustrate both the strangeness to us of the New Testament world-view and also the mixture of categories involved in the Biblical concept of "Powers" than this odd characterization of the Torah. We of the twentieth century can understand by an effort of imagination how the concept can represent a more or less individual angel or demon (which we do

[1] G. B. Caird, *Principalities and Powers* (Oxford, 1956), being the Chancellor's Lectures for 1954 at Queen's University, Kingston, Ontario, cited herein by permission of the Clarendon Press, Oxford.

not readily believe in) and at the same time the hypostatization of a nation (which we, too, operate with); but we find it a strain when the concept also connotes a personalized and individualized abstraction—the Law of Sinai.

Our bewilderment is itself an historical datum, to be explained by our unconscious reception of the extreme individualism of the Christian tradition. For us, the person (in the material realm his analogue is the individual atom) alone is real in himself, while the "national spirit" and the "influence of the Law" are merely modifications of his mind or emotional make-up. He is the subject, they are possible predicates. Our disbelief in spiritual agencies, angelic and demonic, derives from our assumption that they were supposed to be disembodied individuals, and therefore either exist only as such, or not at all. Again, we think of Law as a system of norms, essentially inactive. Neither a Hebrew nor an early Christian would have recognized from such a description the formidable oracles of God. "In the Epistle to the Romans," as Caird puts it,

> the law duplicates those functions which we have seen elsewhere attributed to Satan. The law is the great accuser. . . . The law also carries out the sentence . . . the law is also the tempter . . . "for I should not have had personal knowledge of covetousness if the law had not said, Thou shalt not covet" (Rom. 7: 8–9) . . . Evil in itself . . . is a parasite, which can exist and thrive and propagate itself only by distorting the good gifts of God. . . .[2]

So the Law of Sinai is thus a "power" both for good, as it was intended to be; and also for evil, despite the Law's intrinsic holiness. For Judaism of the first century, the Torah was the temporally revealed but eternally valid word of life. For Paul, at least in Galatians (3: 19) it had been "brought in because of transgressions," to be "our pedagogue until Christ came, that we might be justified by faith" (3: 24).

We also learn, in 3: 19, that the Torah had been "ordained by angels through an intermediary," a commonly received tradition of the time. This suggests the proportion: as its angel or Power is to each Gentile nation, so is the Torah to Israel. On the other hand, all who have been "under law" were now to receive "adoption as sons" by virtue of God's Son, "born under the Law" (4: 4–5). Furthermore, the Galatians are warned that, since they keep the "days, months, seasons, and years" of the Sinaitic dispensation, they have backslidden to the beggarly elements—"by nature no gods"—from whom, as Gentiles and Pagans, the Gospel had redeemed them (4: 8–10). This in turn suggests the proportion: as the Torah has been to Israel, so have their several peculiar sovereignties and laws been to the Gentile nations. And, just as the Christian gospel was not thought to do away with what we should nowadays call the moral aspects of the

[2] *Ibid.*, pp. 41–43.

Torah, but rather to restate them as precepts of conduct befitting the converts to the new way, so the "principalities and powers"—roughly, the law and government—established in each Gentile state were to be obeyed for conscience's sake as "an ordinance of God"—of course, short of apostasy.

I have begun with this hardest case—the Torah as a Power—for two reasons. Firstly, it helps us of the twentieth century to grasp more readily how the "principalities and powers" tyrannizing over the Gentile world, the "cosmocrats of this dark age," may be interpreted as the collective wills and minds of the governmental, legal, cultural, and patriotic establishments of each ancient nation-state. Secondly, by linking the concept of nation-as-Power with a law which is no mere secular system of norms, nor a resultant of natural reason, but a "deposit of Revelation," we can begin to see that loyalty to the nation-state and involvement in the nation-state system (or whatever other form, from feudalism to world-government, the power of the civil sword may from time to time assume) will appear to men as something much more than a nuisance, a burden to be borne or shed, but rather as an imperious exaction of moral and spiritual obedience. In both the Pauline and Petrine traditions, probably going back in this to a common origin in Jesus' own doctrine, a difficult and subtle but important distinction is made: on the one hand, the nation-state has no spiritual or moral authority as such; on the other hand, it remains a "Divine ordinance" and insofar as it is such, its enactments are to be obeyed for conscience's sake, provided they do not conflict with Divine commandments.

Thus—in modern terms—the positive laws of the state, or of any secular equivalent, did not confront early Christians with absolute moral authority, i.e., as a Kantian categorical imperative, nor tie them to the Powers whose laws they were by any absolute obligation. Nor was it a matter of setting another law, even say the Decalogue, to override the laws of the land. It was rather that another loyalty now overrode for Christians all loyalties to systems of law, authorities, or nation-states.

On this subject the New Testament affords as evidence the various accounts of the trials of Jesus. It is not their historical accuracy which is here at issue: whether in the Synoptic Gospel's story of his examination before the high priest's council, where, to the high priest's charge, "Are you the Christ, the Son of the Blessed?" Jesus answered "I am" (Mark 14: 60–62); or whether in St. John's story of the arraignment before Pilate—who asked him "knowest thou not that I have power to crucify thee, and have power to release thee?" and to whom he replied "Thou couldst have no power at all against me, except it were given thee from above" (19: 8–11), Jesus was shown as confronting the representatives of the Powers with no worldly power of his own, but with an authority that claimed to overrule theirs. If Christianity attributed to him the overthrow of all authority such as theirs, it was only because he first defied that authority.

It is in this context that contemporary Christian pacifism has its theological justification. The Christian pacifist at least asks himself the right question—to take the hardest example: "Does loyalty to Christ permit compliance with a strategy of nuclear deterrence?" The pacifist question avoids the nationally centered assumptions of such questions as "Would a nuclear-deterrent strategy be worth the risk to us?" It is not, as they are, logically enslaved to the principalities and powers.

The Biblical outlook, both New and Old Testamentary, also gives the *student* of international politics a liberating standpoint. Otherwise, in such a value-oriented study as his, which in practice cannot be a completely neutral and objective science, his choice of problems to investigate is apt to be determined, explicitly or implicitly, by his sense of the interest of his own nation or civilization. Certainly, the Biblical standpoint does not endow anyone with Divine impartiality; but it does make him aware of the relativity of all other standpoints.

I must now provide some indication of how the context, as well as the standpoint, of thought about international politics has become indebted to Biblical thought. The roots of all New Testament usage concerning the Powers is, according to Caird, to be found in the third of the various Old Testament interpretations of the pagan gods.

> According to this third theory the beings whom other nations worshipped as gods were in fact subordinate powers acting under the supreme authority of Yahweh. These beings are known either as . . . "gods" or as . . . sons of God. First, then, the superiority of Yahweh to the other gods is asserted. "Who is like to thee, O Yahweh, among the gods?" The inferior gods are called to recognize the supremacy of Yahweh. . . . These supernatural beings are conceived as forming a heavenly council around the throne of God. . . . Yahweh, as God of the angelic hosts, exercised control over the powers of nature.[3]

These were the "hosts of heaven," readily identifiable as the stars—e.g., Jud. v: 20; I Kings 22: 19; Job 38: 7. Caird further points out that by the Exile, each Gentile nation has its own angelic ruler, while Israel alone is directly subject to Yahweh. He cites the Septuagint:

> When the Most High gave to the nations their inheritance,
> When he separated the sons of men,
> He fixed the borders of the peoples
> According to the number of the sons of God.
> For Yahweh's portion is his people;
> Jacob is his allotted inheritance. (Deut. 32: 8–9).[4]

[3] *Ibid.*, pp. 2–3.
[4] *Ibid.*, p. 5.

The "princes" of Greece and of Persia, warring together in the Book of Daniel, are inferred to be their angelic guardians, since the intervention of Michael on behalf of Israel is evidently that of no human ruler (Dan. 12: 1 and 10: 13–20). From the prophetic viewpoint these angelic guardians, being subordinated to and servants of God, merely implement the Divine sovereignty over history. On the other hand, the Gentile nations erred and sinned in worshiping and making idols of their several angelic guardian rulers, while, through the logic of myth, "by accepting their worship the rulers had become involved in their sin."[5] This, an historic rather than a precosmic fall of the angels calls forth a prophetic doom against corruption in the heavenly places as well as against their earthly idolaters (Isa. 24: 12 and 34: 2–4).

The widespread reference to the number seventy as that of the nations is answered by a mythology of seventy ministering angels. Caird refers here to the late apocryphal Testament of Naphtali:

> For at that time the Lord, blessed be he, came down from his highest heavens and brought down with him seventy ministering angels, Michael at their head. He commanded them to teach the seventy families which sprang from the loins of Noah seventy languages. . . . But the holy language, the Hebrew language, remained only in the house of Shem and Eber, and in the house of Abraham our father who is one of their descendants.[6]

He then points out the significance of the Septuagint's terms: "Where the Hebrew speaks of God's hosts, the Greek speaks instead of His powers."[7] The word is δυνάμεις—the "qualities," incidentally, of the Stoic universe.[8] The "authorities" of Daniel 7: 27 are alternatively ἐξουσίαι and ἀρχαί; the "princes" of chapter 10 are ἄρχοντες.[9]

We thus have all the etymological apparatus of New Testament doctrine concerning "principalities and powers." More to the point of the present chapter, we have also inherited, through the linguistic transformation effected by the Septuagint, a terminology subsequently used by the New Testament writers and by the Western European philosophers of "Power" politics.

This secular application was delayed more than a millenium: the "world" of the first three or four centuries A.D. was dominated by two great empires, the Parthian and the Roman, not by seventy nations. John's Revelation found a new occult or cryptic representation for the power of pagan Rome, which consolidated into one enigmatic figure the Old Testament's hierarchy of angels fallen because they had suffered them-

[5] *Ibid.*, p. 6.
[6] *Ibid.*, p. 6.
[7] *Ibid.*, p. 11.
[8] *Ibid.*, p. 13.
[9] *Ibid.*, p. 12.

selves to be worshiped as gods. The representation of the nation-state as a spiritual Power thus became a myth element for which there was no obviously current political application. From Constantine onward, the figure of the Christian Emperor complementing the Patriarchate and Papacy began its role in the prolonged Western Christian dialectic of Keys and Sword, Church and State.

Augustine's dichotomy of the Two Cities, significant as it has been for Western political theory, again postponed the borrowing of the Scriptural "Power" as a designation for nationhood. However, his thought provided a strand of that tradition in which the political philosophy of the Reformation and the late Renaissance was to embrace the concept of national "Powers." This was the Augustinian insight that came to represent the great worldly institutions—property, the state, the interstate order—as *poena et remedia peccati,* at once the punishment of and the palliatives for sin. Post-Renaissance thinkers were thus enabled to represent the international system as a rough-and-ready Providential order, and to conceive of partly stabilizing mechanisms such as the balance of power.

That may seem an unimportant because an obvious step, until we remember how the great Greeks, Herodotus, Thucydides, and Polybius, had regarded the inter-state systems of their day. Thucydides, preeminently, had hinted at a sovereign power that brought low the proud. But as with Herodotus, Thucydides' transcendent force was an anti-Providence: a divine mischief-maker who, according to Herodotus, delights in destruction and tossing things about, and who suffers no one to be proud but himself. In twentieth-century terms, this would suggest the theory that the course of politics between nations is a random process; and helps explain why the classical world, which had discovered a typology of internal political systems, and whose brilliant historians anatomized the catastrophes of their city-state order, never so far as we know developed a theory of the inter-state system.

After Machiavelli's study of the Italian city-states, and with the rise of the new monarchies in the sixteenth and seventeenth centuries, European philosophers and practitioners of statecraft were able to develop such a theory. Modern continental writers (e.g., Meinecke) contend that the Calvinist political rationalists who employed the notion of *raison d'état* were the chief originators. For the task they had already to hand the New Testament usage of "principalities and powers," together with the Old Testament historiography of the wars and alliances of the ancient Middle Eastern Kingdoms, which fitted surprisingly closely the Western Europe of the New Monarchies. The complex Calvinist dialectic of obedience to and legitimate resistance against the "powers that be," which are "ordained of God" suggested an analogy between the "New Israel" of the Reformed churches and the old Israel immediately ruled by the Lord. Yet each nation was no less and no more than one of the "Powers." So long as the theorists and practitioners of statecraft saw their own, as much as any nation, merely one among many ambiguous Powers, they could be content with a world-picture of an imperfect and secular but mutually restraining comity of nations in the European system. This philosophy of state, capable of development even though rather self-satisfied and shortsighted, was challenged by two intellectual developments—the liberal vision of a State such as revolutionary France committed to the task of liberating the peoples of Europe, and the romantic and Germanic doctrine of the nation-state as the bearer of ethical values. Lines of descent can be traced from these to the Left and Right totalitarianisms of the twentieth century.

In our own age, the balance of terror has brought the ambiguities of "Powerhood" to a point of crisis. It is no accident that the great theologians of the interwar generation developed doctrines concerning the posture of the church toward power-political conflicts, just as the theologians of the Reformation had to develop doctrines of the duties and rights of a subject toward his own state-rulers.

II

The intention of the foregoing historical sketch was to show how this concept of Powerhood—a term of the greatest generality, in its origins alien to the Greco-Roman language of politics—has come to play its constitutive part in our thinking about external politics. Perhaps a majority of present-day political scientists will consider that its religious origins unfit it for employment in scientific discourse, and may wish to substitute a reformulated concept—say, "the political system in its external-political relations with other systems."

Against any such substitutions must be set the fact that they deprive us of the sense, conveyed to us by the concept of Powerhood, that a Power, looked at from within, is a unity-in-spirit "before" it is a political system—*viz.*, a polity. Let it be clear, firstly, that there is here no intention to suggest that there exist spiritual beings—"Powers"—distinct from the individual human beings who in each of them are integrated into a society: the national (communal) unity-in-spirit is wholly an attribute of at least some of those human beings, the citizens of the nation, the subjects of the Power. Secondly, unity-in-spirit is regarded throughout this study primarily as an *explicandum* and only secondarily as an *explicans;* and its explanation is sought in social and psychological contexts. Thirdly, the expression is not intended to be eulogistic: we do not consider unity-in-spirit to be nobler than, for example, the sharing of a material interest—indeed, an advantage of Powerhood's religious origins is their suggestion that it is precisely the spiritual aspect of the Power that renders it morally ambiguous and indeed suspect. Lastly, everything that can be conveyed, in the traditional language of Western political science, about political systems, their internal constitution, and their external relations, can also be conveyed in the language that makes use of the concept of Powerhood—and, so we shall claim, more.

We now attempt a definition of Powerhood, which will be used in our subsequent analysis of the politics of the Powers and of the systematic relations that they involve. The elements of the definition are so numbered that the addition of one decimal place indicates qualifications of the preceding integer's clause. Thus, element 1.1 is a qualification of 1.0; and both 1.11 and 1.12 are successive qualifications of 1.1.

A Power is

1.0 a set of persons

1.1 believed to be a unity-in-spirit (hereafter usually referred to by just one of its connotations—"society") by at least some members of the set, of whom at least some (the governing set, the "directors," or "rulers")

1.11 are, for their part, determined to preserve both the integrity and the safety of the society—if necessary at the expense of outsiders, whether grouped or ungrouped; and

1.12 who are able to act in a concert (which will always exhibit at one extreme some features of arbitrary power and at the other some elements of polity)

1.121 within the 1.0 set, and also

1.122 against or with outsiders,

1.123 in order to further their intentions under 1.11;

1.13 in the course of 1.12–1.123, they dispose of certain resources (see 1.31) for which, within the society-set, alternate uses could be found;

1.131 it will always be possible that at least some of these resources will be expended when

1.14 from time to time the rulers impose certain of the sanctions available to them—either

1.141 *against* those whom they deem members of their own society (its "subjects") in the belief and for the purposes mentioned in (1.1–1.11)—

1.1411 above all, in order to strengthen the belief of subjects of the society in the integrity and persistence of the society and of their unification in spirit within it, under those restraints upon employment of sanctions against subjects that are exercised upon the rulers by the structure of the society;

1.142 or, without similar restraints necessarily being exercised, *against outsiders*—

1.1421 upon which occasions, though also when cooperating with outsiders, the rulers have to form an idea of how their own actions on behalf of their society, and their collective capabilities for such action, appear to outsiders' rulers, and thus also whether the outsiders constitute another society (or societies) answering to the specifications of (1.1–1.142).

The foregoing numbered clauses are intended to define the essence of Powerhood; without the exclusiveness, the integration, the command over resources, and the possibility of imposing sanctions against outsiders, no set of persons amounts to a Power. On the other hand, it should be noticed that the society-set of 1.0 is *not* dichotomized into rulers and subjects: *all* members of the set are initially subjects (even, e.g., the heir-apparent to a monarch), and the definition does not exclude the possibility that each one of them may be a ruler. But the definition does entail that the concert of rulers must always exhibit some degree, however small, of the arbitrary exercise of power and authority (constitutionally the most limited of executives has from time to time to issue fiats that are not direct derivations from parliamentary enactments of rules). Contrariwise, the rigidest hierarchy cannot exclude all political activity, at least amongst the more numerous classes of rulers lower in the hierarchy.

Nothing so far has been defined concerning territoriality, or concerning the employment of armed force in sanctioning—features assumed to be essential to Powerhood by most political thinkers. They seem not to be absolutely essential: a predator Power might survive without territory peculiarly its own—e.g., nomad horsemen and, fictionally, Captain Nemo's submarine; in the other regard, sanctions might still be applied against outsiders (e.g., by diversion of trade) even though no Power were able to impose sanctions by armed force. Similar considerations apply to the usual requirements that a Power shall have a numerous population (again cf. the fictional *Nautilus* submarine) and that it shall outlast the span of ordinary human life. The following continuation of our definition is therefore not concerned with the absolute essentials of Powerhood, but with characteristics which almost invariably it displays and which, along with the essential features set out above, in practice make a Power the kind of society it is.

The set mentioned in 1.0—

1.2 is too large for face-to-face relationship throughout;

1.3 it usually persists as a distinct set for longer than the human life-span; to be able to do so, it must—

1.31 engage in production, whether as a self-sufficient economy, or along with outsiders, grouped or ungrouped, in a larger economy, or as a congeries of private production groups and individuals, thus generating resources (see 1.13); and therefore it is

1.311 characteristically based on some range of territory, though not necessarily enclosed within frontiers;

1.32 it requires some means (if only by birthright) of admitting new members,

1.33 and also depends upon an educating, training, and initiating procedure, in turn dependent upon memory, tradition, myth, historiography, etc.

Almost invariably, the connection between the features (1.0–1.1421) and those in the second section (1.2 *et seq.*) of our definition is made by the nexus of productive relations, which, as suggested, typically involve territoriality. The system of production also brings to bear upon systems of Powers many of the extraneous (often called "autonomous") innovations and changes that change the relations between Powers—and sometimes, the very nature of those relations. These elements of production together with those concerned with recruitment (1.32–1.33) provide for theorists of Power politics most of the means of enriching their models beyond the scope of strategic theory alone. I include in these elements the production of the means of transport, and in my account of the *causes* of "systemic" change (see below, pp. 108 *et seq.*) I employ the explanatory power of the features (1.31–1.33). This has something in common with the Marxist approach, but in the last resort I regard the productive system as a channel for innovatory currents deeper than those of the mode of production—*viz.,* revolutionary change in fundamental science and other systems of thought.

The *effects* of systemic change, however, are most frequently observed in the features mentioned in the definition's first section (1.0–1.1421), especially in the ideas that a Power's directing group entertains about the nature of outsiders' societies and about the kind of relationships with them that seem possible. It is here that systemic change is exhibited through human responses and actions. Here also, as we have defined the realm, the issue of a Power's internal unity is put in question.

Several other matters need some clarification. What distinguishes the subject of a Power from the "stranger" outside it? Consider ancient Sparta, and set aside for the moment the rest of the Hellenic environment. Were the helots Spartan subjects or outsiders? It seems evident that since nothing in the structure of Lacedaemonian society constrained the Spartans from treating the helots as they thought fit, the Spartans alone constituted the society-set of that Power, while the helots were in practice ungrouped outsiders amongst whom the Spartans permitted no ruling group to arise.

Secondly, though a Power may in practice not survive for more than ten or twenty years, its methods of recruitment and education, and above all its directors' fostering of a unity-in-spirit, indicate a common purpose of self-perpetuation. The criminal gang, however powerful, is not a Power unless and until it is concerted so as to perpetuate itself. Neither, on the other hand, are long-persisting secret societies employing armed force, since their leaders, ostensibly anonymous, maintain no definable relations with other Powers and, moreover, show no compunction in their dealings with their own members.

Notice that the definition makes no mention of external *politics,* as distinct from the external imposition of sanctions—i.e., from coercion. In the final clause (1.1421) of the definition's first section, however, some of the conditions for the undertaking of external-political action by a Power's ruling group are set out. Those conditions are cognitive states of individuals and even so do not embrace all the conditions necessary for external political transactions to take place—e.g., the conditions of 1.1421 would have to be fulfilled for at least *two* Powers and their ruling groups in respect of each other. (There is a case, as is argued later in this volume, for making the condition "at least *three* Powers," since a relation of just two "persons" can hardly be political.) Central to the themes of this study are the following entailments of our definition: (1) that Powers as such are not the collective agents of external politics, but that political activities on their behalf are conducted by "representatives"—individual rulers and small groups of rulers; (2) that political relationships between Powers are necessarily subsequent to the emergence of those Powers as unities-in-spirit, and to the envisaging of them as such, at least by their own governing classes. These two universal propositions are of course open to refutation, and it certainly cannot yet be claimed that they have survived stringent testing and are therefore well supported. I have therefore thought it proper, to indicate both their vulnerability and their formative significance for the whole point of view here expressed, that they be exhibited plainly as consequences of a definition.

Neither those two propositions nor the definition as a whole imply, however, that the practice of external politics is necessarily a development from that of internal politics. Admittedly, it is insisted in our definition (1.12) that within any society being constituted as a Power, the concert formed by its governing group must exhibit some element of polity as well as of merely arbitrary power. But when a ruler (or group) begins to represent the Power in external politics, his activities *may* be quite detached from those of the internal polity. This can happen when the society is closely unified in spirit as against its external environment, and when at the same time the members of its ruling group, and the factions they form, are deeply interested in internal political issues. The Tudor and early Stuart monarchs did their best to keep "affairs of state" within their own prerogative; their styles in foreign politics seem to have had little to do with how they managed business with Lords or Commons. It is quite possible for a tradition of the conduct of external politics to develop, amongst the various Powers' representatives who practice it, that is *sui generis,* which is not to say that it is not also recognizably political.

On the other hand our definition, since it allows the element of polity in a Power's governing-class concert to be widely extended, and by providing that—as in a thoroughgoing democracy—the governing set may approach coextension with the subject set, suggests a variant model in which the Power's representative in external politics is also a member of the internal government. That variant can assist us in understanding the richest and most developed forms of statecraft—when the statesman is Janus-faced. One and the same person acts in both the external and the internal political systems. Moreover, his performance and experience in the one affects his opportunities in the other. His picture of the world takes in both, and by doing so provides in real life the factual connection between the two. Since, as was indicated in Chapter 3, of the whole field of inter-Power affairs, this study focuses greatest interest upon political relations, it is essential that our definition be rich enough for use in the construction of a framework for the investigation of the Janus-faced leader's ideas and actions.

Nevertheless, our interest also includes the matter of systemic change —i.e., change in either the nature of relations between Powers, or in the nature, number, and dimensions of the Powers themselves, or in both—a subject treated of in the next chapter. Inter-Power systems (external systems) must, as we shall contend, always exhibit amongst their interrelations some that are properly styled political. But the political element in inter-Power relations could well be greater or less than at present: such variations are amongst those denoted by "systemic change." Our definition, then, must be logically powerful enough to permit the construction of the most diverse models of Power systems, including those of Powers so primitive that the contacts between them are not perceived as inter-Power relations—e.g., when one tribe's raiding party accidentally comes upon and does battle with another's. Chapter 5 is intended as a demonstration that our definition has, in this respect, the required scope.

SECTION III

THEORY OF DYNAMICS

FIVE

The Criteria of Systemic Change

In this chapter we take up theoretical questions about the dynamics of Power systems. That may seem to be starting at the wrong end: why not begin from statics—i.e., from models of particular systems of Powers in equilibrium? Then, when the analysis shows a system to be moving away from an unstable to a new stable equilibrium, we shall have already found in statics a starting point for dynamics which is "non-autonomous" —that is, is intrinsic to the realm of Power politics.

That would be the more usual order of theoretical development, as followed, e.g., in economics. Briefly, there are several reasons for beginning instead with dynamics. First, the more interesting explanations of systemic change in our subject *are* "autonomous": they often arise, not within Power politics itself, but in the intellectual, technological, economic, and sometimes internal-political realms. This is understandable, for the agents in Power politics are few, so that changes in the conditions of their interaction are less likely to be taken up in and directed by the equilibrating movements engendered within the systems comprised of interacting Powers than is the case with analogous changes in systems (e.g., the market) of numerous agents.

Secondly, the statics of Power politics present a much less tractable problem than the dynamics: if treated as instances of competitive-cooperative interaction, their appropriate model is the *n*-person, nonzero-sum game, notoriously multifarious and often too complicated for computation. Our approach through dynamics may suggest explorable routes into the maze of statics.

Connected with that is the third reason: because so many power-political systems are possible, one must find a vantage point for their study; and with at least two of the more obvious vantage points, contrary kinds of difficulty arise. If, as in an earlier work,[1] we take our departure in the most general terms from a few axioms or principles, and build up from simpler to more complex (from two-Power to three-Power and so on) sequences of modeled systems, until complexity prevents further development, then no doubt one has part of a theory of statics; but it will be sheer chance if any of the modeled systems happens to have instances in the real world. (The venture as a whole does make a pertinent and indeed predictive comment on the real world, but does not furnish specific factual explanations.) If, on the other hand, one begins with a model of the present world situation, the equilibrium point needed for a static analysis is not easy to find. We seem to be just now at a point of systemic change, so that by beginning with dynamics, we may eventually make our way to a static analysis of the situation we have come from, and to suggestions of the various alternate equilibrium points to which our present changes may eventually bring us. But a theory of dynamics will not be of much interest, except perhaps to political historians, unless it has some plausible predictive range. In the present chapter, some major predictive hypotheses will be mentioned, even though the tenor of this study is that the political future beyond a very few decades must be subject to perspective-dissolving surprise.

The idea of very long-run rhythms in world politics—the "age," the "dispensation"—was introduced above (pp. 10–12) by a two-fold definition: during an age, there persists between more or less evanescent Powers a particular type of relation or syndrome of relations; during a dispensation, the constituent Powers themselves are usually of a particular kind (making it likely that they will interrelate in some persistent fashion). The end of an age or dispensation and the beginning of a new, we called a "systemic revolution,"[2] confining the word "systemic" to that kind of alteration and not applying it to changes of "period" or "era."

Before designing a model or theoretical structure to assist in the

[1] *From Balance to Deterrence: A Theoretical Analysis,* A.N.U., Social Science Monograph No. 9 (Canberra; The Australian National University, December 1956); also *World Politics,* IX: 4 (July 1957), 494–529; also J. N. Rosenau, ed., *International Politics and Foreign Policy: A Reader in Research and Theory* (New York: The Free Press, 1961), pp. 350–66.

[2] The present writer owes this expression to Mr. George Pettee, to whose conversation in 1959 he is indebted for several stimulating ideas.

explanation (perhaps, in the prediction) of systemic change, we must tighten up the description of our *explicanda.* For instance, the change from predominantly monarchical to predominantly republican governments does not amount to a revolution in the nature of the Powers constituting the European system; nor does the introduction of a formal and would-be-universal world organization (the League of Nations, the U.N.) suffice for the kind of change in type of inter-Power relation—though it is indeed some kind of change in relation—that is referred to. We are thinking of changes like the conquest of the Mediterranean world of city-states by Rome; or like the Roman Empire's coming to withstand barbarians in the north and to enter into a political relationship of balance and opposition with the Parthian Empire in the East; or like the prolonged process that by the mid-seventeenth century had begun to give rise to the European state system.

Such a sharpening of our definitions of systemic persistence and change will lead us directly to those objections raised in Chapter 3 against the possibility of general predictive theories in world affairs, and against that methodology in social sciences which insists upon the logical equivalence of explanation and prediction. For though there may be some faint hope of classifying all historic changes in the nature of and relations between Powers, and then of constructing a model which might help explain them; yet there is no possibility of making a list and classification of all possible future changes in system. However, a model which was logically rich, thereby having a potential for great explanatory force, would also have a range much wider than the sum of all historical instances, and could thus *suggest* types of possible future change not previously contemplated by the more traditional positive and would-be-predictive international theory. Furthermore, since systemic change is not a process in which men can at all easily intervene, it may prove possible to "set" a general-purpose model for the particular conditions of the third-quarter twentieth century and have it produce an array of likely outcomes—likely in relation, of course, to the logical limits of the model itself, and certainly not in relation to the unknown, indeterminate future as it will be. Again, in mitigation of our warning against predictive social science, we may notice that even nowadays systemic change requires a decade or more, except in its utterly destructive forms, so that the great range of possibilities offered by a good model can be narrowed considerably in view of time lag.

Change in the nature of a system of Powers is here to be understood as that kind which reveals itself in the logical structure of the descriptions of the situation as to Powers before and after the change. The logical structure of those descriptions may differ either in respect of what they state about the kind of relationship obtaining between the constituent Powers (including relationships characteristic only of systems comprising a certain *number* of Powers), or in respect of what they state about the nature or *character* of the constituent Powers themselves (changes of character in the "terms" entailing changes in the kind of relation, but not necessarily vice versa). By contrast, nonsystemic change—e.g., that from a stable equilibrium amongst the Powers to an unstable relationship or, in a multi-Power system, the emergence or destruction of one of them—entails no change in the logical structure of the description.

Are we justified in thus dichotomizing changes of world-political order into systemic and nonsystemic—i.e., into changes in the system's nature and those in its non-essential properties? First, is it justified in principle?

Let us suppose that Powers, as defined above (pp. 86–88), are interrelated in a competitive-cooperation system. Those changes in the nature of *its* constituent Powers that also change the kind of inter-Power relation are allowed for in the second part of the definition—i.e., the elements numbered from 1.2 to 1.33, which concern the Power's connection with territory, with the productive system, and with "outsiders." (The first part of the definition, which more concerns the Power's internal-political arrangements, has less direct consequences—indeed, sometimes none at all—for its external relations. However, see pp. 163–164 for remarks about a systemic change's *effects* upon a Power's disposition toward external factors, and upon its own internal arrangements.) Territoriality, the production system, relations with outsiders, can readily be imagined: consider three kinds of three-Power systems, the first of nomadic steppe-dwellers, the second of city-states each in control of an island, and the third of great land-based empires, each with a *glacis* of vassal-principalities. Compare such differences between systems with those between two city-state systems, one in which all the states are democracies and the other in which some are tyrannies. These two kinds of contrasts indicate the distinction in logic between systemic (the first) and nonsystemic (the second) change; yet when it comes to applying the dichotomized terms to actual instances, one can readily imagine that many doubts about appropriate classification would arise. Secondly, then, is a dichotomy justifiable in practice? Even the question of the number of Powers can be ambiguous; e.g., before Canada achieved Dominion status, the United Kingdom and the white colonies of the British Empire clearly constituted one Power; at the onset of the First World War, Britain and the Dominions acted in so close a concert as to be practically considered as one, even though they were in some respects different nations. At the onset of the Second World War, the legal distinctions were still more apparent, and quite probably the Dominions could have remained as neutral in 1939 as did the U.S.A.; but they chose to join the United Kingdom in declaring war on Nazi Germany: should we then speak of five Powers *simpliciter,* or of five

Powers owing a single allegiance to a Crown, and acting for practical purposes as one? So, if contrary to the facts of this case, the matter of numbers of Powers would have made a difference to the nature of the Power-systems of the nineteenth and twentieth centuries, we should have had doubts as to how to read off this instance against our dichotomized scheme.

Changes in number—*viz.,* the emergence, on the frontiers of an *imperium,* of a second comparable Power; the introduction of a third comparable Power into an essentially two-Power system; the almost impossible case where the number of Powers is so great as to cause system dominance—induce systemic change by necessarily altering the kind of interrelationship that obtains within the system (cf., the differences in "species" between two-person and three-person or other *n*-person games). Other apparent causes of systemic change in the system's characteristic style of interrelationship can be misdiagnosed, and indeed the character of the changes themselves misconceived. For example, the present writer had supposed that the medieval or feudal system of Powers began to give way during the Hundred Years War, under the impact of the longbow, the crossbow, and finally gunpowder, to the European state system (the immediate ancestor of our own) which could be seen to have begun in the sixteenth century, at the latest by the time of the Field of the Cloth of Gold, however long the one took to become fully established in Europe, and the other to disappear without trace.

An eminent historian, F. H. Hinsley, sees an intermediate system—rather, perhaps, a very ancient one revived—that immediately preceded the European state system. He writes:

> Historians are liable to ante-date the completion of massive developments because of their preoccupation with origins. They are given to ante-dating the beginnings of massive developments for the same reason and also because such developments are rarely finally completed: when the end of one phase is usually but the preliminary to the onset of the next it is easy to mistake the onset of another phase for the beginning of an entirely new departure. These opposite hazards have affected our assessments of the origin and evolution of the modern states' system. Only when due allowance is made for the first can it be seen that a new European states' system emerged in the eighteenth century, and not at an earlier date. . . . It was during the eighteenth century that the actuality and the conception of a collection of Great Powers in Europe finally replaced an earlier framework of existing fact and inherited thought in which, while more than one state had always existed, it had been natural for one Power to be rated above the rest and impossible for that Power's pretensions—resisted though they had always been by other states—to stop short of the control and protection of Christendom.
>
> This had been Charles V's conception of his position, and Philip II's and Louis XIV's. The ideas, indeed, of the first Napoleon were still made

> in the same mould. He undertook the domination of the Continent—the refashioning of its kingdoms within a single empire to replace the Holy Roman Empire, which he insisted on suppressing. . . .[3]

Certainly, the "earlier framework" seems to represent a type of interrelation between constituent Powers different in character (because the Powers sought a different objective and had a different vision of world order) from that both of the European state system and of the inter-Power relations of the Dark Ages. One needs sharper criteria than have been so far provided in this study to decide this issue.

We have already suggested above that whereas some types of systemic change in inter-Power relationships are entailed by changes in the nature of the constituent Powers themselves, not all are: some, it may be suspected, spring from what we shall call "autonomous" changes—i.e., those generated in domains outside that of world politics proper, for example, technological developments that transform the possibilities of military pressure and thus affect the scope of sanctions by one Power against another. Others may consist in "non-autonomous" developments—i.e., those arising by evolution of the system of Powers itself, perhaps in the course of a trend away from an earlier position of stable equilibrium, as in the emergence of the Empire of China out of the system of Warring States. One is tempted to classify systemic changes according to their apparent causes; but that would be to make circular one's theory of systemic change. At this stage, at any rate, what we need is to begin upon a list of types of international system, characterized first by numbers of significant Powers, then by other changes of interrelationship not entailed by numbers alone or chiefly, then finally—though to do this thoroughly will prove beyond the scope of this volume—by internal changes in the nature of the constituent Powers. Since in principle the first and the third of those kinds of change could conceivably coincide, we shall begin with a discussion of changes to or from a "system" of one Power only, to or from those of two or more Powers.

The one-Power world (or rather, known world) has occurred several times, both prehistorically and historically. Its instances never have approached and probably never could, at least for long, approach the ideal of a universal world-society in which there were no outsiders, internal or external, and no motivation for the employment of sanctions against subjects simply to preserve social unity (the ideal of a universal Switzerland or United Kingdom). But there really have been cases of a solitary Power amid many small and scattered bands of outsiders: P. M. A. Linebarger has used the word "ecumene" to denote the Andean empire at its zenith, and China in some of its ages. Notice that these were recognizably

[3] F. H. Hinsley, *Power and the Pursuit of Peace* (London: Cambridge University Press, 1963), p. 153. By permission, Cambridge University Press.

Powers: they possessed the essential elements mentioned in our definition —a widespread recognition of and intention to preserve a unity-in-spirit, if necessary by sanctions, against those perceived as not belonging to it. The ecumene is a Power system, though without the immediate possibility of Power politics (external politics). It is probably the least complex type of world organization.

Because the one-Power world appears the simplest, idealists have seen in it one of the two possible paths to permanent peace, the other being world federation. They hope for a liberal-democratic world empire, the rule of law being internally supreme, and all politics being internal politics: the remaining "outsiders," chiefly primitive people, would thus soon be drawn in by the prosperity and the civil liberty enjoyed by the citizenry of the unitary World State. (A liberal-democratic world *federation,* at this stage of the envisioned process, would work in these respects very similarly.) Then, like the postrevolutionary Workers' State prophesied by Marx and Lenin, the Power would "wither away." While this looks quite implausible for a totalitarian world empire—Marx-Leninism in practice strengthens the Power-element in internal society by so imposing sanctions upon citizens as to treat many of them as outsiders—the approach through liberal democracy appears hopeful at first sight because in fact quite populous democratic Powers already exist in which citizens seem to manage their lives as individuals under almost completely contractual relations, and the enforcement of law does not tend to operate (see definition) as a sanction to promote unity-in-spirit. What objections are there, then, to this hope that "the Powers" would wither away after the emergence of a nearly worldwide liberal democratic State?

The objections are much the same as those against the very emergence of such a State. Firstly, representative institutions in very populous nations —e.g., the USA—and in culturally or linguistically diverse societies— e.g., the European Economic Community—tend to be bypassed or transformed, either into "four-year elective monarchies" or into public-relations showcases for a self-selected bureaucracy. In one way or another, smaller would-be-sovereign political communities are apt to withstand the movement to a unitary state or, it being once established, to attempt secession from it. Secondly, the more liberal, individual, and contractual the tenor of social relations, the easier and more desirable for dedicated minorities to establish communities in which a certain way of life is practiced. For instance, Roman Catholic or Orthodox peoples have on the whole resisted corporate dissolution within a Protestant or secularist majority; socialists have tried to found utopias that would practice both social and political democracy, rejecting the more common union of the latter with private enterprise. The national revolutionism of the nineteenth and twentieth centuries has in fact catered for both religious and political "secessions."

One would expect similar movements, even though gradualist and peaceable, in a universal democratic State.

Nevertheless, one feature of the idealists' vision seems much less vulnerable to such objections: the universalizing of the rule of law, at least in respect of individuals. Though Power politics may be perennial, it may also be possible to separate from it the administration of justice. The European Community's initial successes in this regard, and many decades of similar practice in British nations, supports the hope. (The digression on permanent peace in a one-Power world now concludes.)

The distinction between internal and external politics for a one-Power system depends upon the rulers' recognition of some distinction between an internal and an external proletariat. Otherwise, such distinctions as those between intrarulership politics and ruler-subject relations (which will always have at least a residue of politics) are already contained within our definition of a Power as set out in Chapter 4. The theory and philosophy of the subject, in marked contrast with its practice, has usually been characterized—some would say, "distorted"—by a divorce between internal and external theory. In the Second Book of *The Republic,* Plato has Socrates develop his account of the city in which justice may be seen writ large, but with no account of the relations, just or unjust, between it and other cities, up to the point when Glaucon, objecting that a city content with the mere necessities of life is "a city of pigs," requires also the provision of luxuries; and, to acquire more land for the subsistence of the artisans and specialists who will produce those luxuries, the city is then said to be forced to make predatory war, and to resist the armies of other predator cities: without a demand for luxuries, the city's natural condition would be isolation. Hellenic and later Western political thought was thus set on a course in which external politics was to be either an afterthought of internal politics, or a consequence of the more gratuitous of economic demands. The gap has never been completely closed. Other civilizations have come, accidently and by quite different courses, to a similar division.

We have noticed the case of ancient China, where an "ecumene" supervened upon an era of warring states, of which the tradition and even something like a history have remained. But the coming of empire seems to have left an impression upon the Chinese, not of "national" or chivalric freedom and variety lost in a superstate, but rather of a single and virtuous order overcoming petty tyranny and anarchy: so much so that a unitary state for Chinese civilization seems to be a norm to which even the most incursive outsiders and the most aggressive revolutionaries constantly return. The conviction that liberty makes its home in states which are amongst a plurality of Powers developed quite late in Europe, and is by no means universal even there. Is that conviction a political discovery than can never be unlearnt, at least by the surviving societies that have once learned it? Even if so, may it not be made obsolete by a further possible development: that the various demands expressed through a libertarian polity are met most readily by and through an administrative machinery which sooner or later is bound to overshadow the political institutions that brought it into existence?—in which case, unless a countervailing anti-bureaucratic movement arises, the proposition that political liberty is dependent upon the multi-Power system, while not ceasing to be true, ceases to be relevant. We still know little about the relation between international structure and the liberties of citizens and states, though political philosophers since Plato and Aristotle, who believed that liberty belonged only to small cities, have kept on coming back to the question. That we should know more is a theme of this study, which contends that internal and external politics are the same kind of activity. How we *can* come to know more is another question: the variety of Power systems from earliest times to the present day is not large, and the theory that might allow us to say something about the condition of liberty in possible future world systems has not yet been developed. But we can recognize that this ignorance is itself an important initial condition to be mentioned in any explanation of the present state of political affairs.

That concludes for the moment our consideration of single-Power systems. Of two-Power systems, historical instances are almost as scarce. For Westerners, one *prima facie* example is the confrontation between the still-united Roman Empire and the Parthian Power before its internal defeat by the Sassanians in A.D. 250. Each had more in common with the other than either had with the barbarian at his gates—not more in common internally, but as Powers. On the other hand, neither impinged very much upon the other; for their centers of greatest power were rather far apart, so that the effectiveness of the forces they could bring against each other fell off rapidly[4] over distance; further, each was more concerned with civil strife at the center and with barbarian pressures on other frontiers. As their interactions were less intense the system they constituted is of less immediate interest than that of the 1950s, in which the reciprocal preoccupations of the United States and the Soviet Union structured the multi-Power system into a decided though temporary bipolarity. That 1950s bipolarity was, however, by no means a genuine example of the two-Power world; but in the years preceding it, at least from the Chinese revolution completed in 1949, one could see how a collapsing subsystem of several Powers in the politically most evolved area (*viz.*, Western Europe), by causing the involvement of two strong though peripheral Powers, might set off a process by which the latter pair would become rivals in everything.

[4] Kenneth E. Boulding, *Conflict and Defense: A General Theory* (New York: Harper and Row, Publishers, Inc., 1962); on the Loss-of-Strength Gradient, *passim*.

A two-Power system forms most dramatically out of the schism of a single great society—e.g., as might have followed the American War between the States, had the Confederates brought off their secession. Canada and Mexico were in comparison small enough, and the Transatlantic Powers neutral enough, not to intervene: thus the beginning of that war has become a prototype of "world-political" fission. In terms of our definition of a Power, the rulers or governing set (1.1–1.121) divided against each other about the nature of their unity-in-spirit (1.1) along a line which was also a geographic (1.13–1.14 and 1.31), economic, and social (1.141–1.1411) frontier. The salience of that possible geographic (i.e., territorial) division seems to have been the *sine qua non* for a civil struggle, quite like many other internal wars about religious, ideological, class, and straightforwardly material issues, nevertheless almost turning into a quite different political process—the production of two Powers out of one.

Though the attempt to divide in this case consisted in a unilateral bid for secession, other political approaches to division—e.g., acceptance of *de facto* ceasefire lines, *faute de mieux* partition, and so on—are possible. But it is always likely that at least one of the sides or a party within it will take up, in opposition to the seceders, the position of "maintaining the union." In the War between the States, of course, the political and constitutional forms and concepts of unification and division were canvassed with peculiar explicitness and self-consciousness. Thus that great conflict provides evidence that neither political and social maturity, racial or religious homogeneity, nor ardent and widespread patriotism are prophylactics against accidentally arising tendencies for schism in a Power—a proposition relevant to our reflections above upon the one-Power world.

Two-Power systems can also arise out of opposing associations amongst subnational groupings—tribes, cities, syndicalist communities, even when such groupings are socially advanced enough to understand and to wish to avoid such a change from their former anarchic condition. No recent examples spring to mind, but it may be worth considering that some future system, which had devolved the control of sanctioning and coercion upon small and numerous territorial groups (e.g., cities) could easily evolve again into a duopoly of power.

Again, a two-Power system can form from the gradual encroachment upon each other of peoples formerly belonging to widely separated systems. Such a development raises no great theoretical problems. The essential difference between one- and two-Power systems is in the relationship with "outsiders" (definition 1.122). In the *ecumene,* for instance, the ruling group perceives as outsiders only what Toynbee has called the external and internal proletariates—the barbarians on the frontiers and the nonsubjects *within* the ecumenic territory but not *of* the ecumenic society.

In any two-Power world, each ruling group must come to perceive the outsiders as including or comprising another Power, whose ruling group, at least, presumably perceives in turn an alien Power. We may put the difference in semantic terms: the language of authority in a one-Power world need not go beyond the first level of meta-language—"We command you: pay this tax to the imperial officers"; in the two-Power world, both ruling groups' languages must be able to ascend indefinitely the ladder of meta-languages—"Their emperor thinks that *ours* is plotting to deceive him . . . ," and so on. An important methodological consequence follows: whereas the theory of a one-Power system can afford to be positivistic (e.g., a Parsonian sociological model would be rich enough), that of systems of two or more members must employ logical resources of more complex order—at least as intersubjective as those of game theory. This is not merely to say that multi-Power theories are "more complex" in the sense of involving more variables. A two-by-two game-theoretical matrix has fewer variables than has many a sociological model: the difference of logical richness lies in game theory's presupposition of the existence of more than one independent subject, and in its "postulates of rationality." Another way of making this point is that game-theoretical models can often include many sociological models as special cases (e.g., as "games against nature"), but not vice versa.

The two-Power world, then, is intersubjective; but one hesitates to say that the relations between just two "persons" should be styled "political." (Indeed, it goes against the grain to use the word "system" of the relations between less than three subjects—e.g., Pnin's referring to Siamese twins as "this group.") Consider the difficulty of "bargaining" between any isolated pair: the enforcement of a deal depends wholly upon the one's or the other's strength of personality and of will. But for either one, further alternatives will open up as soon as a third interested party enters the situation; for a new deterrent to breaking agreements arises from the reflection that the other may then turn to the third party. Another aspect introduced by the presence of third parties persuaded the author, in a venture ten years ago into the subject of this study, to begin a theory of international *systems* with model of a *three*-Power world.[5] Thus *"pacta sunt servanda,"* the great principle of international law, is, in a three-Power anarchy, a counsel of prudence, as well as a moral imperative. And, given that the matter of the bargain or agreement is not simply economic (*viz.,* some quantity of scarce goods), the deterring reflection—that a third party may offer to the second an alternative outcome of which the consequence for oneself would be worse than that of abiding by one's somewhat inconvenient arrangement with the second—is precisely the sort of reflection we regard as "political." Persuasiveness, force of personality, and strength of will remain

[5] *World Politics,* IX, 494–96.

significant in a three-Power as in a two-Power world (just as, in a two-Power world, authority of rulers over subjects, and unity of spirit in the face of outsiders not concerted in another society, may be as significant as in the *ecumene*). But the possibility of a new quality—"world politics" —emerges with the appearance of the third interested party.

Two remarks in qualification: Firstly, some political philosophers of sound and cultivated judgment have held it improper to call any activity "political" that is not conducted within a State or at least a framework of order. Thus Bernard Crick:

> Politics is one form of human activity; diplomacy or the conduct of international relations is another. The political system exists within a prior framework of order. International "society" is not a political system. It is a proper subject for the study of government; but while it has no common government at all, it is not helpful to call it political.[6]

Let us at once agree that "politics" in the prime and exact sense of the word denotes an activity carried out under a common government; and if to preserve the distinction one decides always to say "statecraft" and never "world, Power, international . . . politics," nothing will be lost. Nevertheless, the "deterring reflection" about alternatives opened up by third parties, which, we have just argued, is commonly considered a political consideration, also goes toward constituting a "framework of order," however weak and tacit, for statecraft. The three-Power system itself is an order of sorts; and when there has grown up amongst the historical community of statesmen a certain common understanding, certain counsels of prudence concerning the directions and bounds of their interrelated activity, does there not perhaps exist as much of a framework for politics as in those undoubtedly political systems whose governments hardly existed or which had no peculiarly governmental means of coercion? If there is anything in the contention that two-Power systems are subpolitical, while those of three or more Powers are not, then we can claim a parallel to the condition supposed to be necessary for internal politics—that there be several distinct agents or centers of power in the society. All that having been said, we can disavow any intention to make Power politics an *instance* of internal politics: it is far from the viewpoint of this work that every social activity has a political aspect. We are contending that politics can supervene at more than one level of social organization; in Australia we have local, state, and federal politics; we play a middling part in world politics; and if it had turned out that intelligent and fallen species were inhabiting Mars and Venus, no doubt the Earth would be engaged in interplanetary politics.

Secondly, it is not here maintained that if our world did polarize into

[6] Bernard Crick, *In Defence of Politics,* revised ed. (Middlesex: Penguin Books, 1964), p. 182.

a genuine two-Power system, that system would thereby lose the quality of politics. These are arts that cannot be lost while the historical tradition of them is kept alive. The (originally Biblical) conception of "this world's Powers"—of "the nations" and their Power politics—was kept alive through several hundred years in which the centers of authority often were certainly not governments of nations, but (if generalization is at all possible) heads of families. The habit of thinking—indeed, of behavior—in the political mode would not disappear the moment the number of Powers decreased below that which would certainly ensure that politics was being carried on. The argument is not only that the rulers of a two-Power world would be slow at changing their minds; but also that they would be well-advised to consider that a third Power might reemerge. In any case, the political arts have been lost and found several times in the history of the race; and it seems that their discovery and rediscovery has always been a swifter process than their gradual loss.

This study has so far done without a formal definition of politics. That it is an activity of rational creatures has been taken for granted; that the paradigm of political activity (though not necessarily the earliest historical instance) is activity "under a common government" or, better, "by members of a ruling group or groups" (see our definition of Powerhood in Chapter 4), has been admitted; and it has been asserted that political activity can occur only if either there are at least three "persons" each with an "interest" that he can freely maintain or, in two-person situations (for no one seems to have supposed that there could be one-person politics—philosophers have alleged that the individual is a society, but not literally that he is a polity), there is a recognition of the possibility, or a memory of the fact, that a third person might come in. But there can be three-person situations of the sort defined, in which the "interests" are merely economic but not also political: in these, the issues at stake, the objects of the interests, are what we call "material"; whereas in the truly political situation the interest for each person comprises, in the internal-political case, "life, liberty, and the pursuit of happiness" (to use the American rather than other equivalent formulations); or in the case of a Power in external politics, "security, integrity, and the unimpeded exercise of sovereignty"— the last at any rate in respect of the Power's own resources. It is these two sets of ends of political activity, internal or external, together with the employment of means appropriate to securing or advancing them, that make it *political*. The feature of the three-or-more-person situation that seems a necessary condition for politics, we alleged to be the set of options opened for each party by the presence of a third party, or from another point of view, its being not only a moral precept but also a counsel of prudence in a three-person situation that agreements be observed: *pacta sunt servanda*. Thus we define politics as an activity pursued by at least three rational "agents" (e.g., individuals, or Powers, etc.) for the above-mentioned sets of ends. Furthermore, our definition of Powerhood in Chapter 4 entails that external politics is the pursuit of the "interests" of Powers, each of which itself must be, or must include, however minimally, a polity (see item 1.12 of our definition of Powerhood). If a non-economic two-person or two-Power situation in which the ends characteristic of politics are pursued is not to be called "political," what is it to be called? The adjective, I suggest, is "strategic," which is used primarily of situations on the conflict-cooperation spectrum where the objectives pursued are not those characteristically definable as "economic." Situations of three or more persons may also have a strategic aspect—e.g., where two allies cooperating wholeheartedly coerce an enemy—but where subsequently options may open for each ally to which the adjective "political," and not "strategic," would be appropriate.

The introduction of a fourth into a three-Power system brings changes —but none comparable to those between one-, two-, and three-Power systems. This is not to say that an adequate four-Power model would be simply a three-Power model altered a little: the history of game theory strongly suggests that the addition of one more or less commensurate "player" involves the working-out of a whole new model, at least until there are so many that, in Kaplan's phrase, the system itself becomes dominant. Indeed, the change—by addition of further Powers—to a situation of system dominance is comparable in significance to that between a two- and a three-Power system, since both are changes in that to which the typical Power responds.

We have, of course, no means of telling at what number of Powers system dominance would set in, though we can be reasonably sure that it never has in fact occurred. This is in part because, even when Powers have been small and numerous, conditions of transport and communication throughout the system have often prevented effective relationships amongst wider circles of Powers than neighbors of neighbors. Therefore, one would expect that during an era—or, during an even longer "period" —the history of such a system would be explicable only by following the actions of each of the many small states that made it up; that is, the "subsystems"—the member-Powers—would be dominant. It is only on a longer time scale that an explanation sketch in terms of the military, productive, and geographic features of the system as a whole will be apt to throw light upon the system's evolution. Even so, the task of historical explanation does not begin to be completed until that explanation is filled out in detail with the particular histories of Powers and constellations of Powers, era by era.

As we have seen, there have been no unequivocal instances of constellations of Powers so numerous and so readily in contact with each other that the adjective "system-dominant" would be appropriate for their interrelations. We need an imaginary instance to illustrate the principle. Suppose nuclear proliferation to break up alliances and federations so far that no *city* could be relied upon to risk utter destruction in order to deter attack upon another. The world order comprises thousands of city-states each with a few ICBMs and reliable means of detecting the source of an attack upon it by ICBMs. Each then can hope to deter a devastating strike by missiles upon itself, and can seal its frontiers against manned invasion. Warfare between pairs or even between small groups of city-states is likely to be isolable so that the actions of one or two of these Powers do not reverberate very much throughout the whole system. On the other hand, this order could be transformed by certain changes in military technology —e.g., proliferation of a cheap and perfect antimissile defense, coincidentally with improvement in the prospects of manned attack across frontiers. In that case, the city-states in large numbers would probably need to take new Power-political measures to preserve their independence, rather as changes of scale or of the structure of the average firm might result throughout an industry comprising thousands of independent producers.

Summarizing in reverse order: we have sketched an imaginary world of Powers so numerous that it might be considered system-dominant, but have noticed that even such a state of affairs is dependent upon the coincidence of many conditions, political as well as technological, and is not necessarily stable. Earlier, we had noticed that subsystem-dominant worlds form a class in which there is a significant distinction between those of just two Powers and those of at least three: in the latter case, the relations between any pair of Powers are under important constraints when each recognizes that there are third, fourth, or other Powers whose policies might offer alternative opportunities to the second Power, thus creating a situation contrasting with that of a two-Power world by its possibility of giving rise to unequivocally "political" relations. Earlier still, we had discussed under several heads the single-Power situation, noting that while it too was liable to disruption and instability, the concept of Powerhood as defined in Chapter 4 was applicable to the solitary Power, as a social and sanctioning unity discernible to its rulers and subjects over against the human environment afforded it by "outsiders."

These are by no means the only ways in which the sheer number of Powers may affect the behavior of the systems they constitute: we shall investigate below (pp. 249–250) whether in several types of *n*-Power system distinguished by the nature of inter-Power relations the number of Powers makes a difference to the degree of equilibrium exhibited by the type of system. Even if so, that would not in our terminology amount to a systemic difference—a difference in the nature of the system; whereas we do attribute such differences to changes between one-fold, two-fold, three-or-more-fold, and system-dominant worlds.

We now introduce a previously unmentioned factor that can make for systemic differences: disparity of dimensions. In discussing the effect of numbers, we tacitly assumed that the various Powers were not incomparable with each other in respect of powerfulness. That assumption is now removed; but we shall first glance at those cases in which its removal makes little difference.

Clearly, when an ecumenical empire like the classical Chinese is surrounded, not by stateless nomads, but by a score of tiny kingdoms and chieftainships, the situation from the imperial viewpoint will still be that of a one-Power system. From the viewpoint of the small principalities, their relations with each other and with the vast imperial Power looming over them will appear to be a multiple-Power system, though not at all as it would if the imperial Power did not exist. Because they can hardly be of any great causal significance, such minor Powers and the marginal systems they form amongst themselves are usually considered of little theoretical interest, except in relation to the locally predominant Great Power.

A more complex case would be provided by a pair of reasonably comparable Great Powers in an environment of many very small ones. (The instance here is not that of the loose bipolarity of the late 1950s; for then a few middle Powers whose presence precludes the situation just described played significant parts, though for the time being in alliance with or as satellites of the two leaders.) Suppose that, even in combination, the very small Powers do not carry enough weight to swing the balance decisively against either Great Power, but that they can act to the short-term advantage or detriment of either.

According to our previous contentions about the significance of numbers, we are probably obliged to classify this with the three-or-more-Power systems, since it would be apt to promote indubitably political activity. But, for the two Great Powers as we have described the case, that political activity might be merely optional, and not, as in the three-Power system mentioned above, an essential method of maintaining a strategic position. Strategically, then, the relations of the leaders might differ very little from what they would be in a strictly two-Power world; and that would certainly lend a distinctive color to the politics of the whole system. Such complex characterizations become the more necessary the more nearly our models approximate to historical reality.

The reader will have noticed that we have suddenly enlarged the number of possible systemic differences between various interrelationships of Powers. Thus far, we have been concerned with only two differences of dimension—the very great and the very small. If we now ask how many ranges of dimension relevant to systemic differences can be found between those two extremes (which for our present purposes means "between the most powerful and the only-just-powerful"), then clearly we are enlarging the total number of systemic differences even further. Is there any sensible method for dividing this range?

A traditional criterion for a Power's being a Great Power is that it cannot be defeated except by a coalition of Powers. This type of criterion can be extended: we may define a Superpower as one that cannot be defeated and conquered—as distinct from being wiped out in a universal holocaust—even by a coalition (this not necessarily implying that it can defeat any coalition); a Middle Power may then be defined as one that cannot be defeated except by a Superpower, a Great Power, or a coalition. The residual class of Minor Powers can, if required, be further differentiated within itself by reapplying the same distinction. Thus for any given world or system of Powers we can devise a dimensional classification entirely in terms of a strategic relationship (whether or not the Power in question "can be defeated") and with no mention of politics in the *definiens,* except insofar as "coalition" carries political connotations.

We have now reached a crucial transition point in building a framework for the analysis of systemic change. The interpretation of dimensionality as a strategic *relationship* moves us on from a consideration of the nature and the number of a system's constituent units to a much closer examination than heretofore of the character of relations between the units. This is because the particular strategic relationship we have hit upon is not merely a matter of comparative quantities—say, comparative sizes of population—but is also a function of the state of military technology. When defensive armaments predominate over offensive, for instance, Powers are harder to defeat than in the contrary situation. Technology in the broadest sense is thus a candidate for the explanation of change in *strategic* systems while, in a different mode of explanation, both the numbers and the strategic dimensionality of Powers enter into the explanation of change in the character of intrasystemic *political* relations. Security and strategic power are not the only objectives of political action by the Powers, but usually they are central ones. Here there is a parallel with characteristic objectives of internal politics, for instance with the economic, racial, or religious objectives of particular interests. In the external case, the link between a subpolitical objective such as security and the realm of political action is made through the kind of interaction, such as alliance formation, mentioned in our definitions of dimensionality.

It must be understood, however, that the concepts of strategic relationships in our definitions, e.g., ". . . can be defeated by . . . ," are quite coarse in the mesh. Firstly, as clauses indicating potentiality, they become ingredient in statements which cannot of course be tested *directly* against matters of occurrent fact—indeed, in many cases they will be decidable only with such a margin for error as makes them somewhat doubtful in application (e.g., one cannot be sure that, in the early Forties before the development of atomic weapons, Japan was not a Great Power). Nevertheless, something can be discovered about a Power's military potential, even in peacetime; and many power-political decisions are made upon the basis of such discoveries and estimates.

The reader may have thought it odd that we measured dimensionality in strategic terms only: why not also (or instead) in terms of economic strength?—that, after all, is amongst the objectives of external politics.

Perhaps in centuries to come, if wars of conquest cease to be practicable, the weaker modes of coercion, including economic measures, will become the indices of a Power's status. Historically, however, strategic relationships have provided on the whole rather more important and immediate objectives for politics—even the hypothesis that wars are "economically caused" presupposes this. Further, a Power's strategic dimensions are in part a consequence of its economic strength; but since, during peace, a time lag often supervenes between changes in economic strength and the emergence of their consequences for strategic status, the relationship between various Powers' economic potential seems a longer-term matter than do their strategic relations.

This is far from saying that the longer-term issues usually overbear the shorter-term in the deliberations of governing groups. Economic potential and prevailing conditions of technology are rarely under their control as, to a limited extent, are the issues of military strength and security. The creation and functioning of such external-political institutions as the League of Nations and the U.N. (which in our chronology are of middling duration) are thus to be explained with the help of accounts of the Power system, its numbers and dimensionality; whereas we shall look amongst technological and economic developments for long-range explanations of systemic change.

We have noticed that a bridge is made from strategic to political relationship by means of the concept of "coalition" or "alliance" employed in our definitions, which remain applicable even to the interrelations of those imaginable (but never as yet actual) systems where it pays no Power to form a coalition, at least for strategic purposes. Thus the occurrence or nonoccurrence of strategic alliances affords one distinctive criterion for differentiating amongst external-political relationships and amongst the systems they constitute. Furthermore, the concept directs us to a second criterion—the occurrence or nonoccurrence of multimember international organizations—for these have emerged, in the two clear cases of the League and the U.N., from coalitions of recently victorious Powers. Yet there are other kinds of inter-Power relation less directly connected with the concept of alliance. In both the Western and Eastern medieval systems, for example, Powers were also distinguished by their rulers' positions in a ceremonial order of precedence which had no immediate relation with the strategic status referred to in our definitions. In the Hellenic system from Marathon to the rise of Macedonia, distinctions perceived between Hellenic and other Powers, including that of Persia, did not preclude intra-Hellenic war. It does not seem possible to make a complete list of all the conceivable criteria for differences between external-political systems, once we have listed the rather more obvious differences produced by the three important differences of number; for, as we noticed above, the range of possible differences in dimensionality is vast.

Thus, a certain arbitrariness seems unavoidable in our selection of criteria for systemic change—there is no conclusive argument against so designating the change from the Bismarckian concert of 1871–90 to the intensifying of bipolarity that led to the First World War, as does R. N. Rosecrance.[7] However, I think it possible to rationalize one's selection up to a point, with the aid of the distinction between theories of dynamics and of statics mentioned at the beginning of this chapter. Statics is concerned with analysis of partial equilibria. In world politics we expect stable equilibrium only within idiosyncratic conditions, any one of which may readily be overset. Nevertheless, those conditions may not be overset all at once: indeed, it is possible that one of a set of equilibrium-producing conditions may be replaced by another that, while significantly altering the status and relative strengths of some constituent Powers, merely modifies, without overthrowing, the weak but stable equilibrium. So modified through successive changes of precondition, a partially equilibrating process may have a history continuous through several centuries, in the sense that there were always some tendencies, however weak and changing, obtaining toward equilibrium, and never occasions when all the conditions were overset at once; nor was the logical nature of the equilibrium transformed. (The equilibrium of a chandelier or a mobile is, for example, "logically" different both from those of an Egyptian pyramid and of a bicycle in motion.) But such processes, even when centuries-long, are not perpetual.

I shall therefore, in this chapter, call a change "systemic" if but only if (1) an equilibrating process of one kind is utterly terminated and replaced by some process of another kind, whether equilibrating or not; *or* (2) though most former Powers continue to exist and though there is no complete absence of equilibrating features in their interactions, nevertheless the nature of the equilibrium (and thus of the most significant relationships between the Powers) is transformed. This of course corresponds with a similar determination of usage in Chapter 1, p. 10, and implies

[7] R. N. Rosecrance, *Action and Reaction in World Politics* (Boston and Toronto: Little, Brown and Co., 1963), pp. 250–57, *et passim.*

that systemic change is extremely uncommon. Some specific implications may be of interest—e.g., despite the emergence in 1945 of the USA and the USSR as Superpowers preeminent above the Great Powers of Europe (France and Britain) which had persisted for several centuries, no systemic change is supposed (on this definition) to have begun for several hundred years before the 1950s, when hydrogen explosives and long-range missiles inaugurated one which is still several decades from completion.

Admittedly, to identify change with the termination or transformation of an equilibrium process lets in a class of theoretically trivial cases. As an example, it appears that in certain Pacific archipelagoes before colonization by overwhelming Western forces, small systems of island Powers had grown up, amongst whom there were recognizably political contests for hegemony over the group. The overthrow of these systems of Powers by the Western advent falls within our definition of systemic change. But we call such cases trivial because, *ex hypothesei,* their explanations are not surprising—*viz.,* involve no discoveries of new principles.

Neither do the last stages of a multi-power system about to be taken over piecemeal by a Power which has grown to overwhelming strength within the system. What is surprising and would seem to require the sort of explanation that involves some element of "discovery" is the prior growth of the potential conqueror (one thinks of Rome's conquest of the Mediterranean world). Systemic change may be in this sense sometimes foreseen immediately before it impends, and, by logical parallelism, the course of the change from then on may be trivially explained. What then are the nontrivial features of systemic change?

As argued in Chapter 3, they are characteristically indicated by those eliminations or reversals of equilibrium process that initially were improbable or counter-expected. Their (nontrivial) explanations, moreover, will involve some aspect of discovery, either about the structure of the preceding system (thus arising from an exercise in "static" analysis), or about some development outside the realm of external politics—i.e., an "autonomous" change. To avoid circularity, we must of course not make any particular explanatory feature part of the criteria of external political change, nor indeed of the persistence of any particular system. To identify the latter, historians and political scientists have employed so far two diverse approaches—the historical and the taxonomic. In this chapter we can say little that is pertinent to the historical approach (e.g., Hinsley's, *loc. cit.*), though for any theoretical structure or array of models the test of historical evidence must be decisive. The taxonomic approach, however, is here entirely to the point, and we shall now consider an eminent example of it in the work of M. A. Kaplan.[8] It should perhaps be mentioned here that the

[8] Morton A. Kaplan, *System and Process in International Politics* (New York, 1957). Quoted by permission of John Wiley and Sons Inc.

line of argument developed in this study is not at all to be laid at Kaplan's door: the terms employed in *System and Process in International Politics* often coincide with those in this work and indeed with those in the present writer's publications of 1956 and 1958. His definitions and theorems will be found, however, to be logically quite different from ours (e.g., the treatment of the concept of equilibrium).[9] One can only record the sense of gratitude and encouragement that Kaplan's eclectic, inventive, and enterprising book inspired.

Kaplan distinguishes six types of international system, ". . . or, with possibly greater accuracy, six states of equilibrium of one ultrastable system . . . ,"[10] beginning with (1) the "balance-of-power" system, instantiated, e.g., in Europe of the eighteenth and nineteenth centuries; (2) "loose bipolar"—e.g., that which in general now prevails, in Kaplan's opinion; (3) "tight bipolar"—*viz.,* the same, but consisting solely of two "hierarchically organized blocs," no grey areas, and no U.N.; (4) "universal"—*viz.,* roughly, World Federal Union; (5) "hierarchical"—i.e., unitary world government; and (6) "unit veto"—i.e., what is more often called the "deterrent" or "standoff" situation, where all possess "weapons of such a character that any actor is capable of destroying any other actor" (or coalition) "even though it cannot prevent its own destruction." Kaplan does not intend an exhaustive list.

The following rules characterize "balance of power":

1. Act to increase capabilities but negotiate rather than fight.
2. Fight rather than pass up an opportunity to increase capabilities.
3. Stop fighting rather than eliminate an essential national actor.
4. Act to oppose any coalition or single actor which tends to assume a position of predominance with respect to the rest of the system.
5. Act to constrain actors who subscribe to supranational organizing principles.
6. Permit defeated or constrained essential national actors to reenter the system as acceptable role partners or act to bring some previously inessential actor within the essential actor classification. Treat all essential actors as acceptable role partners.[11]

One cannot be quite sure of the theoretical work that these "essential rules" are supposed to perform. Later in the book, Kaplan suggests that they might be regarded as "initial hypotheses—in the absence of systematic evidence which would be convincing." But this leaves still unresolved the question whether "essential rules" are meant to describe the subject matter of international relations or to explain it. Since only two of

[9] *Ibid.,* p. 8.
[10] *Ibid.,* p. 21.
[11] *Ibid.,* p. 23.

the six types of system characterized by sets of "essential rules" have had historical instances, the sets of rules can hardly be descriptions, however sketchy, affording material for comparative study. If, on the other hand, the rules are meant to explain in some degree the behavior of the type of system they characterize, then in this first set concerned with the balance-of-power types there is a mixing together of two levels of explanation, one presupposing the other. Rules 3, 5, and 6 cited above presuppose that a balance-of-power system already exists which the constituent actors wish to preserve; if rules 1, 2, and 4 were followed by national actors, even by actors quite ignorant of the possibility that any international system should exist, then, provided the state of the military art were suitable, a balance-of-power system should come into existence without anyone's necessarily intending or even noticing the event. Thus while 3, 5, and 6 could explain little more than postponement of the system's gradual decay, 1, 2, and 4 explain the much more surprising fact that a more or less equilibrating system of nations once existed and could well have done so without any nation's having wittingly fostered it. Moreover, in the sense that 3, 5, and 6 are rules or norms comprising an ethic of statecraft, 1, 2, and 4 are not "rules" so much as maxims directed to the single aim of preserving national integrity (cf. our definition of Powerhood in Chapter 4). The theorist could use them to construct, from a minimum number of axioms, a model which would account for the essentials of balance-of-power behavior amongst nations; then, supposing that some of the predictions derivable from the model did not square with the historical facts (or, in the case of systems which have not yet existed, with the kinds of situation that national actors might be expected to accept without modification), the theorist could formulate, in supplementary hypotheses, the rules —such as 3, 5, and 6—for a policy that would adjust the model to the historical facts, or to our expectations concerning future political behavior. (This, however, is a criticism rather of methodological style than of logic and substance, and is hardly relevant to the present chapter.)

Kaplan nevertheless maintains that the number of these essential rules cannot be reduced. This makes excellent sense if we regard the whole set of six as a specification or characterization of a certain kind of international system, rather than as an explanation. Consider, that is, the list of six essential rules, and preface it as follows: "We shall say that a balance-of-power system prevails whenever, and only when, all the Powers (or, all except the minor Powers) that make up the system (1) act to increase capabilities . . . ," and so on through Kaplan's six rules.

By thus emphasizing the descriptive rather than the explanatory aspect of Kaplan's essential rules, we can take them as criteria for a balance-of-power system, and moreover use evidence for their having ceased to apply as indications of a systemic change away from the balance of power.

Nevertheless the rules, especially 1, 2, and 4, would still retain their heuristic capacity to suggest explanations of the process which, together, they help to describe; therefore the set of them could be applied as criteria for the presence of a balance-of-power system only to a well-worked-over and highly explanatory historical account: each rule specifies a class of purposive acts for each of which a "motivational explanation" (see above, Chapter 3) would be required, and that in turn requires the findings of minute diplomatic historiography.

The scale of the former requirement may be reducible if from the various rules we infer some of their more discernible general effects:

(a) much changing of alliances (from 1, 4, and 6), but, except during wars, no "grand coalitions" (from 5);
(b) occasional additions to the number of Major Powers ("essential national actors") in the system (from 6); and no or very rare eliminations or reductions of Major Powers (from 1, 3, and 6);
(c) wars limited, and less frequent than changes of alliance (from all except 5);
(d) quantitative arms races and mercantilist economic policies (from 1).

This list of phenomena could be used to develop a set of *quantitative* indicators of a power-balancing process, which could be applied (e.g., to ancient multistate systems) with less need for prior detailed historical analysis. From a number of such sets, each indicating a distinctive type of system, quantitative criteria for (unexplained) systemic change could be developed. Furthermore, the background of theoretical invention and criticism should provide some assurance against the dangers of illusory quantification (on which see pp. 225–254 below).

The expression "theoretical invention" is used advisedly: all of Kaplan's sets of "essential rules" had to be invented, that for the balance of power less than the others. Here a great difficulty arises: types of system only now emerging are not easy to characterize correctly. If a bad mistake is made at this point, the theorist's taxonomy and thereby his theory of dynamics as a whole will be vitiated.

That danger can be avoided by a restriction of the role of theory to being an adjunct of historical explanation. The hardheaded scholar who insists that the theorist must choose between history and science fiction can be answered that the public and the politicians are bound to speculate about the immediate future, with or without benefit of criticism, and that it is the business of scholars to see that they have the benefit. Theorizing is mere fiction unless checked by historical evidence; yet it must take the risk of refutation by the future.

Kaplan's six systems are represented by him in a succession from past to future, the loose bipolar system being the present nexus to the other four future possibilities—nor will he allow us to exclude the fifth alternative, of a reversion to the balance-of-power system. Thus his loose bipolar system is crucial. Its "essential rules"[12] when transformed (as above, in respect of those of the balance of power) yield a recognizable description of the Cold War world after 1955. It has proved, as Kaplan anticipated in expounding its features, unstable and ephemeral; nevertheless he regards it as an equilibrium position. It is this latter opinion which must always prove extremely difficult to substantiate concerning any current situation. Since by definition too little time will have passed for us to tell whether a list of phenomena (cf. that for the balance-of-power system, pp. 113–115 above) suggestive of equilibrium does in fact describe the current situation satisfactorily, we are thrown back, for indications that the process is an equilibrating one, upon the explanatory elements in the proposed list of "essential rules." For the loose bipolar system, Kaplan supplies the following:[13]

1. All blocs subscribing to directive hierarchical or mixed hierarchical integrating principles for the international system are to eliminate the rival bloc.
2. All blocs subscribing to directive hierarchical or mixed hierarchical integrating principles for the international system are to negotiate rather than to fight, to fight minor wars rather than major wars, and to fight major wars—under given risk and cost factors—rather than to fail to eliminate the rival bloc.
3. All bloc actors are to increase their capabilities in relation to those of the opposing bloc.
4. All bloc actors subscribing to non-hierarchical or non-directive hierarchical organizational principles for the international system are to negotiate rather than to fight to increase capabilities, to fight minor wars rather than to fail to increase capabilities, but to refrain from initiating major wars for this purpose.
5. All bloc actors are to engage in major war rather to permit the rival bloc to attain a position of preponderant strength.
6. All bloc members are to subordinate objectives of universal actors to the objectives of their bloc but to subordinate the objectives of the rival bloc to those of the universal actor.
7. All non-bloc member national actors are to coordinate their national objectives with those of the universal actor and to subordinate the objectives of bloc actors to those of the universal actor.
8. Bloc actors are to attempt to extend the membership of their bloc

[12] *Ibid.*, pp. 38–39.
[13] *Ibid.*

but to tolerate the non-member position of a given national actor if non-tolerance would force that national actor to support the objectives of the rival bloc or to join the rival bloc.

9. Non-bloc member national actors are to act to reduce danger of war between the bloc actors.
10. Non-bloc members are to refuse to support the policies of one bloc actor against the other except in their capacity as a member of a universal actor.
11. Universal actors are to reduce the incompatibility between the blocs.
12. Universal actors are to mobilize non-bloc member national actors against cases of gross deviancy, for example, resort to force, by a bloc actor. This rule, unless counteracted by the other rules, would enable the universal actor to become the prototype of an international political system.

"Directive hierarchical integrating principles" are roughly dictatorial: it was supposed that the USSR was able to dictate to all members, or at least to all satellite members, of the Soviet bloc. "Mixed" principles are partly dictatorial, partly consultative—e.g., NATO of the Fifties. With the benefit of hindsight, one may notice that these principles are not really strong enough to provide assurance that the bloc members will for long adhere to the blocs. Less unfairly, we may point out that a necessary condition for all bipolarity was a dimensional factor—the emergence in 1945 of the USA and the USSR as Superpowers. Though the positions of both were strengthened in the early 1950s by their acquisition of thermonuclear weapons, that development may also be thought to have introduced into the bipolar configuration certain elements of the "unit-veto" system, in which "any actor is capable of destroying any other actor that attacks it even though it cannot prevent its own destruction."[14] And though the history of the twenty years since World War II has certainly not been that of a balance-of-power system as defined by Kaplan, we must recognize that in the last decade there have been, especially amongst the lesser or formerly "nonaligned" Powers, some interesting realignments.

Such considerations seem to involve us in an unhappy regress: until we have a reasonably convincing theory of dynamics (i.e., one which explains, or in the nonhistorical case, predicts, the shift from one kind of system to another) we shall find it difficult to characterize even the present phase of external politics, let alone future ones; but so long as we confine our analysis to historical instances only, we are unlikely to develop the type of explanation (or prediction) which would allow us to characterize the current situation properly.

The course that suggests itself, for want of a better, is that we con-

[14] *Ibid.*, p. 50.

sider the twenty years from the end of the Second World War as a period not characterized by any single and overriding feature of equilibrium, but as one in which several theoretically distinguishable elements, each one of which could give rise to a distinctive equilibrating process, are emerging and thus making the whole period essentially a transition.

This would mean that Kaplan's "loose bipolar system" is a transition. His balance-of-power system is immediately obsolete in its pure form, and would require for its restoration quite unlikely changes in military technology, though important elements and partial aspects of it continue to have quite obvious application in our time. His "universal system," which may be interpreted as a world ideally guided by the United Nations, is out of the question. So are his hierarchical (or world government) systems, whether democratic or dictatorial, at least for the present century and short of some universal disaster. His "tight bipolar system" which is the Cold War carried to extremes, seems to have been bypassed. The only one amongst his emergent systems that foreshadows a considerable degree of stability is that of the unit veto.

Clearly, the USA and the USSR are now quite near to a unit-veto position in respect of each other. Given that situation, it would follow that either of them could annihilate with something like impunity any third Power, possibly excepting the UK, France, and China in (currently) that order of decreasing improbability. Thus, whether the unit-veto relationship at present includes two or up to five Powers, and whether it will come to include more as further Powers acquire nuclear weapons, depends upon the technology of reducing vulnerability of weapon systems.

In any case, the political and strategic consequences of the thermonuclear standoff are now evidently *not* those of a war of all against all, nor of total peace through terror. The two leading Powers can undertake limited military operations against each other's dependants (and could even do so, though under still stricter limits, directly against each other). Secondly, the other's dependants can be taken as "hostages" by the Power which is under threat of unlimited (i.e., thermonuclear) attack from the other. Thirdly, some of these again—especially those with nuclear or thermonuclear but vulnerable forces—may gain some protection against their major ally's chief opponent by being in a position, if threatened with attack by the latter, to launch a strike against him that would also "trigger" the major ally's thermonuclear forces. (This last relationship is possible only if the chief opponent's retaliatory forces are not quite certainly invulnerable against the major ally; and it would have no point were the forces of the triggering "hostage" Power clearly invulnerable to the chief opponent.) Since it is quite possible that no thermonuclear threat will ever be implemented, the question of the power-political situation engendered by the mere existence of such armaments and of the unit-veto "rules" or standing conditions which they seem to enjoin upon the world, will continue to be a crux for any theory of dynamics.

For instance, events from the mid-Fifties on have shown that conventional warfare is no more excluded than nuclear warfare is necessitated by the advent of the new weapons. Even should more and more Powers arrive at unit-veto status, it is therefore likely that Kaplan was mistaken in inferring that:

> . . . in such a system actors can exist on only one level, though whether these actors will be national actors or bloc actors will depend upon the kind of organization existing when weapons of the indicated level of destructiveness are possessed universally. Universal actors [e.g., the UN] cannot exist in such a system.[15]

One can readily imagine future conflicts between the USA and Communist China confined wholly to conventional or even to limited tactical-nuclear forces. In such a situation, states in North Vietnam's present situation would certainly be "actors," though minor ones: in our own terminology they would be Minor Powers whose actions could affect in some measure the balance within the system.

Moreover, a "universal actor" (world organization) is likely to be an almost essential adjunct to the carrying on of the Powers' interrelationships. On the one hand, an international organization, along with other diplomatic facilities, can damp down minor conflicts that might embroil the Superpowers with each other. On the other, most Powers, especially at either extreme of dimension, can use international organizations to advance their several interests.

In a realm quite different from the military (*viz.*, economic integration), there can be engendered important changes in the dimensions of Powers. This is not a phenomenon of the mid-twentieth century alone—indeed, the demise of the balance-of-power system may well have begun from the Zollverein. Whether in fact the Powers (of Western Europe; of Latin America) who press on to economic integration will also integrate as Powers is still very much an open issue. While the more obvious considerations of economic and military power would seem to favor unification of states and thus a transition to "continental" or bloc Powers, the actual play of external politics, especially as practiced by the Superpowers, has tended to induce middle and Major Powers amongst the potential integrators to preserve important elements of sovereignty in a quite traditional sense of that term.

This somewhat unexpected resurgence of the nation-state system is further encouraged by tendencies in the internal politics of the mid-twentieth century (another ground for dissatisfaction with the fashionable

[15] *Ibid.*

specialization of contemporary social science). Many of the new and underdeveloped nation-states have political systems so fragile and impotent that, except by conquest, one cannot see how they could be politically integrated with each other or with advanced societies. For many of the latter, on the other hand, an opposite disposition may keep them separate: several great liberal nations have demonstrated in the present century an extraordinary dynamic stability, as though they had completed their internal political evolution through the development of polities flexible enough to take up the strains of almost any degree of social mobility. But though, for example, the USA, the United Kingdom, Holland, the Scandinavian nations, Switzerland, and the older British Dominions are all liberal in their political structure, and remarkably stable in their constitutional arrangements, their several forms of liberal constitution—the presidential, the parliamentary, and the unique Swiss constitution—produce a similar liberal environment from political structures that not merely differ from but also seem incompatible with each other. The political integration of such states, and of those of the European Economic Community, might take the shape of confederation, except that there seems good historical evidence that confederations either disintegrate or move further into federal and even unitary arrangements. Other modes of political integration amongst advanced states have yet to be *invented:* at the time of writing, the type of invention foreshadowed within the European Community at the beginning of this decade appears to have come to little.

A consequence of these internal-political tendencies for the theory of external dynamics is that theorists must be ready to develop a wide range of models, from extreme bloc integration to reinforcement of the multistate system, upon the expectation that some kind of mixed international system is rather more likely than either of the extreme cases. Another indicated task is close and ingenious diagnostic analysis of the current situation—not a very hopeful enterprise despite the increasing intellectual resources now spent in political science, since so many of them are taken up by policy-oriented research in which the temptation is strong to work on limited "decision" problems.

In the next chapter we consider hypotheses explanatory of systemic change, having left in an admittedly unsatisfactory state our descriptions of and criteria for the systemic changes which are emerging. However, we can state in summary a few of the important specifications for the *explicanda* of dynamic theory—the theory of systemic change.

The *explicanda* are changes in external-political systems—i.e., the field is almost solely that of clause 1.1421 (p. 87 above) of our definition of Powerhood. Coalitions or alliances, and oppositions of interest are here considered as political phenomena, even though alliances, for example, clearly have a strategic aspect. Our expectation, however, is to use strategic features amongst the predictions or explanation (*explicantes*) of changes in external-political systems—e.g., of, perhaps, the disappearance of the political phenomena of alliance in a thoroughgoing unit-veto system. We would also expect to use technological change in the explanation of strategic change, though we by no means exclude the possibility that political-systemic change will be explicable intrinsically (i.e., by non-autonomous, political features).

In essence, the finish of a particular system consists in the termination of some particular partly equilibrating process. This can be bound up with changes in (1) the number of, (2) the dimensions of, and (3) the logical type of political interrelationship between the Powers systematically connected. These phenomena of termination and change are described in implicitly quantitative terms. No doubt the present advances of political and international studies will soon produce explicit quantitative measures of such phenomena, and these we shall welcome, not for their own sake but because they should enable us to put theoretical questions with more logical precision, and to design more rigorous tests for explanatory models. But even in their present qualitative form, the descriptions of inter-Power systems that political scientists have recently devised have enough logical character and distinctiveness to open up the problem of explaining systemic change.

SIX

Explanations of Systemic Change

In this chapter we shall consider several hypotheses that have been advanced to explain or to forecast systemic change—both changes in the order of numbers of Powers in the system (i.e., substantial changes considerably increasing or reducing the number) and also changes in the nature of their interrelationship. Such hypotheses often refer to worldwide technological and economic developments which, by affecting the mode of Power-relations, also alter the conditions of viability for most Powers in the system. Though those developments have been invariably the unintended and compositive consequences of many distinct actions of individuals—scientific and technical discoveries, investment of resources, technological applications of discoveries—and though their effects upon the structure of the Power system have been as little deliberate, yet is worth noticing that none of them, actual or forecast, eliminate the statesman's freedom to act: rather, they change its conditions.

The theory of dynamics—i.e., of the transformation of systemic relations and of numbers—seems at first sight to be dependent upon a theory of statics, but on closer inspection, the dependence can be seen to be both partial and reciprocal. The conditions for formation of alliances, for instance, depend upon the state of the military art; and that, upon technology. Contrast for instance the 1939 situation, in which the Axis confronted the Western Allies, with the present one: to the USSR and the

USA, the actual or incipient nuclear forces of their respective allies are on the whole an embarrassment, while before, any forces disposed of by an ally were an increment to one's own strength.

Most analysts suppose that there has recently been a major change in world affairs, bearing in some way on the future of the nation-state, our current unit of power; Churchill thought the change would occur because of the thermonuclear weapon, and called the emergent situation "the balance of terror"; Kenneth Boulding thinks it has occurred because of a vast reduction in the cost of transporting instruments of destruction and men-at-arms.[1] He contends that, though formerly some countries were "unconditionally viable" chiefly because of the expense of getting at them, from now on all will be at best "conditionally viable"—i.e., will survive only on each other's sufferance, and that therefore some kind of unitary world government must succeed our present order of many sovereign Powers.

Now, both hypotheses seem relevant to the explanation of a change in the world system—but, of course, only if there *has* been a change of some kind—if, indeed, during the Fifties and Sixties, the Superpowers' allies became, at least in the nuclear context, liabilities. If Churchill were correct, nonnuclear Powers should be viable only by the grace of nuclear Powers, whereas the latter could also rely upon each others' rational fears, so that one should expect those states that can do so to acquire a thermonuclear deterrent, and others to confederate into units or groupings large enough to have nuclear prospects. If Boulding were correct, we should expect the nuclear Powers themselves to be leaders of the movement toward world unification. Both predictions point to an enlargement in the average individual size and a reduction in the number of units of power. Both suggest a decrease in the significance of national geography. In either respect, both should depart from the expectations of traditional power-balancing statecraft, for which geography is a most powerful determinant —e.g., the geopolitical hypothesis—according to which there should be resistances to aggregation of power, even on a regional basis.

Are there really differences between the two systems' rates and nature of change amongst their respective populations of Powers? (It is ten years since I first looked at these broader questions. I have not been altogether disappointed in the more general predictions that came out of these earlier studies;[2] but I am quite dissatisfied with their false simplicity and false precision.) Boulding's approach gives a useful lead because of his connecting a certain change in military technology (i.e., reduction of the

[1] Kenneth E. Boulding, *Conflict and Defense: A General Theory* (New York: Harper & Row, Publishers, Inc., 1962 and 1963).

[2] See Chapter 5, note 1; and *Power Politics and the Growing Nuclear Club,* Policy Memorandum No. 20 (New York: Center of International Relations, Princeton University, June 1959).

cost of transporting explosive weapons) with the question of "viability." However, "viability" connotes only "being exempt from invasion"—tacitly, "invasion from some single Power." We need to think rather of "survivability": there are many actions beside *invasion* that will take a Power, or part of it, off the map. Some have even appeared desirable to minor Powers—*viz., unification* with others into a greater Power. *Secession* of noncolonial peoples increases the number of states, as does *"decolonization."* Sometimes *internal war* reduces a state to quasi-feudal anarchy. Many ancient societies were destroyed by *massacre;* the present nuclear threats to national survival are best classified as massacre, especially since nuclear destruction need not be followed up by invasion or occupation.

Boulding's central idea is to be found in the Appendix to Chapter 12 of his *Conflict and Defense,* entitled "The Loss-of-Strength Gradient." This supposes that at any distance of more than a mile or so from home, 1000 fighting men will need some of their number to become "suppliers," who will in turn require suppliers, and so on. On the imaginary model he furnishes, at 5 miles, a maximum of 667 and a minimum of 621 are available for fighting; at 10 miles, the range is 500–365; at 20 miles, 333–148. Admittedly, this suggests a US-type logistic: for the Japanese, or Marlborough's forces, the slope of the curve would not be so steep. But the point is well taken for any armed force of which the unit of fire-power (e.g., an infantryman) does not carry all his efficacy with him. The characteristic Boulding diagram can be seen in Figure 6.1.

Figure 6.1

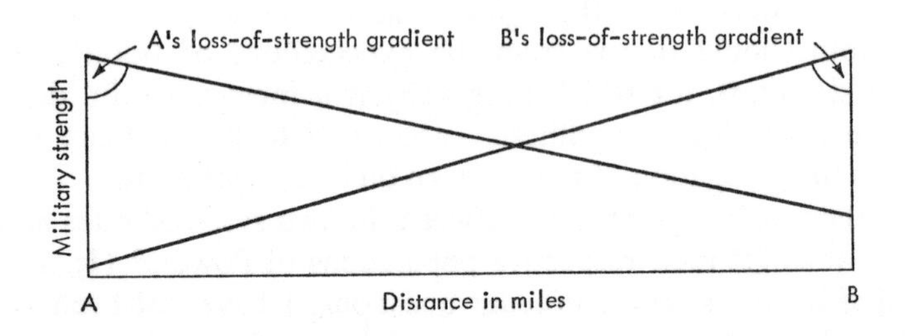

Here the verticals at A and B measure the respective sides' strengths at home, the marked angles measure the (constant) loss-of-strength gradient, and the point of intersection on the interval A-B—which indicates the distance in miles between the two opponents—is the position of equal strength. Thus, given the loss-of-strength gradient angle modeled by Boulding, 1000 fighting men at home come down to *one* at a distance of no more than 140 miles. Suppose, however, that it takes only 10 men to transfer 990 men, with all needed for a 48-hour war, across 140 miles in three hours. This means that, given the new efficiency of transport, the loss-of-strength gradient is at once much less steep. That is the principal element in Boulding's argument for loss of viability, through reduction in cost of transport, by the constituent Powers of a contemporary international system. Elsewhere, he has cited the entirely peaceful unification of the Australian colonies, and the formation of the European Economic Community, as chiefly explicable by the "negligible" costs of "internal" transport; he also has maintained that reductions in transport first set in at sea—hence Britain's ability to maintain her second Empire.

Even a mere military relationship between Powers is not, however, determined solely by the loss-of-strength gradient. Let us consider what Boulding's fighting-manpower might do. It could (1) destroy or capture other fighting-manpower (counter-force); (2) destroy property or capture nonfighting-manpower (counter-resource); (3) destroy or capture some of both.

(1) If it concentrates on counter-force, an important new ratio, the military exchange rate, becomes relevant. As we shall argue below, this can be (i) unitary and constant for all levels of force (e.g., of fighting manpower); (ii) negative to any proportion (i.e., requiring *more than* a unit of force to eliminate one unit of force); (iii) positive to any proportion (i.e., requiring *less than* a unit of force to eliminate one unit of force).

(2) If it concentrates on counter-resource, we can measure its effect by another ratio—*viz.,* the cost of maintaining a unit of force against the "cost" (to the enemy—given international comparability of costs) of the property and lives it could destroy. The latter ratio also may be (i) unitary and constant; (ii) negative; (iii) positive.

If we are prepared to overlook the problem of inter-Power cost-comparison, the relationship of (1), (2), and (3), in degrees (i), (ii), and (iii), can be roughly illustrated on the following diagram invented by Amster and Sherwin, 1955.[3]

Thus, values of (1) are represented horizontally; of (2) vertically; of (3), diagonally. The diagram embodies an explanatory theory, not only of the incidence of war, but also of systemic change, provided we suppose (what is not usually true) that the state of military technology impinges in the same way on all Powers at a given time. A few examples: when forces find it difficult and expensive to get at each other, and weapons are not very destructive, and cities well fortified, the system of military Powers is well down and outward in the lower left quadrant, and very stable; as the first two conditions are reversed, the system is shifted upward—if into the upper right quadrant then becoming highly unstable and

[3] W. Amster and C. W. Sherwin, *Bulletin of the Atomic Scientists,* XII, No. 5 (May 1956), 159–65. By permission of the Editor, *Bulletin of the Atomic Scientists.*

Figure 6.2

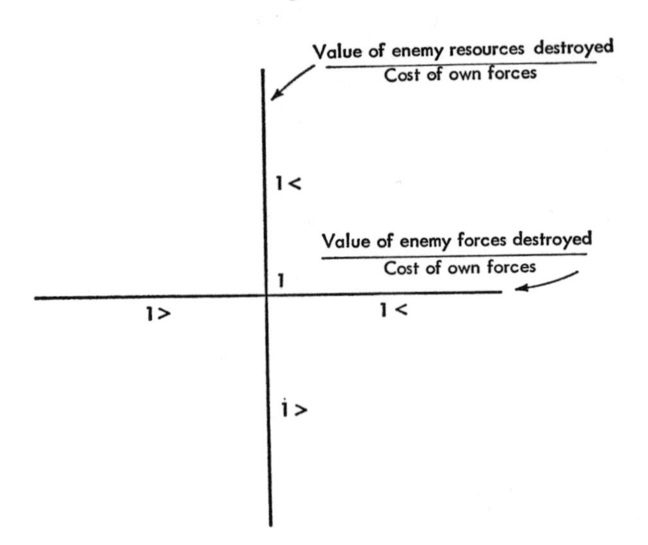

self-destructive; if still in the left, then acquiring the stability of "mutual deterrence."

In Boulding's terms, and in terms of *invasion,* one measures along the horizontal axis. Rightward, the loss-of-strength gradient slopes down. Leftward, it may be level. But, further leftward still (i.e., if tactical nuclear weapons are employed), it will begin by sloping upward, since you cannot explode them near your own population; then further leftward still it will level off, with loss of accuracy and some positive cost for transporting the devices; eventually, at the uttermost left, it must again slope downward.

In terms of *massacre* and destruction of resources, one measures on the vertical axis. The real world is representable above rather than below the horizontal, given ordinary human capacities for destruction. Given thermonuclear explosives, the center of interest is a long way above the horizontal but, depending upon other technologies, may be to the left or to the right of the vertical.

The limitations of the cross-diagram, so long as it is confined to two dimensions, come out when we realize that the military exchange rates between swordsmen and between teams of artillerymen using nuclear mortars probably place both situations near the intersection. We need a third-dimensional axis, rising up from the plane of the diagram itself, to represent the *absolute cost of force*. That is an element which, however we represent it, must be kept in mind, since amongst the important motives for a Power's seeking unification with others in the nuclear age will be its own peculiar ratio: absolute cost of force against absolute national productive capacity.

Still further relationships affect the purely military one: in the pre-nuclear age, many Powers had a more desirable alternative to destruction than final unification with each other: *viz.,* temporary alliance against a common danger. To account for this, and to account more adequately for any propensity to unify in the nuclear age, we need to reckon with yet another element connected with the military exchange rate: *viz.,* the correlation of proportion-of-forces-required-for-victory with the total-of-forces-committed-to-battle. This correlation may be (i) constant; (ii) negative; (iii) positive. Situation (i) is rare. Situation (ii)—i.e., when the proportion of superior size of force required for victory declines with the total of forces engaged on both sides—tends toward a characteristic balance-of-power set-up, in which it will usually be prudent for less populous or poorer states to ally against the more populous or wealthier state. Situation (iii) represents the standoff for long-range protected missiles with single warheads—i.e., beyond certain absolute numbers on either side, security can be maintained by matching the enemy's build-up of launching sites less than one-for-one. Boulding's contention that once upon a time many nations were "unconditionally viable" depends upon our ignoring any possibility of alliances' combining against them. Even the British Empire of the early 1900s feared a coalition of the world against her. The traditional concept of a Great Power was not of an invincible Power, but of a Power that could be conquered only by a coalition.

In the nuclear age, still another correlation is poignantly relevant to survival in general and unification in particular—i.e., the minimum "subscription" to the Superpowers' nuclear club (the minimum resources required to become a Superpower). This is a rapidly shifting figure, dependent in most complex ways on technological development both at home and abroad. It is now being debated whether even the European Community, if federated, could command enough resources to become and remain a nuclear Superpower—one capable of continuing to provide everything, including the research and development, needed for a completely independent deterrent. It is argued that such a capacity is beyond the UK alone, and thus beyond France alone. If that were not true, then we should expect France (and Britain) *not* to join in a thoroughgoing European federation. This would tell against Boulding's hypothesis that there is a tendency for military Powers (national and bloc) to amalgamate into some kind of world government. His case would be strengthened if a united Europe could not become an independent nuclear Power, though all the same Powers like France and Britain might still choose to keep their national independence and for that purpose to maintain minimum nuclear forces. Boulding is right to contend that very soon not even the USA will be "unconditionally viable," but only if "unconditional viability" includes security from *massacre* as well as from *invasion.*

If, however, it includes only security from invasion, then a large number of Powers capable of acquiring tactical atomic weapons could be "unconditionally viable." Switzerland, for instance, could probably defend itself in that way against even an invader himself armed with tactical nuclear weapons. But she would not presumably have a military reply to a Superpower that threatened, "Disarm yourself or we shall stand off and annihilate you with long-range missiles."

Another possibility might well arise in such a case: the threatening Superpower's main rival might offer to retaliate on behalf of Switzerland, on the ground that the use of thermonuclear weapons against population centers except after receiving a thermonuclear attack oneself would make the user intolerable to the whole world. Most Americans believe that the USA has just such a general commitment. If so, (1) lesser nuclear Powers like the UK (and an atomically armed Switzerland) share the USA's formidable "conditional viability"; (2) the "conditional" is so strong that it should prevail against all but lunatics (Boulding calls them "thermonuclear Alexanders") or could deal with some as-yet-unimagined accident. If not, then the short-run argument for federation and military unification, not only of the EEC but of all Western Europe including the neutrals, is much strengthened; and the long-run argument for universal nuclear disarmament is unanswerable. (This is unless nuclear independence becomes cheap enough for the run of European nations.)

Let me now pose part of this chapter's prime question. Suppose we could make a closely articulated formal model (it would have to be far more complex than any we have yet discussed) of the world order of the nuclear age, assuming "cold rationality" on the part of all Powers, which would be thought of as reviewing all the possibilities—massacring opponents; invading them; seeking various kinds of national nuclear force; and so on. Suppose we then asked, "In all the most general senses of 'survival,' what is the 'likelihood' of survival in each of the various grades of national Powers (there being over a hundred nations in all)?"

As we have already seen intuitively, rather small differences in each of a number of distinct quantities and proportions (e.g., in the accuracy and hence the minimum effective numbers of an ICBM force) are apt to determine very different answers to that question. A complete, theoretically respectable answer could be got only by varying separately each of the distinct quantities and proportions; probably, we should also have to allow some random changes in the potentials of the various constituent Powers. The findings would be presented as a "tree" with its roots in the present time, and its many branches reaching forward for two or three imaginary decades into the future. I am quite certain that, even if we could use all present computing and mechanical aids, we could not at present hope even to set out the problem, let alone answer it rigorously. The current theoretical ambitions expressed in this volume, at least as concerns the nuclear world order, are (1) to expose this present limit upon theory; (2) to proceed some way in setting out the problem, or suggesting how it might be set out.

Given these limits of precision in answering the question just posed, there must be consequential limits upon answering theoretically broader questions. Nevertheless, it should be possible to see whether there are important correlations of the "birth and death rates" of Powers with other non-international aspects of history—e.g., Boulding's reduction in transport costs. Something like that, in any case, will be necessary though not sufficient for any theory of international dynamics.

We shall now try to provide a graphical approach to the question of destabilizing change, intended to include the "thermonuclear deterrent" considerations of Amster and Sherwin, and Boulding's hypothesis of the significance of the "loss-of-strength gradient," and thereby to suggest conditions under which Powers are viable—unconditionally, conditionally, or not at all.

Our analysis begins, not with the concept of physically given ratios of force, but with the idea of a political act—the act of surrender or capitulation. "Capitulation" is meant in the most extreme form—the abandonment of a Power's Powerhood by its rulers on its behalf. This is always the enactment of a choice, even though of a hard choice, except in the case where, by enemy action or internal rebellion or both, the rulers' ability to govern and to concert the subjects has been taken away. Otherwise, capitulation requires a motive. We here generalize the various possible motives under the head of *the prospect of losing some proportion of the Power's resources.* In accord with our definition in Chapter 4, *"resources"* includes productive resources; but here we extend it explicitly to include also the property and even the lives of the subjects. Amongst the items of resources thus defined, different Powers' rulers (and, indeed, different sets of rulers in the same Power) are almost bound to differ radically in their judgments of relative value: in a totalitarian Power, the lives and the property of the subjects as individuals will be little valued, but the means of coercion, internal or external, will be valued highly; in a liberal democratic Power, the lives of subjects (who are themselves, in a legal and formal sense at least, the most general class of rulers) and the conditions guaranteeing their personal liberties should be the chief, if sometimes contradictory, ends, to be preferred above property and the instruments of production and of coercion.

However these various components of "resources" are valued, there must be, for rulers of the most limited rationality, some point of indifference *between* the retention of Powerhood *and* the preservation of a certain proportion of "resources."

I say, "there must be" because the point could be at zero, and could be at unity. It would not be "irrational," in the formal sense of that term, for extremely liberal rulers, confronted by an equally liberal opposed Power which would certainly impose a system as liberally democratic as their present one, to declare, "We value our separate nationality and will continue to advocate its reestablishment; but it is not worth the sacrifice of a single human life." Neither would it be irrational, when confronted with a totalitarian foe, to say "We will fight on, if need be with broken bottles, till we are all killed." Neither, therefore, would it be irrational to set the point almost anywhere in between.

Admittedly, some of the places in between, though rational, are not in the least sensible. The practical obstacles, however, to any ruling group's maintaining control over its state's subjects in a situation in which surrender is being considered set some constraints upon where in real life the capitulation point (the point of indifference mentioned above) will be allowed to be drawn. To draw it at zero would obviously require a highly idealistic group of subjects; at unity, an extremely stoical one. *A priori,* the likeliest indifference point is considerably nearer the zero than the unity level, for it is in that general region that venality is greatest. In order to develop a consistent model, we here assume initially (whether realistically or not) that the rulers adhere to their "decision" about the location of the capitulation-point throughout a conflict with another Power or Powers.

Thus, there should be a prospect of almost certain loss of a proportion of resources beyond which a ruling group will resign, on behalf of the "society set," all claims to continue to exist and to act *as a Power.* On the other hand, provided that point is not at zero, it will be consistent for the rulers to be willing to allow their society to suffer the loss of the corresponding proportion rather than capitulate.

Now (without having recourse to the idea of utilities) we shall suppose that the rulers would be rational if they were to convert just this corresponding proportion, but no more, into armed forces to be put at risk, if—but only if—forces of the consequent size could be relied upon to present a physical barrier which an enemy would have to overcome to the extent that he wished to wreak destruction upon "our" resources (putting ourselves in the rulers' place), and which he could not overcome to the extent required to induce "us" to surrender. Suppose that "we" believe that condition to be fulfilled—it does not matter whether correctly or upon what evidence. Further, suppose that a one-for-one relation holds between amount of resources converted to forces and the effectiveness of forces thus obtained, so that the entire sum of resources just up to the capitulation point or surrender-line is transformed into armed forces.

The reader will understand that we are not now generalizing about strategic relations in the real world: we are deriving implications from our definition of Powerhood, from our conception of a rational capitulation point, and from abstract ideas of "resources" and of "armed forces," the latter being conceived of solely as instruments for preservation of the former, and for avoidance of capitulation. Thus any segment of "armed force" is equivalent with any other segment of the same length; and the same with a segment of "resources."

Figure 6.3

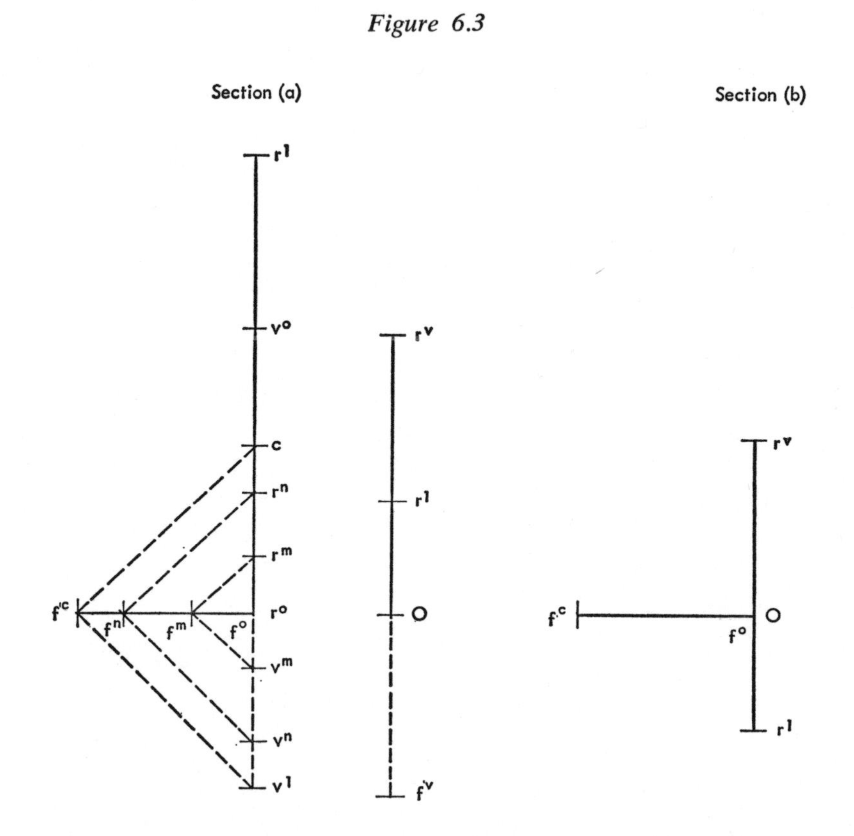

Consider Figure 6.3, Section (a), the left-hand portion. The vertical segment (r^o, r^1) represents the Blue Power's total resources "before" the establishment of any armed forces. The segment (r^o, c) represents that proportion of resources which the rulers of Blue would be prepared to sacrifice, if necessary, in order to maintain the Blue society as a Power. The horizontal segment (f^o, f^c) represents the total amount of armed forces available by investment of the entire segment of resources (r^o, c), so that the Blue rulers should be ready to capitulate if it appears that almost the entire segment (f^o, f^c) is about to be destroyed—unless some militarily effective part of (f^o, f^c), together with the entire segment of resources equal to (r^1, c) measuring down the vertical, or (r^o, v^o) measuring up the vertical, are likely to survive, and unless the enemy would use up his entire armed forces in the process of attacking Blue's. Note that $(r^o, c) = (r^1, v^o)$. Thus Blue's rulers should be indifferent between losing (r^o, r^m) and (f^o, f^m); or between losing (r^o, r^n) and (f^o, f^n). Supposing that by investment of exactly that amount of resources which they would be prepared to lose rather than capitulate, they have in fact established certain armed forces (f^o, f^c)—i.e., converting the whole of $(r^o, c) = (r^1, v^o)$—then it is possible to represent on a vertical line (v^o, v^1), which we have set out separately, on the right-hand side of Section (a), as (r^v, f^v), the sum of resources and forces which Blue's rulers control and upon which they set *value.* (Their valuing, thus represented, since it involves the capitulation point and thus their specific valuing of Powerhood, is political, and not directly translatable into utilities.) On this vertical value-line, the segment $(0, f^v)$ represents the value of the whole of the armed forces (f^o, f^c), and is equal to the segment of valued resources (r^v, r^1), since by construction $(0, r^1) = (c, v^o)$, and $(o, r^v) - (o, r^1) = (c, r^1) - (c, v^o)$.

In Section (b) of Figure 6.3, for mere convenience in later exposition, we have relocated the elements of Section (a). The horizontal segment (f^o, f^c) still represents the total of armed forces, scaled (as to value) linearly with the vertical line representing resources. Below it, and inverted in terms of Section (a), is $(0, r^1)$, which represents that proportion of resources which there is no question of sacrificing. Above the horizontal in Section (b), $(0, r^v)$ is equivalent with (r^1, r^v) on the separately set-out value-line on the right hand of Section (a), and represents the proportion of resources parts of which, under the following constraints, the Blue rulers are prepared to sacrifice rather than to surrender: *viz.*, they would sacrifice up to but not more than $\frac{(f^o, f^c) + (0, r^v)}{2}$.

One's first thought is that this should mean that they would be indifferent between, say, the loss of $\frac{4\ (f^o, f^c)}{10} + \frac{(0, r^v)}{10}$ and the loss of $\frac{(f^o, f^c)}{10} + \frac{4\ (0, r^v)}{10}$. But that does not follow in practice, except in the special case where the enemy must use *n* units of his forces to destroy *n* units of their forces *or* *n* units of their resources, and where *n* units of their forces would be used up in destroying *n* units of his forces *or* of his resources. While, at the present stage of our analysis, we have assumed that Blue's rulers are indifferent between loss of a unit of forces and loss of a unit of that proportion of Blue's total resources required for provision of the total of Blue forces, *considering forces and resources simply in themselves,* we have as yet said nothing about (1) the effectiveness of Blue's forces against Red's forces; (2) their effectiveness against Red's resources; (3) the effectiveness of Red's forces against Blue's; (4) the effectiveness of Red's forces against Blue's resources. Indicators of these potentialities must be depicted in our diagram if we are to justify our step on page 130 in which is laid down the rationale for buying armed forces at the cost of resources up to the level of the capitulation point. Conversely, by representing the significant elements of military effectiveness as being valued solely as they subserve the primary political need of any Power (*viz.,* to avoid having to capitulate), we can do without the supposition that rulers put an independent value upon having military forces, and can thus skirt around the morass of utility theory. Instead of the economic unit of "utility," we employ the political unit of value—"survivability as a Power." What of the cases in which force has been used for genuinely economic objectives—e.g., to annex resources of land and labor, or to capture markets? According to our diagram, the Power doing this would, in terms of Section (b), be investing part of his resources depicted on the resource line *below* the horizontal—i.e., part of $(0, r^1)$—to acquire extra forces—i.e., to protract the force-line (f^o, f^c) leftward beyond f^c. To do so would be rational only if a net increase of $(0, r^1)$ were certain, with the rest of the diagram being unaltered. For the remainder of this chapter we shall ignore that possibility and confine our attention wholly to the proportion of forces (f^o, f^c), and of resources $(0, r^v)$.

Figure 6.4 represents the four above-mentioned elements of military effectiveness. For example, Section (i), Figure 6.4, is intended to convey that Blue, by using up some part (f^c, f^x) (represented by a broken line) of all the forces he has procured at the expense of that proportion of his resources which he is prepared to lose rather than capitulate, could destroy *all* the forces, represented on Red's force-axis by the *vertical* broken line (f^o, f^c), which, symmetrically, Red has procured at the expense of that proportion of *his* resources that he (Red) is prepared to lose rather than capitulate. Blue's and Red's force-lines are of the same length, and also of the same length as the resource-lines of both, as represented in Sections (ii) and (iv): this implies only (1) that we have adopted an arbitrary convention that, to the rulers of each Power, the value of remaining a Power, i.e., of not capitulating, is the same as the value to any other Power—a purely formal convention, since our definition of the capitulation point would, for example, allow Blue's rulers to place their capitulation point at nearly the total of their resources, and Red's to place theirs at almost none of *their* resources; and (2) that each Power has expended resources right up to his capitulation point in order to procure armed forces. But by derivation from these implications, any force-line represents a certain finite quantity of militarily effective armed force—*viz.,* in Blue's case, that quantity of forces (both personnel, trained and untrained, and material) which it has procured by expenditure of its resources up to the capitulation point. That is, it represents by derivation the same quantity as does either of the outermost verticals on Boulding's loss-of-strength diagram (Figure 6.1).

However, the unbroken arrowed line sloping up and leftward from Blue's f^x to Red's f^o represents not only Boulding's LSG effect, but also every factor that contributes to the military exchange rate in respect of the survival of mutually opposed forces—e.g., it includes the *objective and quantitative* aspects, representable on the Amster-Sherwin diagram (Figure 6.2) of the ratio "Value of enemy forces destroyed/Cost of own forces." Since in Section (i) of Figure 6.4, Blue uses up *all* of that part of his total force with which he attacks Red's (in a later diagram, we shall have him use up only part of what he sends against Red's) the Blue-Red battle in this case is perhaps best imagined as between land-based ballistic-missile forces, with just one missile on each (expendable) launching-pad. Blue, using less than all of his forces can eliminate all of Red's, who is thus *not* unconditionally viable in the face of Blue, if we consider forces-against-forces alone.

Section (iii) of Figure 6.4 shows that, symmetrically, Blue is for the same reason and under the same conditions *not* unconditionally viable in the face of Red—the system constituted by (but limited to) their opposed forces is unstable and explosive so that, when they come to see it is so, we should expect each to try to get in the first blow. But if instead Section (iii) were simply a reciprocal of Section (i)—i.e., if it were identical with Section (i) except that the arrow pointed downward and to the right, the implication would be that Blue *was* unconditionally viable in the face of Red (provided we ignore for the time what Red could do against Blue's resources). If, however, Sections (i) and (iii) were transposed, so that the two Powers would each have to use up all his forces to destroy only a portion of the other's, their force-against-force situation would be in stable equilibrium.

If we now superimpose Section (iii) on Section (i), it will become evident that the resulting diagram can depict the force-against-force balance between two Powers. The location, on the resultant diagram, of the intersection of the two arrowed lines, together with the directions of the two arrows, specifies this. The form of this diagram can then be used to depict *changes through time* in these situations—*viz.,* by connecting several temporally successive arrow intersections by lines numbered with the intervals in years between them. Some kinds of the changes thus depictable, as

Figure 6.4

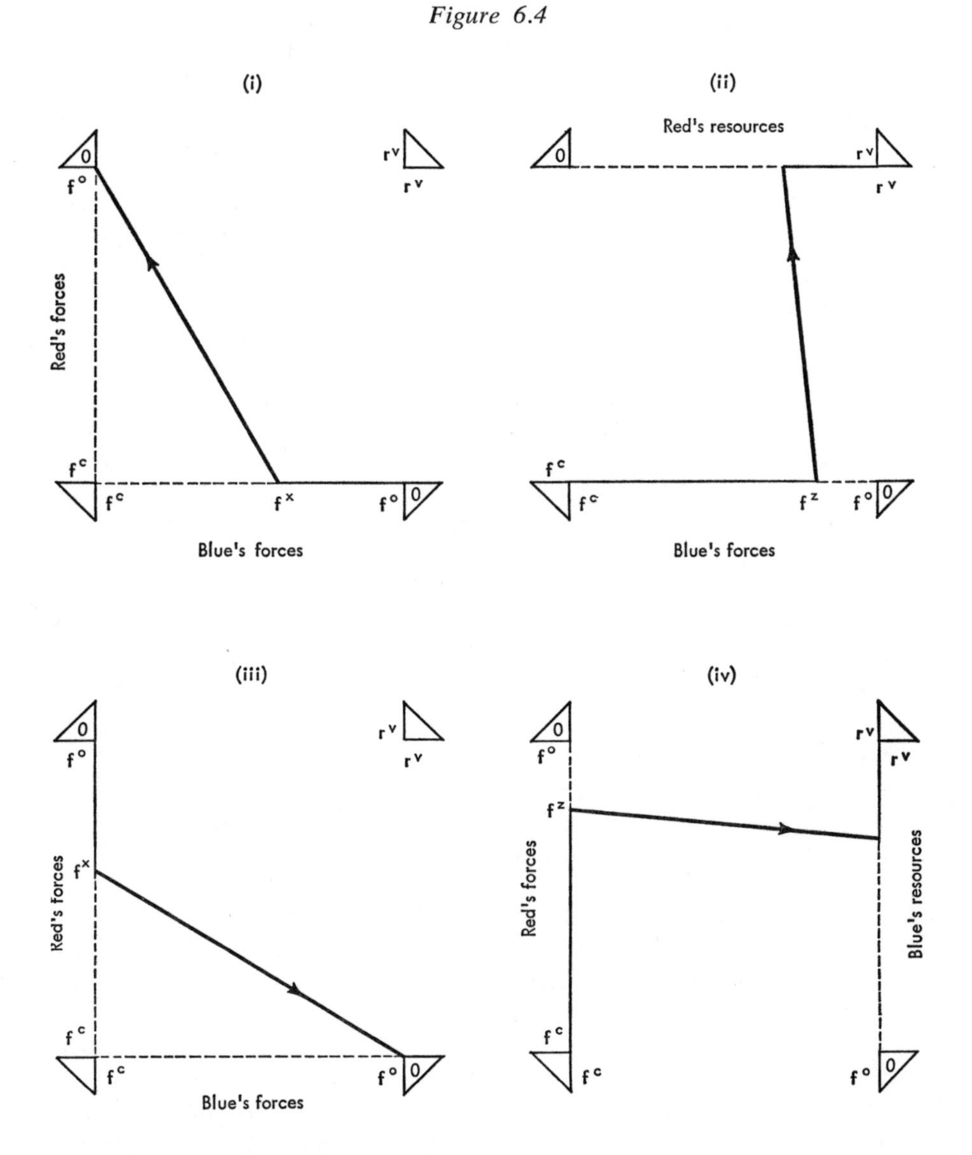

we shall see, can be aspects of systemic change, while others, such as arms races, are central to the problems of statics, discussed in Chapters 8 to 11.

Next let us consider counter-resource (i.e., force-against-resource) effectiveness, as depicted in Sections (ii) and (iv) of Figure 6.4. Section (ii) indicates that Blue, by using up merely (f^o, f^z) of his forces, can destroy more than half of Red's resources. (Forces used up in counter-resource operations are depicted by a broken line stretching from the f^o end of the attacker's force line—unlike those used in counter-force attacks, which come from the f^c end. An arrowed line from some point f^z meets the attacked resource-line at a point from which a broken line, extending to the zero end of the resource-line, indicates the proportion of victim's resources eliminated.) Section (iv), with the situations of Blue and Red reversed, completes the diagramming of a case in which when (i), (ii), (iii) and (iv) are superimposed, both Powers are conditionally viable, and in which both have almost irresistible motives for striking first, *unless* either or both can automate an effective counter-resource attack, to be launched as soon as the other launches his counter-force attack, and can convince the other that he has done so. We should note that if the latter alternative is physically possible, and *if both parties know what they are about,* an otherwise explosive situation will be turned into a quite stable balance of terror. Thus, the situation represented by the superimposition of our four sections will be ambiguous unless we can indicate whether or not any counter-force attack is bound to arrive before any prearranged counter-resource reprisal could be dispatched; whether the resources thus counter-attacked could be protected against it; and whether both parties could be apprised of the situation, and so on.

In Figure 6.5, Section (i), both Powers' counter-resource potentialities are depicted by arrowed lines which are broken, contrasting with the unbroken counter-force arrows: this is to indicate that neither Power can attack the other's resources without first eliminating all his forces. That means that both are far from unconditional viability, and that each has the strongest motives to get in a first blow at the other's forces. Part of each one's segment of forces employed in counter-force attack is solid, to indicate that that proportion is not used up but survives the campaign that eliminates the opposed force. The point is that the counter-resource effectiveness of the attacker is so low (let us suppose, because of a loss-of-strength gradient) that unless he has the benefit of those survivors, he can barely touch the other side's resources.

This depiction contrasts sharply with the combined four sections of Figure 6.4. There, where all the arrowed lines are solid, it remains possible to suppose that, as soon as one side launched a counter-force attack, the other would, without further deliberation, launch a counter-resource strike, and that such a response would beforehand have been demonstrated as inevitable to the opposite side.

To have the counter-resource lines solid and the counter-force lines broken would be to indicate, according to our conventions, that resources of the attacked Power were being destroyed as a necessary consequence of attacks upon forces. Again, this would result in an explosive situation.

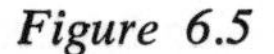

Figure 6.5

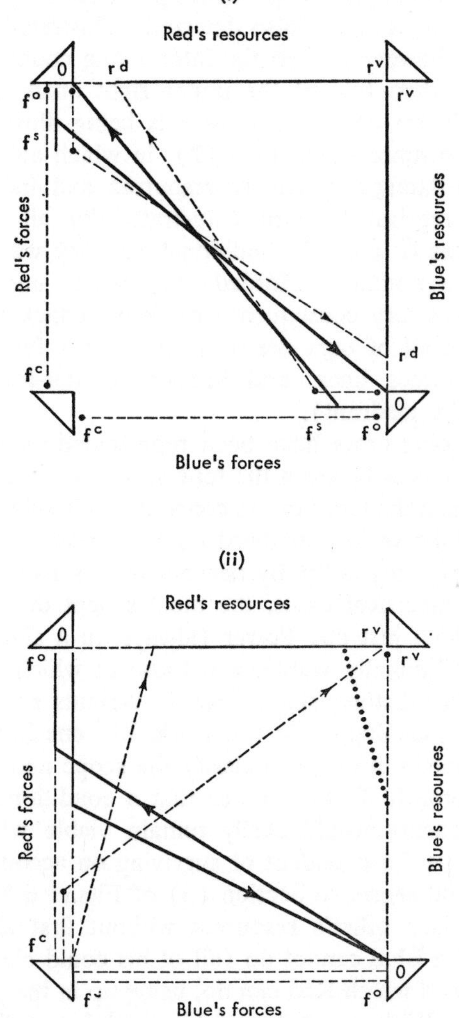

Finally, if all arrowed lines were broken, this would indicate *both* the foregoing, *and* that any counter-force attack would set off an effective anti-resource reprisal: in contrast, an extremely stable and unexplosive situation.

Amongst two-Power situations, we are now able to distinguish (1) cases of bilateral unconditional viability—illustrated by (a) the arrowed counter-resource lines, if any, being broken and (b) the counter-force arrows both pointing away from the upper righthand quadrant; (2) cases of mutually conditional viability, dependent upon each Power's being deterred and believing that the other is also deterred—illustrated by having all arrowed lines solid; however, when the intersecting counterforce lines point away from rather than toward the upper right quadrant, a much more stable and unexplosive deterrent balance is being illustrated; (3) a case similar to but even more stable than (2), in which any counter-force attack both causes damage to enemy resources and inevitably sets off a counter-resource reprisal by him (illustrated by all attack-lines being broken); (4) cases of mutual conditional viability where the conditions are *not* apt to be mutually afforded—i.e., where enemy resources are destroyed as a necessary consequence of "our" attack upon their forces, in which less than all of ours destroys all of their forces (illustrated by solid counter-resources lines, and broken counter-force lines arrowed *toward* the top right quadrant).

All the foregoing cases have been represented as more or less symmetrical: the differences between the four varieties are insensitive to minor asymmetries between the two Powers concerned. (It should be remembered that the slopes of the various arrowed lines are resultants representing the combined effects of many militarily relevant factors.) Once we depart from predominantly symmetrical cases, the most salient distinction is that between cases in which just one Power (always, in a situation of only two Powers) is unconditionally viable, and those in which neither is. Within the two classes thus distinguished, possible variants are multifarious, and quite beyond being catalogued in this work. But one in particular may be worth mention, chiefly in order to clarify the scope and limitations of our diagrammatic approach. Firstly, notice that a conditionally viable Power, whose potential enemy would easily remain viable whatever was done against him, may yet be confident of surviving on account of his estimate of the enemy's good sense. In Section (ii) of Figure 6.5, neither Red nor Blue can attack each other's resources without first eliminating all the other's force, which Blue cannot do (all of his could eliminate about two-thirds of Red's); and which Red *can* do, using up in the process about half of his own forces. With a quarter of his total forces Red can eliminate all of Blue's resources, whereas all of Blue's forces could eliminate only a quarter of Red's resources, even were Blue in a position to attack them, which as we have seen he cannot be. Now suppose, as the dotted line indicates, that from Red's point of view, all of Blue's resources at risk are worth only an eighth of Red's and that half of Blue's total resources are not at risk; then if Red could capture instead of eliminating Blue's resources, and add them to his own, the entire campaign would still not be worthwhile to Red, since after victory over and annexation of Blue he would have suffered a net loss of half his forces. Thus Blue, though poor and weak in comparison to Red, and viable only on condition of Red's not attacking him, might yet be confident that Red will not think it worthwhile to do so. (Note that our form of diagram, though not dependent upon the idea of economic utility, can illustrate it, as in this case.)

Notice, however, that Blue can pose this military deterrent to Red only because he is (1) much poorer in resources; (2) quite expensive, force for force, to attack; and (3) armed up to his capitulation point. In a strictly two-Power world, with capitulation points held constant, if any of those three features is reversed, not necessarily by very much, Red would be apt to attack and to annex Blue. For the dynamics of systems theory, this can be an important consequence: while the three conditions still hold, a quite asymmetrical situation may still be in a stable equilibrium, even though a straitly localized one: when the conditions are removed unstable equilibrium supervenes, and systemic change is likely. Blue's rulers may, when such a change seems to impend, take it into account and (contrary to our initial assumption, p. 130) alter their capitulation point—i.e., by lowering it considerably, they may signify their acceptance of annexation or dependency; by raising it, and consequently by increasing their own armed forces, they would both raise the costs to Red of annexation and reduce its profitability to him through having impoverished themselves. But of course the limits of their resources set a limit to the effectiveness of such a remedy. This matter is mentioned in order to bring out that our predications of the capitulation point and the rational purchase of forces to avoid capitulation are dependent not only upon the rulers' *preferences:* their perceptions of the power-political situation will also be relevant.

We shall return to asymmetrical cases in the course of dealing below with three-Power systems. But next, our discussion of systemic change will take in the bipartisan arms race. In 1959 the present writer developed a different graphical approach[4] to that subject, which however can be included within our present and more general approach through the concept of the capitulation point.

In the earlier work, it was predicated that conditions of military technology imposed upon both parties in a two-Power system certain objective relationships of military *power* and military *security;* then each party, through its intelligence organization, etc., could make estimates about those objective relationships which would allow it to choose between levels of armaments giving it a degree of *subjective* security or power *vis-à-vis* the other, one party's maximum level of power correlating with the other's

[4] A. L. Burns, "A Graphical Approach to Some Problems of the Arms Race," *Conflict Resolution,* III, No. 4 (December 1959), 326–47.

minimum level of security, and vice versa. The present more inclusive approach is depicted in Figure 6.6, Section (i).

Imagine the resource- and the force-lines of both Powers divided each into ten equal segments; and note that for its owner, one segment of force initially equals in value one segment of resource. No resources can be annexed before all enemy forces have been eliminated, but then three times the value (in resources) of forces used up in annexation can be annexed from the vanquished Power (as symmetrically indicated by the broken counter-force lines). The exchange rate of forces is constant for all levels of force—e.g., two segments are used up in eliminating one of the enemy's. This situation is symmetrical, but in order not to clutter the diagram, levels of deployed forces are marked in only for Blue. The uppermost unbroken arrowed line indicates Blue's force-level of highest power: if he has spent right up to his capitulation point on armed forces, he would be able to annex, with forces surviving Red's most effective attack on *his* forces, fifteen segments of Red's resources (assuming that Red has at least five extra segments that he would not willingly put at risk), which would yield Blue his maximum net gain—*viz.*, five segments.

Lying just below Blue's level of highest power is his minimum level of absolute viability where, having procured only eight-and-a-third segments of force, he would break even, by annexation after attack. Lowest of all is Blue's level of minimum deterrence: here, he has procured only four segments of force, to eliminate which Red would have to use up eight segments, having two over with which to annex six of Blue's segments of resources, yielding Red nothing for the whole venture, if we neglect in this case the effect of Blue's savings on unprocured forces. (On the present approach, these two lower lines replace the concept of a "level of security" employed in the 1959 analysis, "security" being ambiguous as between "minimum unconditional or absolute viability" and "minimum conditional or deterrent viability." However the concept of a "level of power" remains unchanged.)

Another concept used in the 1959 analysis involved a distinction between "naïve" and "sophisticated" responses by a Power altering "annually" its level of forces in view of that of some opposed Power: to adapt one's level of force solely to the current level of the other's, upon the basis of one's latest information, was termed a "naïve" response; a barely "sophisticated" response is one based upon a guess at the opposed Power's level in the coming "year"; a stage of sophistication beyond that is reached when one guesses whether, and what, the other Power guesses about one's own expected level in the coming "year"; and so on. In theory there need be no limit—though certainly there is in practice—to increases of sophistication.

The concept is important for dynamic theory, since increasing so-

Figure 6.6

(i)

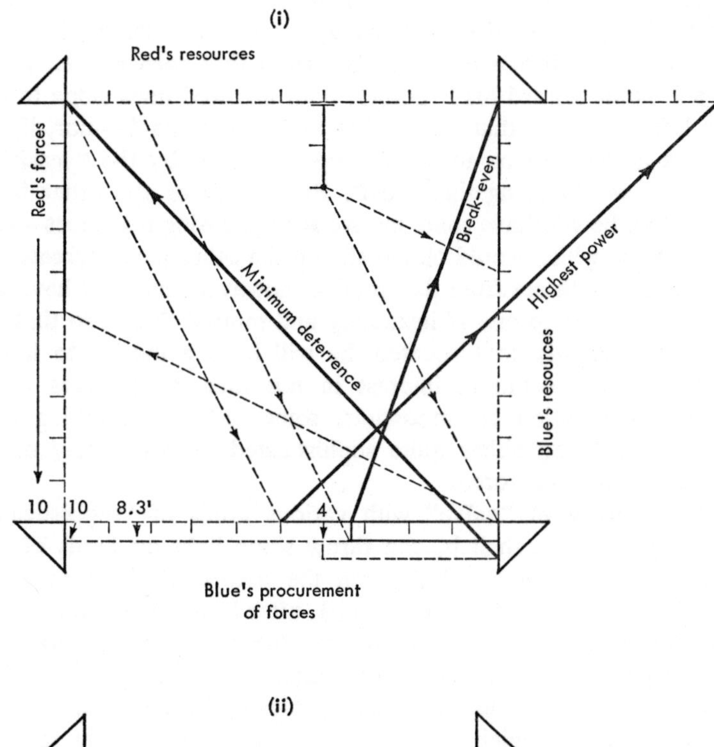

(ii)

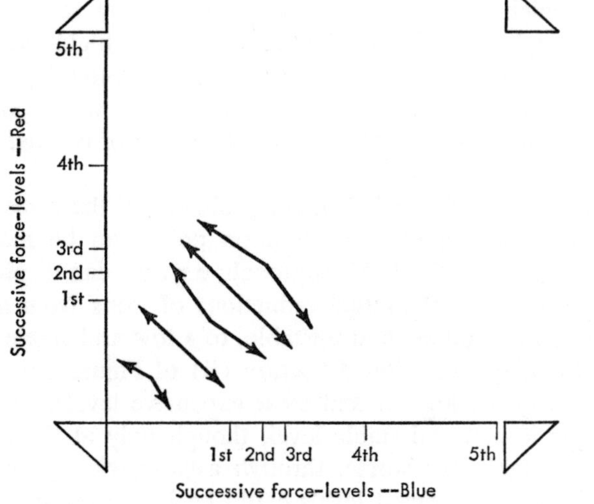

phistication can modify conditions of equilibrium and disequilibrium. Consider Figure 6.6, Section (ii): in the bottom left hand corner, where both sides have procured only small forces (in this illustration, increases of procurement of forces are measured from that corner—i.e., *from* each Power's f^c point toward his f^o point), both arrowed lines slope toward the bottom left corner, so that neither has motive for attack—nor, if either is naïve, has he any reason for increasing his forces by the "yearly" increment which would bring them to f^o. But if one or the other is *slightly* sophisticated, he will have some motive for increasing his forces—*viz.,* fear of the situation which would obtain should the other have increased and he himself not. If both act from that motive, however, they will have changed their joint situation to one of instability and mutual threat; so that if either is more than slightly sophisticated, he will have a motive to inform the other about their common interest in *not* increasing forces and, even should communication be impossible, some motive for taking a chance on the other's being either quite sophisticated or completely naïve, and thus not increasing his forces.

This contrast of "naïve" with various kinds of "sophisticated" response, fantastic though it is, can throw some light on kinds of systemic change brought about by changes in the *nature* of constituent Powers. Suppose that, in Figure 6.6, Section (ii), after both Blue and Red have set their forces at the lowest level, both leave future adjustments to computers which are programmed to make alterations only in response to observed alterations by the other side: the relationships of force should then stabilize at the lowest level, which could not be assured by slightly sophisticated human judgments, though it would also be assured by the highly sophisticated. Such a difference in the Powers' systems of decision-making, which might well appear trivial in the context of internal politics, would amount to a change in their natures, as prescribed by the first part of our definition in Chapter 4.

To conclude the present digression about problems of the arms race: our approach through the idea of a capitulation point can be made to include findings brought out in the 1959 approach; e.g., we can display the difficulties and the desirability of mutual reductions of arms from a high but stable level, through a middling and unstable, to a low and stable level. Suppose that, as in the above-mentioned Section (ii) of Figure 6.6, forces are currently deployed at the highest and most expensive levels, could be reduced quickly to the lowest and stable level, though only at the risk of passing through the unstable (or worse, through asymmetrically unfavorable) middle levels, but at the lowest levels could be increased again only by the "yearly" increments already mentioned. Then the *process* of disarmament would be risky, and *maintenance* of the lowest level, though a great economy, precarious and impermanent because of the dangers of being cheated and made inviable by a rearming rival. Therefore counter-rearmament procedures of all sorts are likely to be essentials of a thoroughly disarmed world, even if only when military technology seems to imply stability at highest and lowest, but instability at middling, levels of force.

We can further use the square diagram to show that the development of long-range weapon systems, notably ICBMs, permits certain conditions of stability not completely accounted for in the reasoning that employs Boulding's distinction between unconditional and conditional viability: *viz.*, by introducing the idea of physical uncertainties—i.e., probabilities—not dependent upon human choice, that a certain proportion of one side's forces will eliminate a certain proportion of the other's. (Further uncertainties could be represented—e.g., that of the physical probability of *being able* to eliminate, with a certain proportion of one's forces, a certain proportion of the other's resources; but since conditional viability is only in a small degree dependent upon that consideration, we shall for present purposes fix the probability for the ratio [resources eliminated]/[forces expended] at unity.) Figure 6.7 illustrates the requirements for mutual conditional viability.

In Figure 6.7 (where we assume complete symmetry between Red's and Blue's position), a slightly different pictorial convention is used to depict the ratios of force-*versus*-resource and of force-*versus*-force. To

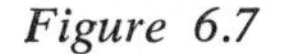

Figure 6.7

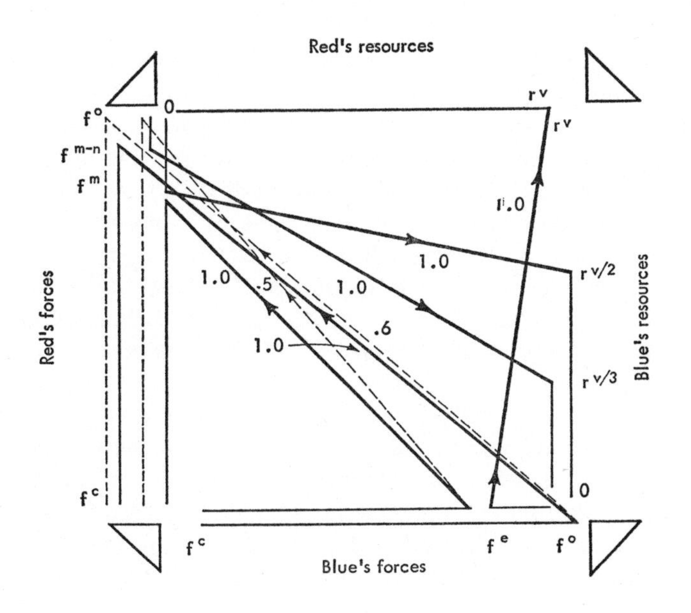

follow this depiction, begin from an axis measuring the attacker's proportion of forces. Thus, on the axis labeled "Blue's Forces," a line (f^o to f^e) measures the proportion of Blue's forces which he would have to use up to be certain (i.e., to have a physical probability equal to unity) of eliminating exactly all of Red's resources represented on this diagram—i.e., Red's resources (0 to r^v): a solid arrowed line leads from Blue's f^e to Red's r^v, and has a probability-indicator of 1.0.

Suppose Red directs some forces against Blue's resources. The proportion (f^o to f^m) of Red's forces will be certain to eliminate half of Blue's resources depicted on this diagram—follow the dogleg arrowed line (f^o to f^m to $r^v/2$ to 0). A smaller proportion of Red's forces—(f^o to f^{m-n})—eliminates for certain only one-third (0 to $r^v/3$) of Blue's resources.

Now consider the force-*versus*-force ratio which, since complete Blue-Red symmetry is supposed, is marked in on Figure 6.7 only for a preemptive attack ("first strike") by Blue against Red: Blue uses up the proportion (f^c to f^e) of his forces preempting against Red's forces, having a probability of 1.0 that he will eliminate not less than (f^m to f^c) of Red's forces—follow the solid arrowed line (Blue's f^c to f^e to Red's f^m to f^c); and a probability of 0.5 that, using up the same amount of his own forces, he will eliminate all of Red's—follow the dotted arrowed line (Blue's f^e to Red's f^o to Red's f^c). If, on the other hand, Blue is prepared to use up all his forces (f^c to f^o) in preemption, he can be certain of eliminating not less than (f^{m-n} to f^c) of Red's forces—follow the solid and arrowed line (Blue's f^o to Red's f^{m-n} to Red's f^c); and he has a two-thirds chance of eliminating all of Red's forces—follow the dotted and arrowed line marked .6· from Blue's f^o to Red's f^o to Red's f^c.

This diagram is supposed to illustrate an instance of "conditional viability" as we have defined it—an instance in which, despite the symmetrical temptations to preemption and the consequent mutual fears of it, both Powers have rational arguments (i.e., arguments consistent with their prior "decisions" determining capitulation points and developing armed forces whose size would be consistent with those "decisions") for withholding. Those arguments, which are both strategic and political in character, are reinforced by considerations of a "meta-linguistic" kind—i.e., involving imputation of arguments to the other fellow, which seem to me to be of a purely political character, falling under the terms of our definition of Powerhood in Chapter 4.

The strategic and political argument, put now from Blue's point of view, is that it would not be rational for him to preempt *either* with all his forces *or* with a proportion (f^c to f^e) of them, for in the former case there would be up to a one-third chance that having used, to the capitulation point, all his forces, he could lose up to one-third of his resources; while in the latter case his Red opponent, if "irrational" and willing to risk a total loss of his own resources, might be able, with a physical probability of up to one-half, to destroy up to one-half of Blue's resources. In the former case, then, preemption by Blue would be formally irrational, and he should prefer to capitulate rather than to take such action! In the latter case, preemption by Blue would amount to a partially irrational gamble on Red's rationality and on Red's not having automated a counter-resource response.

The second—"meta-linguistic" and political—argument against a preemptive strike consists in each side's attributing or *imputing* to the other the first argumentation ("imputation" is further discussed below, pp. 213–221). Imputation in political practice is almost invariably hypothetical to some extent—e.g., it is rare to have absolutely convincing evidence that the other side is, for the time being, rational. On the other hand, no political action (as distinct from sheer "engineering") can be carried on except upon the basis of some imputation, however far to seek the evidence required to substantiate it. In the case of Figure 6.7, however, each side's imputing to the other the first level of argument, even when neither side can be confident that the other is also imputing, strengthens for each side the first-level arguments against preemption. Information that the other side *is* imputing strengthens them further.

It is upon such cases that the view depends according to which "political understandings" make for peace: they allay Hobbesian doubts and anxieties. As we shall see in the next chapter, they need not always do so—sometimes, indeed, they confirm one's worst apprehensions about the other fellow. The concept of imputation as such is important for a theory of dynamics in that, by raising one's analysis to a political level which our Figure 6.7 cannot depict but may suggest, it helps indicate that the origins of change in political inter-Power systems need not all be autonomous (e.g., matters of changing military technology or of productive capacity), but may come from within the power-political system itself. Indeed, we contend that a system in which each member of every pair of Powers envisaged itself in relationship, not merely with the other member of each pair severally but with every other Power, would be *ipso facto* a different system from that in which each had a more limited vision. Again, we shall return to this point in the next chapter.

We have tried to show that in the situation of Figure 6.7, despite the predominance established by the Power that strikes first, there are strong arguments against either Power's deciding to do so. Those arguments depend upon two quite different quantitative considerations. One of these is only in part representable on the Amster-Sherwin diagram (Figure 6.2). For example, when it is almost certain that a small proportion (say, a fifth) of a Power's long-range thermonuclear forces can eliminate almost all its opponent's resources, while all of the same Power's forces have only a fifty-fifty chance of eliminating the opponent's entire (thermonuclear) forces; and when these conditions are symmetrical for the opposed Powers—then any attempt to capitalize upon the advantage of the "first strike" is bound to be risky.

We have now indicated that "conditional viability" on *our* definition (which differs from Boulding's) can be a fairly stable situation, provided one may assume that leaders of Powers have no *unlimited* ambitions. Aspects of systemic change can be reintroduced into our analysis by consideration of the various relationships represented on our square diagrams. The most important of these is the angle of intersect of the lines representing forces encountering or at least launched against forces. Generally, we may assume that if such intersections are obtuse angles falling to the left of and downward from, and pointing away from, the diagonal bisecting the square downward from left to right, then, as between two Powers, the military technology establishes a stable relationship. In the case where such intersections form an angle pointing up toward the diagonal, the area on the other (the upper and right-hand) half of the square may (in circumstances as illustrated in Figure 6.7) reveal features which nevertheless indicate that a stable equilibrium is possible, though barely so. In that half of the square are represented the comparative evaluations, by the rival Powers' rulers, of their several Powers' resources and of their retaining independent Powerhood—factors which make it clear that the "decision" not to render an opposed Power nonviable will often be no mere act of grace, but the result of fundamental political reasoning.

That dependence upon fundamental political evaluations—"is there a price too high to pay for our retaining Powerhood?"—can be illustrated by making alterations to Figure 6.7. As it stands it depicts a situation in which (1) relatively small allocations of forces can eliminate very large proportions of resources, and (2) forces which launch the first strike against other forces have a better-than-even chance of eliminating a *rather* larger proportion of the enemy's forces than is used up of their own; but (3) even the employment of all of the attacker's forces cannot make it more than probable that all the enemy's forces will be eliminated. Holding constant on Figure 6.7 the forces-*versus*-resources ratio, we increase the effectiveness of a first strike: instead of Blue's having to use up all his to achieve a .6· probability of eliminating all of Red's forces, let us suppose that he need use up only half; while by using the amount (f^c to f^e) he can achieve a .95 probability. Now suppose that the relationship is symmetrical—that Red has now the same first-strike prospects against Blue, and that Blue knows this, just as Red knows about Blue's capacities. Each severally must now consider (1) that both are in the position where a preemptive strike using up (f^c to f^e) proportion of forces is very likely to disarm the enemy totally; (2) even if it were not totally successful, the enemy would have to consider that the other one's remaining forces (f^o to f^e) could wipe out his own resources up to his capitulation point—e.g. (0 to r^v); and (3) even if the enemy were not to be deterred by that consideration, but had perhaps pretargeted all his forces against one's resources, the little he would have left to send against one's resources might not be capable of destroying as much resources as, together with the forces one had expended in attacking his, would for oneself amount to losses of which the prospect should rationally induce one to capitulate.

Thus, if one increases the first-strike effectiveness of forces against forces, the rationale of strategy and politics should, in consistency, change also. The change is, indeed, a change in political perspective: the increase in first-strike effectiveness does not *mechanically* upset the deterrent balance and abolish conditional viability. Nevertheless, it would be an important and necessary premise in the explanation of any overthrow of the deterrent balance, which in this case would amount to systemic change.

In earlier sections we pointed out that Boulding takes little account of the effect upon unconditional viability of alliance factors or, indeed, of the copresence of other Powers. A *prima facie* argument supporting Boulding on that issue can be derived from a definition of "unconditional viability," which means that Power *p*, irrespective of what other Powers choose, has the physical means to repel attack if it chooses to employ them. But to depend upon alliances is to depend upon the choice of at least one other Power: so that viability through alliances is mere conditional viability. I shall now try to show that in a three-Power world the physical relations of armed forces can in principle be such that the weakest of the three can so dispose its forces as to make viability conditional only upon the determination of each of the others to maintain his own unconditional viability.

Consider the situation of Blue in Figure 6.5, Section (i), and suppose that Blue has to maintain intact a proportion of his forces *greater than* (f^c, f^s) in order to remain unconditionally viable against a third Power, Green. Further suppose, as is plausible, that Red would be unconditionally viable against a Blue force no larger than (f^o, f^s). Then Red must be viable upon the sole conditions that Blue (1) understands the situation we have just supposed and (2) does not form an alliance with Green (which would free for use against Red the Blue forces previously maintained in reserve against Green).

But does not condition (2) make Red's viability conditional in Boulding's very sense? Let us amplify our description somewhat. Blue is unconditionally viable against a combination of Red and Green in which neither maintains forces against each other, but each has his total forces ready to attack Blue. (Let us suppose, to make this accountable, that, against Blue, Green has a very steep loss-of-strength gradient.) Green is likewise unconditionally viable against a Blue-Red combination.

Now suppose Red, though viable against either Blue or Green singly (since each must reserve forces against a possible attack by the other), is not unconditionally viable against a combination of the two: could there be any strategy open to Red which might restore Red's viability? Under certain circumstances, yes. If Red can demonstrate to both Blue and Green that, in the face of their combined attack, Red forces can be *unequally* deployed so that those against, say, Blue, would destroy up to (f^o, f^s) of Blue's total forces—thus rendering Blue nonviable *vis-à-vis* Green, who would have met with only token opposition from Red—then Blue's determination to stay unconditionally viable against all comers should deter Blue from combining with Green. If in the foregoing sentences the names "Blue" and "Green" were transposable, then Red, threatened with the possibility of a coalition against him, could issue the counter-threat that he would choose one of his opponents—he would not in advance say which—and make sure by concentrating all resistance against him, that that one would cease to be viable when facing the other alone.

Two situations have been described in which the weakest of three Powers has at least a prospect of maintaining its viability by a roundabout threat to that of another. Though this differs from "unconditional viability," based on the fact of a certain material configuration of forces, it otherwise conforms with the definition, in that Red's viability in these circumstances depends primarily upon *his own decisions,* though it also depends upon *perceptions* by the others—they both must recognize the predicament that Red has put them in. Even that requirement of recognition by the others does not make Red's viability any *more* (nor, of course, any less) "conditional," in this context, than it is in the original two-Power situation of Section (i), where nevertheless the whole argument rests upon an assurance that Blue will respond in its own way (i.e., by refraining from attack) on account of a recognition of the situation.

Admittedly, we have had to suppose, in this three-Power situation, rather unlikely and special military and geographic relationships. The first part of our argument—that which suggested that Red would be viable as against Blue upon the sole condition that, a combination between Blue and Green being impossible, Blue would lose his own unconditional viability in respect of Green should he attempt the conquest of Red—sometimes has a real-life equivalent in the case of a competent armed neutral: it has been suggested that, during the Second World War, Nazi Germany was deterred from attempting to conquer Switzerland by the consideration that Germany would lose too many forces against the determined resistance that the Swiss could put up. The second part of the argument—depending upon the victim's deterring a combined attack by threatening to offer an unequal resistance—is much more difficult to instantiate, though something like it is provided by the reasoning behind the maintenance of buffer states.

Conceptually the neatest definition may be to lay down the rule (1) that a Power is "unconditionally" viable if and only if it could repel an attack by *all* other Powers combined, provided it were willing to produce the forces to do so—i.e., provided its capitulation point were at a high enough level; (2) that a Power is viable, "given rationalistic conditions," if and only if other relevant Powers recognize that the conquest of it is possible if but only if at least one of them loses unconditional viability in the process; (3) that, apart from "rationalistic conditions," a Power is "conditionally" viable if and only if other Powers which, singly or in combination, could conquer it without losing unconditional viability, *decide* not to do so; (4) that a Power is not viable unless, given the state of affairs alluded to in (3), the relevant other Powers do decide not to conquer it.

A provoking question is whether, in the strict terms of (1), *any* nation of the last two hundred years has been unconditionally viable. The strongest candidate, of course, is the USA from, say, 1943 to the late 1950s: otherwise, it is hard to think of any case of a Power that could have withstood a coalition of the world against it. Even Great Britain at the height of her naval supremacy before the days of the bomber aircraft might not have been able to stand off, for an unlimited time, all other fleets combined.

A distinction is sometimes made between sheer "defense" and "deterrence." I do not believe that this can be a dichotomy: a Power unconditionally viable in the sense of (1) above surely has a perfect defense, but the recognition of that fact by other Powers ought to deter them from attacking. On the other hand, definition (3), though it makes room for thermonuclear deterrence by threat against the attacking Powers' resources, thus persuading the other to "decide" against attack, does not completely preclude "defense"—e.g., protection—even though limited, of missile sites. Definition (2) represents in the current terminology "counterforce deterrence"; but, as our exposition has suggested, it is very difficult to distinguish this militarily from (1), which is the nearest to "sheer defense."

We do no better by assuming that a policy of "defense" involves considering only the *capacity* of the enemy, while one of deterrence works also and principally on his *will.* "Capacity" is a material and in principle calculable condition—a matter of what the enemy's forces-in-being can do against the other side's forces and resources, or, in the longer term, what could be done by the various sizes of forces which his resources would enable him to maintain against the range of forces his possible opponents might maintain. "Will," as our diagrams have suggested, can be interpreted as the partly arbitrary decision which rulers of a Power actually come to about the circumstances in which they would capitulate, and therefore about the upper limit of forces they are prepared to maintain in being in order to withstand demands for capitulation.

In the present chapter, we have depicted a variety of changes in relationship between two Powers and, when such changes were systemic, have indicated how they might be explained by changes in the military exchange rate. These can be represented on our square diagram (e.g., as in Figure 6.6, Section (ii), by drawing two or more intersects successive in time on the one square); and, as earlier contended, we can make some show of illustrating the effect of considerations about third Powers by the same device. By plotting the movement through time of intersection points, from situations in which they represent an equilibrium to others in which they would represent or create expectation of disequilibrium, we can suggest to ourselves, and even synthesize, hypotheses about the causes of systemic change—*viz.:* Boulding's "transportation" hypothesis; the hypotheses to explain a particular case of systemic change—from "power-balancing" to "deterrence"—illustrated by Amster and Sherwin, and expounded by Kaplan and the present writer amongst others; and finally the highly general hypothesis of the location of a "capitulation point," and of the implications of the choice that locates such a point for consistent decisions about the scale of a Power's military expenditure. We also noticed that recognition by rulers of the situation of their own Power *vis-à-vis* others might well induce them to raise or to lower their capitulation point. In doing so, they change the conditions that make "rational" the various grand strategies depicted on our square diagram, but only because they have achieved a second and higher order of rationality: that of reflecting critically upon the deliverance of their first-order, egocentric rationality.

Notice further that explanatory hypotheses in terms of the technology of transportation and of explosive energy are, in this study, thought to be no more than the beginning of a theory of dynamics. Not only are we prepared to consider intrinsic causes—e.g., that every system of inter-Power *political* relations carries within itself Hegelian seeds of its own decay—it also appears quite possible that changes other than those in the military art, in military technology, or in the cost of transport—most notably, changes in the nature of *internal* political systems—could induce systemic change in the external political order. These nontechnological sources of systemic change are briefly reviewed in the next chapter.

SEVEN

The Dynamics of Power Relations: Further Sources, Especially in Internal Politics

This chapter concludes our discussion of the dynamics of power-political systems. We began by distinguishing systemic change from perturbations within a system that remains despite them the same kind of system. We then identified types of systemic change: that consisting of changes in the kind of relationship between the constituent Powers; that consisting of certain but not all changes in the numbers of the latter; that consisting in changes in the nature of at least the more important constituent Powers. Next, we classified certain sources of systemic change. One source, the power-political process intrinsic to the system itself (styled "non-autonomous"), we saw, could not be discussed until after our postponed discussion of the statics of Power politics. In the last chapter we depicted changes in the military or strategic relation between Powers, classified some of these as systemic changes, and identified the possible sources of those systemic changes as arising amongst "autonomous" processes: in militarily relevant aspects of technology—e.g., in transport of armed forces, projectiles, and other weapons—in capacities for destruction, and in means of detection and surveillance.

Since inter-Power relations are conducted often, though not necessarily, within a structure of strategic confrontations, any pertinent account of the dynamics of Power politics must deal seriously with the technological processes that largely determine conditions of strategic confrontation. But technology is no Uncaused Cause. Nor is it by any means the sole cause of systemic change in the politics of the Powers. At the price of obviousness, some others will now be mentioned.

Most obviously, the technology of communications has changed at least the tempo and the style of our Power politics during the last century and a half, quite apart from the influence already discussed of transport and surveillance upon strategic confrontations. In the earliest few pages of our first chapter, for instance, the recent advent of a quite informal style of political "conversation" amongst statesmen was partly accounted for by the present ease and speed of worldwide communication; and we noticed that this development had also begun to have the effect of making continuous, or at least potentially continuous, the communications between statesmen. American scholars have already noticed the paralyzing effect upon political decision of "communications overload"—of too much information, by too many channels, for a nation's chief executive to digest.

Do these various aspects of the current revolution in means of communication combine into a cause of our century's systemic change? It would seem not, if we consider their effects apart from those already mentioned as arising for the strategic situation from the militarily relevant changes in transport technology. But the distinction between the two is merely abstract—the military is part of the general facility in communication and transport, and could not have arisen without the rest.

A stronger case could be made out for regarding the sixteenth-century advances in maritime transport and to a lesser extent the earlier one of harnessing the draught horse as having been amongst the causes of the ending of the postfeudal hegemonial system on the Western European continent and, less directly, of the emergence of the modern European system in the seventeenth century. Further, one could imagine future changes in initially nonmilitary means of communication and transport that, by making possible a "perfect defense" for even middling Powers, might produce the most far-reaching systemic change. But that, again, would be associated with the strategic situation and with military technology.

Another obviously dynamic factor is economic differentiation between classes of Powers. In the colonizing era, ancient civilizations like the Chinese and the Indian, as well as premetallic cultures in the Pacific and elsewhere, suffered systemic change as Power structures from the sheer economic impact of the European seafarers even when and where muskets and cannon had little or nothing to do with the conquests. The world system of Powers now taking shape reveals a division longer-lasting and deeper than—indeed, often a condition of—the divisions into Super and other Powers, or nuclear and nonnuclear: that between advanced and backward economies. There are anomalies, as in Communist China, where a backward economy contains an advanced echelon—an anomaly because we feel it unnatural that the two should subsist in the same territory and not be separated by oceans, as for instance with the British Empire between the wars.

A less obvious source of changes that sometimes may be systemic is the internal evolution of "social classes" (for want of a better term). Little is known about this process, but it is happily beyond human control. The middle and lower classes of northwestern Europe, who in the last three centuries came to predominate in their native lands and who, transplanted to North America, have from there exerted power, influence, and example, are changing the world system out of all proportion to their numbers. It is not too much to say that what is new in the world of the twentieth century—e.g., the acceleration of discovery in the natural sciences, and its application to technology—has been brought about by those people: the rest of the globe has followed in their train.

Similarly, the Roman conquest of the Mediterranean and Gaullish regions seems to have owed something to Roman social structure—not, as some of the Roman historians themselves contended, to a superior constitution and class-system, but rather to the milieu that made the legionary arrangement militarily practicable. A case even more striking at first is the suitability in culture and *mores* of the successive peoples—first Arab and then non-Arab Syrians and others—who enabled the first two Islamic conquests. The Romans' onslaught produced what we have called a systemic change, inasmuch as they brought under a single Power nearly the whole of "the known world"—i.e., the Power-system known to them. The Islamic feat, perhaps more remarkable as a military phenomenon, did not. The theorist should ask himself whether in the Roman case he should inquire only after the *differentia* of Roman society, or whether he should not also investigate the power-political statics—*viz.,* the nature of the post-Alexandrian system of Powers, to see if that has more explanatory force than any aspect of Roman society. (A consequence of the affirmative would be that, if not Rome, then another Power —perhaps Carthage—would probably have united the ancient world.) It is not contended that, if a satisfactory model of the ancient world's Power-system were invented, there would emerge a unitary explanation plausibly dividing weight between internal social structure and external politics, and entailing a neat deduction of Rome's rise to solitary dominion: much that is properly excluded from the model as insignificant would be bound to have had effects in the form of unforeseeable "accidents," which historians always expect. The enterprise of theorizing should be to replace particular by general explanations, but only where the latter are demonstrable.

We remarked above that technology itself is not an Uncaused Cause —i.e., the sources of technological change are not all technological; in Chapter 2 the world-changing potential of discovery in pure science was acknowledged. The history of pure science, in turn, is interpreted by modern scholars within its context of philosophic and religious history. Einstein's overthrow of the Newtonian world-view can be connected at a remove or two with Berkeley's speculative philosophy. The Galileian revolution in physical science is interpretable through the High Renaissance union of Pythagoreanism and Platonism with New Testament doctrines of creation by the Divine Logos.

Such long and indirect pathways from new light in the mind and spirit to new and infernal weapons are not foreseeable before the event; but in retrospect they are traceable: historians of thought recount the breakdown of a former world-view and the improbable germination, amid Syrian and Levantine fanaticism, of an intellectual life which is now engendering a universal and scientific culture.[1] The ambitions of historians of civilizations —to discern cycles in these former processes and thereby to predict future systemic changes—have been frustrated in many directions, but not least by the twist of events between the World Wars away from the perpetual recurrences expected half a century ago by Spengler and Toynbee; ratios of tempo and magnitude in the processes of demographic, productive organizational, and intellectual development, though not wholly reliable, are now among the few clues to the future. Before the end of this century, systemic changes as impressive as that of the last thirty years could originate, we surmise, in almost any one or combination of the proliferating ventures of science and speculation, as well as in the unpredictable mass upheavals of ideology, class, and race.

Technological and especially military-technological change, moreover, can produce dynamic effects only through a few kinds of power-political structure. The potent decreases in the loss-of-strength gradient detected by Boulding (see Chapter 6) occurred unevenly so that, for example, the seafaring revolution from the fifteenth to the twentieth centuries temporarily elevated a succession of embattled and initially minor maritime states to great power: Portugal, Spain, Holland, England, Japan, the United States. Powers great by land—France, Germany, Russia—were often ill-situated to exploit the seafaring technology. It is not, by contrast, as yet certain whether the thermonuclear transformation will raise to

[1] E.g., C. N. Cochrane, *Christianity and Classical Culture* (London: Oxford University Press, 1940, Galaxy Books, 1957 and 1959).

greatest strength only those few Powers that are amongst the most populous as well as technologically the most advanced, or whether at the other extreme it will become an equalizer of states. The later stages of the firepower revolution, ending the millenium of the armored horseman's battlefield predominance and determining the military exchange rate that conditioned the European state system, strengthened as we know only a certain kind of state—those having the appropriate armament manufactories.

This is a commonplace—great changes in its productive system obviously can affect a Power's economic potential, and thereby its situation within the system of Powers; and more generally, a change in all or many Powers' productive systems can sometimes modify the nature of inter-Power relationships—i.e., can cause systemic change. But can that be done by a change of a different kind: a change in the ownership and control of the means of production? Have the epochs conceived of by the Marxists—from primitive communism to the slave system to bourgeois capitalism to socialism—each initiated systemic change in inter-Power relations?

For the cases of the Russian, the various Eastern European, and the Chinese revolutions and *coups,* the answer is, "No." Though in several of these cases the transition to state ownership and a planned economy has been followed, after greater or lesser intervals and more or less temporarily, by a new access of power to, e.g., Russia, Yugoslavia, and mainland China, those effects did not amount to or cause a change in the very nature of the inter-Power relations of the twentieth century. This negative result is somewhat surprising since, as a phenomenon of Power politics, total planning of the economy keeps it on what is virtually a permanent war footing, a situation accentuated under the totalitarian or Soviet version of socialism by the internal need for a large standing army, irrespective of the level of external threat—e.g., in the USSR during the late Twenties. A worldwide change from market economies to totalitarianly planned economies (whether of Soviet or of National Socialism) might be expected to make all inter-Power relations far more abrasive than under capitalism or democratic socialism. But in reality there were in the Twenties and Thirties so many other and stronger influences upon Power politics—e.g., the resurgence of Germany, the rise of Japan, the relative decline of Britain as an industrial and commercial center, the self-isolation of the USA, that the early overarming of the USSR was not decisive; and after the Second World War, the great increases in cost of armaments and of the maintenance of men under arms, together with the great speed with which certain kinds of attack could be mounted, are conditions that have affected all Major Powers alike (though not equally), whether their economies were centrally planned, or "market," or a mixture of the two. The level of expenditure on armaments for the USSR, the Warsaw Pact States, the Major Powers in NATO, for instance, has been maintained steadily at medium to high rates, except for peaks during the Korean and (for the USA) the Vietnam wars. Any differences made by changes in ownership of the means of production have been masked by other effects.

The hypothesis (vulgarized from the analyses of Hobson and of Lenin) of the causation of wars, at least of colonial wars—*viz.,* that they result from a crisis of investment and relative overproduction experienced by monopoly-capitalism, has also been, if not refuted, then confused by the overlying of many other tendencies. Nevertheless, few authorities now expect a recrudescence of wars for trade or for colonies; and this change, resulting not so much from changes in ownership of the means of production as from increasing costs of warfare and from the emergence into national independence of most former colonial territories, may conceivably be styled a minor systemic change. In short, changes in methods of ownership and control seem, on the whole, not to have been so productive of changes in the nature of Power systems as Marxist and similar analysts had supposed for half a century before the Second World War—though their effects upon the style of national life have certainly been significant.

Thus far in the present chapter, we have eclectically surveyed a number of possible "candidates," beside military technology, for being originators of systemic change. It is hard to see how eclecticism could have been avoided, for no well-attested theory of world-historical processes, which might have lent our inquiry a method and order, is as yet available. But our next step has been prepared for in theory: we are now to consider whether internal politics can produce systemic changes in external—i.e., in inter-Power—politics. Since, as we claim, it is in practice all but impossible for the rulers of any Power to rule their subjects without themselves interacting politically with each other in their own internal polity, and since such a Power's statesmen usually maintain a "Janus-faced" stance—in one direction toward their own polity and in the other toward the external situation—then causal connections both ways between internal-political and external-political change are to be expected. Nevertheless, upon a first view of the evidence much is to be said for the hypothesis that internal constitutions and politics have no significant implications for external relations. Between the political styles of statesmen representing Left or Right dictatorships, liberal democracies, and aristocracies, differences can indeed be distinguished; but the differences are unlikely to be decisive, at any rate in the short run. Admittedly, the kind of world-political public, characteristic of democracies and aristocracies, that participate as critics and ralliers of opinion on the margins of the central "conversation," can marginally change and make more sophisticated the working of the power-political system. It may turn out that in the long run the politics of the Powers can be humanized only by the influence of such people. Yet it is not certain that they bring about systemic changes, according to the narrow and formal understanding of that term in this study.

The hypothesis that internal politics is irrelevant to external or Power politics can be propounded in stronger or weaker forms. The logically stronger (i.e., the one that makes larger and less plausible claims and is thus more open to refutation) would be that internal politics has no effect whatsoever upon the working of the system of Powers—neither (1) by causing systemic change, nor even (2) by affecting the interplay of Power politics or the balance of power during an era in which no change is systemic. Part (2) is surely refuted by well-attested historical counter-examples—e.g., Cromwell's return to an anti-Spanish policy reminiscent of the Elizabethan age. Part (1) however, which is equivalent with the logically weaker and more plausible form of the irrelevancy hypothesis, is by no means evidently refutable; though, since there have been so few known instances of systemic change, it may turn out to have survived refutation because in every case the systemic change was brought about by something that affected the necessary conditions of the Power system more directly and immediately than could the internal political situation of any of the Powers. Our discussion of this question—"Can internal-political developments cause external systemic change?"—must therefore be largely speculative. We shall refer to certain features of internal-political structure suggested by our definition of Powerhood in Chapter 4: do particular modifications of these features suggest resistance against or conduciveness to systemic change? We shall also refer to aspects of the discussion, Chapter 5, pp. 98–101, about conditions for persistence of a single-Power system.

On the last-mentioned page we had observed that it might be possible to remove the administration of justice from the sway of Power politics, and that, of all paths toward a world society in which Powerhood, though acknowledged as ineradicable, might be subjugated and civilized, this was the least utopian. Our definition, clauses 1.14 to 1.1421, distinguishes between the employment of sanctions against "subjects" and against "outsiders." In advanced liberal (though not necessarily representative-democratic) Powers, this distinction is confirmed by several distinctions in law. Very rarely need such societies employ the sanctions of forcible coercion in order to maintain their integrity as Powers (see definition item 1.1411). In other words, few kinds of action are classified as "crimes against the State"; moreover, actions so classified are rarely perpetrated. For instance, opposition to government policy, though carried as far as mass demonstration, public picketing and vituperation, is no crime in such societies. On the other hand, many of them act in concert against nonpolitical crime—e.g., by reciprocal arrangements between such states for extraditing nonpolitical criminals. But the tendency toward such a distinction in the liberal Powers' employment of coercive sanctions—a distinction that enhances the rights and liberties of subjects—is quite evident, and is perhaps best symbolized by a police force that carries no weapons.

The present writer contends that an international organization such as the United Nations will most usefully exercise peace-keeping functions when it has become possible to confine them precisely to the norm of a liberal society's police actions, or at most to the usually circumscribed action of the military "in support of the Civil Power."[2] UN forces, that is, should not, without recourse to the powers of Chapter 7 of the Charter, enforce *policy:* when they do, they reduce the Organization to its original condition as a coalition of victorious Powers; and this would be the case even were the enforced policy agreeable to the great majority of the General Assembly.

The path here advocated toward a world society was already trodden by Dag Hammarskjöld in his endeavor to construe the "military assistance" so that, in the words of the Security Council resolution of 14 July 1960, "national security forces might be able, in the opinion of the Government, to meet fully their tasks"—in Hammarskjöld's view, purely policing tasks. In this doctrine there is a point of fine balance, to put it at its most favorable, between straightforward police action in the safeguarding of life and property, and that kind of action by "security forces" which ensures that a legal government shall be in a position to govern—as in our definition of Chapter 4, clause 1.12, rulers act in a concert "which will always exhibit at one extreme some features of arbitrary power and at the other some elements of polity." Advanced liberal societies, which by definition come close to the extreme of polity and at the same time have securely established state apparatuses, quite easily maintain the balance—e.g., they should not need, as must the governments of certain backward and newly emerging Powers, to suspend *habeas corpus* in order to ensure that no one succeeds in faking the ballot at election time.

I shall use the expression "liberal internationalism" to describe a reformation of the politics of the Powers so as to reduce the opportunities for states in their *external* relations to exercise "arbitrary power" against "outsiders," just as within a liberal polity reformers endeavor to regulate the state's exercise of arbitrary power against "insiders"—i.e., citizens or subjects. This reforming program is called "*inter*nationalist" because it

[2] See A. L. Burns and N. Heathcote, *Peace-Keeping by U.N. Forces: From Suez to the Congo* (New York and London: Praeger and Pall Mall, 1963).

assumes the continued existence of nation-states as Powers and, more, a continuing arbitrariness in their actions toward other Powers *as Powers:* the intended limitation upon arbitrariness is in the sphere of a Power's action against outsiders *as persons*—for example, one would hope to reduce the capacities of all Powers to attack persons and destroy property, to make war, whether declared or not. But the liberal internationalist concedes that, within those limitations concerning actions against persons, Powers may pursue their divergent interests, assuming that there is an international anarchy, a kind of private enterprise system in world politics. The view is that Power politics cannot be eliminated, but may be civilized.

Should such a reform succeed, it would have certain features that would induce one to call its success a minor systemic change. Because it could be brought about only in a world where the dominant Powers were all internally "liberal," we have imagined by means of it, one minor systemic change for which a necessary though not a sufficient condition would be the prevalence of liberal points of view in internal politics. How causally important might this element be?

We may approach an answer to that question by contrasting liberal internationalism with two different internationally reforming movements: one contrast is with a world-ideal common to Soviet Marxist-Leninists, Maoists, and the now-declining party amongst the nonaligned who have shared attitudes like Sukarno's. We might style this "illiberal or totalitarian internationalist," since it rejects what it calls "bourgeois rights and liberties" but is more fiercely conservative of national sovereignty than are the liberal internationalists themselves. Unlike the latter's, however, this ideal involves no specification for the kind of internal-political developments that might induce systemic change in the relations of Powers: if every nation in the world were converted to this illiberal and totalitarian view, there would be no change in the *nature* of our present power-political order, though no doubt the present balance of the system would be shifted considerably.

The second contrast is with what we shall call the "liberal supranationalism" of the idealists of the European Community. Their vision (before the crisis of 1964–65 set sovereign national limits for the time being to the extension into politics of the Commission's methods and influence) seemed apt to produce in Western Europe a society characterized as follows by the present writer in 1963:

> Firstly, a capitalistic free-market economy, embracing a population of some two hundred millions, will be qualified by a well-protected agricultural system, designed to slow down the decline of the European peasantry. Much business organisation will be on a very grand scale and, whether nationalized or privately owned, will be exempt from political

> intervention, though subject to a certain administrative policing intended to keep it "competitive."
>
> Secondly, the executive branches of national governments will be relatively strengthened *vis-à-vis* their own national parliaments and polities, but will be obliged to consult and plan with both the supranational bureaucracy and with other national governments.
>
> Thirdly, as a result, both supranational and national bureaucracies will be enlarged, endowed with effective control, and highly prestigeful. They will provide careers open to talent, and it is to be expected that young people with an ambition for leadership will go into administration and not into politics. In most of the Member-nations, and certainly in the Community institutions, the highest of such officials will be public figures, and not the anonymous, self-effacing civil servant of British antiquity. An administrative career will lead upward to fame as well as to power.
>
> Fourthly, the European Parliament will be much less the focus of a polity—a political community—than the leading echelon of a vast public relations operation on behalf of the European bureaucracy.
>
> Finally national parliaments, in all matters except defence and foreign policy, would have even less constitutional sovereignty than the State Parliaments of Australia. As to defence and foreign policy, their remaining sovereignty would not be exercisable.[3]

A European Community synthesized politically as well as economically on such terms, and eventually deploying a common armed force and, presumably through some sort of bureaucratized Presidency of Western Europe, developing a common foreign policy would, again, significantly modify the present balance of world power; but there seems no reason to suppose that a liberal-supranational Europe alone would change the nature of the Power system. To do justice to the supranationalist hypothesis, we must imagine its universalization—a supranationalist globe.

In effect, this would amount to a liberal World Federation, differing internally in degree from great national federations such as the USA by its formal depreciation of politics and its appreciation of administration and bureaucracy. Even more than the liberal internationalist ideal, it would require a liberal code of law—e.g., by universal extension and enforcement of such instruments as the European Human Rights Convention. We have discussed in Chapter 5, especially pp. 98–101, some of the practically insuperable difficulties in the way of establishing, and once established, of maintaining the unity of such a sole world Power. More importantly, doubts now suggest themselves about the feasibility of the liberal-supranationalist idea even within the European Economic Community itself—supranationalism may be a passing fad and the Treaty of Rome (as

[3] A. L. Burns, *Politics and Administration in the European Economic Community,* Robert Garran Memorial Oration for 1962, published by the Royal Institute of Public Administration, Canberra, Australia, 1963, pp. 29–30.

suggested by the *New Statesman* in 1965) no more permanent than the Treaty of Versailles. Whether or not our doubts are well-founded, variants of the supranationalist concept less closely bound up with the European Community's genuine if less-than-democratic liberalism are worth examining for their potentialities to promote external systemic change.

Consider something that might be labeled "continental" or "regional supranationalism." One of the themes that contribute to this idea is the hypothesis that an advanced economy uniting one or two hundred million people or more can without deliberate intervention or planning approach the condition of autarchy—not in the sense that it is self-sufficient and will not trade at all beyond its own boundaries but in the sense that the volume of its internal trade will be twenty or more times that of its external—a reversal of Hobson's and Lenin's characterizations of imperialism, for such vast economies would be, on this argument, motivated *against* increasing their foreign markets, their foreign investments, and the numbers of the nations in their memberships. On the other hand, the existence of one or more of these economies—e.g., the USA—would motivate smaller nations and groupings of nations to recruit partners and members up to a number that would bring their own economy to the critical size of one hundred or more million consumers. Auxiliary arguments about the advantages to manufacturing of a very large market within a hundred or so miles, and about the disadvantages of oceanic and other long-range transportation (perhaps questionable on account of modern transport technology) are used to reinforce the case that these accretions into nearly self-sufficient economies should be "continental" or at least "regional."

A further stage in this kind of supranationalist exposition is that, with the possible exception of the USA's, these super-economies are bound to be "managed" or "*dirigiste.*" This implies that there must be some governmental or quasi-governmental organization to administer them. It is indifferent for the argument whether the governmental organization is ostensibly capitalist, communist, socialist, etc.: the gravamen is that the super-economy will somehow evoke a "state" entity to govern and direct the area of the economy. Whether the entity has to be a completely sovereign Power is a matter on which the continental supranationalists maintain an open mind. One tendency is to argue that the question of sovereignty can be bypassed by retaining the formal sovereignties of the several member-nations of a super-economy such as that of the European Community, meanwhile insuring that the real management and control of the economy is in the hands of a bureaucratic organization endowed with the needed authority—the "substance of sovereignty."

That line of thought quite neglects issues of military security. But ready to hand is an up-to-date strategic argument which can complement the argument from the "inevitability of super-economies." A fully credible thermonuclear deterrent—so this argument goes—must evince "second-strike invulnerability" against the most that could be done by the forces of either of the two present Superpowers. This would require an investment in military force equivalent at least to the absolute size of the USSR's, which in turn requires a super-economy. The fully credible deterrent also requires geographic depth—large territory or at least access to the weapon-system of the nuclear submarine and Polaris missile. But these are short-run considerations: in the long run, credible deterrence depends upon the ability to keep up with the qualitative arms race (see Chapter 6); and that ability requires not only a super-economy, but also a scientific and technological establishment (so supranationalists maintain) beyond the capacity of any single European nation.

Various schemes are suggested by the strategists for setting up an adequate military directorate for such a bloc. Except for those of the outright advocates of a European federal union, all these are more or less managerial in structure, thus contributing to accretion of the "substance of sovereignty" at the center of the supranational community. Though we have here employed the European Community as our example for exposition, the same arguments would apply to any continental or regional super-economy.

If—and, as suggested, it is quite doubtful—a supranational community could be evolved in Western Europe, one can imagine the example's being followed in other areas of "continental" dimensions, though perhaps not so effectively during the twentieth century. The question for the present chapter is whether this would be (or would cause) a systemic change in the present relationship of Powers.

One's answer must depend in part upon one's view of the present situation. Those who consider that since 1945 it has been and, despite a loosening of ties, continues to be "bipolar" should conclude that the successive emergence of several new blocs of continental dimensions must transform the situation (as, certainly, would be the case given our criteria of Chapter 5). Those who instead interpret the predominance of the two Superpowers as a transient postwar phenomenon should probably judge the adding of new blocs not to be a change of the same order of importance as that brought about by the development of long-range thermonuclear weapons: at present there are two Superpowers, a few second-ranking Powers, and a gradation down to several score dwarf states; in the envisaged situation, there might be from three to six or seven Superpowers, a few important but nominally second-class (would this include "non-continental" Japan?), and still a large number of dwarf states.

Changes within the new blocs and within the polities of the nations making up their membership would of course be considerable. Suppose the United Kingdom had merged its identity in a Western European federation. Much of the insignia of nationality might remain, as at present there remain between Scotland and England constitutionally enshrined differences in minor aspects of law, ecclesiastical establishment, and custom. But, though there might still be Houses of Parliament at Westminster and a Court of St. James, the making of foreign, military, and economic policy, and important lawmaking, would be in other hands. In Great Britain for more than two centuries the "nation-state" (though the United Kingdom is three-and-a-half nations in one) has been exemplified, in that the polity has made itself overseer of every aspect of public life that a Power can treat as politically debatable and still leave its subjects free men. A distinguishing feature of this classic Western State-Power (of which France, the Netherlands, and Sweden are also notable instances) is that the legal, the military, later the economic, and always the political realms have bounds that coincide. That coincidence of bounds is what the supranationalists of all varieties wish to see changed, and changed above all in the direction of widening the economic and military bounds under a bureaucratic aegis. But as far as concerns the nature of the wider system of Powers, supranationality is in effect merely another though antipolitical variety of federalism.

The bounds can be imagined as not coinciding in a rather more interesting way. A minority opinion amongst strategic pundits holds that nuclear deterrence loses credibility the wider the bounds of the military realm: since, they say, it is doubtful whether Washington would sacrifice New York for the sake of avenging Paris, it might be unwilling to sacrifice itself for the sake of avenging New York—the bounds of the military sphere may, in a thermonuclear age, need to shrink, so that if Powerhood is a matter of ability to apply military sanctions, a nation-state such as the USA might come to contain a dozen or twenty or fifty deterrent "Powers," each including a high concentration of population separable as a nuclear target from that of other similar "Powers" within the USA.

If such a change in internal-political systems were to occur, the nature of relations in the external Power system would indeed be transformed—or else the thermonuclear aspect of military force, having shrunken into a thousand independent municipal deterrents, would have lost all importance. These happy outcomes are quite unlikely, for a reason which, though it tells likewise against all supranationalism and against world-unifying aspirations, we have not yet discussed. This is the self-conserving potential of well-established Powers, especially those comprising stable polities: it is not easy, for example, to imagine the USA joining an Atlantic, let alone a worldwide, federation.

Because above all this volume is concerned with political relations between Powers, our definition of Chapter 4 specifies at considerable length the conditions for internal unity—every item except 1.142, 1.1421,

1.2, and 1.31 deals with that. The conditions of and inspiration for a Power's unity-in-spirit have not yet, in the present writer's view, been cogently discerned and verified, let alone explained: even Karl Deutsch's hypothesis of intercommunication[4] seems more to describe than to explain the phenomenon. But his and other work does suggest (1) that dynamic stability in a Power's internal polity increases its capacity to damp down nontechnological systemic change in the Power relationship in which it participates; and conversely (2) that the more equilibrating the process of interaction between Powers, the more favorable the conditions for their several internal evolutions toward stable internal polity.

Those joint hypotheses suggesting reciprocal "feedback" between stabilizing political systems, internal and external, are mentioned here because they are pertinent to our previous hypothesis of irrelevance, and as other ways of formulating, after a general discussion, the kind of question that it raises. We shall argue below that it is possible to design quantitative measures of stability and instability in external systems. Supposing it would be possible also to design such measures for internal systems, then our hypothesis of irrelevance could be adapted to empirical testing, and not merely discussed as a speculation. Decisive results either way would certainly further the theory of dynamics.

We have been considering the systemic effects of possible departures from the coincidence in territorial and populational bounds of the several criteria of Powerhood, both essential and accidental, mentioned in our definition of Chapter 4; and conversely, the conditions promoting that coincidence. The implications of great changes of population should now be looked at.

Some of these have already been dealt with in our review of supranationalist proposals. We could be confident (to take an improbable example) that if the population of a unified and advancing Indo-Chinese area grew in three or four generations to 500 million and formed a supranational bloc, the nature of the world system would not be much affected, though the South Asian balance of power undoubtedly would. More puzzling problems arise in considering even longer-run implications of sharply differentiating population changes.

Suppose that while populations of partly European descent, and those of other largely Westernized countries—e.g., Japan—level off, those of Asian nations, especially of India and China, continue to grow until together they exceed four billion and comprise at least two-thirds of the global population. Suppose further that Communist China alone of those populous states achieves preponderance of technological power. Holding constant the conditions for a continuation of the present thermo-

[4] See, e.g., Deutsch's *Nationalism and Social Communication* (New York: John Wiley & Sons, 1953), *passim*.

nuclear stand-off, would that kind of Chinese predominance fundamentally change the world Power system?

Once again, our answer is "No," provided that a new bipolarization, produced by a combination of most other advanced Powers against the Chinese, is not to be regarded as a fundamental change. But if we remove the assumption of continuing thermonuclear stand-off, and suppose instead a reversion to the balancing of much more limited military force (assuming megaton weapons to have been considered unusable in support of policy) the resultant change in world-political relations would obviously be systemic: a different combination of populational and strategic change is thus expected to have a different *order* of effect.

The foregoing speculation is intended merely to illustrate the possibility that, though the internal-political disposition of Powers may not, of themselves, much affect the inter-Power system, combinations of such changes with other large-scale alterations—e.g., in population, in technology—are quite another matter. The comparatively crude and simple argumentation of our theory of dynamics would have to be much refined if the probably impossible enterprise of prediction for several decades ahead were ever to be carried out.

SECTION IV

THEORY OF STATICS

EIGHT

The Theory of Statics and the Enterprise of Quantification

The subject matter of the theory of statics is the interaction of Powers *within* a system, or at least their interaction in a systematic fashion. The time scale of statics (using the terminology of our first chapter, pp. 10–12) includes the "era"—the duration of a distinct constellation of major Powers—and also the longer "period," "in which various regions of the world maintain despite gradual change a certain relative order of importance." The "era" may last as long as a generation, the predominance of a region as long as one or two centuries; but because the era is the basic duration for the study of interaction between Powers, the time scale of statics is characteristically that of the cooperation and conflict of human purposes. A few statesmen have remained in control of policy for as long as a generation; sometimes, as we have already observed, the tradition of statecraft can be perpetuated in a fortunately situated Power for as long as one or two centuries. Thus, in contrast with the typical explanation which we have employed in the theory of dynamics (i.e., constitutive and compositive explanations), we begin in the theory of statics with motivational explanations and synthesize these at a later stage of analysis into the constitutive and compositive forms.

We pointed out in the preceding chapters, especially the last, that some explanations in dynamics are logically dependent upon the development of models in statics to a point where the latter can show how and why equilibrating processes evinced in the interaction of Powers have broken down. For this and for several other reasons an adequate theory of statics must be more complicated than that of dynamics: even in systems of the same kind, displaying only minor differences in numbers (e.g., between five- and six-Power systems) or in dimensions, it may not be possible to generalize about interactions—distinct models may well be required even for such small differences of degree. In those circumstances it seems overwhelmingly probable that the theory of statics will never be completed. Nevertheless, we devote this and following chapters to seeing how far, on certain lines of approach, it may be advanced.

Three approaches, two of them already in common use, and various combinations of these, are now to be considered. All the distinguishable combinations are quantitative, at least in intent. The present chapter therefore begins with a philosophic and methodological review of difficulties in and objections to the quantitative approach to external politics as such. The chapter concludes with an examination of an instance of one of the three approaches—that to which we attach the label "inductionist": the collecting and correlating of statistics about international behavior. Broadly speaking, our objection is made, not to the useful enterprise of collecting and correlating, but to the inductionist conviction that correlations are or can be refined into explanations. Such an approach stops short of explaining, though it provides invaluable quantitative *explicanda* for qualitative explanation.

We devote a separate chapter in the present section to theorists who have employed, and to one who has criticized, the assumption that there exist "real" or "objective" or even physical probabilities inherent in purposive actions (as distinct from the phenomena of behavior which derive from actions). That probabilistic approach is sometimes combined with another and quite different one—the pure game-theoretical approach—though the two are, as we shall maintain, incompatible, except of course in the case where a game-theoretical solution enjoins mixed strategies.

The approach of game theory is considered in several distinct subdivisions. In Chapter 10, we analyze a two-person model under conditions (cf. Chapter 2 above) of real uncertainty about the future. This leads us to the difficult methodological problem of representing the way the contenders impute points of view to each other.

In Chapter 11 we raise a crucial question for statics—the theory of alliances or coalitions, and examine an approach through the theory of *n*-person games. Concluding that in the path of orthodox game-theoretical solutions for alliance-games there are insuperable obstacles, we examine but are at last compelled to reject a recent promising "short cut" to the theory of coalitions.

Since, then, demonstrative game-theoretical solutions, whether orthodox or unorthodox, seem unavailable, we discuss as a third approach certain Monte Carlo methods of exploring the theory of statics and especially of formation of alliances, by the playing of table-stakes games, directly by human players.

Eminent critics of all three approaches and their combinations have charged them with heteronomy—that is, the importation of alien categories into the study of external political action, and the failure to employ or to illuminate that category itself. Our subsequent analyses are intended as an answer to part of that accusation, by showing how the various game-theoretical approaches open out in their ultimate elaboration toward a synthesis of quantitative and qualitative reasoning, which has analogies with the style of thought characteristic of action in the realm of external politics. Therefore our discussion of the problems of statics culminates in the sketching of a theory of negotiation, which begins to bring us back to the world of Powers and of the statesmen who in "conversation" represent them, introduced in our first four chapters.

In the following Section I, we put a case that anything worth calling a science of politics must be qualitative. It is intended to represent a philosophic attitude which, while seeming generally valid despite the recent advances of quantitative behavioral politics, makes no claim to supply a critique on their own terms of the quantitative approaches.

I

Politics is action, not behavior; or, if "political behavior" is a fitting characterization of something that does go on, it characterizes only those consequential, passive processes that necessarily accompany and follow from the political act. (The behavior of subhuman animals cannot be "political" upon this understanding, for they do not act, politically or otherwise.) Much behavior, doubtless including political behavior, is numerable —ordinally if not cardinally—so that there *is* scope for the study of numerical patterns in political behavior. But that study cannot possibly constitute the science of politics: no study is a science until it explains; political behavior is consequent upon political action, and explicable only if action is explicable; but not vice versa, at least not necessarily or wholly. Action on the other hand is not numerable; all attempts to impose number upon it betray their own arbitrariness. Even that temporal and logical order which is of the essence of action—"before, after," "prior to, subsequent to," "in intent"— affords no ground for the meaningful assignment of ordinal numbers to actions.

"But voting is an act, and votes can be counted." Precisely: the effects (ballot-papers) and the instances (occasions on which the voter voted) are countable; but whenever some citizen's voting can be fittingly styled "a political act," the concern of political science can be only with his intentions in voting as he did—with "Why?" The explanation of an act can only be qualitative. All political action is explicable by, and only by, reference to the political end in view. But the explanation of a political man's having a particular end in view and therefore acting requires as context an interpretation of the current constellation of his political ends. Such a constellation is describable only as an historian would describe it —in literary, i.e., qualitative, terms. The scientific study of politics must be explanatory, and the explanation of political action can in the end be nothing but qualitative historical explanation.

Yet the political actor at least sometimes prefers one genuinely political end to another genuinely political end. And since one pair of these ends can be ordered (i.e., into his first and his second preferences), why not the whole constellation? But once it is so ordered, we may be able to arrange a thought-experiment which would allow us to translate that ordinal array into a finite allotment of cardinally numerable political values (cf. the capitulation point in Chapter 6). The scope of political interaction afforded by any political system, however, is likely to upset the "rational" ordering of one's political preferences, even while inducing one to choose (or at least to come to prefer) one of a pair rather than the other. We shall not understand political behavior unless we assume as the usual or typical case a citizen-politician whose schedule of preferences is partly but only partly rationalized. He is not absolutely irrational—he does not prefer A to B *and* B to A; A to C *and* C to A; B to C *and* C to B. He is not absolutely rational—he does not, as might a wholly rational creature, prefer A to B; B to C; A to C; and A to B and C. But he may prefer A to B, B to C, but C to A; or, more likely, A to B and C, but perhaps B to C *and* C to B. Further, he is not bound forever by any particular irrationality—sooner or later he will sort out his preferences for B and C. But by that time a new end (or object of preference), D, may well have presented itself to him—if he did not allow it to, he would be not irrational but mad—bringing for the time being another potential source of paradox and contradiction into his schedule, so that perhaps he then prefers A to B, C, and D; but B to D, D to C, and C to B. Meanwhile he will have to have kept on acting, from a constellation of political ends that, until he resigns and writes his autobiography, is perhaps never really well ordered. Explanations of political action begin from descriptions of individuals' always imperfectly ordered, occasionally revised, and occasionally augmented constellations of ends. But as was contended in Chapter 3, after discussing motivational explanation, political theory like history is built compositively from accounts of action.

Thus, such explanation of the actions of individuals is necessary to the science of Power politics, but not sufficient. Statesmen are not, as such, creative artists. Each, acting out of his vision and from his constellation of ends, interacts with the others; and these interactions produce—sometimes they *are*—resultants often unintended, rarely intended. An explanatory account of those unintended resultants is an essential of the science of Power politics in its historical aspect, and constitutes a model of the system of Powers as it actually is evolving.

That science nevertheless is not simply historical. The imagination that lets us enter into past thought, action, and system can construct models of Power systems that have never existed, and in them foreshadow deeds that have never been done. Logically, there can be no distinction of type between models that approximate actuality and models that do not at all. Whether or not models are ever needed for explanation, some will be needed for prediction—supposing that the other conditions necessary for prediction are obtainable. To the degree that any model needed for prediction has to be specified quantitatively, a similar quantitative specification, very likely corrected somewhat, will be required for the model when used after the event in explanation of it.

Further, to the extent that the event, as *explicandum,* can be adequately characterized partly or wholly in quantities, the *explicans* must also be quantified—though of course, in that kind of explaining, it may well turn out that we never get anything better than an explanation sketch. The quantifiers have succeeded impressively with some cases of power-political behavior, but action, of its nature, has eluded them.

Nor are single actions the only *explicanda* that there is little point in quantifying: systemic change, for instance, is often a unique process. Most experts would now agree that, whereas the Power system is much changed by each of the first few nuclearizations of particular Powers, the motives for acquiring nuclear weapons differ for different Powers, even for the same Power at different times, and that while two or three well defined conditions are necessary for nuclearization, we know of no set of conditions sufficient for it, or even adequate for a fairly reliable prediction. Admittedly, on the rare occasions when a particular Power system settles into more or less stable equilibrium, we have some idea of how a formalized or mathematicized account of that system would look. But most of the time most systems are being changed, sometimes changed in unique and novel ways, and often changed by the acts of no more than a handful of leaders. After the event, historical explanations of such singular changes can sometimes be found, but so far the adequate ones have always taken a literary, qualitative form.

To recapitulate: if we could develop a genuine science of Power politics (and thus far we have only the rudiments of it), its core would be qualitative, because first and foremost it would have to incorporate—or at least furnish the leading ideas for—the explanation of political *acts;* and because secondly the explanation of much *inter*action is similarly qualitative. (Even in dynamic theory, when we explain a change in the quality of a system by the fact that one new member was added—i.e., quantitatively—our explanation will always presuppose qualitative facts—e.g., about dispositions to further one's Power's interests.) There is a place for quantitative thinking about power-political *behavior;* but that, as has been argued, is a phenomenon dependent upon and resulting from political action.

Nevertheless, the core of power-political science—the "pure science of Power politics"—is merely a slim axis, though a controlling one, in the body of the subject as a whole. Beyond the qualitative core, the scope for quantifying is virtually unlimited. This is not to say that it would always be cogent, or very significant, or in every case worth the trouble. However, adventures in quantification are bound to be frequent during the next decade or so in many branches of international studies, and we shall now examine a promising instance.

II

It is no longer a plausible criticism that political scientists quantifying world affairs merely reproduce in statistical disguise what everyone knows already. Hayward R. Alker, Jr., referring to voting support at the 16th General Assembly (1961–62) for motions enjoining supranationalist tasks upon the UN, points to the "universal" correlation *between* votes cast in favor of such motions *and* percentage of previous trade with either the USA or France or the UK.[1] In another paper of the same date, he adds the following information:

> The Arab states increase in their supranationalist voting [correlation coefficient of $r = 0.87$] at an even higher rate than the universal one . . . [$r = 0.55$]. For other regional categories of states, in particular the Soviet Bloc ($r = -0.24$) and [the USA + South Africa + Western Europeans + white British Commonwealth =] Old Europeans ($r = -0.20$), the higher traders with the West [i.e., with USA + France + UK] are *less* likely to support supranationalist positions. . . . In these latter areas Western

[1] "Dimensions of Conflict in the General Assembly," *American Political Science Review,* LXVIII: 3 (September 1964), 654–56.

trade appears to *decrease* supranationalist voting, while among Arabs and Latin American [$r = 0.40$] it tends to *increase* UN supranationalism.[2]

Incidentally, the "supranationalist" resolutions dealt with "nuclear testing, economic aid, the renewal of the Committee on Information from Non-Self-Governing Territories, . . . votes on Rwanda and Burundi, and most of the questions regarding the financing of the Congo Operation."

I selected this particular correlation for examination because it interested me more than any other in the two above-mentioned papers by Alker (his and Bruce M. Russett's large work, *World Politics in the General Assembly,* not being available in Australia at the time of this composition). It is fair to point out that the methodological objections concerning it did not occur to me until after I had begun to write of it as an example of the interesting discoveries that might be made through the quantitative approach. *World Politics in the General Assembly* provides other such examples, but I have been able to discover none as compact at this. The important point about it is the non-obviousness of the correlation: the methodological difficulty about it can be generalized for any hypothesis about politics that seems to equate a correlation (or any combination, however complex, of correlations) with explanation—as will be argued later. Meanwhile, the following are some of the striking features of Alker's discovery of a relationship between Arab and Latin American pro-supranationalist voting and the percentage of previous trade by countries in those regional groupings with the Western Big Three.

Firstly, the correlation of Arab and Latin American voting for UN supranationalism with a percentage of US-or-French-or-UK trade is *surprising*—it certainly had not struck me before, and I have made some study of the UN at this period. Secondly and more importantly, a practically necessary condition for making this kind of empirical discovery is the employment of quantitative methods and analyses of a complex and sophisticated kind. (I had originally styled it a "necessary condition" without qualification. That was a mistake in logic, since it should be theoretically possible to state any relationship in many different ways, including qualitative ones. Nevertheless, it seems a practical certainty that political analysts working with a coarser mesh than that of such quantitative models as Alker's and Russett's would not have stumbled upon so recherché an association.) In other words, the (non-additive) quantitative form of this correlation is not just an incidentally more precise way of stating what could have been translated without loss of information into ordinary qualitative English—the form is practically indispensable for communicating the substance.

Thirdly, the fact of the correlation would presumably have come as a

[2] "The Long Road to Mathematical Theories of International Politics: Problems of Statistical Non-Additivity," republished in *World Politics,* 1966.

discovery to the "supranationalist" supporters themselves: the Arab delegate, even though possessed of the information that his own state traded heavily with one or more of the Western three, and that his fellows in the Arab group were likely to be supporting, say, finance for UNOC, would hardly connect the one and the other. That a correlation holds whether or not the actors themselves are conscious that it does is a necessary though not a sufficient condition for the correlation's candidature to the status of a law of society (cf. the more notable "economic laws"). Alker clearly has in mind the raising of his correlations to some such status, for in the *A.P.S.R.* paper he points out:

> A significant finding is that in each of the two main geopolitical conflicts, *trade, not aid,* is the better predictor of voting behaviour.[3]

One of the "two main geopolitical conflicts" is that between East and West—*viz.,* between the USA and USSR, each with their entourages of allies, satellites, and clients. This factor of East-West conflict "accounted for"—i.e., correlated "about 64% of 'explainable' voting alignments"[4] in the 16th Assembly. The other factor is styled "North *versus* South," and envinces a conflict between developed countries (preeminently the USSR and its bloc) and underdeveloped countries, the majority of which of course are located in the Southern Hemisphere. Overlapping (as far as one can judge) the North-South conflict is the anti-*versus*-pro-supranationalist issue mentioned above.

Furthermore, in the *denouement* of the article, he argues,

> American foreign aid has increased in its relevance to the Cold War struggle in the UN, but still remains fairly uncorrelated in a world-wide basis with this conflict. If it were to become highly correlated in this manner, an effective neutral and supranationalist role for the anti-colonial countries would be increasingly difficult. . . . The Soviet Union failed significantly to make the Congo crisis into an anti-European and anti-American self-determination issue, although she and the Casablanca states tried to do so. Many of the elements of such a conflict were certainly there; but fortunately (for us) Russia misperceived Afro-Asian and American supranationalist predispositions. . . . The American opportunity—and challenge for our policy-makers—is to persuade others and ourselves of the United Nations' universal supranationalist possibilities.[5]

Thus the argument seems to have been that by playing upon the Afro-Asians' willingness to support a supranationalist role for the UN, which the Soviet bloc was opposing at the 1961 Assembly, the United States could enlist more Afro-Asian Powers on its own side in the East-West conflict; and (directly to our point) that a large measure of trade with the USA, the UK, or France, would dispose Latin Americans and

[3] Alker, p. 654.
[4] *Ibid.,* p. 647.
[5] *Ibid.,* p. 657.

Arabs particularly to favor the UN-supranationalist interest—i.e., Alker regards that connection between trading patterns and Arab-Latin voting patterns not just as a correlation to be explained, but as itself a promising candidate for the status of a causal explanation. In the "Long Road . . ." address, replying to an objection that factors such as trade impinge differentially (display a "regional slope effect") on distinguishable political groupings, and that such differences may be the causally significant ones, he points out that

> . . . the non-additive "slopes effect" accounts for only about 5% of the rather high (76%) *explanatory power* of this simple "regional contingency hypothesis" relating trading inter-relationships to supranationalist voting in the United Nations.

Alker adopts[6] Herbert Simon's method "of algebraically deriving predictions from causal models," while noticing[7] that "several different causal models"—e.g., both "intervening" and *spurious* correlations "make the same predictions," and that the assumptions of various causal models may "always be proved wrong at some future date by the poor fit of model predictions with actual data."

It is at this point in the quantifying enterprise, where *explanatory power* is ascribed *simpliciter* to high and surprising correlations between some nonpolitical, temporarily prior condition and the pattern of political action by members of a politically distinguishable group, that one begins to demur again.

Firstly, though (I agree) the explanatory power of an explanatory hypothesis can be measured (with results that conform very well indeed to common everyday usage of expressions like "a powerful explanation") by various recently designed algebraic indices, it does not follow, simply from the obtaining of a high score on some such index, that an hypothesis is an explanatory hypothesis: it must also, and initially, *increase understanding.*

Another of Alker's high-scoring hypotheses does just that though not to any great degree: being a military ally of the United States correlates very highly with voting on the US side at the 1961 Assembly, and one can understand why—so much so that one would be surprised if on that issue the correlation were not high. But the high trade-supranationalist correlation, for Arabs and Latins, is surprising and worth the trouble of discovering—in short, cries out for explanation—just because as an hypothesis it does *not,* merely by being formulated, promise to increase our understanding of why Arabs and Latins voted as they did on this issue. How could heavy trade with the USA *or* the UK *or* France (one of whom was strongly for, one of whom was highly dubious about, and the

[6] H. R. Alker, *Mathematics and Politics* (New York: The Macmillan Company, 1965), Chapter 6, pp. 112–29.

[7] *Ibid.*, p. 125.

last more and more disapproving of the methods of conducting UNOC in August and in December 1961) dispose ten Arab Powers to support UN supranationalist activities? One imagines oneself in the position of an Arab delegate, and cannot make the connection between two issues which, qualitatively *a priori,* seem to have nothing to do with each other.

It is impossible, in political studies, entirely to replace these qualitative and imaginative ventures in understanding by quantitative (even non-additive) indices of explanatory power. We know on the one hand of any number of adequate, strong, and demonstrable explanations which are qualitative; and on the other hand, we draw up an array of those hypotheses which, whether explanatory or not, might reduce the variance remaining in a finite and well ordered tabulation of some exhaustively listed assemblage of historical facts (such as Table I in Alker's *A.P.S.R.* article, where the roll-calls of the 16th Assembly are objectively correlated with voting components). Further, qualitative explanations (or at least, explanation sketches) are indispensable for the *direction* of quantitative inquiry: (1) Since we already understand very well why Soviet-bloc states voted nearly always with the USSR even on the supranationalist issue, we do not look for further explanation of that very high correlation: we look rather for explanations of why it is not 100 per cent—in terms of "missed signals," "inadvertent absence," etc. (2) We need a qualitative "world-picture" of preliminary imaginative explanations, in terms, e.g., of political interests and motives, to develop arrays of initial (or *"a priori"* or "unconditional") likelihoods of political actions by states, since any satisfactory algebraic index of explanatory power somewhere within its structure employs the ratio between an event's initial or unconditional probability (P e), and its probability when given a hypothetically explanatory condition (P c,e).[8] The contention of Raiffa *et al.*[9]—that, in ignoring subjective estimates of initial probabilities of actions, one is simply throwing away promising information—seems sound.

Since, then, in choosing conditions for the role of independent variables, we have to imagine qualitatively plausible explanation sketches, I suggest, as at least a useful safety precaution for quantifiers of Power politics, that one admits to candidature for *explanatory* power (in contrast with close connectibility *simpliciter*) only those hypotheses for which one can recite an initially plausible chain of argument by which the actor *could* have connected the hypothecated condition to the action which he takes. For example: "I am the delegate of Arab State *A,* which trades heavily with (USA-or-UK-or-France) . . . *therefore* I shall support the maintenance and increase of the UN's supranational functions." The dots indicate the missing "chain of argument." A chain of some though not

[8] See above, Chapter 3, *passim.*

[9] H. Raiffa and R. Schlaifer, *Applied Statistical Decision Theory* (Cambridge: Harvard University Press, 1961).

much plausibility could be produced if "*or*-UK-*or*-France" were struck out of the above, and there were inserted, "It will pay us to please our trading partner; the USA would be pleased by our supporting its policy of UN supranationalism." But presumably, *that* hypothesis would fail in its aspirations to explanatory power for a "quantitative" reason: trade with the US alone has some but not much correlation with pro-supranationalist voting![10]

To summarize: high scoring on some index of correlation is not enough to make an hypothesis explanatory. It must also explain.

Being unprepared to regard trade with the Western Big Three as even a candidate for explanation of the Arabs' and Latins' pro-supranationalist voting, I must accept the onus for suggesting explanations of the puzzlingly high correlations: Arab States had benefited much by UN supranationalist action at Suez (which of course pleased the USA, but was wryly received by the French and British governments); most of them had been not displeased with the limited UN responses over Jordan and Lebanon, the latter of which had not wholly satisfied Washington; well before the convocation of the 16th Assembly, several of the ten Arab States had taken the lead in initiating UNOC along lines much in accord with Hammarskjöld's thinking—Mongi Slim, the Tunisian delegate on the Security Council, had been a proponent of the three enabling resolutions (14 and 22 July, and 9 August, 1960). In short, six years' political experience had inclined most of the Arab States to vigorous support of UN supranationalist activity: that most of them traded extensively with both France and Britain was *sheer coincidence*—if, indeed, by 1961 those trading connections were not mitigating against their supranational attitudes.

The foregoing is an explanation sketch: it requires amplification, and substantiation by evidence. But if those could be provided, it would *explain away* the surprising correlation, and would do so by providing qualitative, historical, idiosyncratic explanations.[11] But even thus ex-

[10] Alker, *A.P.S.R.*, Table IV, p. 654.

[11] Pp. 162–163 may suggest that I assume that all high correlations are *either* self-explanatory (e.g., the USA's military allies voting with it against the USSR; the Soviet bloc voting with the USSR against the UN supranationalists) *or* are to be explained away by several qualitative, particularist accounts of why the individual members of a group of Powers adopted their several policies. I do *not* suppose that those are the only alternatives: for instance, one can sometimes detect a previously unsuspected *rationale* that helps explain a surprising high correlation—a nation, or group of nations, is under some common precondition which correlates highly and suprisingly with its political actions, and then it turns out that the nation (or group) has some very good though *recherché* reason, connected with the precondition, for taking just such a policy line. That—and not the mere prospect of explaining away a correlation—is what makes the work of the quantifiers inviting to the qualitative theorist, and perhaps involves the quantifiers in going beyond their data and formulating hypothetico-deductive explanations on their own account.

plained away, the correlation can hardly be called "spurious": it is not as though there were some prior third variable correlated with and explanatory of both the terms in the correlation. That is another ground for dissatisfaction with the explication, which Alker adopted from Simon, of the ideas of "cause" and "explanation." I believe that the weaker correlation in respect of the Latin Americans' voting can also be explained away historically.

Alker's application of covariance analysis, which we have been criticizing, has significance for policy-making—a significance brought out by Alker himself in the passage from his A.P.S.R. article on the predictive power of "trade, not aid." I think it would be agreed that since 1961, United States policy in the UN has been pursued on assumptions resembling Alker's both in substance and in form—e.g., the US endeavored to retain initiative and leadership in the pro-supranationalist group opposing both the Soviet bloc and the European ex-imperialists, and to turn this leadership to advantage in her confrontation with the Soviet Union by insisting on the application of Charter Article 19 (the paying of dues that would finance Assembly-authorized peace-keeping operations). That policy may have fallen short of success because of an oversight in its making analogous with the oversight that we seem to have detected in Alker's model-building: in trying to manipulate groupings of nations—groupings discernible in the way members line up from time to time on issues in General Assembly voting—a major Power's policy-maker is apt to overlook the individual nation's peculiar viewpoint which, in the same way though probably not to the same degree as his own, can help explain past processes in the Assembly, and perhaps help predict future ones. The requirement suggested above—i.e., that no condition can be explanatory unless (directly, or after decomposition if *the explicandum* is an interaction of several parties) it can be plausibly imputed as a reasonable motive to some individual member of what are after all rather small aggregations (ten Arab, nineteen Latin American states)—may be paralleled by the maxim that the several and distinct attitudes of one's potential allies and opponents should be taken note of as carefully as the composition and behavior of the more or less temporary grouping into which they enter.

The quantitative data which Alker analyzes is enlightening when presented in completeness—i.e., initially as all the roll calls of the kind he deals with, for every meeting of the General Assembly from the first one onward, and including the votes of each member-nation for all roll-calls. The "factors"—groupings of members on various issues discernible in the subject matter of the motions voted on—could be displayed for each year. We would thereby possess a quantified chronicle for Alker's entire universe of discourse. For first-order empirical correlations (which the study of world politics has thus far gone in want of) this would provide much more severe tests and, therefore, if they passed them, stronger evidential support. It would also provide more promising arrangements of data for the testing of synthesizing models of the General Assembly *system.* There can be no objection to quantification, or to correlation of quantities, provided that in the process no eccentric information is lost, and provided it avoids the fallacy of inductionism—that if one takes enough data, and rearranges it in enough different ways, sooner or later explanations are bound to come out.

On the other hand, as we have suggested above, the *devisers* of explanatory models tend to be so concerned with the internal consistency of their models, and with the order that they bring into one's thinking about the world-political system, that they neglect to formulate their model-scale hypotheses in ways that make them easy to set against the evidence, and more particularly to be testable by a "crucial" observation—i.e., the kind of observation which *either* disagrees with consequences of the model and therefore undermines the model as an explanatory hypothesis, *or* by fitting well with a prediction derived from the model, confirms it. This pitfall in systemic model-building can be avoided. But there are other, intrinsic limitations upon the building of would-be explanatory models—e.g., inability to conform with the Postulates of Rationality; generation of orders of numbers that will never be calculable in practice; the intractibility of "surprise" and of creative novelty. These seem to be insuperable, and, thus, a *general* advance along those lines impossible. But there may be approaches along certain lines that do not strike these limitations, or that postpone their onset.

This chapter has dealt with quantitative enterprises concerned only with a special time scale—"two to twenty years" was mentioned. More could have been said about longer time scales: the evolution and revolutionary change of power-political systems may turn out to be more readily quantifiable and more easily explicable than are intrasystem changes—e.g., changes of alliance and of the balance of power.

Nothing, on the other hand, has been said about quantification on a short time scale—e.g., minute analyses of brief crises like that preceding the outbreak of the First World War. (Even Alker's 16th Assembly met for nine months.) On general grounds it seems likely, however, that even in the management of the most urgent crisis, long-term intrasystemic considerations will not be wholly set aside; so the middle time range may be necessarily prefatory to the shorter one. There seems little possibility of transfer of method from one time scale to the other. Indeed, much of the apparent contention between methodologists arises from ignoring the time scale issue. Decision theory, for example, is more likely to have application in the shorter than in the middle time range, and can of course not apply at all in the range of a century or more.

NINE

The Concept of Probability Misapplied

In the previous chapter we examined an interesting application by H. R. Alker, Jr., of data derived from an extremely complicated system of inter-Power relations—*viz.,* voting in the UN General Assembly. Alker stops short of attributing to the actions which he analyzes and correlates in quantitative terms intrinsic or real or objective probability. In the present chapter we shall review the work of theorists who in one way or another do seem to make that attribution, and also of one theorist-critic with whose conclusions we shall on the whole agree, while disagreeing with some of his arguments.

No objection is offered here against the *subjective* application of the Calculus of Probability to actions: indeed, we do just that in the hermeneutic analysis of historical explanation in Chapter 3. What is under attack in this chapter is the practical consequence of a metaphysical conviction—that while perhaps some classes of events are determined or necessitated, all members of all other classes "happen by chance" of varying degrees of objective probability; and that amongst the latter set of classes of "chance events" are human actions. We reject that in favor of distinctions close to those of the 1647 Confession of Faith of the Westminster Assembly, according to which (V:2) "all things . . . fall out according to the nature of second causes, either necessarily, freely or contingently." In that threefold categorization, we place actions under the rubric of those events which "fall out . . . freely" and neither "necessarily" (*viz.*, deterministically) nor "contingently" (*viz.*, probabilistically in the objective sense).

Metaphysical differences are relevant to political theory, not of course immediately or of themselves, but because of the differences they induce in the arrays of views of the real world which are made visible under their several lights, and which guide the actions of those who hold them. The objectionable feature of the kind of probabilism here attacked is that it induces its believer to act as though his own (or his side's) actions are free while all others', as it were, "happen by chance"—chance to which an objective probability measure can be attached. Many well-intentioned reformers hold such views: "Find the probabilities of actions by Powers; calculate the resultant probabilities for all possible outcomes; then act so as to maximize *our* expected value." Exactly the same formula is applied by nonreformers in what they believe to be particular national interests.

At a second and more sophisticated level, it is argued from the evidence of certain matrices in the Theory of Games: "The meet or outcome of two pure dominant strategies, since rational players *must* employ just them, has to be a deterministic event; *pari passu* the meet of two mixed strategies is an array of alternative events, determined probabilistically; once a rational player—as he must—has adopted the correctly calculated strategic mix, the outcome is out of his own and his opponent's hands, and in the hands of chance." This second line of argument is at first sight extremely convincing, and might purport to provide a rationale for a sophisticated probabilistic approach to politics. It has seemed worthwhile to attempt a criticism and refutation of the whole approach *via* objective probabilities, before going on to consider the contention that from the Theory of Games there can be developed a complete theory of competition and cooperation.

Lewis F. Richardson in *Statistics of Deadly Quarrels,*[1] calculated the statistical probability that at least one of the "quarrels" which resulted in 3,163 or more deaths and which began between 1820 and 1929 would have broken out in any given one of those years. From that and from similar findings of "mathematical history" he hoped to discover both the causation (perhaps remediable) of such deadly quarrels, and also their incidence, if not remedied, in the future.

Richardson's conclusions (inferred from but by no means identical with his findings of statistical probability) could be inputs for practical military planning: they could influence the planner's guesses about the

[1] L. F. Richardson, *Statistics of Deadly Quarrels,* ed. Q. Wright and C. C. Lienau (London: Stevens & Sons, 1960).

"likeliness" of alternative Soviet actions—influence, but never replace them. It is not merely that Richardson's original data are often ambiguous in themselves, sometimes perversely characterized or out of perspective, and never the whole story (Richardson disavowed exhaustiveness for them). It is rather a matter of logic, and of logical category: first, even if a war begun in 1968 by Soviet attack were to prove assignable to the same *class* of event as were Richardson's deadly quarrels 1820–1929, no probability statement about the latter *set* of events could be applied to or extended to the 1968 situation. And supposing, secondly, that there were many more kinds of, and better-tested, statistical generalizations than even Richardson's diligence has been able to afford us, we would still be unable to devise a law of combination of social forces enabling us to calculate the resultant Soviet behavior. A planner's statements of subjective probability are at best quantitative and mutually consistent expressions of the planner's guesses about future Soviet behavior. Richardson's are statements about what proportions of a set of past events belong to which various subclasses of warlike and peaceful events.

The arms races of 1908–14 and 1929–38 are examined and reexamined in Richardson's *Arms and Insecurity*.[2] He begins with a pair of comparatively simple equations, in which either party varies his own defense effort directly with the product of "the menaces by which he is surrounded" (chiefly, others' defense efforts) and a constant called the "defence-coefficient." The next step is to introduce a countervailing constant "representing the fatigue and expense of keeping up defences." Thirdly, a positive element—the effect of "grievances"—is included in every contestant's equation. Lastly, another and important countervailing element, representing participation in foreign trade, is taken in. This last-mentioned, apparently inappropriate quantity was brought in partly because Richardson's mathematical tastes called for a formal contrary of threatening armaments, and partly because, like the good liberal he was, Richardson believed that trade was something from which both parties stood to benefit. Now, given four such terms (some incalculable and several of opposed tendencies), a formula certainly can be found flexible enough for any competition in armament—whether the competitors are spending more, or less, than pound-for-pound against each other. So Richardson made the theoretically crucial move, by inventing the first quantitative rationale for a class of contests that many in an obscure way already knew to be quantitative.

Compared with the significance of his achievement, it does not matter that he made a rather poor choice of indices: for instance, he included no strictly *military* terms, even after such broad hints as the naval

[2] L. F. Richardson, *Arms and Insecurity,* ed. N. Rashevsky and E. Trucco, (London: Stevens & Sons, 1960).

race of the 1910s and the naval disarmament of the 1920s. He seems to have been overanxious to produce explanations and predictions of actual trends in the gross—the arms expenditure of European nations before 1941, and of half the world before 1939. We learn from some of his editors[3] that in submitting his 1939 study to an American journal (which rejected it), "Richardson urged that the paper be published immediately because its publication might avert an impending war."

He appears also to have supposed that, whether the arms race involved two or ten nations, each responded to the "lumped" effect of the rest of the world's armament, as that stood at each successive budgetary epoch. These assumptions deprived him both of an understanding of the phenomena of alliances and threats, and of a specific clue to the occasions of outbreak of war. The saddest and most honest pages of a wholly honest book[4] are entitled "The Great Surprise" and refer to the Ribbentrop-Molotov Pact, which should never have come about according to Richardson's index of armament expenditure. (For extensions of a simpler equivalent of Richardson's model, see Chapter 6, pp. 130–145 above.)

To analyze the arms race of the 1960s, we should need an array of terms much more complex than Richardson's. We should have to notice several subcontests—some exponential, some not—in several different *types* of weapon. We should distinguish those contests from the "qualitative" or "technological" arms race—*viz.,* the search for *new* weapon systems. We might notice that secular fluctuations of cost usher Middle Powers into (and later, perhaps, out of) the nuclear club. We might observe how a rise of ten billion dollars in US defense expenditure replies to pressure from and exerts pressure on the USSR, while permitting US government expenditure in acceptable guise.

Statistics of Deadly Quarrels, on the other hand, makes a number of durable contributions to "historical mathematics." One example: Richardson classifies his "quarrels" killing 3,163 or more people 1820–1939 according to the numbers of nations on either side. (Quincy Wright has an independently derived collection of noncivil wars 1480–1941, similarly classified. The two resultant tables are much more alike in their distributions than could be explained by their overlap alone.) Another example from a different domain: bandit-groups in Manchoukuo 1935, arranged according to the logarithm of the number of bandits in each group, relate inversely in the ratio (-2.29) to the logarithm of the number of raids conducted by each size of group. The logarithm of the number of members in Chicago gangs relates inversely in the ratio (-2.30) to the number of gangs per unit range of membership. Both ratios also agree very nicely with that between the number of wars per unit-range of war-dead and

[3] *Arms and Insecurity,* p. ix.
[4] *Ibid.,* p. 211–12.

the numbers of war-dead in Richardson's list of wars 1820–1945. These are regularities of historical fact that ask as pointedly as do economic regularities for theoretical explanation.

In this book Richardson was charier than in the other of offering theories, but he offered one which on publication misled some critics. He hypothecates that the world of quarreling nations is a "chaos restricted by geography and modified by infectiousness" of warfare; and he offers this to explain why wars, throughout his selected century, have occurred in time according to a Poisson distribution—very crudely, as though at random. The anti-military intellectual is apt to seize on this, saying "So the makers of wars, who claim they fight by military calculations and from reasons of state, are shown to be *governed by sheer chance* after all."

The contrast is a false one. The Poisson distribution fits other kinds of event beside "deaths by kick from a horse" and "emission of alpha particles from radioactive substances." In particular, one would expect the conflicts of more or less rationally led armed nations to be distributed in just that way: only a few of the rulers of Powers have deliberately and consistently sought warfare—wars, being standard examples of "unintended consequences of intended interactions," may thus be thought of as *accidental* clashes of purpose, the purposes or purposive actions being, *ex hypothesei,* non-accidental, unlike the failure of different persons' purposes to harmonize. The leader of one Power accidentally puts his state in a position where it comes into conflict with another, as a trooper in the cavalry might accidentally get himself into a position where a horse kicks him.

Glen H. Snyder[5] defines rationality as acting in "the manner which gives best promise of maximizing one's value position, on the basis of a sober calculation of potential gains and losses, and probabilities of enemy actions." ("Values" can include honor, prestige, revenge, and so on.)

Professor Snyder believes that there is a *real probability* of enemy action for his planner to guess at—otherwise, the planner could not even estimate "expected values"—i.e., he must be able to say of a possible enemy response[6] "not less than 10% but not more than 50% probable." Now, contemporary theorists of probability and of decision-making have shown how it is possible to assign "probabilities," on the basis of informed judgment, to an array of alternative outcomes and their antecedents, according to rules that ensure consistency amongst the probabilities and thus enable one to make the most efficient use of one's information, guesses, and judgments (see, for instance, Chapter 3 above, pp. 54–55). Gen-

[5] G. H. Snyder, *Deterrence and Defense: Toward a Theory of National Security* (Princeton and London: Princeton University Press, and Oxford University Press, 1961).

[6] *Ibid.,* p. 30. (The first "not" is lacking in the text.)

erally, one bases one's numerical assignments upon such qualitative judgments as, "The enemy would have such-and-such grounds—far from conclusive ones—for so responding." Most philosophers, however, would agree that it is a mistake in categorization to assign such numbers to one's own acts of policy in the immediate future (cf. the distinction between first-person and third-person sentences). In a quite different sense of "probability" it is sometimes possible to discover physical facts to support a statement of the probability that some planner, sane at present, will become insane. With this kind of probability there is no similar difficulty in assigning a figure to the probability of one's becoming insane oneself. Because of the above considerations I contend, against Professor Snyder, that there cannot be an *objective* probability of a rational agent's response, though there can be of his continuing "rational" in a different sense—*viz.*, sane.

The implications of this disagreement can be brought out by an imaginary example of Snyder's.[7] D is a deterrer, who can either "retaliate massively" or not if an aggressor, A, should launch against D's ally, B, a conventional attack which could not be warded off even by D and B together. If A so attacks, and D retaliates massively, the resultant all-out war will cost both A and D 100 units of utility each. If D does not retaliate massively, he will lose control of B to A—i.e., A will gain and D will lose 20 units. If A does not attack B, no one gains or loses anything.

So far, D seems "rationally compelled" (i.e., induced by considerations of prudence) not to retaliate; and if A takes that as certain, he is rationally impelled to attack. But, Snyder points out, A should be indifferent between attacking and not attacking if he is sure that it is approximately 17 per cent (or exactly one-sixth) probable that D would retaliate. I shall now suppose that D decides to probabilize his response, which was before (as I believe) neither probabilistic nor determined: D connects his retaliation-button to some stochastic device—say a roulette wheel which is set to give an 18 per cent probability of absolutely automatic retaliation by D if A should attack B; and D somehow demonstrates to A that the button is connected and cannot be disconnected.

On Snyder's definition of rationality, D could now be certain that if A is rational, he will not attack. Already the situation is rather bizarre: both A and D must "know" that, given A's "rationality," the probability of A's attacking would be: *100 per cent* if instead he knew that D's roulette wheel was set at 16 per cent or less; *fifty-fifty* (construing ". . . is indifferent between . . ." as ". . . would let even chances determine . . .") if he knew instead that it was just under 17 per cent; and *zero* when he knows it is at 17 per cent or more.

[7] *Ibid.*, pp. 16 *et seq.*

The oddity of the case results from my having made D's response objectively or physically probabilistic, so that A's task is no longer to assess the *reasons* D might have for retaliating or for not retaliating (a task for the imagination), but to ascertain at what precise *odds* D's stochastic device has been set. I think the methodologists of strategy are seduced into confusing those two tasks by the temptingly plausible assimilation of "indifference" to "even chances." One's considerations for and against (say) launching an attack may be so nicely balanced that one might even be prepared to make it depend upon the toss of a coin. But if a new consideration—however minor and inconclusive in itself—comes in on the affirmative side, one presumably decides outright to attack. One does *not* substitute, for the even chances of a coin-toss, the spin of a wheel set at, say, 55 versus 45 (not, that is, unless—in some situation far more closed than that of world security—one deliberately chooses to adopt a mixed strategy as formally defined in game theory; and that would be itself a second-order strategic choice between strategies).

As to *pay-offs:* both A and D now neither "gain" nor "lose"; for D by setting his wheel at 17 per cent has cost A—and saved himself—20 units of expected value. He would have saved himself at least three units even had he estimated A's insanity as 98 per cent objectively probable, given that it is even chances whether or not an insane man presses any button. D could be deterred from thus automating his retaliation at 17 per cent only if A could have got in first with the roulette wheel trick, and had automated the probability that *he* would attack at at least 60 per cent.

But, given 60 per cent probability of A's attacking, D on the one hand had better demonstrate that he will *never* retaliate; for he will then be sure (given he is certain that A is "rational") of an expected value of *minus* twelve units, whereas if he maintains an 18 per cent probability of retaliation, it would be *minus* rather more than 20. A, on the other hand now has about *plus* 12 units expected value. But as he is sure that a "rational" D is certain not to attack provided the probability of A's attacking is at least 60 per cent, it would seem to pay him to raise that probability to 100 per cent (thus guaranteeing himself 20 units), provided he is certain that D will stay rational and therefore generate no probability of insanely retaliating. But the nearer A's attack approaches that unitary probability, the nearer D's expected value approaches *minus* 20 units.

D would have had only one hope of averting such a loss of expectations—*he* should have got in first with the roulette wheel and set it at 100 per cent probability of *retaliation,* demonstrating immediately to A that he had done so. This foreshadows a terrible exponential arms race, in the setting-up and exhibiting of roulette wheels. Alternatively, we could suppose that both A and D had to *choose* whether or not to go in for roulette wheels—each estimating the "subjective probability" of the other's choosing so or not. But since, if one believes in the objective probability of a choice, it is rational in certain circumstances to automate one's response, we must suppose that, for the making of this decision whether to employ roulette wheels, a second-order roulette wheel should be employed; and so on.

My fanciful extension of Snyder's mathematical example is meant to show that a "rational" contestant in the game might well have strategic reasons for *making* his own response mechanically probabilistic, and for manipulating the degree of that probability. And that, it would appear, presupposes that the rational contestant's response has of itself *no* determinate objective or physical probability.

The idea of a "probability of rational action" is thus inapplicable and indeed incoherent. Even if the human strategist were contending not with another human but with a mechanical stochastic device, the modification by probabilities of Snyder's positive- and negative-signed values would be logically objectionable in at least one respect: it would prevent the expression of the participants' possible preferences in regard to gambles or risk-taking—surely a significant issue in the context of deterrence. In the above example, for instance, A is said to be indifferent between the alternatives of: a certainty of neither gaining nor losing, or a gamble of five-to-one on winning 20, and five-to-one against on losing 100. Professor Snyder's calculus of valuation sometimes appears, indeed, inconsistent in his own terms—e.g., he distinguishes "intrinsic" (or "end") values from "power" (or "instrumental") values, but then alleges (my italics) that "the aggregate value of any given asset is the *sum* of its valuation on both scales."[8]

Amongst the dissenters from the enterprise of using game-theoretical models in the explanation of world politics is Anatol Rapoport. A critique of "Theories of Rational Decision" and an exposé of "Hazards and Pitfalls of Strategic Thinking" comprise the first two and more significant parts of his *Strategy and Conscience.*[9] A third part pleads for understanding between the United States and the Soviet Union, and for "ideological disarmament": it presents "another mode of thinking in which conscience is central."

This last essay has great educative value in loosening imaginations too long fettered to a "strategic mode" which at first promised much but seems now unable to resolve its own dilemmas. Strategic thinking begins with a question both instrumental and partial; what *means* will increase *my* country's security, or its military power? When two or more countries severally promote power or security in relation to each other, they jointly

[8] *Ibid.,* pp. 31–32.

[9] A. Rapoport, *Strategy and Conscience* (New York: Harper & Row, Publishers, Inc., 1964).

form a "system." Thought about the system as a whole requires but goes beyond partial strategic thought. Rapoport is quite right to push us beyond the limits of a self-defeating concentration upon our own country's or alliance's partial interests and to make us ask questions about the system as a whole; but he is mistaken in supposing that if all parties take into consideration the interests of the system as a whole as well as their several partial interests, then there will cease to be a system. In a recent article, contrasting strategic with "systemic" thinking (Adam Smith's, Pareto's, Marx's, Freud's, Lewis F. Richardson's), he argues that the latter is concerned only with "determinants in human affairs which operate independently of anyone's rationally designed actions or consciously perceived goals."[10] The determinants of a Richardson arms race are not "independent of" rationally designed actions: they are the unintended consequences of rationally designed but particularistic actions. If, contrariwise, the national leaders enlarge their perspective and contemplate the consequences of some or of all other nations acting from particularistic designs only, or, as well, from designs in similarly enlarged perspective, then those individual leaders will have some dispositions to act differently, as a result of which the behavior of the system they comprise will change. But it will still be a system. Only if a worldwide and barbarizing nuclear war occurs, or if all nations merge in a single world state (and we have suggested, in an earlier analysis, that that is not *strictly* impossible) do they dismantle the system of external inter-Power relations and constitute another, "internal," political, and social system. No strategic or political system subsists without the rationally designed and mutually responsive actions of at least two parties; and conversely.

Furthermore, it must stand initially as an open question, to be determined by systemic analysis, whether a particular group of persons or societies systemically related is more likely to survive when severally *pursuing* egotistic or, instead, altruistic ends. The question, of course, cannot be asked without *considering* altruistic goals (as Rapoport would say, without considering conscience) and other parties' egotistic ends; but it must remain a possible conclusion that affairs will go best for all if each can be counted upon to pursue his own interest. Such a conclusion though derived from a quite informal analysis, underlay the classic doctrine of the balance of power. Underlying the doctrine of deterrent balance is a mixed conclusion: the system is supposed to be stable (and thus nuclear war is avoided—the overriding interest of "our" as well as of "their" side) only when each of the parties in the nuclear system has an "invulnerable second-strike force." On the other hand, so-called stable de-

[10] A. Rapoport, "Systemic and Strategic Conflict: What Happens When People Do Not Think—and When They Do," *Virginia Quarterly Review,* XI (Summer, 1964), 342.

terrence certainly depends on the conviction that each party would be egotistic enough, indeed vengeful enough, to *launch* its second strike if attacked.

Rapoport's criticism, however, is directed not only against the alleged objectionable morals of strategic thought, but against its *validity*. The remainder of this discussion will concern the latter criticism.

Let us first notice that most of Rapoport's criticism is directed to something that strategists contend exists only in Rapoport's own mind: to a special and narrow variety of strategic thought—that in which game theory, particularly the theory of the zero-sum two-person game, is apt to be applied to, or used to illustrate, strategic issues. (He refers much more briefly to stimulation, war-gaming, and scenario-writing.) There are other styles and varieties of strategic thought: it is perfectly possible to develop a strategic doctrine without using any game-theoretic concepts; one need never assign a numerical probability to any military-political event (though one might, presumably, to the performance of military hardware), let alone assign "utilities" to "outcomes." Indeed, a telling methodological criticism of any single variety of strategic thinking, which Rapoport overlooks, would be that it takes no cognizance of the effects of the other varieties: except where "we" know we have a dominant strategy, it is not rational to choose the strategy containing a saddlepoint unless we are convinced that "they" believe themselves to be playing the same game as we do. Unless it can be shown (as some decision-theorists think could be shown in principle) that a game-theoretic approach, by virtue of its greater generality, somehow contains any other consistent approach as a special case, it will not follow that a critique of game theory amounts to a critique of all strategic thinking. If, for example, your country is a hostage to the Russians or Chinese for American good behavior, and unless you are convinced that the inordinate power of Russia and America is counterbalanced by a quite unusual prudence and care for the interests of the least of their allies and dependents, you may consider yourself a little safer possessing a nuclear strike-force of your own; and the world no more unsafe as a consequence. Neither Rapoport nor the most game-theoretical strategist could prove such "commonsense" strategic thinking mistaken.

Rapoport has a section on "the neo-traditionalists" (broadly, those who deal in *realpolitik*) in which Kissinger and Morton Kaplan are mentioned, and which he may consider to subsume all "commonsense" varieties of thinking in the strategic mode. What he misses is the neo-traditionalists' sense of tragic and inescapable dilemma. Especially in Western Europe, their peoples and governments cannot extricate themselves from the predicament of nuclear power-politics. Dutchmen and Belgians, for example, have seen the nuclear stand-off between the United

States and the Soviet Union build up regardless of anything that Holland or Belgium might do. The stockpiles, the bombers and missiles are deployed and in production: thinking in a non-strategic mode will not get rid of them. That is now true for United States citizens also—or, at least, the American neo-traditionalists will suppose so, all the more because other nations, responding to the predicament in which the Superpower stand-off places them, are acquiring nuclear forces. Thinking "in the strategic mode" (which, to repeat, need not mean thinking in the terms of game theory or of anything like it) could hardly be avoided even by, for example, a Western European country that adopted a policy of "conscience." Suppose that France had decided to abjure all force except a token conventional frontier guard: even so, its government would have to decide for or against a counter-nuclear shelter program, since its population could still be imperiled by a Russian-American nuclear war set off, perhaps, by events in Cuba. What steps could it take, in such a case, to promote the survival of Frenchmen and French society? That is a strategic question though asked under the promptings of conscience, for it involves an assessment of how others might employ their armed forces, and of how to respond to various uses.

In short, the present writer cannot accept a distinction of modes—only of levels—between strategic and conscientious thinking. On the other hand, Rapoport seems quite right to expose the pretense to logical completeness of thinking at the strategic level: the supposition that there is or could be a calculus of strategic thought, built up "objectively" and adaptable as a ready-made instrument for any inquiry into the allocation of all possible values, can and should be challenged; and in choosing the game-theoretical variant of strategic thought as the subject of his critique, Rapoport has certainly chosen the variant on behalf of which the strongest claims to logical completeness are made.

On one count Rapoport seems to be quite in the wrong: not as to his purpose, which is to reaffirm the difference between estimates of probability based upon "objective" frequencies of events and those based upon "subjective" (i.e., personal and estimated) assessments; but as to his calculations in a particular example. He imagines the following game:[11]

> The deck consists of eight cards, namely, four aces and four deuces. After shuffling, you take two cards, and your opponent takes two. After seeing your hand but before the opponent sees his, you can offer a bet, giving or asking any odds you choose that your hand beats your opponent's. Aces are high; so the highest hand is two aces, the next is ace-deuce, and two deuces is the lowest hand. Suits do not count. If the two hands tie, you lose the bet. You have just drawn an ace and a deuce. What are fair odds? . . . To fix ideas, suppose we hold the ace of diamonds and the deuce of clubs.

[11] *Strategy and Conscience,* pp. 26–30.

At this stage, Rapoport correctly concludes that the chances of our opponent's holding a hand that ours would beat (*viz.*, a hand of two deuces) is $\frac{1}{5}$. He sets out the "fifteen possible hands" our opponent could hold, only three of which comprise two aces, and then supposes that a spy tells us that *one* of the opponent's cards is a deuce, but without telling us of which suit, and concludes that now

> . . . the first three hands do not come under consideration. Only twelve hands are possible, and our hand still beats three of them. Therefore, if we know that the opponent has a deuce (but do not know any more), we should estimate the probability that we shall win our bet as $\frac{1}{4}$ instead of $\frac{1}{5}$.

Next, he has the spy report that our opponent's previously mentioned deuce is the deuce of spades, and concludes that since now the opponent's "possible hands" are only five, of which two are pairs of deuces, "the probability that we shall win the bet becomes $\frac{2}{5}$. . . . But if the change in odds is the same no matter what suit he reports, why should his report make a difference?" Rapoport answers this question by saying that

> the two-to-three offer was justified by a certain betting policy. . . . Thus it is not only probability that determines betting policy (how much to bet). Betting policy (*when* to bet) determines probability. In the case of a single bet, this probability is entirely in the mind of the policy maker.

That last proposition is not necessarily true, and Rapoport's example in support of it contains an error. For as soon as we learn that our opponent's hand contains at least one deuce, even though we do not know the suit, we know that the chances that the opponent's other card is also a deuce are $\frac{2}{5}$. That other card must be equiprobably one of three aces and two deuces. We know he has a deuce, we know that (in terms of the example) it is *either* the deuce of spades, *or* of hearts, *or* of diamonds: the question of a fair bet boils down to that of the identity of his "possible other card," rather than of his twelve "possible hands." In fact, the information that he has at least one deuce does more than merely eliminate from the original fifteen possible hands the three all-ace hands: it determines, within the twelve remaining, three *alternative* sets of five which nevertheless have some overlap of membership, and indicates that the opponent's actual hand belongs to just one of those alternative sets. The example is unfortunately chosen in another way. "Probability" in that kind of card game is as objective as it could be—we already have all the relevant information for determining what would be a fair bet in this case: nothing more would be added to our knowledge if from a pack of three aces and two deuces we made ten thousand draws of one of the cards. Furthermore, the bet is "fair" in the interpersonal sense that, having offered our opponent the odds, we would be rationally indifferent as to whether he *or* we wagered at those odds that his hand would beat ours. Indeed, we could offer him the choice as to who should wager when we offered him the fair odds. If, as in the game described by Rapoport, our opponent has no such choice, then it will not necessarily be in our interest to offer him a fair bet. Rather, we should select the odds we offer him at the "*un*fair" extreme of a range bounded at one extreme by the fair odds, beyond which we should decide to make no offer at all, and at the other extreme by odds, *un*fair to him, beyond which to the best of our knowledge, he will decline our offer. If haggling is allowed, our opponent would be rational to decline all our offers within the range until he had pushed us to the "fair" limit beyond which *we* would decline. But since such a haggling process should (if both parties are rational and have, in respect of the sums wagered, a "constant-return" utility for money and gambling) settle at an accepted offer of odds which coincides with a fair bet, then it is false that as Rapoport concludes, "in the case of a single bet, this probability is entirely in the mind of the policy maker."

There are, indeed, grave difficulties with the notion of the probability of a strategic or political event, but it is not always true that "betting policy (*when* to bet) determines probability." Rather, betting policy should be determined (1) by our preferences for money and gambling; (2) by our estimate of the probability of any relevant decisive event (e.g., the turn of a card); and (3) by our estimate of the "probability" or "likelihood" that our opponent will accept odds within a certain range. To both the second and the third of these determinants, information can be pertinent. To the second, information about frequencies, even when available, is not always necessary; but singular information—e.g., about the constitution of the pack of cards—can be both necessary and sufficient.

What information is pertinent to the third, the social or "personal" determinant? For example, what kind of information is relevant to the likelihood that at least one of the present nuclear Powers will launch a nuclear attack, using most of its delivery vehicles, within the next hundred days? Let us at once agree with Rapoport that there exists no probability or improbability somehow residing in such an event; but let us not suppose that this is because no nuclear attacks have occurred, or are likely to occur in large enough numbers to justify a statistical estimate. Rapoport devotes a chapter to an account of an experiment in which pairs of college students at the University of Michigan were set to play the game, Prisoner's Dilemma, several hundred times in succession. This game has been alleged to bear some resemblance to the nuclear dilemma (if both attack, both lose relatively heavily; if only one attacks, he gains and the other, correspondingly, loses even more heavily; if the pair cooperate, both gain, but only a little). The evidence of Rapoport's experiment suggests broadly that, after a stretch of unilateral attack, a majority of pairs "lock in" on cooperation, while a minority lock in on mutual attack: i.e., it suggests that the members of both majority and minority pairs "learn" about their opposite numbers' dispositions, including their dispositions to learn. But it gives much less guide as to how a pair, playing the game for the first time, would initially dispose their strategies. Obviously, we should rather want to know about the members of that particular pair, their characters and capacities, and about the particular pay-offs in the actual matrix they were to play. About the nuclear Powers we want to know what they believe they can do to each other, what they think of their several prospects for staying in the advanced-weapons race, and how the leaders of each are disposed toward the use of extreme violence and toward the conduct of Power politics.

Now, it is no doubt possible, and may be demonstrably rational or "consistent," to impute, on the basis of such information, estimated prior probabilities to various courses of action, relevant to the provoking or launching of a nuclear attack, which each of the various Powers may undertake. If so, however, we should remember that each of the Powers, in their different ways, will be doing much the same thing in relation to each of the others' possible actions; so that the information that each has or thinks it has about the others will provide one of the determinants or influences on its own action. So the probability-estimates which we as onlookers impute to them should take cognisance of each one's predictions of the others' behavior, *and* of the others' predictions, *and*. . . . But it is extremely doubtful whether anyone has this kind, or the more obvious kind of information about the characters and policies (even if about the capacities) of Powers, in anything like the quantity and quality worthy of delicate and subtle display as an array of prior probabilities. Rapoport is wise to consider the possibility that the notion of the "calculated risk" of nuclear war is "only eyewash"—again, *not* because "a single man" (or a single Power) "is not a population," nor even because a check on such personal estimates of probability "can be made only if we agree on the class into which we shall put our unique event" (though on that difficulty Rapoport is astringently corrective of much shoddy thinking), but because we know very well that we lack the information that might begin to justify the epithet "calculated."

On this theme, Rapoport is excellent: "Probabilities are often simply 'estimated,' and estimates are solemnly offered as if they were estimates of next week's price of wheat. These estimates lose all significance when we are dealing with events which are extremely improbable."[12] He supplies a matrix in which the opponent's strategies are treated as "states of nature" and therefore as subjects for probability estimates. "Our" pay-offs are:

[12] *Ibid.*, p. 102.

both cooperating, 10; we back down, he stands firm, minus 100; the reverse, plus 100; both stand firm, minus 20,000:

> . . . if we estimate as one in a thousand the chance that the other will be as stubborn as we are, the "expected gain" (whatever it may mean in the present context) of standing firm is greater than that of giving in. But if we estimate that there is one chance in a hundred that the other will stand firm, then the "expected gain" of giving in is greater. In this way either decision can be easily rationalized.[13]

Notice that this is an objection about the *practical* difficulties of relying upon probability estimates which are severally arbitrary though doubtless capable, in principle, of being made jointly self-consistent. The present writer considers the objection both compelling and adequate; we do not need an additional objection-in-principle, which in any case is not evidently supplied by Rapoport's card-game example.

Very much the same applies to his treatment of the inadequacies of arbitrarily assessed and unidimensional utility scales. His following argument applies to the situation of decisions under certainty. *A fortiori,* it holds against decisions under risk, under uncertainty, and against the direct application of game theory to those strategic and political decisions which are under strict conflict-of-interest (where zero-sum games look deceptively promising) or under conflict-and-cooperation (where non-zero-sum games do):

> If the decision-maker is a group (or a population) the problem of constructing a consistent rank order preference becomes still more difficult. Since such a scale is essential before a normative decision theory can be developed, we are forced to the conclusion that even in the context of decision under certainty, we have nothing approaching a usable and general normative theory of rational decision: Preferences cannot in general be unambiguously deduced from actual choices.[14]

Taken together, Rapoport's objections to unidimensional utility scales and to arbitrary probability estimates sufficiently refute the possibility of an applied science of strategy: we cannot have optimizing decision rules, except perhaps in limited and repeatable tactical situations (e.g., fighter-plane combat). Rapoport is, however, anxious to reveal even more serious defects in strategic thinking, especially when it is designed to provide advice for governments.

Thus, he begins, in his Introduction, by distinguishing "three modes of decision theory . . . the formal, the prescriptive (or normative), and the descriptive (or empirical)." The formal mode "is confined to the construction of a deductive apparatus to be used in deriving logically neces-

[13] *Ibid.,* p. 104.
[14] *Ibid.,* p. 72.

sary conclusions from given assumptions." The prescriptive mode "is concerned with the determination of *optimal* decisions. It depends upon a set of given *goals*." Lastly:

> a descriptive theory seeks to find principles which guide real people's decisions. It must therefore rely on *behavioral data*. Such a thing accomplishes its aim if it can say (and support the statement with empirical evidence) something like this: "People make decisions *as if* they were guided by following such and such decision rules. . . .[15]

Rapoport concludes his Introduction by remarking that it will sometimes turn out that the data required to construct a prescriptive upon the basis of a formal theory will be unobtainable without a descriptive theory of decision.

This seems impeccably orthodox methodology; but two very different kinds of objection to it suggest themselves. Firstly, in respect of the art of inventing descriptive theories of the decision process and of the social and political system to which it gives rise: before testing an hypothesis which states that such and such decision rules appear to be acted on in political behavior, it is often a good idea to have elaborated one's hypothesis in some complexity—i.e., to have made a rather intricate model. Such models do not consist wholly of logical deductions from axioms: they must also set up hypothetical initial conditions, singularly describable. Decision theory and game theory in their *strictly* formal sense are powerful means for examining the *feasibility* of such models. For example, game theory can be useful in helping to decide whether it is feasible to attempt to test a model of coalitions sufficiently complex to be of interest in a real-life descriptive theory—sometimes we find that a model just complex enough to be interesting is far too complex to be testable. The present writer therefore finds it methodologically convenient to split "the formal mode" of decision-theorizing into a strictly formal and purely general level, from which canons for model-construction can be derived, and a rigorous but partly singular or particular level, where one constructs and tests the models.

The game-theoretical matrix, then, probably never provides *directly* an hypothesis about strategic or political events in the real world, as some of the broader and more vulnerable of Rapoport's targets amongst the strategic thinkers have imagined. The use of game theory and its matrices is to set a standard of explicitness and rigor in the discussion of acts that are competitive and, in a constrictive and almost obsessional sense of the term, "rational." In the place of hunches about the working of the balance of power, for instance, game theory provides an exact grammar which for the most part simply exposes the arbitrariness and untestability of our

[15] *Ibid.*, pp. 5–6.

hunches: we now know what it would be like to have knowledge of these matters; and we know we cannot have it.

Secondly, in respect of formal models' *suggestiveness* in a prescriptive or normative direction: Rapoport's methodology implies that both data obtained through descriptive investigation *and* formal models obtained deductively are together always necessary and sometimes sufficient for prescription. To be brutal: it is hardly ever the case that the most respectable combinations of behavioral data and formal theory are strictly sufficient for *optimal* decisions in politics. On the other hand, a clearly expressed formal notion, unsupported by data, can be *psychologically* "sufficient"; i.e., it may catch on politically. It will have Schelling's "salience." Thinking back over the history of nuclear policy since Churchill's coinage of "the balance of terror," one is impressed by the attractive and organizing power that has been displayed by the strategists' models, distinctions—their very phrases. By sheer elegance, and often without benefit of any "behavioral data" at all, they have had themselves adopted by the political "decision-makers," and at last by the military.

Now that kind of thing seems inevitable in politics. If the world-political community does some day manage to make safe its destructive nuclear capacities, this will quite likely have come about by grace of well-presented and suggestive ideas produced by disarmers like Rapoport, quite untested and without the help of "behavioral data." From Adam Smith through Marx and Keynes, the most exact and advanced of the social sciences has been "applied," not by virtue of exhausting all the alternatives (a necessary condition for optimizing, unobtainable in human affairs) but usually by incantation.

Rapoport's psychological expertise, on the other hand, helps him bring to light a defect in strategic thinking of almost all varieties: the habit of regarding each Power as a single international "actor," and of attributing a rather jejune Hobbesian disposition to each of them. "The strategist will not get the sort of (psychological) knowledge he wants because he does nothing to inquire into its underpinnings, namely, the deep commitments of people."[16]

But even on this subject, Rapoport has the defects of his qualities: while affirming that strategic and political acts are not the work of the abstractionists' utility-maximizing robots, but of flesh-and-blood politicians and administrators with deep personal commitments, he gives far too little weight to the political context that makes their acts and thoughts something other than the simple expressions of their personal psychic dispositions. In the same way, while understanding that the greater part of the national leader's environment is formed by his people's corporate impulses, preconceptions, and character, he does not bring out how the latter, also,

[16] *Ibid.*, p. 124.

have their effects in a political context and (even in a totalitarian state) through political activity. Strategically oriented thinkers have erred in reducing political to strategic considerations—i.e., to the bare calculation of advantage in a conflict or cooperative-conflict situation. Rapoport errs in supposing that when he has put back the psychology, he has put back the politics as well. But the truth about international politics is not derivable only from a conjunction of the truth about strategy and the truth about individual and group psychology. To have politics in the conclusion, you must have had it in at least one of the premises. Again, Rapoport's focus upon just two Powers, the USA and the USSR, obscures his vision of the real world of multinational politics. (A two-person system is hardly political.) The vision of many strategic writers is obscured by the same bipolar restriction.

TEN

Game Theory, Real Uncertainty, and Imputation

I

We have defined "the Power" as a self-preserving, self-nurturing collectivity, and we have supposed that all constellations of Powers are, or are apt to be, interrelated in systematic ways. In the enterprise of theory-making about the politics of Powers, we try to determine the nature of these supposed systems. Since their constitutive relationships seem to be partly competitive and partly cooperative, the hypothesis readily suggests itself that Power systems can be interpreted as games, analyzable by means of the Theory of Games. Morton A. Kaplan and others, including the present writer, began working on that hypothesis in the middle Fifties. This chapter will try to show why in the long run the hypothesis, or at least any strong form of it, has to be abandoned; but this can be done only after a persistent effort to apply the Theory of Games directly to the politics of the Powers. Most of this chapter, then, consists of a serious attempt to refute our hypothesis: that no game-theoretical game can be designed which would be used to explain an actual power-political conflict.

The hypothesis does not entail that any and every relation between states, nations, or peoples is power-political and thus suitable for the application of game theory. Some international *economic* relations are not amenable to such an interpretation, though others—notably the "trade war"—are so, given certain drastic simplifications. Some aspects of international affairs are better understood upon a sociological or cultural model. But in both economic and sociocultural relations, the foci of attention certainly differ from, though they partly overlap with, that of the power-political relationship.

Again, there was never any question of applying the matrix of a single game to processes drawn out far beyond the time span of human decision, such as the age-long relationship between Islamic and Christian, or between Eastern and Western Christian, civilizations. At most two or three generations of statesmen, inheriting a common mind about their Power's interests in foreign policy, set the extreme limit for the duration of any process that could be regarded as a single "game." Much more frequently, we think in terms of a few years, sometimes even a few weeks. Nevertheless, on the hypothesis that Power politics is amenable to game theory, the single distinguishable "game" would provide the briefest and irreducible unit-event. When a series of these were strung together, the skeleton of an explanatory narrative of world politics would be built up. Of course, the concept of the "game," though necessary, would not be sufficient to account for all the shifts and changes in this narrative: demography, scientific and technical innovation, philosophic and religious change, as well as internal politics and economics would determine new "pay-offs" and thereby help establish successive arrays of possible outcomes. But the game would provide the indispensable nexus by which the effect of any such extraneous change could make its appearance.

An immediately evident objection is that politics does not proceed as a sequence of distinguishable games. Even more than in the case of competition between business firms, the game applied to some stage in a political process is a thoroughly artificial construct. The most that can be said is that its application need not be wholly arbitrary: an "issue" or a "crisis" typically arises when two or more partly opposed Powers join in a conflict for which each has some idea of the others' preferences and intentions, and makes some guesses—bearing a degree of resemblance to the others' guesses—about the range of possible outcomes. It is not unthinkable, though no doubt it would be extremely pedantic, that as a crisis-situation began to be defined, some statesman should arrange his estimates of his own and the other party's alternatives in a game-theoretical matrix, even assigning numbers both to his own preferences for various outcomes and to his guesses about the other's preferences. Provided the theorist avoids hindsight in imagining that kind of operation, and provided above all that he has evidence as to what the statesman's estimates and preferences were *before* the crisis, the delimiting of a single crisis-game, though artificial, need not be entirely arbitrary. Perhaps a more serious difficulty arises from the need to link one crisis-game to the next.

Firstly, since crises can and often do overlap, and since distinct matters can remain at issue during the same period, the image of a simple sequence of games is certainly misleading: before an issue is disposed of, another will arise. A serious attempt to apply the gaming model to some actual era of world politics would have to produce many overlapping matrices. How could these be made consistent with each other?

The answer is simplest for two matrices strictly contemporary with but quite independent of each other, except for having at least one player in common: for any such player the pay-offs in the two games must be expressed in the same or in completely intertranslatable units.

If on the other hand, for at least one player-in-common, the matrices are *not* totally independent—if, for example, Column cannot simultaneously choose Strategy 1 in Matrix A and Strategy 2 in Matrix B—the condition of equivalence in the pay-off units, though still necessary, would not be sufficient: we should have to construct a supermatrix showing just what permutations of strategies were available to the several players.

For consecutive matrices having at least one player in common, it is also necessary to devise a supergame. Obstacles to this mount up discouragingly, and are discussed later in this chapter. Suffice it at this stage to refer to Hao Wang's elegant treatment of the subject in "Games, Logic, and Computers" (1965).[1] Wang's concerns differ from ours—he seeks to delimit the type of problem in principle solvable by a computer (i.e., by algorithm), and to explore the nature of mathematics. But for our purpose, the interest of his logical investigations lies in what they tell us about types of game.

A game is said to be "unfair" if one player always has a winning strategy; but "futile" if each player has a nonlosing strategy (thus eliminating the possibility of a winner). Wang records a theorem: "Every game is either futile or unfair if there is a fixed, upper boundary to the length of each path on its tree and only finitely many branches come directly from each node."[2] If we could show that, for every game at all applicable to the politics of the Powers, there was such a fixed finite upper boundary, then we would know that, insofar as the game actually applied to real-life affairs, systems of Powers were either stable (corresponding to the "futile" game) or were likely to throw up a predominant Power (corresponding to a run of games mostly "unfair" to all but one player). Unless one or another of these conditions could be fulfilled, it is hard to

[1] *Scientific American*, CCXIII, No. 5 (November 1965), 98–106.
[2] *Ibid.*, p. 102.

see how the application of game theory could possibly add positively to our understanding of world affairs.

On the other hand, to show that for a strictly logical reason (e.g., failure to have a fixed upper boundary) some exemplary game cannot be applied to world affairs does in a negative way comment upon the nature of the real-life process. Few differences are greater than that between problems which, no matter how complex or complicated, could in principle be solved by the same method, and one which, whether or not it is solvable at all, is not solvable by any regular, teachable, or programmable method. At least since the eighteenth century, Europeans have been haunted by the dream of rational (i.e., teachable) solutions to political problems. That hope is still alive, especially in the USA. Against it there stand, not only the irrationalist philosophies, but also several older strands of rationalism, which hold that while politics consists for the most part in the actions of rational creatures, the issues it presents cannot be conceived of as methodically solvable problems. (Later we shall see that there are certain coalition games which, though they have a solution in principle, are not solvable in practice because the numbers involved are too great to be dealt with by any actual computer—*viz.*, any having a finite "memory." This is not the same point as that there are games which, solvable or not, cannot be solved by algorithm—i.e., not even by an imaginary computer having an infinite memory.) We proceed in this chapter to ask whether any game-theoretical representation of world politics that would be even *prima facie* plausible would have a fixed, finite upper boundary.

The equivalent real-life question is whether we must suppose that the human race in some form or another, and thus possibly the system of Powers in some form or another, might in some circumstances go on forever! If that had to be supposed, then though no present Power need be supposed to persist indefinitely, it would be entailed that at least one present Power might possibly always have a "descendant," though one transmuted beyond recognition.

The Biblical religions which, as we have seen in Chapter Four, largely formed the dominant view of Power politics give to this essentially metaphysical question the answer that "this world" of Principalities and Powers is not everlasting—the Powers are not gods. Marxism yields a secular variant of the same doctrine. This suggests a rather widespread supposition that the Power system or its transformation will have an indefinite but not an infinite future. So the equivalent supergame will have a finite but not a fixed boundary—not fixed, at any rate, according to our knowledge. Now, Wang shows by use of the "infinity lemma" that such a game must be either "futile" or "unfair";[3] which entails that *in principle* a game-theoretical solution for it exists—though, as just argued, such a solution

[3] *Ibid.*, pp. 102–103.

is likely forever to remain unavailable, because of the difficulty of computation.

Another objection in principle, however, also arises: given the distinct possibility of drastic changes, both in the players and in the rules, from one subgame to the next, is it logically feasible to string them together into the requisite supergame?—In principle, yes. For we could ask each player in a chess game to evaluate for himself the outcomes, supposing that one of the latter was an entry-fee to membership in a pair about to play in a bridge tournament—for which, in turn, one of the outcomes was an entry-fee to a poker game; and so on. Once the tree of outcomes has been valued in this way by one of the players (and similar evaluations imputed by him to the other and the theoretically possible later players), the supergame simply is this tree of evaluated outcomes, in which the subgames—chess, bridge, poker—are embedded. The difficulty of principle is not with the changes in nature of the subgame, but with the players' ignorance of such future changes.

Suppose, nevertheless, that we decide to try out the interpretation of international politics as an *n*-person nonzero-sum game. The first specification for constructing such a game is that, since the players cannot know when it ends, they cannot assume an end to it amongst the stages they envisage.

The major objective, then, for every player, must be the assurance that he will be in the game as long as it lasts. This means that, at the very latest stage—*L*—in the game he is capable of envisaging, he will put an indefinitely high valuation on being still in it. Since he can be so only if, but not necessarily if, he is still in it at Stage $L - 1$, the all-up valuation he puts on *that* outcome must be even higher than the one he puts on being still in the game at Stage *L*. This is because the value to him of survival during $(L - 1)$ is made up of an instrumental part (roughly, the possibility it affords of also going on to survive in Stage *L, multiplied by* the net payoff for survival during *1*) and an intrinsic part (all the payoff attached to his surviving through $L - 1$); and so backward through the series of envisaged stages $L - 2$, $L - 3$ . . . to the initial stage—i.e., to that immediately after the present moment. And since, once he has been eliminated, he can claim no other elements of pay-off, any other objectives in themselves, such as the acquisition of resources or the elimination of other players, must in sum have far less value than that of remaining in the game (unless of course those other objectives happened also to be necessary conditions for his survival). This premium upon survival represents in a gaming interpretation the preservation of a unity-in-spirit mentioned in our definition of a Power.

A consequence is that each player has some clue as to the structure of the others' pay-offs, though he will be very far from having perfect information about them. A principal reason for the imperfection of his information is that he certainly will be ignorant of the others' suppositions about the outcomes of the game (no player, of course, *knows* for certain what the outcomes will or even might be), and even ignorant of the distance any of them can penetrate in envisaging the later stages of the game. This, as we shall see, is one of those conditions that in the *long run* make it impossible to interpret world politics in game-theoretical terms. Nevertheless, we must try to take the gaming interpretation as far as it will go. What are the features of a game in which a given player takes the outcomes to some stage S^L and imputes to the other(s) a similar extrapolation to some stage S^L, $S^L - 1$, $S^L - 2$, . . . ? (For he cannot consistently *specify* some precise stage S^n which the other arrives at, though he can always consider the possibility that the other thinks beyond him to some *un*specified extent—see Chapter 2.)

Suppose two players—C for "Column," and R for "Row"—are doomed to play a sequential game in a series of stages. For each stage an entry-fee is charged which, if a player can afford it, he must pay; and he must go on to play that stage. The sequence of stages stops if and only if one or more players cannot afford a particular entry-fee. The foregoing rules are known (given as certain) to both players.

The outcomes for each of the successive stages, on the other hand, are not given as certain to any player, at least beyond the first stage immediately after the present moment. (It may not be unreasonable to suppose that national leaders often safely discount surprise in the very short-run future.) For later stages, we must suppose that each player projects his own corrigible guess at the pay-off matrices for those later stages as far forward as his imagination permits, at the same time making guesses, also corrigible, about each of the other players' projections, and their limits. The latter kind of guess we call "imputation." More will be said below about the incorporation of corrigibility into the gaming model. At this stage the important thing to notice is that each player can plan his long-term strategy for the *series* of stages only upon his "best guess" at the numbers in the pay-off boxes of the successive matrices (and at the entry-fees for each particular stages), knowing full well that his guesses are likely to err—the more likely, on the whole, the further they go—and are also likely to differ from those of the other players. This implies that a player has to assume that when the other's differs from his own best guess, the other will be wrong (except by accident), and that the other has probably not managed to guess any stages further ahead than he himself has—though rationally he should admit the contrary *possibility* and, if he can, insure himself against the chance of having been thus outguessed.

Figure 10.1 is a game-theoretical representation of how Column (C) might project a series of future stages, and of how he might impute a

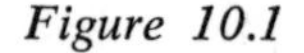

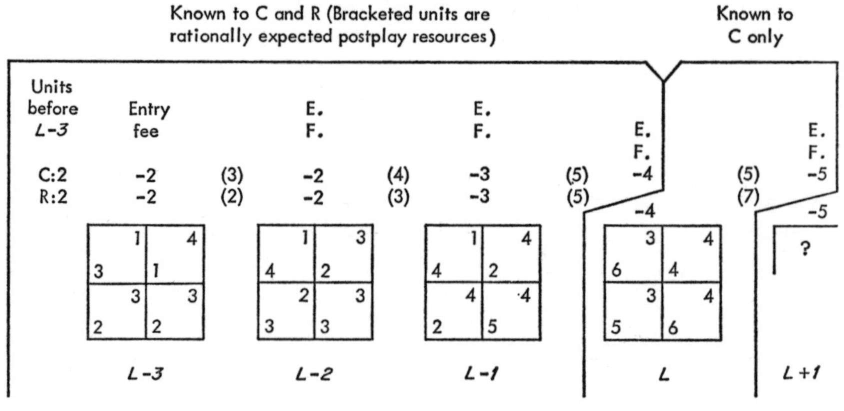

similar though shorter projection to Row (R). In this particular representation, C does not suppose that R differs from himself in his guesses at the matrices or at the entry-fees for the first three Stages $L-3$, $L-2$, $L-1$; but C does suppose that while R has guessed correctly at the entry-fee for his own furthest-projected Stage L, R is ignorant of the contents of the matrix for Stage L, and also of R's entry-fee for it (which C has correctly guessed) and for the "unknown" next stage, $L+1$.

In this particular example, it happens that the two players start with equal resources (2 units each), that at each stage they pay equal entry-fees, and that the matrix for every single stage presents a positive-sum game. At each of the stages, considered in itself, C has a dominant strategy, his second; and there seems to be a "rational solution" available through R's also playing *his* second strategy. Moreover, as it turns out, both players can guarantee to stay in the game, for both will have the required entry-fees.

Yet because C has guessed the successive matrices up to and including the entry-fee to $L+1$, but has imputed a shorter-ranging guess to R, the series as a whole looks to be turning into an elimination game. C's resources accumulate to 5 after $L-1$, and would not be increased by his playing Stage L; whereas he guesses that all five units would be consumed by payment of the entry-fee to $L+1$. On the other hand, he can stop the game for good, with all five units in hand, should he succeed in eliminating R after $L-1$.

C can eliminate R by playing, in $L-1$, his first strategy (even though his second patently dominates it) so long as R persists with *his* second strategy. The game would then conclude with C having five and R having two units (cf. the state of affairs after L: C, + 5; R, + 7). But in seeking thus to eliminate R, C runs the risk that if R for some reason changes to *his* first strategy in $L - 1$, it would be C who, by playing his first, was eliminated at that stage, giving the final carve-up: C, + 2; R, + 4. But what reasons *could* R have for playing his first?—only a strong persuasion that C was not going to play his second, dominant strategy; for if C actually plays his second, while R plays his first, the same result occurs as would if R played his second and C his first. What might give R that strong persuasion?

Supposing all the while that R's guesses, until just before the L matrix, are assumed by C to be identical with his own (and throughout this exposition we have indeed been seeing R and his cogitations solely through C's imputative eyes), it is clear that the *prima facie* case for R's playing his first strategy would only be R's own well-supported belief that C was going to play *his* first in order to get R out of the game, thus insuring himself a solid 5 and eliminating subsequent risks. But of course R would not continue to entertain that "well-supported belief" at all if he were to acquire reliable information to the effect that C was convinced that R would play his first on the belief that C was going to play *his* first; for if C *were* thus convinced, he would certainly play his second, thus avoiding the outcome for $L - 1$: C, 1; R, 4—which eliminates from the whole game, yielding an all-up score C, 2; R, 4.

In the last resort, then, C must ask himself whether R might not attempt to guarantee for himself, in respect of the supergame representing the series as a whole, a return of at least two units, by playing in any case his (R's) first strategy at $L - 1$. The worst that could happen to R (as always, on C's reading) would be that he was then eliminated, but with a guaranteed 2 against C's 5, should C play a second strategy at $L - 1$.

Can we, however, consistently represent the imputation that some player would be willing to settle for elimination, though with a positive return? Yes!—for as long as the return *is* net-positive, elimination from the game does not represent, say, national annihilation, but rather something like merging one's sovereignty in a federation of kindred Powers. Elimination with zero returns, or with finite returns but also with the prospect (*not* represented in Figure 10.1) of "infinite" gains at a later stage, *would* violate the Postulates of Rationality.

The alternative to the worst for R is that, underestimated by C, he plays his first while C plays his first at $L - 1$, ensuring the all-up result C, 2; R, 4 eliminating C. But again, if R were confident that C had anticipated these inferences and was therefore bent after all upon playing his second, R could considerably improve his own position (without in fact making C's worse) by playing his (R's) second at $L - 1$—a fact about the game that, if C reflects upon it, could again make him consider playing his first at $L - 1$, starting the cycle of speculation about R's possible cogitations all over again.

Thus C has to impute to R not only a certain degree of *fore*sight, penetrating to further *stages* of the game, but also a degree of *in*sight into the nature of the game, so far as R can be supposed to foresee it. Indeed, C cannot afford not to impute to R the imputing to C himself of similar foresight and insight. In the particular example we are considering, a great deal hangs upon that ignorance of the pay-off matrix for L and/or the entry-fee to $L + 1$ which we have made C impute to R. From C's own point of view, his reasons for attempting a coup at $L - 1$ through "R, second strategy; C, first strategy" do not consist solely in a consideration of the $L - 1$ matrix plus the entry-fee for L; they also include C's belief that the L matrix and entry-fee for $L + 1$ are as represented in Figure 10.1. Further, they include C's belief that R does not appreciate the latter and weighty reason for C's attempting the coup. In other words, C thinks "It is just as well that R is in ignorance of the dangerous position I would be in after L. For now, by considering only the state of affairs before L, he will probably conclude that at $L - 1$ my strategy will be the second, and will therefore play his second—so that I shall have him. If, on the other hand, he knew about the L matrix, *and knew that I knew he knew,* then I would not have my present slight psychological advantage over him—both of us would be in the same state of radical uncertainty about the other's propensity for being adventurous in the face of radical uncertainty about outcomes."

The uncertainty of the game is referred to as "radical" because even C has nothing upon which he can make a guess about the contents of the $L + 1$ matrix or beyond that. Yet he is sure that, provided both he and R play their second strategies at all preceding stages, they *will* be playing some game or another at $L + 1$, from which game he will emerge *either* eliminated, *or* having eliminated R, *or* both, *or* ready to go on and play $L + 2$. This uncertainty, or rather nescience, is of a much stronger kind than that about the strategy an opponent would choose in a game having a definite and known conclusion—which again is stronger than "uncertainty" about the turn of a card or the toss of a coin.

Is there a feasible *a priori* approach to the strongest of those uncertainties—the "radical" uncertainty? Suppose C were to argue as follows: "Given we play $L + 1$, four equiprobable alternatives exhaust the outcomes: (1) I alone am eliminated through being unable to pay the entry-fee for $L + 2$, in which case my final pay-off could be anything from zero upward (but the probability that it will be more than a few units declines, the greater the differences between our final pay-offs), while R's final pay-off will be at least one unit greater than mine; (2) R alone is eliminated, in which case the amounts of our final pay-offs will be reversed; (3)

we are both eliminated, in which case our final pay-offs could be anything from zero to a few, and of any proportion to each other including equality; (4) neither of us is eliminated, in which case for $L + 2$ I have to repeat the foregoing *a priori* analysis. The more stages we stay in the game, the more—on the whole—our total winnings increase and the less the chance (unless entry-fees rise prodigiously) that either of us will be eliminated." (Notice that this last bit of reasoning corresponds only with those real-world situations in which a continued increase of resources is expected. If "entry-fees"—roughly equivalent with the expenses of security, government, and major capital expenses—increase with the increase of accumulated pay-offs, or if pay-offs correspond very closely to prior entry-fees, C's motive for ending the game to his own calculable advantage as soon as possible grows stronger, not least because R's does also.) C continues: "Making these *a priori* assumptions about the future, and imputing to R similar assumptions, I have an interest in the game's continuing indefinitely (an interest in survival) to be counterbalanced against the immediate profitability of ending the game, and the permanent possibility of loss that the game carries with it, by eliminating R. R, if rational, has the like interests, partly opposed to, partly in common with mine. What I need now is more information about R: as to whether his motives are rational, but above all as to whether his insight and his foresight matches mine."

Before we take up the next crucial question—how to represent in the game this need for information about the other players—it will be as well to examine the *a priori* approach. A more sophisticated variant would be to dichotomize the future into: "Either the game stops with L; or it continues at least for $L + 1$." C might then assign equal probabilities to these alternatives; or, considering the series of games already played, and the sizes of the several players' net accumulated pay-offs, he could weight one more than the other. Within the "Game stops!" moiety, he could then distinguish two classes—"C's elimination stops the game!" and "R's elimination stops the game!"—noting the possibility of those two classes overlapping but not as yet treating the overlap as a third class. He should then assign equal probabilities to the two classes of occasions for stopping the game, if but only if C's and R's accumulated pay-offs after L are the same; while if one is greater than the other, he will have to weight its probability accordingly.

The logical difficulty lies, not in the dichotomizing, but in the weighting. No doubt his weightings can be self-consistent (i.e., can comply with the Calculus of Fair Bets); but since they are in the last analysis estimates as to whether he and his opponent will or will not undertake certain deliberate actions, and whether therefore they will or will not have particular reasons for acting in those fashions, his guesses will be in a very real sense, not attempted perceptions, but—in themselves—anticipated actions. So he can hardly use those anticipations of action as a rational basis for planning the very actions thus anticipated. Perhaps the most that can be said for this *a priori* approach is that, revised and revised again, and perhaps applied with many different parameters, it exercises the mind and helps illuminate the structure of possibilities. Nevertheless, out of sheer nescience, only nescience can come.

Thus far we have been working on the implicit supposition that the range of possible outcomes represented in the pay-off boxes of the successive matrices are determined solely by Nature (though of course the pay-offs in Figure 10.1 represent only C's guesses at those determinations of Nature). In some respects, this is oversimplified: sometimes, for instance, an outcome other than that at the saddle-point of a given matrix would create a whole extra matrix for the next stage alternative to that which would follow from the outcome at the saddle-point—i.e., our game-tree in Figure 10.1 has no branches. Since in such a case the matrix for a given stage would be determined at least in part by one's opponent's choice of strategy at the prior stage, information about the opponent's information, opinions, and intentions would of course be indispensable for deciding one's strategy at any stage. But in order not to overcomplicate our present discussion by proliferating the game-tree, we shall continue to assume that only Nature determines the pay-offs, and therefore merely note the above-mentioned additional source of the need for information.

Considering just the situation in Figure 10.1 as we have discussed it above, it is clear that C will often wish to conceal from R—but will occasionally wish to *reveal* to him—C's own information and opinions about the sequence of matrices, and his own preferences and intentions. It is also unfortunately clear that we cannot announce any general principles valid for any sequences of matrices whatsoever, for his deciding just when to conceal and when to reveal. Suppose for example that in Figure 10.1 we substitute for matrix L the matrix in Figure 10.2. C's expecting a stage at L like that in Figure 10.2 might very reasonably inspire in him a certain confidence in the future of the system, and if so he would wish R, firstly, to share his own expectations concerning the matrices, and secondly, to realize that he was sharing them. But should C be unable to convey that impression to R, and should he feel compelled to assume that R's understanding of the matrices was limited to that extent which we have supposed in discussing Figure 10.1, it would still be in C's interest for R *not* to suppose that C, by playing his first strategy at $L - 1$, would be attempting to terminate the game. Indeed, it would be worth C's while to have paid out one unit after $L - 2$ in order to get that notion across to R.

The situation as represented in Figures 10.1 and 10.2 happens to allow C, at the cost of one unit to himself though at no cost to R, to alter his strategy at $L - 2$—playing his first instead of his dominant second—so

Figure 10.2

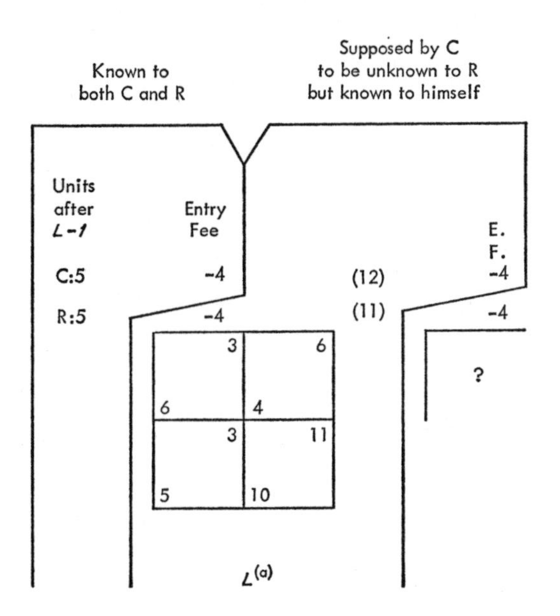

as to call R's attention to the facts of C's own comprehension of the implications of the sequence of matrices, of C's anxiety to continue the game even at some cost to himself, and therefore of his intention to play his second, game-prolonging strategy at $L - 1$. This device of playing an unexpected strategy in order to signal information to another player is analogous with the procedure recommended by American strategists—of "signaling" one's intentions to an opponent by means of some sort of military action—e.g., bombing North Vietnam or suspending the bombing. It is open to similar objections: the signal, since it makes no statement but merely invites attention to a general situation with many distinct facets, can be misunderstood all too easily—such signals are not statements to be understood, let alone demonstrative arguments to be followed, but hints.

Nevertheless, to drop a hint, even in the course of a formal game as in Figures 10.1 and 10.2, can be "rational"—i.e., "in accord with right reason." One is playing against someone whom one must suppose to have the same capacities as oneself for imaginative foresight and for imputation. On the other hand, such action is not prescribed by the Postulates of Rationality, though not forbidden by them either. We shall see in a moment that this has important consequence in assessment of the logical status of our game-theoretical models of world politics. First, however, it should be noticed that, by allowing this stratagem of the hint, we have grafted onto the conflict-game a communication-game.

That this is possible is of some theoretical interest: a frequent criticism of the game-theoretical approach is that by abstracting from the world-political process only the elements of conflict and cooperation in the pursuit of power, it reduces politics to something a-political, removing precisely that network of communicating individuals referred to in the first chapter of this volume as the world-political "conversation." We now see that, though many other criticisms of the game-theoretical approach may have to be accepted as valid, this one need not. Furthermore, it is not merely the dropping of hints that is shown to be graftable onto the conflict-game. Diplomacy considered as a means of eliciting and communicating information (and misinformation) can be represented in a supergame model, not usually in so crude a form as in our example above, but in principle similarly, provided it is clear both that out of the stakes a price must be paid for communication, and that sending or receipt of information may call in question the dominance of a strategy considered simply in terms of conflict and cooperation.

We have examined just one series of games whose properties made difficult the generalizing of any theory from it: (1) though each game in the series happened to have a saddle-point at a mutually advantageous outcome, the series as a whole, though not zero-sum, turned out so competitive as to deserve being characterized as an elimination-game; (2) while at first sight there was a straightforward path for both parties through the successive saddle-points, and thus a solution on certain terms for the series as a whole, the player who in each several game had happened to have a dominant strategy could attempt to divert the series as a whole from its straightforward but non-ending path and to terminate it to his own advantage, if he preferred limited gains to the prospect of a completely unknown future; (3) this diversionary strategy, however, would not be rationally acceptable to him if he should impute insight into it to the other player; (4) there turned out to stem from that third property an indefinitely extendable tree of imputations, which permitted us to graft an "information-game" on to the series as a whole considered as an "elimination-game"; (5) since the introduction of the operation of "imputing" considerably proliferated the game-tree and cast in question the preferences for various sequences of outcomes on account of uncertainties about the unknown future and also about the "other" player's range of insight and foresight into the game, the defining of a sense for "a solution" to the game as a whole greatly increased in difficulty. What produces these ramifications of the game is the imaginative act of *imputing,* which we must now examine. (It has nothing to do with the *technical* term, "imputation," employed by mathematicians.) The following section originated in reflections upon reports of the use of a computer to create artificial "players" (in the form of schedules of preference) for a political war-game previously played as a table-stakes game by human players. We begin by considering the activity of imputing motives in real-life political situations.

II

To think politically entails to impute motives. President de Gaulle was reported in 1965 as speculating aloud that the overthrow of Ben Bella in Algeria had been intended by Peking to help exclude Moscow from the Afro-Asian conference. He was imputing a motive. The import of the present section is that a *political* system cannot arise unless some of the constituent agents of the system impute motives.

This is not to say that no one can lead, or rule, or represent a Power unless he imputes motives: he might very well regard all the other Powers as being governed either so stupidly or so pluralistically that to impute motives to them would be a "category-mistake"—"By their very nature they are incapable of entertaining motives" or "Their leadership is so divided that the motives they entertain are so confused and contradictory as to be indistinguishable." A system in which *every* Power's leader—necessarily in error—refused to allow that any other could entertain a motive could not, on the present line of reasoning, be styled "political."

To impute a motive is, *inter alia,* to impute a disposition to declare some intention (to express some resolve). President de Gaulle might actually have said, "Mao perhaps said to himself, 'If I have Ben Bella overthrown, the Afro-Asians will be more inclined to exclude Moscow.' " The sentence between the inner quotes could be reinterpreted as a conditional statement—imputed by de Gaulle to Mao as a cogitation that Mao was supposed to have gone through in forming his (imputed) resolve to exclude Moscow from the conference—in which he deliberated how to create a resolve in the minds of the Afro-Asians: "If I have Ben Bella overthrown, at least some Afro-Asians will be inclined to decide, 'We will exclude Moscow.' " Now, the last sentence, "We will exclude Moscow," which in the imputation by de Gaulle of intentions to Mao we have had Mao conditionally impute as an idea to the Afro-Asian, does not make a statement, but declares a resolve. Resolves, though neither true nor not, are pertinent or not—i.e., because of a contract, implicit contract, covenant, constitution, established political system, informal political relationship, etc., some Powers' leaders expect that if any of them (severally) votes, declares, moves, etc., that the USSR be not admitted to the Afro-Asian Conference, that will make it in some degree more likely that the USSR *will* be excluded—*viz.,* that no Russian representative will be handed accreditation cards, and so on. But it would not, of course, be pertinent for a mere private person to resolve, "I will attempt to exclude the USSR," since he could do nothing about it. The resolve which de Gaulle was said to have imputed to Mao was primarily a resolve to have the Russians excluded; secondary to it was his supposed resolve to have Ben Bella overthrown, because this would create a resolve amongst the Afro-Asians to produce the effect desired by Mao.

If motives in politics are, amongst other things, dispositions to form resolves, and if the formation of a pertinent resolve can be the ground of a prediction (subjectively probabilistic, or, as in an alliance-permitting game, interpersonally uncertain), then we may say that political discourse always has some aspect that is relevant to the occurrence of future events. It is most important to notice that we must not say *simpliciter,* ". . . is *about* future events." By contrast, much natural-scientific discourse is about future events—e.g., oceanologists predict tidal waves. (Even here a well-known difficulty arises whether for natural-scientific predictions or for those about human action: both the sentence "Athens' fleet will be overwhelmed the day after tomorrow" and the sentence "Athens' fleet will join the sea-fight tomorrow" presuppose what is not necessarily true—*viz.,* that the fleet of Athens will exist at 0001 hours tomorrow morning. Some have, therefore, concluded that neither sentence states anything that must be true *or* false.) But someone who declares a resolve does not *ipso facto* predict. He does, however, give himself and perhaps others some basis for expectation, if not, exactly, for prediction.

Now, the reciprocal affording of grounds for expectation of interaction begins the constructing of a political system. Of course, a political system can exist and yet the events expected from it not occur—e.g., either because the actors' mutual expectations were in the first place unreal, or if, say, the delegates were to attend, with their minds all firmly made up, and an explosion were to kill them all as the chairman opened the first session. This proposition can be generalized: a political system may even exist upon expectations alone, though only briefly, like a conversation accidentally interrupted. On the other hand, expectations fulfilled in some merely mechanical fashion do not prolong a political system, any more than they do a conversation.

Statements about objects-other-than-statements—e.g., "The Athenian fleet sank yesterday"—are said to be in the "object-language." A statement about a statement about objects is in meta-language (language-level 1). A statement about a meta-linguistic statement is in meta-meta-language (language-level 2)—and so on. Politics entails at least the meta-meta-language —at least two language-levels up: at least the imputation of motives. Of course, there would be no point in thinking about others' motivations if none of them ever formed resolves; or if they formed only resolves that were not pertinent; or if they were known to be bound never to implement their resolves; and so on. Whereas, as we shall see, it is possible in principle to invent games which share this feature of political systems (indefinitely ascending levels of language), no gaming model can reproduce the peremptory quality of real-life politics, which may issue in capitulation, war, impoverishment, social disintegration. (In modeled games of war, no one is really killed.) Such possibilities constrain politicians from making a mere "game" out of politics for very long. The element of sanction in anarchic world politics no doubt prevents it in *most* cases from becoming very subtle; but this is an uneven limitation of practice, not a logical limitation in principle. There is no logically coercive reason why one should not go on imputing a motive for imputing a motive for . . . indefinitely.

For instance, assuming that President de Gaulle did "speculate aloud" as above, *we* may wonder why. Did he wish to incite the Russians and pro-Russians to attempt the restoration of Ben Bella? Was he trying to expose American impotence? Notice that such questions have a common presupposition—*viz.,* the *public* imputation of motives is itself a political act; it is a way of contributing to, because it may have an indirect effect upon the course of, the world-political conversation. This is as we should expect, since world-political action is for the most part pertinent utterance by the rulers of Powers. Before we consider the import of indefinitely higher reaches of language (e.g., imputation upon imputation), a brief digression is in order concerning nonverbal communication in politics.

Military action may be construed as political discourse. T. C. Schelling in *The Strategy of Conflict,* and more recently H. Kahn in *On Escalation* and in earlier works, have accustomed us to consider the possibility that even nuclear attacks can amount to political demands for a reappraisal by the attacker of his assessment of his own situation. Herman Kahn, for example, presents a scenario in which the Soviets have, in a crisis, invaded West Germany, and are continuing their advance:

> The Americans might then use two or three nuclear weapons to destroy bridges in the Soviet rear. . . . The purpose of the destruction is less to degrade logistics than to say, "Having used two or three nuclear weapons, are we not likely to use many more? Don't you want to reconsider putting such pressures on us?" The Soviets are then, indeed, likely to want to reconsider, but they might not be willing to admit it. They might themselves use two or three nuclear weapons. . . . But they are nevertheless likely to be frightened—as the Americans are likely to be by their own temerity. One can thus easily imagine a cease-fire being called immediately after the Soviet retaliation.[4]

Notice that the imagined American nuclear strike "says" that the Soviets would be wise to reconsider their imputation of American motives and resolves—i.e., the "statement" is now three language-levels up. But there are moves in games such as poker that have the same logical form: what is missing in the poker, and present in the political-military case, is that both

[4] H. Kahn, *On Escalation* (T. Walker and Son, 1965), p. 111.

parties are "frightened." That reciprocal fact may also be thought to "say" something: it should not only induce reciprocal reappraisals of each other's motivations, but also remind both Russians and Americans of their systemic relations—*viz.,* that each can destroy up to half of the other and all of Europe. What would "remind" them, presumably, would be their *feelings* of alarm: "being frightened" is an emotional state; "being deterred by considerations of reciprocal danger" is a rational disposition, which may but need not be engendered by fright.

Diplomats and statesmen, on the other hand, also speak the language of power. They, every bit as much as two or three nuclear weapons, can and do convey the conditional threat of three thousand nuclear weapons. "Negotiate rather than fight" means neither "Use moral rather than military sanctions," nor "Abjure power," nor even, in all cases, "Save lives." Political and diplomatic communications convey, in logical terms, more "information" than does communication by military initiative. The latter are to be preferred only when there is no time or opportunity for the former, or when the language of diplomacy is so primitive, as between newly met societies, or so debased through bluffing and equivocation, that deeds alone convey meaning.

The hierarchy of language in political discourse has only practical limits. When—to a number of persons or parties each trying to assess (1) upon what, if anything, each of the others is resolved, and (2) how each is assessing each of the others—an additional person or party is visibly added, the assessments of the original number must go up at least one level in the hierarchy of languages. Further, each person can always go on assessing how A is assessing how B is assessing how C is . . . , thereby adding extra levels to the hierarchy at least of his own internal languages. There is no reason in principle why any assessment, at any level of language, should not be imputed, or frankly declared, or dissembled, or denied, or otherwise discussed. In practice, the number of levels that any human can entertain must be finite at any given instant, but there is no reason why at the next instant he may not add another level.

The subconscious and intuitive hierarchy may be vastly greater than the conscious and explicit. That, of course, is merely an hypothesis in psychology. But we are accustomed to mathematical and strategic—so why not to power-political?—intuition. A statesman may go through the equivalent of far more cogitations than he could ever declare. If necessary, particular chains of reasoning within this subconscious web (though never the whole) can be brought to consciousness and even spelled out. Scenario-writing and war-gaming are amongst the devices used to effect this, in some leading Powers' forming of foreign policy. But it is quite certain that the most creative statesman cannot possibly set forth for himself all the alternatives open to him. As Herbert Simon has taught us to say, political choice is at most a "satisficing" and not an optimizing procedure: the statesman *invents* just a few promising lines of policy, imagines how they might be developed and how other Powers would react to them; then, presumably, settles upon the least unsatisfactory of them. It is in that (subconscious) scanning process, one supposes, that the upper levels of the hierarchy of languages are reached. Evidence that the hierarchy is subconsciously ascended obtains in the fact that occasionally the steps are consciously recapitulated in a fashion which logicians might translate into a hierarchy of languages. For instance, the politician arguing amongst his fellow-countrymen for a policy he has invented will recapitulate, more or less guardedly, the one or two alternatives which he has consciously explored and rejected, in order to show that his accepted policy is preferable. The hierarchical structure of imputations and so forth becomes apparent in such recapitulations.

Declaring his policy publicly—i.e., so as to affect the rulers of other Powers—he will not usually display any very elaborate hierarchy of imputations: open avowals of the latter would be for the most part tactless. (It is hard to believe that Athenian envoys, sophistically trained as they were, would really have stated their position with the ruthlessness that Thucydides attributes to them in the Melian dialogue.) The public communications of world politics bear to the statesmen's thinking that explains them a relation much like that between the overt dialogue of buyer and seller, and the several hypothecated arrays of their preferences that economists adduce to help explain the hagglers' dialogue. It is chiefly the nonquantitativeness of the political *explicandum* that distinguishes the two types of relation. Their resemblance is significant since, amongst other reasons, in either case the suggested *explicans* can be construed as a reinterpretation: a reinterpretation that begins from a commonsense answer to the practical question, "What was he getting at?" and develops and abstracts such an answer only so far as is needed to make it a plausible, sufficient, and accurately fitting interpretation. The difference from many types of explanation in the more exact of the natural sciences consists in the political and economic explanations' not causing us to look for any undiscovered existents (e.g., subconscious processes and implicit lists of preferences somehow "in" the brain); whereas in a well-developed physical explanation of, say, the phenomena of heredity, we find our expectations satisfied by the discovery in the organism of such substances as DNA and RNA. Further, the hope of working out a rigorous analysis, in some formal logic, of the nature of political discourse and its explanations is by many orders more forlorn than that for the logical formalization of the exact sciences. Though the terminology of politics is comparatively impoverished, its "syntax" has all the richness and variety of "natural-grown" language.

World-political action consists for the most part of public utterance. Anyone who takes the necessary pains can put himself in a position to follow it on most occasions. But the necessary pains involve sympathetic identification with other and often opposed Powers' points of view and perceived situations. Since their leaders' "perceptions" of their situations must include their images of still other Powers and leaders, which are in turn made up in large measure from the imputations of the "percipients"; and since those of us who are private students and not leaders in politics have not, any more than the leaders themselves, better routes into the minds of others than by imputations which survive the test of confrontation with—and explain—the evidence of the national leaders' actions: then there can be no point in looking "behind" the public utterances for some supposed social force which *is* political reality: the public utterances are themselves objective enough, even when tendentious, declaratory, and subjective. Indeed, they constitute most of the power-political process; but, as we have said in previous chapters, internal-political conflicts and decisions relevant to foreign policy "issues" do sometimes condition the national leader's acts. If that is what we are looking for "behind" the leader's pronouncements, well and good. But the internal-political process itself is not a "force": the lobbying pressure-group consists of people who form resolves and impute motives. Our analysis of imputation applies universally, to any political process whatsoever.

Furthermore, it rapidly becomes an accepted convention, amongst the rulers of Powers in contact with each other, just at what level and in what manner their statements must be pitched in order to take political effect. Or to put it another way: so far as a number of Powers share an understanding of how to make pronouncements politically significant to each other, their rulers, together with entourages and informed critics, make up the *rudiments* of a world polity. The tenor of political exchanges is not constant, and is modified by the outbreak and conclusion of major wars, great shifts of the internal balance of power within influential states, and so forth. Previous diplomatic or equivalent experience improves a statesman's ear for the prevailing tenor. But there remains some information about it to be procured by academic analysis. Amongst this procurable information might be findings about the complexity of response to other Powers, severally and jointly, by any particular Power: and about the number of rungs in the ladder of language that could be inferred from the leaders' public utterances. Let me illustrate this point.

Abstractly considered, there are at present about a score of countries, out of the total of more than a hundred, that might well be classified as significant Powers. Potentially, then, we live in a multi-Power system. But if the Kremlin, for instance, holds that there are only three "essential actors"—the socialist, the imperialist, and the nonaligned camps—and regards the action of states which does not fit in with that vision as so much "natural" background noise; or if, like some strategic thinkers of the 1950s, one deems the US-USSR confrontation by so much the most important conflict that all others should be in effect discounted; and if, at the same time, most other Powers, while admitting the primacy of the Big Two and of their quarrels, take note of at least a few private opponents and allies: then the history of the system as a whole will be fitted neither by a two-person, nor a three-person, nor an unqualified twenty-person model, but by something much more complex. We would need, in fact, a model in which (1) there were great differences of capacity between players; (2) very few players attended to the actions of all of their number, and most were variously interested in a small range (within the total) apparently relevant to their own environment but always including the two or three very strongest players; (3) there were considerable differences in levels of language-hierarchy to which the various players were prepared to go—some would go no further than imputing motives to the several players they were concerned with, while others would impute to their opposite numbers the imputing to themselves of imputations about the latter's motive—and so on; (4) all such imputations would be more or less corrigible and confirmable interpretations of what the other players were about. In other words, imputation is *not* knowledge, not even partial knowledge, but hypothesis—until evidence comes to hand that confirms it, after which it is better classified as background information. But political action has to be taken on assessments that always include a large element of as-yet-unconfirmed imputation, which is *not* "imperfect information": even though a careful policy-maker may privately assign some subjective numerical probability to it so as to make his array of estimates at least internally self-consistent, his doing so is not a necessary condition for his action. Therefore, models of a multi-Power action-system may be appropriately designed so as to allow the actors a certain room for *invention* both of assessments and of policies.

This is especially important if we take due cognizance of the verbal character of most political action: we cannot say what the action was except by discovering what, on the face of it, the communication meant—an objective though nonquantitative matter—and then by guessing what it was intended to achieve, and how third parties would guess what it was intended to achieve.

Contrast the political situation with a model for a game of contract bridge: as far as concerns bidding, the actions (making a bid, passing, doubling and redoubling) are, similarly, verbal. But they are also essentially quantitative. Furthermore, the number of permissible bidding sequences in any hand is finite, and, even more significantly, so is the number of interpretations (imputations) of why a given bid, etc., was made, assuming very stringent specifications about the "rationality" of the bidder. But that last-mentioned number is in any case enormous, so much so that a strict game-theoretical solution for contract bridge is not likely in practice to be available to our present resources for computation.

Now, when bidding goes into a second round, the first bidder in that round must presumably attribute some information and intention to each of the other three players. The questions arise: (1) Should there be a limit to the regress of attributions (imputations) which we might expect to be made by a rational player? (2) In modeling the course of a game of bridge, how satisfactory would it be to substitute, for human players who guess about and attribute intentions to each other, artificial players who employ at worst a rule-of-thumb strategy for bidding, but do nothing equivalent to attributing intentions?

These questions are of course intimately connected. Suppose, in answer to the second of them, that we give each of the four artificial players the kind of instructions for bidding that involve no more than responding to (1) the general features of the hand dealt to himself, and (2) no more than the two previous players' calls. Then, clearly, we have set a *very* low limit to the regress of attributions—*viz.*, zero. But if, as contended above, we have live players to work our model, then we cannot tell, in advance of any particular play, to how many levels of attribution (imputation) each several player will attempt access.

In the matter of contract bridge, as in chess, there is an obvious means of telling whether—indeed, how far—Monte Carloing with artificial, non-attributing players yields a good model of how intelligent and consistent living players would go: we can have the living play against the artificial gamesters several times. After a few rounds of experience, the live players should begin to have, on the average, more wins than the artificial ones. Then we could segregate them so that live plays only with live, and artificial only with artificial, expecting (upon the basis of our contention that rationality and insight is unevenly distributed, and by no means predictable, amongst human agents), that when hands were dealt that might seem not amenable to the conventional bidding norms, the live players' bidding sequences would differ from the artificial players'.

The "Game of Power," invented 1958–9,[5] unlike contract bridge, permits a free choice of "allies" and "opponents," and also of degrees of alliance and opposition. Though, unlike actual Power-politics, its pay-offs are strictly quantities, its rules do not enforce the observing of pacts or

[5] See M. A. Kaplan, A. L. Burns, and Richard E. Quandt, "Theoretical Analysis of the 'Balance of Power'," *Behavioral Science,* V, No. 3 (July 1960), 240–52; and A. L. Burns, "Prospects for a General Theory of International Relations," *World Politics,* XIV, No. 1 (October 1961), 25–46, and simultaneously in *The International System,* ed. K. Knorr and S. Verba (Princeton: Princeton University Press, 1961) pp. 25–46.

contracts, so that in this one respect at least it approaches real-life conditions: a shrewd player will consider the motives of an offer of alliance or demonstration of opposition; and even if he puts some subjective probabilistic quantity upon the observing of such pacts, that quantity is of a different kind from those prescribed, deterministically or probabilistically, by the rules of the game. Since it is a competitive table-stakes game, it of course allows a much smaller proportion of politicking and a much larger one of naked coercion than does the real world system. Nevertheless, the prudence of considering the motives of one's opponents in the Game of Power does assimilate a little to world politics, as does another feature: the possible outcomes of a play of the game, and the branches of the game tree, are so numerous that no player can possibly optimize amongst them; but he may "satisfice." Thus the Game of Power gives scope for creative strategic thinking, not only in the sense in which chess does, but also (because bidding for membership in alliances occurs) in something of the sense in which world politics does.

In the latter sense, one peculiar development is *not* encouraged by the Game: it provides no motive for a transvaluation of values. In real life a national ruler may come to value other ends beside or above territorial integrity, national security, and prosperity—e.g., national membership in a supranational community; national honor, or benevolence. Diplomatic action can result from such transvaluations in oneself, and can be directed to producing them in other leaders.

Since, however, the Game of Power provides in its pay-off system a stable set of ultimate motivations, it permits changeability in proximate policies. Changing fortunes of the game sometimes can (and rationally ought to) redirect a player from a hegemonial to a power-balancing policy, and so on. What is the force here of ". . . rationally ought to . . ."? *Not* that the Game's game-theoretic solution prescribes for him a change of policy at some stage—for no one has a hope of discovering the game-theoretic solution; *but* insights and premonitions extending to a change of policy may be called for from him at a certain stage.

Artificial players can be created—e.g., by a computer. Why cannot they reproduce *all* the propensities of a human player? One kind of reason is practical, though practical to such a degree that it may as well be a reason of principle: the simulation of any human propensity in this Game uses up a great deal of computer capacity. (E.g., the propensity to make errors of calculation would take a little capacity; the propensity to estimate and give a probability to another artificial player's future actions—upon the basis of what the estimating player "knows" about his capacities and about his actions to date—would take more capacity than most current computers could afford.)

Another reason, this time of principle, arises out of that. Suppose we want each artificial player to simulate the imputing of motives to one other player. But, as earlier parts of this section have tried to show, the whole range of *types* of consideration that go into making up one's own mind also go into guessing how someone else is making up his mind. Though I cannot attribute to another person precisely my own cogitations (otherwise, I could simply take my own conclusions to be his), I may reasonably assume that, abstractly speaking, he goes through the same kind and degrees of cogitation that I do. Of course I need not consciously work through all of that—a great deal of it, we suppose, goes on "subconsciously." But in a computer every detail of it must have some kind of representation unless there is some way of demonstrating that part of the process is already duplicated, one for one, in another process available to the first-considered of the artificial players. So every artificial player simulating just a single-level imputation of motive to another must reduplicate the formal features of those of the other's inferential steps analogous to its own. Thus, suppose n artificial players whose construction and operation use up a certain amount of computer capacity; then an additional amount of computer capacity equal to $(n^2 - n)$ times the first amount would be used up if each were required to impute to every one of the others just one level of cogitation. For every additional player and for each additional level of cogitation, the additional amount of used-up computer capacity increases geometrically. So a computer will soon exhaust its capacity doing what a live person does in a quite ordinary political situation.

An objection to the foregoing line of argument suggests itself. Herbert Simon and others have shown that a computer can be programmed to satisfice. In playing chess, a satisficing machine will explore only a few branches of the game-tree, but will explore them many moves deep, instead of optimizing at the third-move level (say) as a computer employing the same capacity would do in exhausting the alternatives as far as it could. The computer programmed for satisficing could no doubt save enough on one player's development to allow "him" to impute to another player an overlapping process of satisficing cogitations. Difficulties arise, however, if there is evidence that limbs of the game-tree which the other player looks to be climbing do *not* overlap with those that interest the computing player. The nature of the game in question need not always guarantee that they should. There is no evident way of helping a computer to benefit by informed advice. Before the coup of September 1964, one of Her Majesty's Ministers might have asked an expert on Indonesia, "What *is* Sukarno up to?" and have expected to understand the answer in a general way without having to take into his head *everything* that went to inform the expert's imputation of motives to Sukarno.

For these reasons I do not believe that the satisficing program, useful as it may be for simulating human cogitation about the proliferating possibilities of a game-tree, is likely to be of great help when the problem is not merely to explore the more promising branches of such a tree, but also to explore other parties' exploration of it. Ingenious programs can be devised that go some distance in this direction; but it is still worth distinguishing between the kind of game-play produced by inerrant but artificial players, and that by erring but human ones.

Indeed, it seems a useful policy, for research into stakes-game meta-models of generally received concepts about systems of Powers, to run human and artificial playings in parallel—i.e., for games that produce situations resembling those of multiperson conflict and of politics, the kind of Monte Carlo solution procurable by a computer which creates artificial players and endows them with the inhuman capacity to follow inerrantly and to the letter a self-consistent strategy, could be sought also by human players. Suppose that, given certain initial conditions in the game, machine-created artificial players produce in a long run of the game what we call a "stable equilibrium"—*viz.,* no player is eliminated; then it is a matter of great interest whether or not the same result is procured by human players. If so, there would be a presumption that the strategic propensities programmed into the artificial players constitutes the rationale of a solution to the given version of the game. If not, then it would be interesting to inquire whether it was human frailty or human ingenuity that destabilized the situation.

Similar results, secondly, may be achieved by the employment of differing and even logically incompatible strategies. If this happens, it suggests that the stabilizing propensities belong neither to the artificial nor to the human players, but somehow to the situation and system themselves. For example, the modeled system's equivalent for the military exchange rate can make it extremely difficult to eliminate a player even while providing some, but not absolutely compelling, motivation for initiating warfare.

On first consideration, the trend of this chapter suggests that (1) any strategy with which it is possible to program an artificial player could in practice be employed by a human player, (2) but not necessarily *vice versa.* But closer thought indicates that conclusion (1) is not necessarily true: the artificial player's inerrancy, the logical impossibility of programming it to "use its own judgment"—e.g., to invent a "personal" probability—allow it some strategic options not available to humans. Recourse to these types of strategy should be precluded if a model is to be even theoretically relevant to world politics. If that is ensured, then fruitful experiments might, as suggested above, be designed in which humans replicate artificial players' games. The explanation of the course taken by an artificial player's game must lie somewhere within the conjunction of the game-system's imposed constraints and the strategies specifically programmed into the artificial players. If human players are then set exactly the same task while being left free to design their own strategies, but if subsequent analysis of the game shows that, in some degree at least, part of the strategies they employed were identical with those programmed into the artificial players, then we have also obtained some clue to the explanation of the course taken by the human game—a clue, that is, to the formal and logical explanation of a particular system of human conflict and co-operation. It would be important in such an experiment not to resort, in analysis of the human game, to asking the players what they had in mind; the information we need must be objective—i.e., objectively inferred from consideration of their actions.

To summarize: The Game of Power is a game of skill comparable in difficulty and inferential depth with contract bridge. One can alter the course of a rubber of bridge by altering that game's pay-off structure—e.g., one could reduce the incidence of high bids by increasing considerably the penalties for failing to win the contracted tricks when doubled. In the same way, one can influence the human playing of the Game of Power by altering the pay-off structure (as well as the number of players, the exchange rate, the methods of building up one's power and resources, etc.). The theoretical advantage of influencing the players in this way, rather than of directly instructing them to follow some particular set of strategic maxims or to adopt some particular style of play, is that if from all this free interaction some systematic pattern of play does emerge, then one knows that the pattern is quite firmly established. It has established itself amidst great variations between human stupidity and human ingenuity.

On behalf of the balances of power and of terror it has been argued that they are maintained both by fools who cannot understand their working and by brilliant knaves who labor to circumvent them. This is a theoretical hypothesis—indeed, an implicitly mathematical hypothesis. But it *is* an hypothesis about theories of the behavior of human systems—not of computer systems. States of equilibrium or disequilibrium amongst artificial players can be a partial guide to similar states amongst humans. But if taken as the sole guides, they could be most deceptive.

ELEVEN

Theoretical Laws of Statics Undiscoverable: The Example of Alliance Theory

In the foregoing chapters, we have emphasized personal initiative in world politics. But a general theory must, of course, be propoundable without reference to particular names, whether of persons or of societies. So we consider the general theory of politics as dealing with two distinguishable kinds or levels of system: systems of Powers (external); and systems of polity (internal). We suppose the two levels to be connected as follows: the outcomes of external-political interaction are taken up as "issues" by internal political parties and politicians; developments in internal politics, when they impinge upon the external-political processes affected by them, do so as *demarches* by the Power which has engendered them or by other Powers perceiving and responding to them; or, if two or more Powers coincide in engendering them, as systemic crises, sometimes as world crises.

A complete general theory of Power politics would, amongst other things, propound the laws of behavior of all power-political systems. What sorts of law?

No law of the political process (which is, in essence, "act" or "deed" in response to "act" or "deed") can be a "law of nature," either deterministic in the so-called Newtonian sense, or stochastic as under the rubric of post-Heisenberg physics (though strictly stochastic—i.e., chance—elements can and do affect powerfully all kinds of political behavior, and would have to be allowed for in any complete general theory of politics). Nor are such laws merely normative, though normative corollaries are closely related to them. We assume, rather, that they are most akin to the laws of that branch of economics that deals with the behavior of firms under oligopoly. They would presuppose more or less rational, more or less informed activity, and they would state the necessary consequences (outcomes) of interactions of various kinds by various kinds and numbers of Powers. From another angle, they would state the sufficient conditions, comprising actions by Powers, for given states-of-affairs in Power systems (or, more often, for disjunctions of alternative states of affairs). In the present section of this whole volume—having in the previous one considered possible laws of the system's dynamics—we have been criticizing various attempts at a theory of the system's statics. This concludes our recapitulation.

I

We now try to show that a general theory of statics is unavailable in as much as it would require, for completeness' sake, a general theory of alliances (or "coalitions"), and that the latter runs into difficulties at the simplest, most quantitative levels. Most inter-Power systems have more than two members; and, amongst such systems, conditions of stable or unstable equilibrium are usually affected one way or another by the possibility of Powers' making common cause against a threat. Common advantage, or common fear of being attacked or overwhelmed, are rarely the sole, but usually the essential and the strongest, motives for allying. But since the making or breaking or refusing of alliance is rarely costless to the Power that does so, we shall suppose that its rulers prefer the expected consequences of their action above the expected consequences of their not taking it. If such a difference could be expressed quantitatively, the Powers might find it informative to do so. In Chapter 6, pp. 148–149, we propounded a potentially quantitative rationale for alliance formation: developing our idea of the capitulation point—itself a quantitative indicator of the value put by a society's ruling set upon the *desideratum* of its remaining a Power—we derived measures (1) of the value, to one Power in a three-Power system, of allying with a second Power, and (2) of the disvalue, to the other Powers, of the prospects of being excluded from the alliance. But we admitted that the application to reality of such measures would require information, both about others' capabilities and about their intentions, never directly and often not even indirectly available to statesmen; furthermore it was clear that for n-Power systems our diagrammatic approach would need to be multidimensional, and would become incalculably complicated. While this approach through the concept of a capitulation point dispenses with game-theoretical utiles, and thus avoids the "economism" bound up with the applying of game theory to politics, I cannot at present see how to depict through it the cluster of problems about n-person situations which we are now about to discuss by means of game theory.

There is no shortage of rules-of-thumb about alliance policy. For twenty-five centuries or more, the sages of statecraft have supposed certain maxims to be discoverable which would direct a "prince" how to make the most advantageous choice in respect of alliance. "Your enemy's enemy is your friend." "Ally yourself with the Power next-but-one to your borders." "Try to form a coalition against any Power about to become predominant." "Break up any coalition of the whole world forming against you." "When in doubt, stay out."

Such maxims, no matter how many, never add up to a general theory of alliances; but they all do presuppose or call attention to certain features of and interconnections in reality that promise upon first reflection to afford the points of departure for a general theory: the maxims, for example, all presuppose the existence of at least three Powers, each disposed in some degree to cooperate with or to oppose, or on the other hand to be indifferent to, each of the others—i.e., an n-Power, mixed-motive situation, which seems to invite the application of game theory (*viz.,* the theory of the n-person game in which coalitions and "side-payments" are permitted). How far such an abstract-mathematical theory of alliances is already available, and how far, if available, it can be applied to power-political phenomena, we shall now investigate.

We begin by trying to show that abstract alliance-games can be devised for which several equally plausible outcomes exist, and from that try to prove that game theory cannot provide a specifically predictive (sufficiently explanatory) applicable theory of alliance phenomena; we then conclude that, since game theory appears quite the most promising candidate for being the source of such a theory, no *complete* theory of alliances is available.

Our method shall be to analyze several games of bargaining. These games are devices for exploring the logical limits of theory: in no sense at all are they simulations of international politics; but the rules for the bargaining in the game are intended to permit a rich variety of choice and a wide range (1) of preferences for risk-taking or for caution, (2) of imputations—i.e., guesses that any player might make about the other players' risk-taking propensities, foresight, intelligence, capacity for bluffing, and so forth.[1]

Games are restricted at this stage to three-person, zero-sum, coalition games in which no player would have a dominant strategy if no coalitions were permitted. We are seeking a game in which (a) for any coalition, there is no dominant strategy available; (b) for every coalition, and for each of the three players, at least one rationally supportable strategy is available; (c) for every coalition and player, no mixed strategy is available. The form of such a game will go through three stages, as in Solo: (1) Prop! (2) Cop! (3) Play! We shall describe these in the reverse order.

Stage 3: Play! Each of the three players implements either of just *two* alternative strategies. (Any player may, or may not, have bound himself at either Stage 1 or Stage 2, conditionally or unconditionally, to some particular alternative, or alternatives.)

Each player's gains or losses are determined by his and the other's choice of alternatives, unless he or some other(s) has previously agreed to share, in some ratio or another. They may not divide units into fractions, and they may divide only what they have gained—e.g., someone who gets zero may receive but cannot give away anything.

Stage 2: Cop! At this stage, any player to whom in Stage 1 a proposal or proposals has been made may (but need not) accept any one proposal (P) even if at Stage 1 he himself has made some contrary proposal, unless he has already (at Stage 1) bound himself not to accept any of the classes of proposals containing (P).

But if any two or more players, having made proposals to each other, accept each other's offer, any gains at Stage 3 resultant to that partnership must be shared equally. However, if such reciprocal proposals contradict each other, not only or at all in respect of pay-offs, but in respect of the actual strategies proposed for either or both players, then they shall be deemed void.

If a player, who (i) has himself received no proposal at Stage 1, or (ii) having received such a proposal, does not at this Stage 2 accept it, has some proposal accepted which he had made at Stage 1, he is bound to implement that accepted proposal during Stage 3. That is, each player is bound to implement his accepted proposals unless at Stage 2 he accepts a proposal made to him, or unless all proposals become void on account of some other rule.

Only transitive proposals and acceptances take effect. Otherwise (unless he has bound himself unconditionally at Stage 1) no player is bound by intransitive Props and Cops—e.g., if A proposes a joint strategy to B who does so to C who does so to A who accepts C's proposal, while C accepts B's and B accepts A's, no one is bound.

[1] See above, Chapters 2 and 10.

If at Stage 1 a player has made mutually contradictory proposals, he shall be assumed to have made none at all—i.e., no one may accept any part of them, and he cannot be bound by them. Similarly, a player's acceptances, if mutually contradictory, shall be deemed void.

When each player has written "Cop—," or nothing at all, as the case may be, Stage 2 is to be completed by the reading out of all the players' returns.

Stage 1: Prop! At this first stage, any player must do one of two things. Either he

1. says nothing. Having said nothing, but having had an offer(s) made to him, he may at Stage 2 agree to accept any offer or self-consistent set of offers made to him; having said nothing at Stage 1, and having at Stage 2 not accepted for any reason an offer subsequently binding upon him, he may at Stage 3 play either of his two final alternatives. Or he may at Stage 1
2. make an offer(s) to either or both of the other players, conditionally or unconditionally, provided the offer(s) is certain to be in his power to carry out. It is essential to notice that, so long as his set of offers remains self-consistent and within his power to implement no matter what other players do at Stages 1, 2, and 3, the offers may be as *conditional* as the player likes to make them—e.g., A may propose an arrangement to B conditional upon B's having received an offer from C which A specifies in his proposal to B—and so on. Reciprocal offers by players specifying these kinds of condition can be shown to be either mutually consistent or mutually inconsistent by application of the ordinary rules of logic—e.g., those concerned with self-referring propositions. The significance of this provision is that it makes the type of game potentially infinite at the bidding stage: otherwise, some mixed strategies in bidding would have to be optimal, and discoverable *in principle;* thus the type of game would be solvable—again in principle. In practice no doubt (as, surely, in power-political practice) there would be various limits to the number of conditions which any particular player could include in his proposals. But (i) we could not predict, of any particular player, just where his limits would lie, and (ii) in any case such a prediction could be self-defeating—*viz.,* if the predicted player were to hear of it and to include in his proposal one condition more than had been predicted.

This game is like contract bridge, and even more like Solo, in as much as the strategies for the "bidding" stages of the game (Stage 1—"Prop!"; Stage 2—"Cop!") are rationally decidable solely in terms of the range of outcomes available at the conclusion of the "playing" stage (Stage

3). And at that stage, the range is determined by the way the "hands are dealt," or, in this game, how the matrix happens to be arranged.

In Matrix 11.1 (taken from Kenneth Boulding[2]), each combination of letters represents one out of eight possible outcomes of the "playing" stage of the game. This follows from the rule that each player has to choose at that stage between just two strategies. Those numbers will decide what pay-offs each player is initially allocated before the dividing of an alliance's spoils, if any, which we have seen is determined at the "bidding" or bargaining stages of the game. Boulding's is a zero-sum game, in which A does best to play his second strategy, no matter what the other two do; and given that, B does best to play *his* second strategy; and given both, C limits his losses by playing his first strategy. So the outcome is at the outside bottom right. The reader will also notice that no pair of players can improve their joint pay-off by alliance.

Matrix 11.1

A^1, B^1, C^1 0, 0, 0			A^2, B^1, C^1 2, −1, −1
	A^1, B^1, C^2 0, 1, −1	A^2, B^1, C^2 1, −1, 0	
	A^1, B^2, C^2 −1, 2, −1	A^2, B^2, C^2 2, 0, −2	
A^1, B^2, C^1 0, −1, 1			A^2, B^2, C^1 1, 0, −1

Next, we have a matrix which is also zero-sum, and in which, unlike Boulding's Matrix 11.1, no player has any rational ground for preferring one strategy to another if all alliances are forbidden. As it turns out, each player is also indifferent between joining and not joining a coalition. It follows that at every stage of the game as played with this second matrix, bidding or playing, each player may as well toss a coin to decide his strategy.

Thirdly, we set out a matrix (11.3) which is three-person, zero-sum, and which would, if all coalitions were forbidden, leave each player indifferent between his two strategies. It is clear that at the bidding stage of this game a quite obviously dominant agreement for coalition suggests itself between A and B: if each plays his second strategy, C is bound to lose

[2] For the form of the concluding (postbargaining) stage of the game I am indebted to Kenneth Boulding's *Conflict and Defence,* pp. 53–57.

Matrix 11.2

A^1, B^1, C^1
1, −1, 0

A^2, B^1, C^1
1, 1, −2

A^1, B^1, C^2
0, 1, −1

A^2, B^1, C^2
−1, −1, 2

A^1, B^2, C^2
0, 1, −1

A^2, B^2, C^2
−1, 1, 0

A^1, B^2, C^1
−1, 0, 1

A^2, B^2, C^1
1, −2, 1

whatever he plays, so that it will be a matter of "chance" which he plays, and therefore also a matter of "chance" whether it is A or B who gains 2; C cannot bribe or threaten either into any position more favorable to himself.

Lastly, we introduce a matrix (11.4) which offers inducements quite different from any of the preceding matrices, even though it is (i) zero-sum; (ii) productive of rational indifference between playing strategies if all alliances are forbidden; and (iii) not productive, at the bidding stage, of any obviously dominant strategy for forming alliances. But unlike Matrix 11.2, no player is *indifferent about alliance formation.* It is far from the case that he may as well toss a coin to decide between partners. For each, the argument for either partnership is strong but never conclusive; and though the balance of argument is certainly against being excluded by a partnership of the other two, there is nevertheless quite a case for the strategy of waiting for others to make the approaches and, sometimes, the threats (against each other) which may redound to one's own advantage.

Matrix 11.3

A^1, B^1, C^1
−1, 0, 1

A^2, B^1, C^1
−1, 1, 0

A^1, B^1, C^2
0, 0, 0

A^2, B^1, C^2
−2, −1, 3

A^1, B^2, C^2
0, 0, 0

A^2, B^2, C^2
2, 1, −3

A^1, B^2, C^1
1, −3, 2

A^2, B^2, C^1
1, 2, −3

Matrix 11.4

A^1, B^1, C^1 2, -2, 0			A^2, B^1, C^1 4, -2, -2
	A^1, B^1, C^2 -2, 2, 0	A^2, B^1, C^2 0, 2, -2	
	A^1, B^2, C^2 2, -4, 2	A^2, B^2, C^2 0, 0, 0	
A^1, B^2, C^1 -2, -2, 4			A^2, B^2, C^1 -4, 6, -2

Out of a hundred plays with this matrix, the "unlikeliest" outcomes (e.g., inner bottom left and inner bottom right) have been arrived at on at least two occasions. Apart from that, the writer has been unable to find a single strategy that any one of the three players could profitably employ in any two consecutive plays of the game; or, indeed, any which would give him a reliable expectation of better than zero at any single play. Since it is a zero-sum game with indifference for each player between either of his playing strategies when all alliance is forbidden, each player has an *a priori* expectation of zero returns. That, of course, does not mean that for any given playing of the game, he is entitled to expect at least zero; but only that, at first sight, and given that he plays an indefinite number of times against players no more intelligent than himself, he is entitled to expect zero returns over the long run of plays.

This has in principle an important consequence: in the long run it will not pay any player consistently to make an offer to another which would involve himself in losing one unit in order to "make sure" of not losing two units (I put "make sure" in quotation marks to indicate that even an offer so tempting to his ally is not *logically* certain to be accepted): if he could be counted on *always* to make such an offer, the others could find a way to win from him, perhaps by turns, all the time. Nor will it pay him *always* to say "No bid" at the bidding stage of the game, for similar reasons. If we put these two conclusions together, we find that the outcomes that comprise the set offering net joint gains to each one at a time of the three possible pairs of allies, will be those shown in Matrix 11.5.

N.B. Against (A + C), B is indifferent between his two "playing" strategies, as is C when against (A + B). Against (B + C), A minimizes loss by playing his first strategy. The net gain in each case is a net gain for the allied pair jointly: there is no overriding consideration why they should not divide the spoils equally. But it does not follow that these are

Matrix 11.5

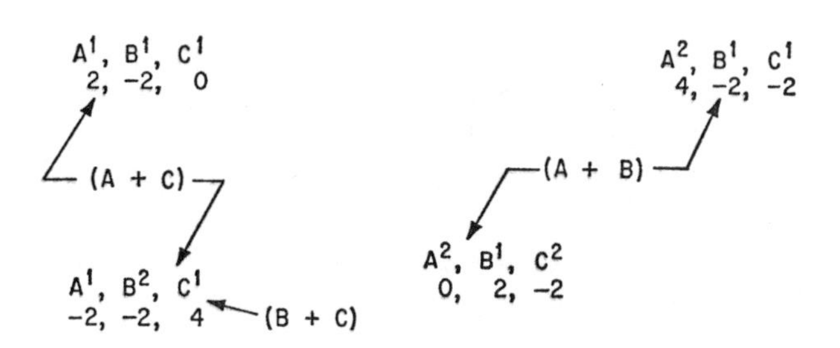

the *only possible* outcomes if all players are technically rational. If, in a finite zero-sum game, no player has a dominant strategy (i.e., a strategy he would be advised to employ every time), then each player must have, in principle, a mixture of strategies. When all (rational) players should employ mixed strategies, the outcome of any particular game is not determined, but "stochastic"—i.e., a matter of chance. However, the chances are calculable—in principle. But how is the optimum mixture of strategies decided for each player?

The answer is: only by examination of the entire "game-tree," or by an analytic procedure which requires as much information as would such an examination. A complete game-tree consists of the distribution of all the possible playings of the game that are consistent with the rules of the game (many of the possibles will turn out to be silly). For some games (including that of the Matrix 11.4) there are many sets of distinct branches which lead to common outcomes, or final results. It is not enough to survey merely all the distinct outcomes (i.e., all the possible final distributions of winnings and losings)—one has to survey all the branches in order to calculate optimum mixed strategies. Our point is that in even as simple an alliance-game as that of Matrix 11.4, it would not be practicable to calculate these numbers, even were it in principle possible (contrary to our provision for "infinite" conditional bids at Stage 1) to do so. Thus, there is at least one elementary alliance-situation in which, even given rational players, there is (i) no method of determining how alliances *will* form; and (ii) no practicable way of determining how alliances will *probably* form. But if the theory of statics in Power politics ought to embrace a theory of alliances, and since for the above reasons there is at least one elementary *quantified* situation in which no rule for alliance formation is in practice available, there can be in practice no complete theory of statics of Power politics. For instance, there can be no prospect for completion of the theory of the balance of power which I set out at the end of 1956 in *From Balance to Deterrence*.[3]

[3] See Chapter 2, footnote 2.

To illustrate the order-of-numbers difficulty: if we add up all the ways of dividing the pay-offs in Matrix 11.4's eight pay-off boxes, we get a total of 92. Since at Stage 1 each of the three players could propose any one of these ways of dividing one or another of the pay-offs, there cannot be less than 92-cubed possible branches after Stage 1. If we also suppose it to be possible that, along with such a proposal, each player also may (but need not) make just one specific threat, the number of possible branches becomes not less than (2 × 92)-cubed. Since, finally, we allow that each player can propose or threaten conditionally upon another player's simultaneously proposing or threatening in accordance with the rules, we are allowing meta-linguistic escalation; and if we permit condition upon condition, the meta-linguistic ladder becomes open-ended—i.e., we produce indefinitely many branches at Stage 1. Even without that provision for conditional proposals, there would be many millions of branches after Stage 2.

At most we have shown that *a complete rationalistic* theory of alliances is unavailable. Some matrices (e.g., Boulding's and Matrix 11.3) are readily determinable. In real-world politics, there are sometimes overwhelming commonsense motivations for the formation of a particular alliance. The reader will have noticed that our game would become much more predictable if each of the players had—and was known by each of the others to have—deeply entrenched dispositions and capacities: for risk-taking or caution; for vengefulness, forgiveness, gratitude, or ingratitude; for intelligence; for foresight; for the avoidance of elementary logical blunders. Let us consider risk-taking first, and let us suppose that the game in Matrix 11.4 allows no explicit bargaining. Then let us suppose that each of the players prefers, and is known by each to prefer, to minimize possible losses, provided (as in this game) there is no rationally preferable choice between strategies. Then, on *first* thoughts, A would prefer his left-hand strategy (he can lose no more than 2, whereas with his right he may lose 4); B would prefer his top strategy, for similar reasons; C would have a preference, though a much slighter one, for his inner strategy. But if each played on first thoughts only, C would get zero (and presumably be satisfied); B would get 2 (delighted) but A would lose 2.

Now let us suppose each player to have, and to be known by the others to have, *second* thoughts. A's second thought would then be to prefer his *right* strategy (giving 0, 2, −2). C would then have preferred A to have had first thoughts only, but could not directly improve his position by shifting to an outer strategy (giving 4, −2, −2). B would be indifferent between the consequences of A's first and A's second thoughts, since he would gain 2 by either.

Next, let us suppose that each has, and is known to have, *third* thoughts. C would then consider shifting to his outer strategy, since indirectly this should induce B to change to his lower (−4, 6, −2). But that, in turn should induce A to shift back to his left strategy (−2, −2, 4).

Fourth thoughts: C has an immediate reason to change—back to his inner (giving 2, −4, 2); and B a consequent one to move upward (−2, 2, 0); and A consequent upon *that,* a reason to move rightward (0, 2, −2).

Fifth and final thoughts: B "remembers" where C's third thoughts led them all and, giving up 2 for zero, moves down to his second strategy, giving (0, 0, 0), the others having stayed put. This is a stable position, if and only if each player prefers minimum risks, thinks as far as the fifth move, knows that any sixth-thought departures by A or B would merely restart a cycle, *and* knows that the others prefer, think, and comprehend like himself. But given all that, one would have supposed that from the very beginning they would have hit upon this outcome—after all, it is very salient—in the first place.

It should not be surprising that in a zero-sum game, universal preferences for minimum risk would lead to such a result—one which, though possible upon other assumptions about preferences, is not amongst the most expected outcomes. This suggests an hypothesis within the field of statics (a field which, so we have tried to show, is partly open).

The hypothesis suggested (though expected by the present writer to turn out false) is that the dispositions of national leaders are causally more efficacious in Power politics than are the structures of the Power systems they operate in. With the aid of another game, the "Game of Power,"[4] I believe that this hypothesis could be experimentally tested.

Here, we can do more than outline the kind of test in mind. One sets up two distinct variants of *pay-offs* in the Game of Power, each variant played by the same number (about five) of players. (In the Game of Power, each player has a stock of capital which he can *either* keep in reserve, *or* spend upon instruments of destruction, *or* invest to gain further stocks of capital. He can also set aside stocks of capital which give him a chance of increasing the efficiency—"destructiveness"—of those instruments. "War," in the sense of mutual destruction of instruments of war, can be waged, during any one particular move of the game, only with those instruments *already* deployed along the common frontier between the pair of players warring against each other. Deployment of such instruments against another player is therefore a way of putting pressure on him, since

[4] M. A. Kaplan, A. L. Burns, and R. E. Quandt, "Theoretical Analysis of the 'Balance of Power,'" *Behavioral Science,* V, No. 3 (July 1960), 240–52 (see esp. "Rules of the game" and "Rules to extend the game," pp. 248–52); R. E. Quandt, "On the Use of Game Models in Theories of International Relations," *World Politics* XIV, No. 1, simultaneously, ed. K. Knorr and S. Verba, *The International System* (Princeton: Princeton University Press, 1961), pp. 69–76; and A. L. Burns, "Prospects for a General Theory of International Relations," *ibid.,* pp. 25–46.

defeat in "war" entails loss of all one's forces on that frontier and the payment of some indemnity; counter-deployment, on the other hand, immobilizes scarce resources. The procurement of *highly* destructive instruments—corresponding very roughly to the order of destruction of thermonuclear strike-force—enables one to destroy at small cost large quantities of other players' stocks of capital as well as armed forces. "Alliance" consists in an agreement between two or more players not to deploy forces against each other but instead against a common enemy.)

Motivation of the players—i.e., the creating of either risk-taking or cautious dispositions—can be effected by arranging two different kinds of pay-off at the end of the game. One of many possible arrangements now follows. In the risk-taking case, very high rewards are paid to a *sole* survivor in the game, much smaller rewards to *two* survivors, and very small rewards all round to more than two survivors. In the other (cautious) case, rewards are paid in proportion to the players' several stocks of capital at the end of the game, there being no *direct* incentive apart from that to attempt to eliminate other players. In both cases, the game ends at some number of rounds of moves above six or eight, randomly determined but in such a way that there is little chance indeed of the game's continuing beyond a dozen or eighteen moves.

The experiment would consist in determining whether and by how much players were eliminated from the game faster in the case that put a premium on risk-taking and sole-survivorship. (A game-theoretical solution to the question is unavailable: computers unaided by humans can no more exhaust the Game of Power than they can that of chess.) My own guess is in line with the classic assumption of the balance of power: the structure of the system itself, and the possibility of switching alliances in particular, is causally far more important than whether leaders have a lust for power and conquest or a love of peace and prosperity. If that is correct, there would continue to be plenty of point in going on with the exploration of statics in those parts where it is logically possible. If my guess is wrong—if leaders' "dispositions" in respect of risk-taking make a great difference to the behavior of the system as a whole, there will be correspondingly less point in bothering with a general theory of statics in Power-politics. The center of interest would then switch back to "current history"—to the study, on the one hand, of national leaders, their character, and the various nations' modes of selecting them; and, on the other hand, of comparative government, comparative foreign-policy formation: back also, to *internal* politics.

Not all political scientists are ready to concede that the deductive or demonstrative approach to alliance-theory through the *n*-person game should now be abandoned in favor of the inductive approach arrived at in this study. Ingenious workers in the field of bargaining theory still hope, by modification of the Postulates of Rationality and by other special assumptions about coalition formation, to produce rigorous normative-deductive solutions for the multifarious *n*-person game. Along another line, an eminent theorist has attempted to deduce a general theory of alliances, which if successful would have refuted the argument of the present section. In the next section we examine his attempt.

II

William H. Riker's *The Theory of Political Coalitions*[5] develops the hypothesis of a "Size Principle" which purports to explain why, in situations approximating the *n*-person zero-sum condition, coalitions and alliances form up as they do.

The prospect is theoretically most inviting, for the hypothesis, if validated, would have great and surprising explanatory power. In its early and simplest statement the Size Principle is: "In social systems similar to *n*-Person, zero-sum games with side-payments, participants create coalitions just as large as they believe will ensure winning and no larger."[6] In subsequent definitions, it is laid down that:

> The complement of a winning coalition is a losing one. The complement of a blocking coalition is a blocking coalition. A *minimum winning coalition* is one which is rendered blocking or losing by the subtraction of any member.[7]

Now, the Size Principle could be supported (i.e., found never to be falsified and sometimes to be instantiated) as a straightforward empirical hypothesis only. That is, experiment and historical analysis might establish a sort of law of political interaction for all systems of three or more (in the significant cases five or more) independent agents (*n*-person), each believing he was in a competitive system where winners won just what losers lost (zero-sum), such that these agents *always* divided into a coalition of winners against the rest—the losers—and, moreover, that the winning coalition *always* contained, in the opinion of each of its members, just enough to ensure its winning and not more.

That, as presented, would be an unexplained universal connection of fact (supposing that it had survived stringent attempts at falsification, which as yet it has not, though Riker provides a number of quite persuasive supporting instances). In fact Riker explains (or, more precisely, predicts) it with the aid of a game-theoretical model, meant as a precise version of common sense. Now, there is no logical necessity why the explanation of such a universal connection should take the rational-individualistic form that game theory and allied mathematics provide; it

[5] W. H. Riker, *The Theory of Political Coalitions* (New Haven: Yale University Press, 1962).

[6] *Ibid.*, p. 32.

[7] *Ibid.*, p. 40.

could turn out to be nonrational and collectivist—perhaps every person has a ritual compulsion to join and build a coalition that looks as though it is capable of "winning," and then to stop just when the coalition has enough members to do so.

But the game-theoretical explanation of why the Size Principle should hold in practice powerfully suggests itself to common sense. We readily imagine illustrative examples—e.g., suppose there are five thieves, each owning three horses; it will take at least three of them to defeat no more than two of them; if three manage to gang up, each of the three can take two horses as his share of the plunder; while if they include a fourth member in the gang on the same terms, they can have only three horses as plunder to share among four.

However, this case of the five thieves exemplifies only one particular type of *n*-person zero-sum game. I shall describe a different type, which I believe invalidates the game-theoretical explication of the Size Principle in respect of the second part of that principle—*viz.*, ". . . coalitions just as large as they believe will ensure winning *and no larger.*"

Figure 11.1

	a	b	c	d	e
1st	H	H	H	H	H
	2	2	2	0	-6
2nd	H	H	H	H	T
	2	2	2	0	-6
3rd	H	H	H	T	H
	2	2	2	0	-6
4th	H	H	H	T	T
	2	2	2	0	-6
5th	T	T	T	H	H
	2	2	2	1	-7
6th	T	T	T	H	T
	2	2	2	0	-6
7th	T	T	T	T	H
	2	2	2	-1	-5
8th	T	T	T	T	T
	2	2	2	1	-7
9th	H	H	T	H	H
	1	1	1	1	-4
10th	H	H	T	H	T
	1	1	1	1	-4
11th	H	H	T	T	H
	1	1	1	1	-4
12th	H	H	T	T	T
	1	1	1	1	-4
13th	H	T	T	H	H
	2	1	2	1	-6
14th	H	T	T	H	T
	2	1	2	1	-6
15th	H	T	T	T	H
	2	1	2	1	-6
16th	H	T	T	T	T
	2	1	2	1	-6
17th	T	H	T	H	H
	2	2	1	1	-6
18th	T	H	T	H	T
	2	2	1	1	-6
19th	T	H	T	T	H
	2	2	1	1	-6
20th	T	H	T	T	T
	2	2	1	1	-6
21st	H	T	H	H	H
	1	1	1	1	-4
22nd	H	T	H	H	T
	1	1	1	1	-4
23rd	H	T	H	T	H
	2	2	2	1	-7
24th	H	T	H	T	T
	2	2	2	1	-7
25th	T	T	H	H	H
	1	2	2	1	-6
26th	T	T	H	H	T
	1	2	2	1	-6
27th	T	T	H	T	H
	1	2	2	1	-6
28th	T	T	H	T	T
	1	2	2	1	-6
29th	T	H	H	H	H
	1	1	1	1	-4
30th	T	H	H	H	T
	1	1	1	1	-4
31st	T	H	H	T	H
	1	1	1	1	-4
32nd	T	H	H	T	T
	1	1	1	1	-4

Consider the coalition-bargaining game depicted in Figure 11.1. (We shall be dealing with five players fixed in five roles—*a, b, c, d,* and *e*—but if the game were frequently repeated one could be sure that at least one of the players would try to insist that allocation of the five roles be determined by lot before each future round of the game.) At the final move of each round, each player chooses between just two strategies—H for Heads, T for Tails—to determine the direct part of the pay-off (i.e., *not* including any side-payments). Figure 11.1 is the exhaustive list of these final direct pay-offs, and is available to all players.

The game begins with bargaining to form coalitions. A coalition is formed by two or more players binding themselves to play *specific* strategies at the final move. One player may offer side-payments to another (or others) as inducement to bind him (them) in a coalition. Upon agreement to the coalition and to its specific strategies, all side-payments must immediately be paid. Reneging on the strategy is excluded by the rules of the game. All proposals and contracts for coalitions and for strategies must be made public—each proposer and coalition must announce to all players just what side-payments are offered and what combination of strategies the coalition will employ at the final move. (Players excluded from all coalitions are free to use either of their strategies at the final move: this, and the rule that side-payments must be paid immediately upon contracting, effectively preclude certain coalitions.) Though, in the bargaining, any player may entertain incompatible coalition proposals, and may switch his own proposals (i.e., he may be enticed from one "proto-coalition," in Riker's terminology, to another), there is no way of breaking a coalition agreement once it has been made.

If no agreements are made, the final choosing between H and T is left to each individual player. For the sake of the present argument, tacit agreements are ruled out—except through the making of contracts no player is supposed to have evidence other than the table of pay-offs as to how another will finally move.

It will be evident from a consideration of Figure 11.1 that the unfortunate *e* cannot do better than −6, cannot effectively *and* rationally bribe or coerce *a* or *b* or *c,* and can only propose to *a, b,* and *c* jointly a set of strategies (i.e., that entailing the 1st or 3rd outcomes, *or* that entailing the 2nd or 4th) which would be just as good as the best that all of them jointly could insure for themselves otherwise.

Similarly, *d* cannot do better than +1, and can only propose to *a, b,* and *c* jointly a strategy (i.e., that entailing the 23rd or 24th outcome) which would be just as good as the best that any of them could insure for himself otherwise—he too cannot reasonably attempt to bribe or coerce them.

On the other hand, *a* and *b* and *c* each has, as well as the option of a place in those two alternative four-man coalitions, the following equally attractive three-man options: an agreement that all three play H (entailing the 1st to the 4th outcomes) *or* that all three play T (5th to 6th). But there is nothing in Figure 11.1 or in the rules of the game to make them prefer the three-man coalition to either of the four-man coalitions, or vice versa; therefore: "there exists at least one *n*-person zero-sum game in which the Size Principle does not hold at any rate as a matter of necessity."

Riker anticipates this kind of objection by two types of counter-objection. The simpler is that

> rational players would not expend energy to change positions [e.g., to adopt one of the four-man coalitions rather than their three-man coalition] if the most they could expect would be the same payoff.[8]

But in the game-theoretical contest, considerations of "energy" are irrelevant: energy there is free; and in political practice, it need not always be the case that the forming of a larger winning coalition is more exhausting to the potential members of a minimum winning coalition than the forming of a smaller.

The subtler objection[9] depends upon its being possible, in the game which Riker considers, for at least one of the members of an initial *smallest* winning coalition to be replaced by his equivalent from among the initial losing players, during the course of a haggle over the composition of a subsequently proposed *larger* winning coalition, perhaps with some redistribution of pay-offs among the surviving winners. Thus, haggling over enlargement ensures that no coalition larger than some smallest winning coalition occupies a position of stable equilibrium in the bargaining space.

It is clear, of course, that the foregoing cannot apply to my Figure 11.1 game, where neither *d* nor *e* can prize *a* or *b* or *c* out of some winning coalition or another. But that does not dispose of Riker's line of argument (here stated not in his but in the present writer's version of it): that, up to the level of numbers imposing system dominance, the larger the number of independent agents in a situation, the greater the real uncertainty about the outcomes; therefore the less the *expected* utility of the outcomes; and therefore the stronger the inclination to dispense with unessential partners. Thus if in the Figure 11.1 game there were a rule that all bargains were off unless agreed to before an unknown, randomly determined instant, *a, b,* and *c severally* might decide beforehand to ignore both the four-man options since at least one extra player would have to come to agreement on them. But it would be just as sensible for each of them to count on the certainty of proposals from both *d* and *e,* and to decide to accept whichever proposal was made first.

[8] *Ibid.*, p. 250.
[9] *Ibid.*, pp. 268–70.

Riker's second line of reply takes its departure from two distinctions that are implicit, but not, I think, always preserved in distinction from each other in his argument. The *first* of those two distinctions[10] is that *between* being a subcoalition of one member who in the outcome is a winner (or loser; or neither) of a pay-off, *and* being a subcoalition of one member in a coalition of more than one member which, in a second (corporate) sense, "wins" (or "loses"; but not neither). The *second* distinction[11] is *between* the "value" possessed by that subcoalition of one member in a zero-sum game who when playing alone loses the total of pay-off that all pay-off-winning players gain (his value is measured by the negative of that amount), *and* on the other hand, the "value" (similarly measured by the negative of his maximum loss when alone) of a certain one-member subcoalition whose "weight" is the least of all subcoalitions' weights except for those whose weight is zero.[12] "Weight" means the addition to the capacity to "win"—in the corporate sense of "winning"—that the adhesion of any subcoalition of one member may make. My difficulties are that the two distinctions are confused with each other, and that the concept of "winning in the corporate sense" has, in the Theory of Games, no unequivocal meaning, and that therefore "weight" is also an equivocal concept.

In the Figure 11.1 game, which at the bargaining stage (not represented in the Figure 11.1 matrix itself) is not an "essential" game, it is nevertheless always the case that exactly what pay-off one *coalition* wins (even when, jointly, it wins zero), the remainder of the players jointly lose; *and* it is the case that the pay-off winnings of all positively winning individual *players* together exactly equal the losses of all losing players jointly. Furthermore, we have noticed that, if and only if they contract to play severally in certain ways, the mutually exclusive groups *a, b, c; a, b, c, d; a, b, c, e,* can obtain for each of their members severally the highest pay-offs that each of them *can* obtain, given a "rational" use by each of the others of that "bargaining power" which the structure of the game affords him. Together with the quasi-two-person zero-sum condition of the relation between the various pairs of coalitions we have seen to emerge in the Figure 11.1 game, the last-mentioned condition provides, I think, as near as one could get to a full-blooded simulation of the real-life event of "winning" an election, a war, a struggle for hegemony.

Now, there are other connotations of "winning," or "total victory," which Riker has in mind but which I do not think can be represented in game-theoretical terms. Game theory is individualistic throughout, and will not allow one to make a single "individual" out of several formerly distinct individuals.

[10] *Ibid.*, p. 23.
[11] *Ibid.*, p. 254.
[12] *Ibid.*, pp. 258–62.

This comes out most clearly in Riker's candid discussion of the allocation of pay-offs, which, he notes, can hardly avoid being paradoxical when the joint gains of a more-than-minimum winning coalition are *greater* than the joint gains of any minimum winning coalition. Perhaps I may be allowed to put my objection as follows: suppose it is correct, as Riker suggests, to represent the penultimate stage of such a political contest as a Presidential election, in terms of a two-coalition zero-sum game: then, as soon as the winning coalition has *won,* and the losing "coalition" (as Riker styles it) *lost,* then the allocations of pay-offs should *also* be plausibly representable as, in both the winners' and the losers' case, further political contests whose penultimate stages are two-coalition zero-sum games. Only when every constituent coalition has been broken up exhaustively into subcoalitions of just one member each, is the problem reduced to the (notoriously elusive) problem of bargaining on the contract curve. *But* every individual who is "rational" in the sense required by game theory must have had his eye on those problems of ultimate allocation of valuables to individuals, from the first moment he contemplated associating himself in the Presidential campaign with his earliest proto-coalition. Indeed, in the "perfect information" case, his "rationality" requires him to infer his initial strategies by working back from an appreciation of all the individual allocation situations he could possibly arrive at as a result of associating or of *not* associating with each of the available proto-coalitions. Of course, no one in any real-life situation has much of a prospect of doing that.

Meanwhile, we must consider Riker's argument[13] that, *if* there are winning coalitions larger (*viz.,* containing more individual members) than the minimum winning coalition(s), the former are unstable and only the latter are in equilibrium. I can best make my point by reference to the Figure 11.1 game, even though that is a highly contrived counter-example. In the Figure 11.1 game, we found several minimum winning solutions for the three-person coalition *a, b, c,* two winning solutions for the four-person coalition *a, b, c, e,* and one for the four-person coalition *a, b, c, d.* We noticed that, while *a, b,* and *c* had a veto over all the four-person solutions, collectively they had no reason for preferring *any* of the winning solutions, four-person or three-person, to any other. (Incidentally, if any of the indispensable three had an extra-game-theoretical preference for, say, an "all-Heads" strategy, the other two would have no game-theoretical reason for denying him that personal satisfaction.) But since the indispensable three are indifferent between any winning solutions, any particular one of those solutions is in *un*stable equilibrium. Generally in contrast with all nonwinning solutions, the class of all winning solutions is in *stable* equilibrium: so that if we begin with a particular three-person, or a par-

[13] *Ibid.,* pp. 262–71.

ticular four-person, solution, we shall stay with it, if but only if there is no extra-game-theoretical occasion to shift; for there can be no game-theoretical reason.

Notice, again, that the same condition would apply as between four equipossible three-person winning coalitions in some other five-person game—(*a, b, c*), (*a, b, e*), (*a, c, e*), (*b, c, e*). If, for example, *a* and *b* in a proto-coalition (*a, b, c*) were simultaneously persuaded by extra-game-theoretical reasons that *e* should replace *c,* and if they as a pair had authority to make the change, then nothing in game theory would prevent their doing so.

Concerning Riker's concept of "weight" in a coalition-game: this is a development of the concept of voting-power where an absolute majority of votes decides, the development consisting in removal of restriction, "one member, one vote," and imposition of a restriction excluding single-member dictatorial majorities. As he points out[14] it is extremely difficult to assign weights in international politics.[15] Nevertheless, the concept of quasi-voting weights is clear in itself. The difficulty lies, as previously suggested, in the confusion of the idea of "winning" in the sense of a member's belonging to the coalition that achieves the majority, thus maximizing the gross returns to itself and minimizing them to the rest, with the idea of the member's maximizing his individual returns. Consider the Figure 11.1 game: in both the available strategies for the three-man winning coalition, gross returns to the coalition equal six. In the four-man coalition including *e,* they equal zero (1st to 3rd outcomes). In that including *d* (23rd or 24th outcomes), they equal seven. Yet *a, b,* and *c* are indifferent as between these winning alternatives, and all the winning coalition-outcomes are zero-sum both for coalitions and for individual players.

My conclusion is, then, that the Size Principle in its present form, but considered *only* as a derivation from game-theoretical considerations, required amendment by adding, after the words "and no larger,"

> . . . at least except so far as any participants added beyond the minimum to an initially agreed proto-coalition do not reduce the pay-offs that would be expected by any of the members of any otherwise minimum-winning set who are all members of the aforesaid more-than-minimum proto-coalition.

In case that should seem to vitiate the Size Principle altogether, we

[14] *Ibid.,* p. 257.

[15] In the Game of Power a quantitative measure of short-term weight is afforded by the relative sizes of "armed forces" deployed on the several "frontiers," and by the ruling "military exchange rate." Even this short-term weighting is difficult to calculate. When the term is lengthened, first by including relative sizes of reserved "forces," then relative sizes of "income-earning capital," and lastly relative possible alliance-potentials in later stages of the game, the order of numbers becomes literally impossible of computation.

might add that all the winning coalitions, whether minimum or costlessly enlarged, which it permits will be in *un*stable equilibrium with respect to each other, though in stable equilibrium with respect to those enlarged at cost.

The tendency of my argument thus far has been that Riker's original Size Principle cannot be regarded as an *entailment* of the mathematical theory of *n*-person zero-sum games. This is far from saying that the Size Principle is quite unsupported by that mathematical theory. In any case, however, my next difficulties are with the *applying* of the Size Principle to actual power-political situations.

What could be tests to determine whether an *n*-Power international situation in fact approximated the zero-sum condition? Throughout his work, Riker insists that even the deliberate limiting by its leaders of a winning coalition is not conclusive evidence—one would have to be sure both that they could not without risk limit it very much further and that they were not limiting it for some quite extraneous reason—e.g., purely ideological opposition to Fascist or to Communist regimes. Nor, I suggest, is it necessarily the case that a situation in which no winning coalitions form is *not* zero-sum. Thus, a rational gambler pays exactly zero for the right to play a zero-sum game. In a five-person zero-sum game where each round is ended by taking of a simple majority vote, just two players each bent upon getting exactly zero can hope to do this by tacit collusion, provided each of the other three players is a maximizer—e.g., the two can always offer +1 to one of them. They can even contrive, if they wish, a four-person winning coalition, by offering a third player $\frac{63}{64}$ and threatening to expel a fourth player unless he accepts $\frac{1}{64}$. Similarly they can threaten any two players seeking to recruit a third with the prospect of *their* topping any such offer, and by repeating such tactics can presumably prevent the formation of any winning coalition.

This, of course, is the classic role of the balancer of the system. Since it cannot be played either in a universally negative-sum situation (Kaplan's ideal thermonuclear unit-veto system), nor in a universally positive-sum situation (hard to imagine, but presumably like Lewis Carroll's caucus-race, in which all who join even "losing" coalitions get positive pay-offs), evidence of its being exercised by someone is presumptive evidence that the exerciser believes the international game to be zero-sum, but would as soon see it not played out. Balancers are non-authoritative *preventers* of the allocation of values. (Riker, of course, is aware of this consideration, which he attempts to meet[16] by introducing two dynamic possibilities, in his view severally necessary and jointly sufficient to disequilibrate an *n*-person zero-sum situation and eliminate the balancers' role.)

In conclusion: Riker appeared to have discovered a shortcut from

[16] *Op. cit.*, pp. 189–90.

general considerations of game theory to a powerful truth about the formation of coalitions; and it has seemed worthwhile to spend all these pages on considering it. I believe it turns out that the shortcut cannot be taken. The long way round—through analysis of many types of *n*-person game, both zero- and nonzero-sum, probably exists, but is not *directly* accessible to human calculators, or to practicable computers.

Having considered for two and a half chapters the case for game theory as *the* theory of Power politics, we shall summarize here our reasons for rejecting it.

Some are reasons of principle: the formal requirements of certain important types of game cannot be *demonstrated* to obtain in the situations in which we are inclined to *suppose* that they might obtain, and in which, therefore, we would either look for a game-theoretical explanation, or give up hope of finding any explanation.

Some are reasons of "practice," but in the restricted sense of practice: that the conditions of the universe, which presumably might have been constituted otherwise, preclude our deriving solutions for some classes of games—those in which the order of numbers that would need to be employed in the solving of the games is beyond the physical capacity of any contrivance that could be used to procure a solution.

Some are reasons of practice in a less restricted sense: there are yet other classes of games for which we could find solutions if we were prepared to go to the trouble. For any given game in this class, it is impossible to predict that nobody will ever go to the trouble. But it is a fairly safe prediction that *some* games in these classes will never in practice turn out to have been worth anyone's bother to solve.

The reasons of principle are concerned with the following conditions, amongst others: (1) Human affairs are beset by real or radical uncertainty. A weakened form of game theory *can* be devised for situations of real uncertainty; but it is so weak as to have very little explanatory power. (2) In the course of a competitive-cooperative conflict, someone may introduce a *novel* prospect. Concerning this obstacle to the application of game theory, enough has been said in this and earlier chapters. (3) We shall always have reason to doubt, about some power-political situation for the direct explanation of which we are designing a game-theoretical model, that the Powers involved in it so envisaged the possible outcomes as to warrant our filling in the pay-off boxes of our game-theoretical model with certain exact numbers. But, as is well known, the shape of the solution of a game can often depend very finely on just what numbers go into the pay-off boxes. Notice that *this* difficulty need not arise when, as in the stakes-game Monte Carlo device that I sketch in this Chapter, pp. 247–248, we are not attempting directly to explain a real world power-political situation, but instead are explaining the structure of certain widely held qualitative intuitions about how certain quantitative models would work out. (4) We cannot be certain that all of the Postulates of Rationality required by game theory are complied with in the real world. (5) We know that many types of *n*-person coalition-games have no unique solution. It would follow that though some such game afforded an accurate analogue to a real-world situation, it could not by itself explain the actual outcome of that situation.

Riker's Size Principle hypothesis about the formation of coalitions was characterized above as a "shortcut": since *n*-person coalition games differ radically from each other, they cannot afford us a general theory of alliances. Riker tries to reduce their infinite variety, first, by restricting them to the class of zero-sum games—but see point (3) above, p. 245 and, secondly, within the zero-sum class, by further restricting the range of acceptable solutions. I have contended that Riker is not entirely successful.

Another kind of shortcut through the jungle of *n*-person games consists in eliminating the capacity of any player to impute to any other a sequence of strategic thought. Notice, for example, that, given the matrix in Figure 11.1, above, a coalition of *a, c, d,* and *e* against *b* (in order to have some prospect of obtaining the 13th outcome) would be excluded by their considering that, though *b* should be indifferent, as to the pay-offs, between the two alternative outcomes (13th or 9th) from which, if the coalition were to form, he could choose, nevertheless he should also be able to consider himself safe by imputing to *a* and *c* the realization that if they were to join the coalition, *b* could insure the 9th outcome so as to punish them. In this shortcut, players instead choose their strategies on other grounds and with other information—e.g., by complying with some general strategic rule or maxim. Computer-played coalition-games must in that fashion forbid imputing.

The restricted sense of the practical impossibility of solving some important classes of *n*-person game derives from the orders of numbers of the branches on their game-trees. It may be objected, "If no computer could ever handle that order of numbers, how can any human?" The answer is (as in contrasts between the chess-playing of computers and of humans) that in any case they handle games in quite different ways, and that the human organism seems to be physically equipped to make "insightful" probings far into the proliferations of game-trees.

In conclusion, we must abandon the hope of developing a complete array of models of Power politics based upon rigorous game theory. Nevertheless, the field of study of Power politics offers many less general opportunities for employing game-theoretical concepts—e.g., the concept of a "dominant" strategy. (A remark on method: it would have been far more satisfactory to deal with this and earlier problems—e.g., those about the prospects of a theory of alliances—by a pure-mathematical analysis of coalition- and other *n*-person games; but I have had to content myself, in attempting to refute general hypotheses about various supposed applications of the Theory of Games, merely with inventing counter-examples. These, if valid, should be sufficient for their immediate purposes, but they cannot, as might a formal mathematical analysis, throw light upon the logical scope of coalition-games.)

Highly particularized game-like models remain a possibility. I do not refer to the growing body of important and interesting findings developed by techniques of simulation and political "war-gaming": a just consideration of those approaches would in themselves take up another major section of this already large volume, so it has seemed better not to deal with that subject at all. What we suggest is the playing-out, mechanically or by humans, of what Richard Quandt[17] calls "meta-models" in ways sufficiently surprising and complicated to suggest lower-order models that might be tested against quantified evidence.

One issue, the logical structure of which can be readily explored by stakes-game Monte Carlo methods, is the question of nuclear proliferation and its alleged destabilizing tendencies. The Game of Power mentioned above is easily adapted to these purposes: briefly, the capacity to destroy is greatly increased, but this and the capacity to use it against others' resources are made to require a high level in the player's own invested resources. Though the latter introduce great complexities, and though one would certainly need, to represent the relationships, at least three-Power, of nuclear hostage-taking, and of "triggering" an ally's nuclear forces against an enemy, the number of players can be kept down, in this case, to no more than ten at the most; for the syndrome of issues clustered around that of nuclear proliferation seems to be fairly isolable from other power-political issues (e.g., only some of the balances of conventional force are pertinent to it, and these can be included). Alliance-structures, such as NATO in the late 1950s, can also be represented by restrictions imposed in the early stages of the game. But it is essential that we should recognize that what the game as a whole represents is *not* the real world, but an abstraction from the logical skeleton of an informal and qualitative model of the real world, discernible in the elements common to the world-pictures envisaged by statesmen of leading and rising Powers in the last decade or so.[18]

Unfortunately, there are very few issues as suitable as is the nuclear

[17] See footnote 4 above.

[18] For an approach to the same question by a simulation method properly so called, see Richard A. Brody, "Some Systematic Effects of the Spread of Nuclear Weapons Technology," *The Journal of Conflict Resolution,* VII, No. 4 (December 1963). In contrast with that method, the stakes-game method requires that players approach the playing simply as a stakes-game—if analogies persuade them to play roles instead, the effect of the game's logical structure is obscured—hence the stakes.

question for this kind of treatment. The calls for conventional forces, for instance, are even more unpredictable than is the willingness to respond to them, though one can be fairly definite about various nations' ability to respond. But alliance, so far as one can distinguish it from political coalition, boils down to a willingness to use conventional force for political ends entertained at least temporarily in common ("nuclear alliance" is a different and simpler, perhaps cruder, concept). Nuclear deterrence *is* a numbers game, although in the disastrous corner of the board the numbers share in the paradox of Pascal's gamble. Conventional military power has again become in the 1960s a political instrument, which means that the indispensable numerical calculations are logically subsequent to just that kind of political consideration that in the first pages of this chapter appeared essentially qualitative.

The stakes-game device I have been advocating can be useful in the exploring of only those models concerned with the actions of Powers (1) within a limited time span—say, two to twenty years, (2) limited spatially and geographically by very general features—e.g., distance, transport cost, (3) rather less susceptible than are most political actions to pressure of domestic opinion (e.g., the long-term ineffectuality of CND in Britain), and so (4), presupposing a degree of integration in an industrialized, administrative state high enough to allow its being regarded, for nuclear purposes, as a single Power.

I have suggested elsewhere[19] how into that game there can be built constraints abstracting quantitatively from the qualitative and quantitative features—the geographic, demographic, economic—of real-world situations. The reason for having such games played competitively is, in the last resort, to open up more possibilities of action than would be produced by role-playing—in which the actors perform as they think their roles demand, whereas in competitive play, while a "role" (as conceived by a political scientist) might in fact be followed from competitive considerations, so might many other unpredicted courses of action. A competitive-cooperative situation provokes the agents to particularized insight into its *possibilities,* in contrast to the *probabilities* brought to light by role-playing.

One of the reasons for abstracting, from the largely qualitative real-world situation, as many quantitative measures as any justification can be found for depends upon the historians' practice of explaining power-political events partly by use of terms which are at least implicitly quantitative. Even in the "motivational" explanation (see Chapter 3) of individual statecraft, it is extremely difficult not to attribute to the statesman's reflections a more quantitative form than one knows he was likely to have consciously cast them in; whereas for "constitutive" and "compositive" ex-

[19] See "Prospects for a General Theory . . . ," *op. cit.,* footnote 4 above, esp. pp. 26–30.

planations of interactions, a quantitative framework is not only natural but appropriate.

Historical modeling, however, would be of more value to theorists than to historians. This study, admittedly, has been destructively critical of the prospects for a complete general theory of Power politics; yet something useful may perhaps be done about the linkage of statics with dynamics: amongst dynamic problems—e.g., causes of systemic change—previously discussed, we left in the air the crucial question of non-autonomous causes—i.e., disequilibrating processes—arising within a partially equilibrating system of Powers, and occurring strictly within the realm of external politics itself, that at the last bring the system as a phenomenon of statics to its end. Here, in our concluding chapter on the theory of statics we return briefly to this problem—perhaps the central one for all power-political theory since the eighteenth century.

III

Classic balance-of-power theory can be interpreted as an hypothesis that in a more-than-two-Power world there are *no* non-autonomous causes of systemic change; in other words, that provided a system includes at least three significant Powers, the purely political aspect of the system's power-political process always tends to produce a stable equilibrium which can be upset, if at all, only by autonomous changes—e.g., by changes in the military art and in military technology, or by economic changes in "the wealth of nations" such as raise just two (or just one) Powers to solitary significance, eliminating all balancers. In its logically strongest form, most vulnerable to refutation, the balance-of-power hypothesis would assert that the political process can stabilize the system even in face of the most extreme autonomous changes, through the mechanisms of alliance-reversal and limited preventive war. But even in its weaker forms, that hypothesis implies that (1) a two-Power process can reach only an unstable equilibrium; (2) a three-or-more-Power political process, other things being equal, tends toward stable equilibrium.

In *From Balance to Deterrence,* 1956–57, the present writer proposed a modification of balance-of-power theory: when the number of significant Powers increases beyond a few—five was the suggested optimum number for stability—the individual statesman has increasing difficulty in calculating the effects upon the power-balance of a prospective change in his own Power's policies, whereas the "hidden hand" in the balance of power can work only insofar as the constituent agents make such calculations. That modifying hypothesis then, asserts that the non-autonomous (i.e., power-political) process, which tends to bring new Powers to significance, thereby also tends to produce systemic change by destabilizing the formerly stable five-Power system.

Since the Second World War, certain American theorists in particular have propounded a view directly negating the classic balance-of-power hypothesis. They hold that a "bipolar" (two-Power) situation tends more toward stable equilibrium than does any *n*-Power situation. A few hold this irrespective of whether the ruling military technology is thermonuclear, and do so on grounds of the incalculability of the *n*-Power situation, similar to the present writer's 1956 grounds for his modification of the balance-of-power theory when the number of significant Powers exceeds five. But most hold the view specifically in respect of the thermonuclear age—an example from a British analyst: "Other things being equal the greater the number of authorities in the world that are able to decide to use nuclear weapons, the greater the likelihood that they will be used." This hypothesis is often supported on simple probabilistic grounds: since it is possible to initiate a (destabilizing) nuclear conflict if but only one disposes of nuclear weapons, since a possibility entails a non-zero probability, and since such probabilities are additive (except for the shift from one to two thermonuclear Powers, at which point the effect of deterrence is alleged to be maximized), then nuclear proliferation beyond two Powers arithmetically increases the destabilizing tendency.

In Chapter 9 we gave reasons for expunging all such considerations of simple probability from the theory of power-political statics. But the thermonuclear bipolar hypothesis could be restated, without misuse of the concept of probability, in strictly political terms—i.e., in terms of the overloading of the political decision-making process as a result of proliferation.

Contrary hypotheses about the stability of nuclearized Power systems have been advanced by others, including the present writer: a Power gaining sovereign control over a more or less credible deterrent thereby politically deters others from taking that Power as a nuclear hostage in order to restrain its major nuclear ally; one nuclear Power may be afforded reasons, over and above that of the second Power's being nuclear, against attempting a surprise attack upon the latter, by learning that a third Power is also nuclear and believes its security maximized by striking against the first striker's remaining delivery systems; and so on.

Thus already in the field there are contrary groups of hypotheses about the stabilizing tendencies of political processes involving various numbers of Powers, one group associated with the age of conventional and the other with that of thermonuclear armed forces. To formulate and test them is, of course, to proceed with the enterprise of the theory of statics (which, as we have seen, cannot be completed) at that level where its findings would provide an important element, so far missing, of the theory of dynamics. Does the world-political process make always for order and sanity, until frustrated by some brute economic expansion or population explosion? Or is every political order heavy with its own decay and destruction? Our argument so far has suggested that such questions must remain forever unanswered. Along the straightforward lines of inquiry, that conclusion would be justified; but before we give up, we should ask, first, whether the questions can be formulated better.

The idea, developed in Chapter 6, of a capitulation point (*viz.,* that for at least some governing classes, their state's capitulation would *not* be an infinite evil) can help to do this. In order to investigate the influence of the political aspects of a power-political process, we must be able to distinguish them from the economic, strategic, and other aspects, upon the perception of which a Power's ruling group can reasonably take its political decisions. Amongst those political decisions, the rulers' determining of a capitulation point is primary: assessing their own and other Powers' current military deployments, their own and others' potential, in manpower and economic resources, for maintaining and if necessary increasing military deployments, the rulers may calculate whether their society is in a position to remain a Power (i.e., physically surviving and sovereign); and, if so, they may then indicate whether they are willing to put at risk enough of their society's resources to sustain the economic and military means to Powerhood. The last-mentioned decision, we call "political." Amongst the considerations bearing on the calculations upon which that decision is grounded, there may be the questions of whether allies can be secured from amongst other Powers and, on the contrary, how far others may ally themselves against the rulers' own Power: those two kinds of question, and the decisions that may be consequent upon answers to them—whether or not to enter into or to oppose alliances—are external-political, i.e., power-political. Upon such calculations and decisions, action is taken, and similar action responds to it: that interaction is the political aspect of the power-political process.

Such interaction may lead to some Power's rulers being induced to relinquish sovereignty and independence on behalf of their society, or to some constituent society's being physically destroyed in warfare. If either of these occur, political theorists characterize the power-political process as having been to that extent "destabilized." We decided in Chapter 5 to call certain but not all destabilizing changes in the number and dimensions of Powers constituting a system, "systemic changes." If the considerations and actions leading to such destabilizing changes were simply economic or military-technological, they were to be called "autonomous" causes of systemic change. But if they also displayed a purely political aspect—e.g., if rulers decided to shift their Power's capitulation point, choosing to put at risk a lesser or greater proportion of their society's resources in order to sustain Powerhood; if the political task of assessing alliance-potential had grown so complicated as to be beyond the political capacities of statesmen; if world-political elites had altered their evaluation of external-political forms and structures (of the nation-state, of international and supranational organizations, of the balance-of-power or nuclear-deterrent systems)—we were to call development of that kind "non-autonomous"—i.e., power-political causes of systemic change.

The foregoing helps us give a specific meaning to the term "political" in such questions as "How if at all does the political aspect affect the equilibrium of one or another type of power-political system?" Even so, such a question presupposes one particular interpretation of world affairs, and that interpretation can be most clearly spelt out by the constructing of models of Power systems. But having seen in the present and the three preceding chapters that deductive (or *a priori*) analyses of the workings of such models are not available, we must now ask again whether our reformulated question can be answered instead by indirect methods—e.g., by an inductive approach. We have already suggested a possible inductive or "Monte Carlo" approach, through the turning of models of Power systems into experimental games.

Radical objections to any inductive gaming procedure present themselves, upon the very basis of our reformulation of the question about the effects of the world-political process: such games as the Game of Power are numerical—they involve imaginary quantities, and since their players' task is to allocate scarce resources to the greatest individual profit, they must be quasi-economic and not political. But, while not being *reducible* to economic categories, a genuinely political situation can present issues calling for political choice that *includes* quasi-economic decisions about allocation of scarce resources; and the latter type of decision situation can be reproduced, we submit, in experimental games.

Firstly, by rewarding players for surviving as agents in the game from one round to the next, we reproduce something like the incentive that moves a ruling class to maintain its society, at a certain risk to its resources, as a sovereign Power. If the trade-off between the risk, the reward, the greater reward for achieving "hegemony," and the converse loss for being eliminated, were calculable in the game, we would have been simulating a quasi-economic process (like the survival of a business firm), and not a political one; but in the Game of Power, that calculation can be made only in rare situations sometimes analogous to those in which a prudent and responsible ruling class might regretfully decide that the price to its society in terms of lost lives and destroyed property was not worth paying for the maintenance of sovereign Powerhood. In other situations of the game, no calculation can be made, since the power position is both too complicated for calculation, and also dependent upon others' responses of the kind that are radically uncertain—i.e., unpredictable in principle.

Secondly, such games can reproduce a similar radical uncertainty and practical incalculability about the situation in which the number of causally significant agents is increased beyond humanly manageable limits (at a guess, between six and nine) though probably not by so much as to induce system dominance.

Thirdly, we can induce in players the impulse to attempt an impressionistic assessment of the nature of the entire gaming situation—e.g., to consider whether or not the balance of power in the game has been so upset as to call for an alliance of all the others against one preeminent player; for the recognition of such an imbalance is not only a matter of discounting each player's *current* position against all the rest, but also of *imputing* to each of the others a certain perspective upon possible future stages of the game. In the same way, real-world imbalances of power are not only a matter of current distributions of armed forces and resources, but also of "alliance-potential" (i.e., of imputing to others certain inducements for lining up one way or another in the more or less indefinite future), and thus of a certain characterization of the process of world affairs as a whole.

Two features reproducible in a game would indicate instability: (1) an incidence of destructive conflict; (2) more significantly, the incidence of elimination of players from the game. Amongst both types of destabilizing effect, some possible instances will induce "systemic change" and, if the latter occur during experimental games, will suggest formulations connecting the statics with the dynamics of Power politics. Comparisons could then be made between the effects of "autonomous" changes (e.g., a marked increase or decrease in the capacity to eliminate other players' "forces" or "resources") with those that we have agreed to call "non-autonomous"—i.e., political.

Findings from games, nevertheless, must not be used directly for forecasting: all competitive-cooperative models are built up out of abstractions from initial conditions; models as such are prescribable by singular propositions, however many universal and quantitative-particular clauses those propositions include. The predictive power of the most elegant and highly articulated model is directly dependent upon the truth of those singular historical propositions from which, by abstraction, its own singular propositions, prescribing the initial state of the model, will have been derived. And the defect of singular propositions about the current situation is that, on the whole, the nearer their date-line to the present moment, the less criticized and the less soundly established they are. This is particularly the case with our information about the several pictures of the world entertained by the representatives of active Powers, and about the error and out-of-dateness that all such pictures are bound to involve.

There is a line of investigation, nevertheless, that may be rewarding for students of Power politics: the comparing of the *tempi* of themes in the political process. We introduced this concept in Chapter 1, pp. 10–12. Rates of change in many fields—population, economic growth, development of weapon systems, and of course political and electoral change in stable polities—can be established from data often quite roughly ascertained, escaping the strictures directed above against "scientific" prediction from models of current situations. Furthermore, extrapolations of *tempi* of development can be made with benefit of criticism from theoretically advanced and quantified disciplines such as demography and economics, thus avoiding the fallacy of prediction from an unexplained trend. The principal difficulty for such projects is that social and political changes themselves do not always move to a settled *tempo:* they can occur in a day. Formal models comparing rates of change must have structures solid and broad enough to allow for those cataclysms.

There can be no general theory of statics; yet as we have seen in these four chapters, a number of particular explorations of the field appear quite promising. The past forty years' revolutionary advances in empirical investigation of world politics is now being accelerated by means of remarkable new facilities for collecting and analysing data, especially those developed in the United States. Conceptual invention, on the other hand, has lagged behind these empirical advances, and indeed behind recent striking innovations at the conceptual level in internal-political theory. The following chapter applies our doctrine of radical uncertainty to the problem of characterizing the external-political conversation.

SECTION V

THE HUMANIZING OF POWER POLITICS

TWELVE

Negotiation and the Commitment of the Political Critic

Can anything be learned about the scope for theorizing in world politics if we turn from the most general aspects of the subject to one particular topic included in it and perhaps peculiar to it—negotiation? We shall consider three approaches to the question, all to some degree theoretical, but one more formally so than the others.

"Bargaining theory" is for the most part an extension of orthodox game theory. Its broad methodology is the same; its postulates include or are strengthened formulations of those from which game theory was derived. A study by J. C. Harsanyi illustrates the method.[1] His purpose in extending by four postulates[2] the original two "weak postulates of rationality"—*individual utility maximization* and *mutually expected rationality*[3]—is to provide an otherwise unavailable determinate solution to the bargaining problem. Can we consider as pertinent to international "bargaining" (i.e., to negotiation) Harsanyi's six "strong postulates of rationality"? As he has renumbered them, these are

[1] J. C. Harsanyi, "On the Rationality Postulates Underlying the Theory of Cooperative Games," *Journal of Conflict Resolution,* V (June 1961), 179–96.
[2] *Ibid.,* pp. 183–84.
[3] *Ibid.,* p. 179.

1. *individual utility maximization;*
2. *efficiency*—"A. Out of the set of all decision rules consistent with postulates 1, 3, 4, 5 and 6, the players will select a pair (R_1, R_2) of most efficient decision rules. B. However, if there is an alternative pair ($R_{1'}$, $R_{2'}$) even more efficient than (R_1, R_2), then the players will adopt ($R_{1'}$, $R_{2'}$) instead of (R_1, R_2) so long as $R_{1'}$ and $R_{2'}$ are consistent with postulates 3, 4, 5 and 6, even if they are *not* consistent with postulate 1";
3. *acceptance of higher pay-offs* (this means that any player will accept from the other better terms than he himself has offered the other);
4. *symmetry* (as between the mathematical forms of the players' decision rules);
5. *restriction of variables;* and
6. *mutually expected rationality.*[4]

I shall not here consider the logical properties[5] of the set of postulates as a set, but rather the connotation of one of them—Postulate 5—as that applies to "open" negotiation.

The bargaining theorist restricts his use of the concept "rationality" to situations which are, of necessity, closed. As Harsanyi acutely points out, his Postulate 5 performs just that function—and correctly so, if the bargaining situation to be resolved *is* a closed situation. But, as argued in Chapter 8, international situations are not closed in this sense—for, since one may have to allow something for the other party's (and one's own) propensity to create and to innovate, one cannot be sure, at the beginning of a bargaining situation, what are and what are not the "irrelevant variables extraneous to the criteria of rational behavior."[6]

But if international negotiations (in contradistinction to some cases of economic bargaining) are essentially open processes, what is the status of a negotiator's schedule of preferences at the beginning and the end (however we define those termini) of a negotiation? As in orthodox game theory, the postulates of orthodox bargaining (e.g., Harsanyi's Postulates 1, 3, 5, and 6) require that the preference schedules must remain constant, except in the case where a subgame is played which includes among its

[4] *Ibid.*, pp. 183–84.

[5] Note, however, that Harsanyi's postulates form a partially *self-referring set:* (2A) refers to (1), (3), (4), (5), and (6); (2B) refers to (2A) and to (3), (4), (5), and (6), while permitting an exception to (1). Such sets cannot be guaranteed free from—though for Harsanyi's immediate purposes, they may well not give rise to—paradoxes of *self-reference.* Agreed, it may be possible so to restate and reorder Harsanyi's set of postulates as to remove the self-reference. But intuitively it would seem that the process of reciprocal imputation, which is of the essence of bargaining and strategic situations, somehow has self-reference built in.

[6] Harsanyi, *op. cit.*, p. 185.

pay-offs (i.e., end-points) the acquisition of power to alter some other person's schedule of preferences. In other words, bargaining theory presupposes that it can never be rational during a negotiation to change one's own ordering of preferences (or to seek to change that of an opponent) in respect of the substance under negotiation. But in negotiation (as distinct from "horse-trading") there is always recognized to be the possibility of such a change. We shall now put forward as a second kind of approach to the analysis of negotiation, the outline of a negotiating model built upon this possibility of a change of preferences.

The abortive negotiations on disarmament in 1960, for example, proceeded by the putting forward of *sets of proposals.* Such political proposals are unlike the offer of a price in a bargaining negotiation, since the ingredient proposals, unlike monetary unit, or better, unlike units of utility, are *not* indefinitely substitutable units. Each set of proposals is rather a part-picture of a possible world—part of what the logicians call a "state-description." We shall refer to them as "possible worlds." Each negotiating party, even before the other(s) has published his (their) proposals, must have at least two "possible worlds" before him—the present world, and the world of his own first set of proposals. Unless the latter is not a genuine offer but instead a negotiating feint, it must be rational for him to prefer the latter to the former. When the other negotiating party makes public *his* set of proposals, the first party will have to decide whether or no he prefers the other party's proposals to the present world. (If the unlikely occurs, and he finds that he actually prefers the other's to his own proposals, he would then be wise to envisage a fourth possible world—i.e., another set of proposals even more to his liking than the first proposal of the other party, because the revelation to him of the fact that the other party's preferences are eminently in line with his own should suggest to him that in such favorable circumstances he might do even better for himself.[7]) If he *wholly* prefers the present world to the other's proposed world, he may reasonably indicate that the negotiations seem hopeless. But he may be able to derive from the other's proposals a reduced set which, by leaving out some particular objectionable item, appears to him as a possible world preferable to the present one. Logically this possibility implies that a finite number of other possible worlds can be telescoped out of the other's proposals by each negotiator. Of *this* set of derived possible worlds, he may wish to offer to the other party the one most preferred by himself. He may also assume that the other already has, implicitly, some orderable preference or another for each item in the derived set.

[7] J. C. Harsanyi, in "Bargaining in Ignorance of the Opponent's Utility Function," Cowles Foundation Discussion Paper No. 46 (New Haven: Cowles Commission for Research in Economics, December 11, 1957), concludes from this kind of situation, among others, that it is always irrational to enter into bargaining when all parties are ignorant of each other's utility function.

There will be, however, an alternative way of proceeding open to each negotiator, once the other, by publishing a proposal or by criticizing another's proposal, has given some indication of his preferences: each may try to create a *novel* or partly novel "possible world" in the hope that it will prove more desirable to both (or all) the negotiating parties than does the present one at least. Now since, *ex hypothesei,* the other party has not yet conceived of this possible world, even implicitly, the publishing of it as a proposal is apt to alter the other's schedule of preferences, either by the simple addition of a new item to the schedule, or also by a subsequent reordering of the original items as well. The model here sketched presupposes that it can be rational to alter one's preferences in the light of new information. The orthodox postulates of rationality (e.g., Harsanyi's Postulate 5) imply that the addition of a wholly new item to an already consistent schedule of preferences must not be allowed to alter the order (or even the cardinal degree of utility) of the items comprising the original set.

I doubt whether this condition implied by the orthodox postulates of rationality can be met in every case, or whether, if it were, we would regard the sort of person who always met it as rational in an ordinary human sense. Indeed, we often take as a mark of insanity the kind of inflexible consistency *not* open to drastic amendment by truly novel information. But such a commitment to openness can have awkward implications: while one is in process of reordering one's preferences to allow a proper place to some newly recognized possibility (a process more like art than like logical inference), the chances are that one's schedule will become quite intransitive (see Chapter 8). That is, we have to buy long-run rationality—"right reason"—at the price of short-run irrationality. I can see no way, given the orthodox postulates, around this difficulty.

Here and elsewhere in the present chapter, then, we are maintaining that the requirement—that in situations of political debate it must be considered possible (i.e., not subversive of the peculiarly *political* character of the encounter) for any participant to add to or take away from the items listed in his schedule of preferences ("constellation of ends"), and that having done so he may reorder other items in the schedule—violates one of the "strong Postulates of Rationality," styled "restriction of variables" or "irrelevance of independent alternatives." Let me suggest an imaginary but not fantastic case.

There was in 1957 an English Liberal who happened not to have considered at all the possibility of the United Kingdom's *politically* integrating with the Six. He then preferred an increasingly close and, if necessary, dependent alliance of the UK with the USA, to a retention by Britain of the means of independent initiative in foreign policy. At the lower level of defense preferences, this made him reprobate Duncan Sandys' White Paper of 1957, which intensified the nuclearization of UK armed forces, inducing the Liberal to advocate unilateral renunciation by Britain of all nuclear weapons. Then in late 1958 the prospect of Britain's becoming part of the European Community was suggested to him. It answered to his intuition that his country had to find a new and in any case subordinate international role. But the more he reflected on it, the more the "idea of Europe" attracted him. This new commitment revolutionized his political attitudes: while now preferring Britain-in-Europe to all other arrangements, he came to prefer UK independence to closer assimilation to the USA. Unlike most of his fellow Liberals, he became a supporter of the "independent British deterrent," partly having in view the prospect of a future European Defense Community, but also because the idea of an Atlantic Community had, as such, now lost favor with him.

A third approach, this time on an empirical level, to the analysis of political negotiation is expounded by Joseph Nogee.[8] The chief premise is that in some types of negotiation (e.g., for disarmament), agreement is very nearly the last thing that any party wants to reach. Only more does each one of them dislike the prospect of appearing to have broken off negotiations, or to have taken up such a recalcitrant position as would "force" the other party to break off negotiations. Therefore a frequently preferred strategy is to offer a set of proposals "calculated to have wide popular appeal" but containing a "joker"—i.e., "at least one feature that the other side could not possibly accept, thus forcing a rejection" of the whole claim.[9]

This kind of negotiation, it is clear, does not approximate either to a bargaining situation, or to the model that I have just sketched. Rather, it resembles an ordinary contest, in which the pay-offs are gains and losses of prestige, and the possible strategies are "quasi-proposals," complete with "joker." Such contests may well be open to game-theoretical analysis, even of the orthodox variety. But if so, it would be a "game" parasitic upon the phenomena of genuine negotiation. Therefore the empirical theory of it, though very likely valid and sufficient in its own universe of discourse, cannot purport to be the one and only Theory of Negotiations (Nogee does not suggest that it is). The model that we have suggested, however, could be developed to include Nogee's suggestion.

Thus, a quasi-proposal is "quasi" only because of the joker that was calculated to preclude its acceptance. But if we neglect this element of calculation (itself a concomitant of many disarmament negotiations), we can describe the negotiating situation as one in which (1) each party is willing to offer the other a possible world which he himself prefers to the present one, but which the other does not; (2) each envisages a (common)

[8] See Joseph Nogee, "The Diplomacy of Disarmament," *International Conciliation,* No. 526 (January 1960).

[9] *Ibid.,* p. 282.

third alternative—a world like the present world, except that in it negotiations have been broken off; and each prefers the present world to that third one, but the fourth one to the world first proposed by the other; and (3) each may then try to think out a set of proposals which, while appearing to the other less preferable than the breaking-off of negotiations, also appears more preferable than the offer which the other negotiator would initially have been willing to make. This variant of the game, it would seem, must be in danger of being broken off by one party or another, sooner or later. If, however, there is anything in the later-expounded parts of our model, each party must recognize that there remains the bare possibility of his wanting to accept some quite novel proposal himself. Indeed, the game described by Nogee could hardly continue if that were not so.

Let us now consider briefly the 1960 disarmament negotiations. At first glance it is clear that Harsanyi's, Nogee's, and our own theories of negotiation will need to be complicated a great deal in order to take care of the fact that while the USSR could design its proposals and therefore modify them quite freely, Western proposals were themselves the products of negotiation amongst allies, and had therefore to be put forward in a much more uncompromising fashion. Further, Soviet proposals were not necessarily addressed to the West as a unitary "negotiator,"[10] and therefore telescoped into a number of alternative outcomes agreeable to the Soviet Union in varying degrees.

The proposals of June 2, 1960, represent the Russians' last major move before the walk-out with which they ended the negotiations of that time. The course of negotiation in the following three weeks fits in only too well with Nogee's hypothesis. Though the Russians' new proposals discarded a joker which the West had been indicating as such for some considerable time, they retained another in the form of a timing of conventional disarmament which, as the West maintained, would have jeopardized the security of Europe.

On the other hand, the Soviet representatives seem to have gauged correctly the likelihood that at this time the United States would certainly prefer the breaking-off of negotiations, even at great cost in prestige, above any far-reaching measure of disarmament. The US proposal forestalled by Russia's walk-out also threw away a number of jokers, but retained at least one, the Controlling Principle No. 5: "The treaties shall remain in force indefinitely subject to the inherent right of a party to withdraw and be relieved of obligations thereunder if the provisions of the treaty, including those providing for the timely installation and effective operation of the

[10] E.g., the Soviet delegation's conciliatory attitude toward the French in respect to their proposal for control of vehicles used for delivering nuclear weapons.

control system, are not being fulfilled and observed." One striking feature of the last stages of this particular "game" was the close approximation between the two parties' final sets of quasi-proposals.

Nogee's informal "theory of quasi-negotiation" thus receives further support—i.e., the disarmament negotiations of 1960, like their predecessors for many years, can be interpreted as a contest for prestige. If gains and losses of prestige were measurable (in fact, they are not), the "negotiating" contest would begin to look like a different kind of zero-sum game, in which each contestant's objectives were (1) to increase his own prestige before a world-political audience by offering proposals that would look reasonable and conciliatory, and (2) to reduce his opponent's prestige by forcing him to reject such reasonable proposals or to break off negotiations. Even so, however, the contest would not be strictly amenable to orthodox game-theoretical treatment, if only because neither the columns nor the rows of the matrix would be finite in number or definite in quality. These indefinitenesses are irremediable in the real world. Furthermore, by being open to creative innovation, the negotiating contest is apt to induce violations of at least one basic postulate of "rationality"—*viz.,* that each contestant's preferences remain transitive.

For the latter reason, if for no other, interpretive insights and valid empirical generalizations such as Nogee's cannot be formalized into a rigorous formal Theory of Negotiations. I do think, however, that they can be subsumed under still more general interpretations—one of many of those being our scheme of "possible worlds" that rival each other in the process of negotiation. But even that scheme cannot be called a General Theory of Negotiations; it is merely a sketch of an approach more hospitable than is orthodox bargaining theory to the possibilities of novelty and inventiveness, and to the brute fact of real, nonstatistical uncertainty in human affairs. Moreover, it resembles a philosophy rather than a science; for it takes cognizance of a second order of rationality, to which we come when revaluing our former preferences in the face of some new possibility to which we cannot remain indifferent. Agreed, only transitive preferences are rational; but closed and impregnable rationality is less than human.

Creativity, and rationality that is open to new information and to the transforming of evaluations, are presupposed in the approach to a theory of negotiations favored in this chapter. Now, it may well be that very rarely in inter-Power negotiations have genuinely novel and creative proposals been put forward; and that even less often have the recipients of such proposals been so open to new information and to new evaluations that they were prepared to see in the novel proposals a possible world that suited them better than either their current world or any of the transformations of it which *they* had conceived. Even so, the reader may be willing to consider a thought-experiment to decide whether our approach to negotiation is utterly irrelevant or, instead, of infrequent application.

Does it seem to the reader that it would be *impossible* either for a negotiator to advance such a novel proposal, or for those to whom it was directed to accept it? If so, then the matter of presupposing creativity and open rationality does not arise. If not, then those presuppositions are unavoidable, and are in fact presupposed in the hypothesis we have advanced in the course of theorizing about the politics of the Powers. Moreover, the context in which such a novel proposal could be put forward and openly assessed can be described only as strategic and political—no other category of rational interaction allows of that kind of development. Our thought-experiment is intended to bring out the point that politics of any kind (*viz.,* in the present case, the politics of Powers) is not merely an instrumental activity, or one that could be turned over without impoverishment to administrators, or made a subject of routine, but is a mode of action that allows of the exercise of talents no less preeminently human than those in scientific and humane discovery and in the creations of the great arts.

From that angle, we may reopen the questions whether the study of the politics of the Powers can be value-free, and whether amongst its students there may be expected a "commitment" to the idea of an inter-Power polity corresponding to the commitment to the (internal) polity which Leicester Webb (see Chapter 1, p. 25) imputed to political science as such. The features of politics in general—amongst others, its omnicompetence—which he indicated as supporting his imputation are related to the openness and creative potential attributed above to the negotiating relationship. Since negotiation occurs in all politics, internal and external, but in internal politics within some formal or informal framework (e.g., a constitution), except after revolutionary change, the sole clue to the above questions suggested by our approach to negotiation is that in political interaction between the Powers the potential for creative proposals and responses need not inhere in the representatives of any particular type of internal polity, or in the advocates of any particular type of inter-Power organization, though there may be some types that inhibit creative potential in their representatives (see Chapter 7). One is inclined to remark upon this, for it would indicate that *if* some evaluation or commitment is involved in the study of Power politics, it is not a commitment to any idealism, or to any one kind of Power system or form of international organization. We are not reopening the realist-idealist controversy. (Chapter 1 acknowledged the common interest of mankind in avoiding universal destruction; but here, assuming that common interest, we are asking whether in *other* respects the study of Power politics is value-free.)

We contend that that study is like the study of one of the great arts, or of the history of philosophy or religion (and unlike, say, entomology). The study of English poetry entails of itself no prejudice in favor of a particular poet or school, even though no student or critic individually can rise above particular prejudices, preferences, and evaluations. But even if he could become so disinterested, he would not be ascending into some value-free realm of the "exact science of poetry": his most profoundly objective judgments would also be evaluations, inasmuch as they distinguished the depths of creation in poetry from the shallows of fashionable imitation and clever unimaginative writing.

The "critic" of Power politics is, we suggest, in the same situation. The more objectively he works, the more he must be able to distinguish between the act of imaginative statecraft, despite his being out of sympathy with it, and the routine diplomatic performance along the lines of a policy he happens to agree with. Such distinctions seem to the present writer to be objective matters of fact, and at the same time discernible only by acts of judgment which are evaluative. Nor are they imported into the field of study from outside, but are as it were native to the Powers' politics.

It may not be necessary to add that "an imaginative act of statecraft" can very well be unsuccessful, and certainly need not entail that the statesman who performs it is unusually powerful, or that he increases his own or his country's power thereby. The act need only "succeed" to the extent that the agent carries it out. Furthermore, the political critic's implied commitment to the activity of Power politics can only be to its quality as politics, and not to the inescapable but incidental and instrumental Powerhood associated with it. Our definition of Powerhood, and the argument of the present chapter, share a common philosophic direction: the Power is defined as a set of persons; the source of its unity is a half-conscious view, that informs the minds of at least some persons in the set, and thus affects the interrelations within the set—in which condition the interrelations are styled an internal system; on the other hand, the external system of relations between Powers chiefly consists in the interrelations between the several Powers' representative leaders ("statesmen"); and the actions and interactions that make up the power-political process are for the most part the actions of the individual representatives, it being allowed that as a rare achievement some of these might be acts of creative imagination.

What the critical student of Power politics is committed to, from this point of view, is the recognition of excellence in the thought and action of certain persons, who act on behalf of Powers or of inter-Power organizations. The internal systems, with their varying elements of polity, and even more the external systems of Powers, have no intrinsic excellence, though the former, since they provide structures for real societies, thereby help to make possible that life in the polity which has been one of the prime matters for evaluation from the beginnings of civilization. Systems of Powers, together with the coercive aspect of the internal systems, are—as systems—partly instrumental; moreover, the Powers' representatives gathered in "conversation" with each other do not as a matter of course form a community capable of an approach to the good life. But severally they can contribute to the humanizing or to the depraving of the power-political process. In that respect, their actions within their systematic interrelationship are more than merely instrumental.

If so, power-political activity should be evaluated in terms of its approach to an end—the "humanizing" of the process itself. From such a conclusion it may be thought possible to construct an ideal humanized world order. I believe that the conclusion is to be avoided, and that acts of statecraft are to be judged by the humane quality of their method and mode, and not by their tendency to produce Utopia.

THIRTEEN

Philosophic Progress and the Humanizing of Power Politics

A mystery remains, unresolved in these pages: the spell that Powerhood has laid upon mankind. The evils of submission to a Power are today as evident as when Samuel told the people of Israel the manner of the king that should reign over them, and the folly of it no less apparent than when they replied, "Nay, but we will have a king over us; that we also may be like all nations; and that our king may judge us, and go out before us, and fight our battles" (I Sam. 8:19–20). In this concluding chapter, therefore, hypotheses are advanced to account (by social mechanism) for the maintenance of already emerged Powers, and (by genetic psychology) for the origins in individuals of allegiance to a Power.

Most of the clauses in our definition of Powerhood in Chapter 4 concerned the internal structure of the Power: amongst them, 1.12 contained the proposition that, at least among the governing set (the rulers), some element of polity was unavoidable. We were careful in the defining to make no necessary connection between such internal-political relationships and the external politics of the Powers: for the nature of the connection may be specific to every case—see Chapter 7, pp. 156–64. Our first chapter opened with the contention that interlocutors in the power-political conversation must always be few, which is enough to make it hard to imagine a single worldwide polity integrating the diverse polities of the Powers. Obversely, one doubts with Aristotle whether a polity of free men can be expanded without limit—certainly not so as to include thousands of millions, even by the representational devices of the last five centuries. So after formulating our hypotheses about the springs of Powerhood and about the maintenance of Powers, we shall touch in this chapter upon the connection between Power and polity; upon their several and joint effects on the course of the power-political process; and upon the much debated question of historical priority as between internal and external politics. Lastly, recognizing the possibility of philosophic and theoretical progress in the "language" (i.e., the categories and presuppositions) of Power politics, we shall inquire whether such conceptual progress may issue in a humanizing of actual inter-Power relations; and, if so, what changes need to be made, on account of those possibilities, in this study's exposition of the theory and philosophy of Powers and their politics.

I

Most institutions and activities, it is fashionable to suppose, have a "political aspect"—hence studies of "the politics of the business corporation," "of science," "of the college faculty." This is a legitimate extension, beyond the recognizably "political," of the concept of politics. But the concept has an unextended and original sense, and in that sense—we have maintained—it properly denotes external as well as internal politics.

On p. 10 of Chapter 1, we interpreted as inputs into the system of Power politics certain outcomes of each nation's internal politics, whether the matter politically at issue were economic, military-technological, or explicitly foreign-political. On the other hand, we treated outcomes of the world-political conversation as inputs into the several internal polities where, as we said, the internal systems' fairly efficient "receptors" took them up as "issues"; but the external system that emerges out of the conversation of the Powers' representatives, being (as in some measure an anarchy) ill-equipped with common receptors, responded—we thought—with "crisis" to the more disturbing of inputs from the internal systems. Such an interpretation is valid only on the whole: there are polities more labile than the Security Council. Yet something can be said for that characterization of an input-output reciprocation between internal and external politics, provided we can disabuse ourselves of the engineering analogies.

Still earlier in our first chapter, on p. 6, we had interpreted the input-output connection as "the information or impression which issues from the informal political interchanges of world statesmen and passes to the directing echelons of military, economic, and political organizations"—i.e., as a relation of communication. Throughout the study we have referred to statesmen as "Janus-faced," emphasizing that interpretation. But during any exchange of political messages, some information will be lost or debased: no statesman can represent without some distortion, in the world-political conversation, such consensus as his government—let alone his entire polity—may have arrived at; not the best press in the world can wholly avoid vulgarizing the issues of an interchange between the representatives of Powers. Were there no such distortion in the flow of information, it might be worth considering the citizens of every polity as all participants to some degree in the world-political conversation. As things are, the difference we make between internal systems and the now-integrating external system still appears well established.

Distortion, however, does not occur at random, but along the boundaries of the power-political map. (Despite the same language and excellent media of intercommunication, the pictures of the USA mostly presented by the English press are quite awry, and American reports of the United Kingdom are even worse.) The ancient and obvious frontiers of coercion still mark off one polity from another, and distinguish them as a class of systems from the web of their systematic interrelations. But, as we have contended throughout this study, coercion is usually no more than potential; indeed, if a society could maintain that potential though without ever employing it, one of the two essentials of Powerhood would remain to it.

The other essential, which we have called "unity-in-spirit," has a far more continuous effect upon the conduct of politics between the Powers: there is usually no need to coerce the national representative into concerting with his fellow citizens on behalf of what he feels to be the dominating assessment of the national interest. It is this cohesive inward subjection to one's Power that was said above to be an unresolved mystery, often taken for granted by political scientists precisely in those highly developed States where it is remarkably strong, and chiefly inquired into where it is weakest—in newly formed ex-colonial nations. (Since it is from the viewpoint of Power politics that the unity amongst a State's subjects is most apparent, an analysis of internal political systems which began from and connected them with their external political relations should contribute something to an understanding of the conditions of *internal* cohesiveness.) We may be able to dispel the mystery somewhat if we can offer explanations for the maintenance of distinct Powers in the face of movements to break down their exclusiveness, and for the widespread individual propensity to owe allegiance to a Power.

The explanations we require then, are for a class of ubiquitous processes (which in Chapter 4 we made a matter of definition—see items 1.0 to 1.123—but which are quite apparent in the real world): certain subsets of people, notably ruling groups, come to discern the larger sets in which they are severally included as uniting-in-spirit, and act upon their determination to preserve the integrity and the safety of that larger set; furthermore, these convictions and the Powers they generate persist and are socially effective, sometimes for centuries and millenia. The former aspect of the problem seems to call for a genetic-psychological solution, capable of accounting for a universal human disposition; the latter obviously requires some references to the structure of internal and external systems. We shall deal first with the latter.

We hypothecate that the typical Power's internal cohesion is promoted, and movements to disrupt it hindered, by a sharp difference in nature and *tempi* between the complex of all interchanges internal to it as social system on the one hand, and on the other those external interchanges, political, strategic and economic, carried on by the persons "representing" the Powers (whom we have let "the statesman" typify). The locus of our explanation is at the nexus between internal and external networks of communication and not within either the external order or the internal systems alone. The frequent, regularized, day-by-day interchanges—both competitive and cooperative—within each society-as-Power cannot be suspended for a while now and then, as can those that constitute inter-Power relations; nor, unlike the latter, can the internal system usually be revolutionized in a matter of weeks. Competitive and cooperative *action* and, even more, the daily round of habitual and unreflective *behavior* within the society greatly complicate the task of enlarging or otherwise changing from outside (e.g., by an agreement reached amongst the Powers' representatives), any community already "united in spirit" and carrying on even the minimum of those interchanges which, in the first half of our definition, we postulated as constituting the community a Power. By contrast, the statesmen who are the agents of the external system are rarely bound together in similar customary and cooperative bonds (the European aristocracy of the *ancien regime* was something of an exception) by which they might hope to unite their respective peoples. Internal cohesion is hardly subvertible except by rival communities of the spirit, amongst which we include not only religious but also revolutionary political movements. The origin of these and of "purely national" unifying movements is not accounted for by our explanatory hypothesis at the present level of exposition; what it explains, if it explains at all, is the *maintenance* of a typical Power's internal cohesion. The reader will have noticed that it is a hypothesis in "social mechanics," and is implicitly quantitative: we could state it so as to be testable by such evidence as is now being collected, for example, by the Yale Political Data Program.

Earlier accounts also have been quasimechanistic—e.g., both those contending that internal cohesion is maintained because of apprehensions of external military pressure, and those that look instead for explanation to the structure of the internal system, in particular to the political relationship between classes. Hypotheses of both those kinds have some explanatory power: it may be a merit of our explanation by conditions at the internal-external nexus that it can be reformulated to include them. Thus, reformulated, it would explain the maintenance of (randomly and extraneously originated) sentiments for the internal unity of a group-as-Power by the multiplicity, variety, continuity, habituality and practical necessity of internal interchanges as compared with the intermittency, infrequency, singularity, incalculability and gratuitousness of external interchanges which because of the latter qualities cannot foster loyalties contrary to patriotism. Furthermore, patriotic sentiment can be reinforced both by perceptions of external pressure and threat, and also by a long-run stable equilibrium in the internal structure of relationship between the ruled and ruling groups. (In the last-mentioned condition, we emphasize the word "structure"; evidently, equilibrium of structure is compatible with much disequilibrium in the individual and class membership of the groups; beyond that, we cannot elaborate the matter here.)

At the level of analysis of our social-mechanistic hypothesis, a group's unity-in-spirit is said to originate "randomly and extraneously"; i.e., the possible sources of origin are clearly multifarious and widely distributed. What, then, is there in the human situation that prompts people everywhere and at all times to see themselves at one with some and not others of their kind, and to concert themselves against others—i.e., as a Power?

Philosophers, usually conflating "Power" with "body-politic," have offered, broadly, four different kinds of answer—(i) from the social (specifically "political") nature of man (e.g., Aristotle); (ii) from the inward structure of the human soul (e.g., Plato in *The Republic*); (iii) from the allegedly evident rational advantages of social union (e.g., all theories of the social contract), and; (iv) from the "inheritance of a pattern of congregating for livelihood and company in extended families" (e.g., Hegel in the introduction to his *Philosophy of History;* Marx, *passim;* and the contemporary animal ethologists). The first answer—(i)—though propounding a necessary, fails to provide a sufficient, condition for grouping of persons into Powers—why should the many human societies be exclusive, potentially by armed force, of each other? The third answer—(iii)—also fails to be sufficient and further has application only to civilized polities and mainly Western ones at that, though it has made a permanent if at present wrongly slighted contribution to the philosophy of the polity. The fourth, so far as it proposes to "reduce" power-political action to resistant animal behavior, embodies a category mistake: Powers, though at first glance resemble, are a different kind of community from the hunting groups and extended families of presapient man, let alone from animal communities exclusive of each other, even upon a territorial basis. The leaders of Powers, at least, act with deliberation and foresight, e.g., they make alliances. In certain Australian aboriginal communities, for example, there exist, apart from the linguistic and religious-ceremonial unity of the tribe and the endogamous unity of the moiety, rival groups of males within the same moiety that are bound by custom to compete for wives. These are the clans, and they are recognizably "Powers":

> The clan is the largest social unit that does not have armed conflict within it. It is usually the war-making group. The causes for warfare are the killing of a member of a clan by a man belonging to another clan, and interclan rivalry for women . . .
>
> The kinship system of the Murngin, with its attendant set of obligations, duties, and privileges, which surrounds the social personalities of the various relatives within it, tends to enlarge the scope of a feud from within the radius of two warring clans to four, or possibly the whole of the clans of the several tribes.[1]

The propensities to wage war and to form alliances, and the collective disposition to vindicate by force the honor of a clan member, are by our definition adequate indicators of Powerhood. They involve speech, unlike the territorial groupings of animals; they cannot be spontaneous reactions, as presumably with presapient human groups "instinctively" warding off attackers. Nevertheless, human warfare mobilizes passions and bodily reactions evidently inherited from archaic and animal ancestors.

It is the second answer—(ii)—which this study's philosophy most nearly approximates, though here the debt is owed more to Freud than to Plato, and more to Paul and Augustine than to either. Elements of idea that inform an adult's disposition to belong to a Power, to promote its integrity, and to stand against the outsider, derive from that aspect of the inward economy of the person (less evidently in the female than in the male) which takes form rather before puberty. Our hypothesis is that at that stage the (male) child internalizes the authority which he has apprehended to be exercised over him by his parents (pre-eminently by his father, or by the father-surrogate whom his community may happen to license), and then projects it out again as the idea of a spirit (his Power) that unites all those and only those subject to its authority—an authority which, like that of the parents themselves, can be, but by no means usually need be, coercive: forcibly but within definite limits against its subjects; if necessary without limit against aliens.

This hypothesis does not refer to initiation into the *polity* (i.e., reaching one's majority), a later and by no means universal phenomenon

[1] W. Lloyd Warner, "Murngin Warfare," *Oceania,* I, No. 4 (1931), 478. Quoted by permission of the Editor of *Oceania.*

touched on below. Nor does it refer to every aspect of what a child internalizes of his parents' position and attitudes; e.g., it is not concerned with the origin of conscience or of moral codes, or with what an infant internalizes from one parent or another. Nor is it concerned with patriotism in the sense of love of childhood landscape. Though that may be later incorporated into the sentiment of loyalty to one's Power, it need not be since, by our definition and from a few historical instances, we suppose that Powerhood does not necessarily involve territoriality. Nor, finally, is the parental authority we refer to precisely the same as that dealt with in psychological analyses of "the authoritarian personality": it seems that both authoritarian and nonauthoritarian types can owe equally unwavering allegiance to their Power—perhaps the authoritarian will always seek its concrete external embodiment. But was Kent an authoritarian character?

> *Lear:* What wouldst thou?
> *Kent:* Service.
> *Lear:* Whom wouldst thou serve?
> *Kent:* You.
> *Lear:* Dost thou know me, fellow?
> *Kent:* No, sir; but you have that in your countenance which I would fain call master.
> *Lear:* What's that?
> *Kent:* Authority.

Kent does not submit to Lear's power, which is negligible: he pledges his allegiance to Lear's authority, an act consonant with his own honor. What makes a Power is the allegiance of a loyal subject, offered freely, in honor, out of a certain self-respect, to an authority created by the subject's recognition of it: Lear himself is not absolutely needed. This complex of sentiments is not an infantile but an adolescent acquisition (though Kent is forty-eight); on the other hand, it is not yet fully adult—Kent is not a political man, a free citizen, entering into a contract with Lear by which both would be accepting the authority of a positive but impersonal law. Nevertheless, the adolescent status of subjecthood to a Power's authority always lives on, however subordinated and transformed, within the adult's free citizenship in a polity: the political covenant can never be wholly rationalized into a business contract. Patriotic allegiance to one's Power can mature into responsible citizenship in one's polity—we may even assert that it should; for though throughout this work Power and polity tend to be opposed as sickness and health, and though one admires, for example, Germans of the Resistance who chose democracy at the expense of patriotism, the feeling that their choice was a tragic one indicates a conviction that normally allegiance should be an element though a subordinate one in political responsibility. Certainly, a liberal democracy survives by the honor as well as by the rectitude of its citizens. Hobbes precedes his statement of principle:

> . . . the right men have by nature to protect themselves, when none else can protect them, can by no covenant be relinquished.

with the important distinction:

> . . . When armies fight, there is on one side, or both, a running away; yet when they do it not out of treachery, but fear, they are not esteemed to do it unjustly, but dishonourably.[2]

Since there are many occasions besides battle in which the polity's interest and security can be undermined by dishonorable conduct, should not Hobbes have mentioned, amongst things that "tend to the dissolution of a commonwealth," the want of honor amongst its subjects?

We have contended above that what creates a Power is the disposition of people to owe it allegiance as subjects; yet in our definition of Chapter 4, items 1.1 to 1.1421, we assigned to its rulers the active concerting and promoting of its indispensable unity-in-spirit. The contradiction is seen to be merely apparent when we recognize that every ruler is normally also a subject (the element of polity inevitable in any Power entails that the solitary and absolute ruler is a limiting possibility, in practice ephemeral); and because anyone who is as conscious of his own identity and integrity as to pledge his allegiance to some authority has it in him to rule in some degree. For what we have to explain—the universal tendency to incorporate into a Power—and for the genetic-psychological explanation which we are offering, we require only the *abstract ideas* of ruler and of alien: nobody need *be* either; but our hypothesis requires that the typical male adolescent actually aspires in some degree to be a subject. Anyone against whom mere power (as distinct from authority) is exercised by a Power cannot be a subject but by that fact must be an outsider.

How would this disposition to owe allegiance to a Power arise in the individual? By late infancy, the child has entered unquestioningly into the relationship of being "subject to his parents" (cf. Luke 2:51). His possibly ceasing to be so, he apprehends as a great disaster, which would occur *either* if he should totally surrender the identity which he won, also in infancy, when he learned to say "No" to them, *or*—a more credible and immediate fear—by their betraying his faith in them: by their suddenly becoming, not hostile or punishing, but indifferent to him as they evidently are, though benignly so, toward other people's children. In thus losing faith in them because of this primal fear, he enacts as it were the Fall of Man. That is, "eating the fruit of the tree of the knowledge of good and evil," he establishes in himself the rule of his parents by coming to "know" it as comprising a finite authority—finite in scope because there could be some-

[2] Thomas Hobbes, *Leviathan,* Chapter 21.

one (himself!) excluded from its sway—which was the disaster he was guarding himself against by enthroning within himself the parental authority. (Such internalization of authority may but need not be assisted and celebrated by some public rite of initiation.) He is now its subject for certain, by virtue of its presence within him; and, according to the strength of his hard-won identity mentioned above, he is also a ruler of himself as subject. As ruler he must maintain the integrity of his internalized structure of authority and foster respect for it. In this way, *loyalty* or allegiance begins as an inward-directed disposition to maintain at all costs the unity-in-spirit of the child himself with his internalized authority and to exclude that . . . traitor, the disastrous alien self whom he had fearfully imagined as cast out by the parents.

The fear of being cast out to which he has succumbed is now the fear that the traitor-self will be realized; and this is what gives the inward-directed disposition to be loyal its aggressive, vengeful, indeed death-dealing force—it is the traitor pre-eminently who "deserves death." The emotion of loyalty to one's authoritative principle mobilizes and concerts together the aggressiveness which maintains personal identity, along with the anxiety that one might be shamed, i.e., might become an object of indifference and scorn to whomsoever happens to embody that to which one owes allegiance. Whoever has thus internalized parental authority is thereby ready to externalize his commitment to a finite embodiment of authority and his rejection of the potential traitor-self.

The will to exclude others not subject to one's own principle of authority is not directed against the others (outsiders) as necessarily traitorous: one may be allied with, indifferent to, or at war against, the outsider. The latter is normally not a traitor—only one who has been a "subject" can betray. Indeed the will to exclude outsiders is derivative from the desire to "include" those who share one's source of authority—primarily, oneself. Feelings of pride in being a worthy subject and of dread of being shamed as an unworthy one constitute the sentiment of patriotic loyalty, which is thus potentially combative but not necessarily aggressive in the primitive sense: the patriot is first ready to die for his *patria,* and only by derivation to kill for it. Above all, the sentiment is in origin secular—finite authority is not uncanny nor necessarily sacred, though objects of worship can readily be annexed by it; equally well, a unity in sacred things amongst Powers who share a common worship can mitigate or suspend conflicts. On the other hand, inter-Power conflict is typically less than total, while "religious" war (e.g., that waged from the motive of supernatural dread and terror) typically cannot be limited.

The foregoing excursus into genetic psychology was undertaken in order to fill out our account of the origin as well as of the maintenance of human groups-as-Powers. The propensity to originate Powers appears to be universal (i.e., endemic) in *homo sapiens;* yet evidently it is not instinctual, and we rejected as a category-mistake the hypothesis (e.g., of animal-ethologists) that it is biologically genetic, though it brings into play and indeed could not possibly be manifest without, many biologically inherited patterns of behavior, e.g., the warrior's stance. If it were culturally derived, its ubiquity would be highly improbable. We have supposed, then, that the disposition to patriotic loyalty (of which the infant knows nothing, but the adolescent male is possessed) is in a class with the incest taboo, acquisitiveness, and religiosity—something that calls for genetic-psychological explanation, and is already apprehended in Biblical phraseology as one of the "traces of original sin": the Augustinian theological tradition singles out—as consequences of the Fall—idolatry, familial and sexual subjection, property, and the "civil sword" or Powerhood.

The account given above is not an hypothesis testable (as is that previously advanced to explain maintenance of Powers) by historical evidence; but psychological experiment might well test it, even though indirectly; so might evidence from anthropology and sociology. A sketch of the topic seemed worthwhile at this point, as having been indicated by convergent assumptions and presuppositions in this study—those, notably, of methodological individualism, impaired rationality, and the perpetual recurrence of the phenomena of Powerhood.

Our account of the psychological disposition to patriotism, furthermore, has been prepolitical. Psychologically and historically, the Power is prior to the polity. The Power is defined in Chapter 4 as logically prior, inasmuch as minimal "elements of polity" (1.12) are there alleged to be merely a characteristic, though an ineradicable one, of the concert in which one set of members of the Power—the rulers—are bound to act in maintaining the Power's integrity: our definition does not entail a *necessary* connection of any kind between politics as an activity and the conserving of a Power. Nevertheless, if all transactions between Powers were to be thoroughly politicized (e.g., if armed force were never employed, if economic conflicts were always susceptible to negotiation), one would expect both that the harshness and danger of external relations would decrease and that the emotional basis of popular allegiance to Powers would be weakened, or at least would remain strong only amongst those peoples who had developed rich and complex internal *polities,* and had a deep understanding of their national histories. Allegiance is poetry; politics is prose. Even the politics of the Powers is prose, contrasted with the epic poetry of war to the death between them.

II

Throughout this work, we have been at pains to argue that any political transaction, external or internal, is made "political" by the nature of the relationship it involves and the hierarchy of language that it necessarily employs, and not by the framework of political constitution, if any, that encompasses it. Having now developed our hypotheses about the origin and conservation of Powerhood, we can interpret any external shell or constitutional framework that a society may happen to possess as the politicized form of the primitive bond which will always remain in some degree, or at least recur however transformed, to subjugate men and to divide them from their fellows. As Power, the exclusive "community" exercises "sovereign" authority over its members, securing their "allegiance" so far as they submit willingly, but their "subjection" so far as they are not willing. As polity (some elements of which are present, at least amongst the rulers, in any Power) the upper segment of the community forms a more or less open "society," exercising sovereign control over its resources, but "legitimate" authority over its "citizens," to which they "consent" freely—that is, conditionally; for so far as its authority *is* legitimate, they will have certain rights of recourse to "constitutional resistance" or political opposition, while so far as it is *not* legitimate, they will have as free men the "inalienable right" to "secede," even if their sole practicable recourse for secession is to go into exile.

Our use of inverted commas in the foregoing sentence indicates that we have been attempting to distinguish the "language" of the polity from that of the Power. The former is irreducibly normative—it carries connotations of what *ought* to be done, since the core of political behavior (see Chapter 8, pp. 171–4) is action, directed by right reason; whereas the language of Powerhood when from it, so far as is possible, the language of the polity has been abstracted away, is not properly speaking normative (for all the internalization of parental authority which we have supposed to be at its origin), but expressive: its syntax is that of the particularly-directed and self-effecting word of command (*impero tibi*), not the generally-promulgating sentence (*iubeo ut*) of the legislator and the judge. It would seem, then, that the "language" of the polity is logically the richer. If so, all attempts to derive the concept of legitimate authority from that of sovereign authority (or, politics from the imperatives of the Power) must necessarily fail.

On the other hand, an historical case could be made for external or inter-Power politics' being the primal form of political activity, and evolving the earlier into developed forms of statecraft. Though all politics is the politics of rulers, the internal form is often the struggle toward rulership of those formerly subjects, as individuals or as classes. But from the beginning of external politics the ruler recognizes, in the alien, his fellow ruler. Furthermore, it is imaginable that the "origin" of the polity, in the sense of a social compact, tacit or explicit, between free individuals, out of prepolitical (e.g., kingly or priestly) rule might be genetically explained as a copying of agreements between sovereign rulers of Powers; but not the other way round. The pact that concludes a war of all against all amongst *individuals* in a state of nature has always seemed implausible: "the individual" seems to have been a late discovery, made indeed within the polity. But a treaty between the rulers of clans or of hordes, enforced by rational fears of being the odd party out of an alliance, could imaginably develop by precedent and convention into an aristocratic polity, and in some historic instances seem to have done so, though never, perhaps, without the motive of apprehension about possibly hostile outsiders. Our paradigm of the social compact would thus be the league of *socii* ("allies") constituted in order to mitigate rationally foreseeable conflict, i.e., from interested and not altruistic motives, from calculation and not from brotherly fervor, but perhaps confirmed by exchanges of oaths made to the divinities of a common cult.

In short, politics would have begun as external politics, based upon divisive allegiances to opposed primitive sovereignties, and would have been then, but only then, as the contract-philosophers have it, transformed by agreement into the internal interactions of a polity uniting within one Power the former rivals. Such a polity would be no special creation, but the resultant of action following from the chieftains' reflections about the consequence of unreflective, Power-dominated behavior. This is a paradigmatic hypothesis, restricted in application to cases of a polity amongst peoples historically ignorant of the idea of politics. Most contemporary polities, by contrast, originated from historical traditions about earlier or coeval polities.

That evolutionary paradigm may suggest new approaches to two other interconnected problems which have recurred throughout this work —(1) the scope and limitations of the statesman's causality and rational participation in the power-political process, and (2) the durations or time scales proper to a theory of the politics of the Powers. We observed above that though twenty or thirty years was, naturally, the utmost duration of an individual statesman's purposes and policies, a tradition of foreign policy is not merely the unreflective and perhaps unconscious maintenance of a certain posture toward a persisting constellation of outsiders and their Powers, to be in part explained, perhaps, by the transmission as folklore of popular prejudices and sympathies; rather, it is also something transmitted to the successive governing groups of a continuing polity through critical historiography (which need not be encumbered with the scholarship of official scribes or academics but can well be conducted in the unpublicized memoranda of a Foreign Office). One instance is England's policy for the last three hundred years (perhaps contrasted with her posture toward the King's lands in France until Mary Tudor); but Byzantium and Venice might also be regarded as having produced instances of historically transmitted policy. Polity is necessarily connected with criticism: the rulers even in an unlettered polity "give counsel" which must survive criticism, being assessed by their fellows, and perhaps commemorated by the bards, more or less as wise or foolish.

In a literate society critical historiography educates the statesman in two ways. By exercising his mind in the vicarious reenactment of the former conducting of statecraft, it helps train him. By tracing the evolution of policy, he learns to specify his people's and his own current conditions for action. The history that he reads will have been written from the characteristic perspective and colored by the values of his own Power and polity, i.e., it will not be claimed to approach the unattainable ideal of detachment sought by the "Critical" historians of the nineteenth century. On the other hand, historiography that can reconstruct the perspectives and the value systems of alien Powers will be quite the most helpful in specifying his own country's situation in the world. But are not the new social sciences, including behavioral world politics, about to supplant history as preferred training for the national decision-maker, especially in the greatest Powers?—quite possibly: though if, as we have argued in the first chapter of this book, the decisive transaction of statesmen is their "informal conversation," it is hard to imagine that abstract and generalized disciplines can illuminate it as naturally as can historical criticism.

Agreed, the simulacrum of a Power-polity can be constructed upon "roles" and "goals" imputed to one's nation, and these presumably are to be "enacted" and "reached" by the application of generalizations derived from research in the social sciences. But today's nation-states identify themselves and each other through their several peculiar histories, and conduct their international affairs by those lights. The dependence of policy upon the historical approach is thus deeply entrenched.

To recapitulate: the modern statesman typically represents a Power the ruling group in which constitutes a polity; that polity is identifiable by a common history, more or less criticized, inasmuch former policies and their proponents are judged according to their wisdom and effectiveness in furthering the legitimate interests of the polity-as-Power. None of the latter during the Christian era has continued to be a sovereign and unconquered Power for more than a dozen centuries (though the citizens of some may be able to identify themselves with a longer ancestry of Powers, e.g., Frenchmen with the empire of the Frankish Charlemagne—but how many with the Arvernian clan of the Gaullish Vercingetorix?), and in only a handful has the polity more than three centuries' continuous history.

The last-mentioned duration seems to represent the utmost temporal limit of secular and corporate human causality. The great religions have far longer and more profoundly continuous histories, for in most of them a return to the fountainheads has evidently remained possible; but their founders, humanly speaking, formulated no *policies* for their communities' future. Their visions and their claims could not begin to be answered through the achievement of any Power's corporate purposes. The pathos of historically apprehended Powerhood, by contrast, arises from its evident finitude and the passion of its subjects' commitment to the advancing of its interests.

Our idea that the "first-generation" polity of a Power typically originates in external politics, out of a pact of alliance between chiefs of clans or other minimal Powers so small that the irreducible element of polity in each is confined to the ruling family, can help explain a certain mutual exclusiveness between polities (which is clearly distinct from that exclusiveness defined into our conception of Powerhood and answering to the wish to exclude the alien that we have posited to be universal in the adult human male). The free unification or federation of two or more fully formed and sovereign polities is difficult even amongst kindred peoples sharing a common (liberal democratic) political ethos, and having strong incentives, of security or power, for combining. The Swiss counter-example represents an impressive political feat, in which the historically understood precedents seem to have suggested, for once, the linking of canton and city polities at the level of sovereignty. More often, it is the very achievements that historically have won for a polity its character, which close the road to unification with others of similar ethos but distinct histories.

The two excluding tendencies—in the polity and in the Power—combine when the polity-cum-Power exercises *sovereignty*. This ineluctable concept denotes both the matter-of-fact propensities (until what we have called—see Chapter 6, pp. 129–31 *et seq.*—the "capitulation point" is exceeded) for a Power through its rulers to have its way alike against outsiders and against recalcitrant subjects, and also the need for a polity's citizens to be assured that, when they have determined some issue in debate, their collective determination will be carried out. Thus the lawful liberties of citizens are necessarily dependent upon the maintenance of a power or capacity that, in relation to any inter- or supranational consensus, must be arbitrary.

Retention of unimpaired national or, better, State sovereignty has been criticized this century as disposing to war and totalitarianism. However that may be, it is also a necessary condition for liberal democracy, and thereby for the sole possibility of rational political control over the inter-Power process, the evils and arbitrariness of which can be mitigated by only two means: by each polity's constraining exercise of State sovereignty, or by the fortunate counterbalancing and offsetting of each Power's destructive ambitions through its confrontation with the other, i.e., by a happy arrangement of the power-political system. The latter, now called "conflict management," was once known as "maintaining the balance of power": it is and will always remain a chancy though indispensable means of preserving freedom and peace, the statesman who employs it neither wielding, by definition, unimpeded control over the process, nor being able at the most to do more than seize opportunities when, along with his own Power's interests that he must pursue, there is coincidental good to be done for a greater part of mankind. International organizations, like the League and the UN, should be thought of as general alliances, existing merely to make such opportunities more frequent and more readily exploitable; they do not contradict but presuppose unimpaired national sovereignty.

Supranational organizations, on the other hand, are intended to constrain exercise of sovereignty by States, through a new "division of powers": in the European example, member-States by treaty relinquish control over many *economic* affairs, which are thereafter at the disposal of the members' ministerial representatives, but often only upon the proposal of an allegedly independent, non-national bureaucracy. If the relinquishing were extended to such other realms as military and foreign policy, the members though still not formally federated would be jointly exercising their sovereignties dispersed through different levels of government, as in a federation. Other supranational or rather non-national methods of dispersing sovereignty might, however, equally restrain Powerhood while less enfeebling policy: in Chapter 5, pp. 100–01, we mentioned the universalizing of the administration of justice and, on pp. 106–7, the devolving of control over weapons of mass retaliation upon units very much smaller than Powers.

Such changes in the structure of the external system—possible, though admittedly implausible—illustrate the protean shapes that both sovereignty and Powerhood may take, perhaps contrasting in this with the well established polity. Within the latter, nevertheless, freedom of collective choice and concomitant responsibility are real and serious—the partial theory of statics which we expound in Chapters 8–11 implies no determinism: the equilibrating and disequilibrating models there constructed depend upon avowedly imaginary postulates of "rational" behavior in artificially simplified competitive-cooperative situations; in the real world, men are able to change the principles from which they act, and even to some extent their perceptions of the situation. Yet they are not the freer the more arbitrary the changes they are able to make: freedom indeed arises from the recognition of necessity, and every situation in which political action is possible has many features that are necessary, i.e., inescapable and insurmountable. But these, the statesman may be as apt to misdiscern as to overlook, failing in action through inadequacy in contemplation. Right action in statecraft is the fruit of sound contemplation, which has two aspects: firstly, historical reflection, appraising the evolution of the situation up to the very moment of action; secondly, the launching of potentially creative imagination into the void of that moment's radical uncertainty. The latter (as we asserted in the first paragraph of this study) is one perennial aspect of necessity for man; and an unalterable past, the other. There is no further kind of "necessity," somehow determining or structuring the moment of action and its future: knowledge of the past, and knowledge that there can be no knowledge of the future, wholly comprise that knowledge of necessity from and in consistency with which the policy-creating imagination takes its departure.

Though in this work no room is made for Fate or Destiny, our concern with the conditioning effects of political *tempi,* and of the time scales and durations pertinent successively to the power-political "crisis," to a temporary constellation of Powers, to localizations in the globe of central Power-balances, to styles in the nature of interrelationships of military force between Powers, and lastly to the cycle of a whole civilization, forbids us to suppose that Man is the master or architect of his own destiny. The youth does not select the Power to which he is involuntarily loyal; the statesman does not create his situation *ex nihilo;* revolutions in the mode of armed force happen and are not made; lastly, the creeds and great philosophies that inform civilizations appear more as revelations than as deliberate rationalistic constructions: the "historical" aspect of the contemplation that guides action no doubt reaches consciously back, for most statesmen, only over the previous few months, rarely more than a few years but, at least for those whose countries have had a few centuries of Christianity or Islam, their historical perspective upon civilizations, faiths, and sciences should dispel the illusion that statecraft and Powerhood can ever be more than briefly and restrictedly creative in mankind's affairs; and yet they demonstrate a certain scope for creation in politics.

Restrictions upon political action are not imposed only by circumstances or by others' freedom of action: the severest restraints are imposed from within. Of these, the present concluding chapter has mentioned a psychological pull toward subjection under a Power. But as yet we have made too little of limitations upon the concepts and ideas about Powers and their politics set up by the *Weltanschauung* of the time and the culture. The implicitly held theory of Power politics—the aspect of theory applied in practice, which is not often coincident with the views of scholars outside the political struggle—has a history of its own, continuous in some civilizations for several centuries, and certainly so in our own for the last millennium. Contemporary theorists and historians understandably have been chary of making overmuch of this dynamic cognitive process in their constructions, the historians from suspicion of its having been oversimplified and tendentiously exploited by propagandists, the theorists on account of its complexity and impalpability, and because in the last resort it defies universalization, e.g., though one may be able to go some way toward generalizing about the Power-system in all maritime city-kingships using bronze and little iron, oar and sail at sea, and fighting on land with infantry and from chariots, Mycenean Greece's concepts of inter-Power politics are bound to be a singularity—witness their imperfect translatability. Yet our critique and exposition of power-political theory cannot stop short of dealings with something so causally significant for power-political action as the developing idea itself of the politics of the Powers.

It is alleged that pre-Hellenistic Greeks assumed that none of the obligations of justice extended to the citizens of alien states, whereas by the end of the Republic, Romans held that some did. Let us suppose that classic Greek political discourse was indeed so restricted. That supposed fact could well assist our power-political explanations, e.g., in accounting for the collapse of the Hellenic system. But it also calls for explanation, through a reconstruction of the Hellenic Greeks' philosophies of life and nature. In Chapter 4 our account of the Biblical origins of the idea of the Powers, borrowed from G. B. Caird, involved an interpretation of still more fundamental Hebraic and Christian thought. The latter's limitations are obvious: internally, it had no conception of the polity; externally, some of its prophets deemed every alliance a failure of faith in the providence of God; that creed was made in and for hard times. In Greco-Roman philosophy one can see the possibilities of evolution and development, since after a thousand years' pause, those possibilities began again to be actualized. The tradition of faith, on the other hand, served and serves men most evidently for whom there is no Power to belong to, and when the rest of the Powers are against them. From different ages and civilizations, yet other illustrations of contrast in scope and limitation between differing concepts—or, better, languages—of Power politics could be derived; and in all cases, since the propensity to owe allegiance to a Power is (we claim) universal in man, we expect that the cues for interpreting those "languages" will be discoverable only within the several civilizations' living philosophies and religions.

In the last millennium, some of the "languages," chiefly those of Christendom, have gone through a recognizably progressive evolution. By that, we mean internal differentiation and enrichment. In Chapter 4 we considered an earlier evolution of the concept of Powerhood itself. During the last six or seven centuries, the notion that the Power, as identical with the nation-state, is to be governed by its own peculiar polity (or, in the totalitarian and in some of the newly emerged nation-states, by one or another dictatorial corruption of the polity) has been universalized—in thought, from the middle of the nineteenth, and in practice from the middle of the twentieth, century. Though at first sight this world-encompassing process appears to have been a devolution and degeneration, reducing local and communal diversities to the jejune uniformity of nationalistic *realpolitik,* it has in fact compelled recognition of distinctions between aspects of society formerly identified—nationality, territoriality, polity and Powerhood. That at least two nations can be united as a single Power with a common polity has been evident in the West since the Union of 1707. Pacific Islanders' French citizenship makes it clear that common polity, nationality and Powerhood do not necessarily involve common nativity within a territorial frontier. The nineteenth-century free-traders' case presupposed the possibility of a global economy quite independent of the Power system, even though few States have been interested to deny themselves control over the commercial basis of their economic potentials.

Has anything in this study suggested possible advances yet to be made in the language of Powers and their politics? Yes: for it appears that our elaboration of the idea of Powerhood has put us in a position to question at least two assumptions, mostly implicit, about the logical import of and connections between the concepts of "the polity" and of "the Power"; hitherto these have been taken pretty much for granted in both popular and theoretic political discourse. It has been assumed, *firstly,* that any independent and sovereign polity that freely enters into external relations is necessarily (i.e., "means the same thing as") a single impermeable sovereign Power; and *secondly* that the quality or status, "Powerhood," at any given time and everywhere, inheres wholly, solely, and without residue, in just those mutually impermeable and atomic Powers that then and there exist. Our having discussed as a logical issue (as to how the situation could be properly described—see Chapter 5, pp. 96–97) whether the British Dominions before the Second World War should be considered as having been many diverse Powers or one single Power together with the United Kingdom indicates that the two foregoing propositions are about matters of logic: the denotations of and necessary connections between the terms they mention.

The first assumption may be thought to have been falsified by the emergence of the United States of America, every sovereign State in which comprises, some have claimed, a single polity, formally sovereign, though only the federation itself constitutes a Power. But (1) we need no longer consider sovereignty to be capable of residing in just a single organ[3] of the body-politic: federal constitutions parcel out sovereign powers amongst central and local legislatures without thereby either dividing the metaphysical substance of sovereignty or leaving irremediably confused the

[3] See Hinsley, F. H., *Sovereignty* (London: C. A. Watts & Co., 1966) *passim.* I am much indebted, throughout the present chapter, to that work; but Mr. Hinsley would, I think, quarrel with me in several places, e.g., the conclusion of the sentence here annotated.

matter of which legislature has which sovereign power; and (2) the federation as a whole (e.g., the Commonwealth of Australia) constitutes a single polity, even though the electors of New South Wales may return a non-Labor government to their State House, but a majority of Labor MPs amongst their share of Members of the Federal House of Representatives. Federations do not contradict but presuppose the sovereign independent unity of the polity. The objections we shall raise to the two allegedly assumed propositions do not concern their sharing that last-mentioned presupposition, but are directed against the notion of the impermeable atomic Power.

The identity of polity and Power seems to be necessitated by the polity's need for unmitigated sovereignty over legislation and over the means of coercion (whether internally or externally directed): if the sovereign polity cannot be made subject to anyone else's positive law, and if to be a Power means to be a sovereign disposing of internal and external means of coercion, then are not the two assumptions valid? Our criticism of them must pertain, then, to the topics of legislation and coercion.

Much daily-enforced positive law is in practice now common to many distinct and sovereign polities: national police collaborate internationally against drug traffickers and certain sorts of murderers. It may not be long before they collaborate against private individuals and organizations buying or selling nuclear explosives. Nothing, indeed, can coerce a major Power into collaboration: the United Kingdom fought wars to traffic in opium. But that need not prevent our conceiving the possibility that Powers might collaborate in the enforcement of law against collective as well as against individual violence.

The conceiving of the latter possibility enables us to reformulate the conception of Powerhood established by definition in Chapter 4 and adhered to, so far as we were able, throughout this study. We too have considered Powerhood as a quasi-individuality, i.e., as inhering without residue in certain numerable and nameable societies, so that there could be no Powerhood apart from some particular Power or Powers, impermeable to each other. It is now, by contrast, possible for us to consider the Powers as so interpermeable at certain levels that there might one day be a worldwide stratum of Powerhood which inhered in internationally cooperating police forces. On the other hand, *ultra vires* of that stratum, extreme inter-Power violence (e.g., nuclear, and conventional attack above the level of insurgency) might be universally deterred, and military immobilism thus established by the diffusion to all Powers, of almost invulnerable, unalerted retaliatory forces, all violence at or below the insurgency level being dealt with by the cooperating police, enforcing positive law universally acknowledged and adjudicated upon common principles in all sovereign polities. In short, we imagine a world of sovereign independent polities that have in practice eliminated war or its threat as a device of inter-Power politics, which nevertheless could still be carried on, even to the extent of allying with or of isolating another Power, by economic, fiscal and scientific cooperation and competition in the short run, and in the long run by increasing one's potential through economic development, growth of population, and improvement in education. Though as polities the nations would still be distinct, numerable, and absolutely impermeable (for at this stage we have included no inter- or suprapolitical world organizations in the picture) they would not be so as Powers.

We are trying to show that: though, by definition, an internal-political system must be closed in the sense of being able to enforce laws (1) as to how persons may become and remain its citizens (i.e., potentially members of its governing group), (2) as to the disposal of its resources, including territory, and (3) as to the public conduct of its subjects: and, therefore, it must always be a distinct individual society possessing the means to maintain its own corporate integrity: yet there is no necessity in logic, i.e., in the structure of concepts concerning Powers, why the shell of Powerhood must also be closed around each polity and similarly institute an order of mutually excluding Powers. A Power-political dispensation *not* consisting of impermeable atom-like Powers would by no means be certain to maintain itself in perpetuity, and indeed could not do so except by the common political will of its member-polities. Material circumstances also, for example the situation in military technology, would have to be favorable if it were to be established in the first place. But, for our present thesis, an important necessary condition for its being established would be a widespread understanding that the two assumptions we have been criticizing were invalid.

What needs to be "understood" in all such cases is, formally, something negative: some particular connection is *not* necessary. Consider an analogy from the question whether "he that hath the sovereign power is subject to the civil laws." Hobbes maintained as a necessary truth, the negation of which was "repugnant to the nature of the commonwealth," that the sovereign was free of the civil laws, and used an argument from the infinite regress to prove it: the negation is an "error," which:

> . . . because it setteth the laws above the sovereign setteth also a judge above him, and a power to punish him; which is to make a new sovereign; and again for the same reason a third, to punish the second; and so continually without end, to the confusion, and dissolution of the commonwealth.[4]

But many developed "commonwealths" now make provision for suit by private and corporate individuals against the sovereign (e.g., the Crown),

[4] Thomas Hobbes, *Leviathan,* Chapter 29, Section 5.

with no risk of dissolution. Hobbes's otherwise-valid argument, which does indeed establish that a single sovereignty must inhere in some finite (though, partly open) set of persons, i.e., the Power-polity, is vitiated by one of its presuppositions—that this single inherent sovereignty can be exercised only by *either* a single supreme person or supreme assembly, free of the law, *or* by a hierarchy utterly subordinate to the supreme person or persons: ". . . all judicature is essentially annexed to the sovereignty; and therefore all other judges are but ministers of him or them that have the sovereign power."[5] By analogy: though the exercise of Powerhood is ineradicable from politics, and though (by our definition) every actual Power consists of a finite, open set of persons, it need not be the case that Powerhood is exercised in a system of Powers only by each of the latter severally. Internally, legal sanctions might be executed by "officers of the law" against the person(s) exercising other aspects of the sovereignty inherent in the Power-polity, e.g., against a royal person or a Prime Minister: externally a Power might be subject to coercion—not by the other Powers' severally internationalized or supranationalized police forces but—by the working of the system of Powers insofar as what issues from it is not the specifically intended effect of any particular Power's or Powers' policy.

We have been in a position to criticize and, perhaps, to correct the two assumptions under discussion, only on account of our having previously singled out and defined the concepts of a Power and of Powerhood, and having sketched in the history of thought about them. Now (as was evident in our brief account of Chapter 4, pp. 77–85, and elsewhere in this work) the idea of the Powers began as mythical, and—after more than a millennium of assimilation to the unitary ideas of the *imperium* and of the City of the World, when it was juxtaposed in various ways to the idea of the Church—was secularized as a *practical* term chiefly employed by statesmen and critics of statescraft. As a distinct concept, it has not been much used in the debates of traditional political philosophy; indeed, "power politics" and the German *"Macht Politik"* are not quite at home in the other political languages of Europe: *"En français, l'expression 'politique de puissance' rend un son étrange, comme si elle était traduite d'une langue étrangère."*[6] So it seemed necessary to coin the word "Powerhood" for the abstract quality (cf. "nationhood"); to force the meaning of "a Power" into formal definition; and yet to use capitals for these words, partly to avoid confusion with "power" or with the interpretation of "power politics" as maximization of State power by "political man"; and partly also to keep in mind those mythical overtones of "Principalities and

[5] *Ibid.*

[6] Raymond Aron. *Paix et Guerre,* 3rd Ed. (Paris: Calmann-Lévy, 1963), p. 58. The writer has learnt much from Professor Aron's trenchant work.

Powers" which even nowadays the political usage of the expression still gives forth. The writer's hope, in so distinguishing the aspect of Powerhood in Power politics, has been to open up ideas for the diminishing of its influence, and for the increasing of that of the polity, which alone ensures the outward liberties of the person and which creates part of the room essential for their exercise.

III

If demonstrable progress in articulation and enrichment of the philosophy of external politics might contribute to the civilizing and humanizing —limited, insecure—of its practice, we ought to be careful to anticipate how that extending of the abstract language may affect the concrete theory of Power politics, especially as developed in this study. We have already noticed somewhat disrupting consequences for the theory of dynamics, as expounded in Chapter 7, pp. 151–165. Firstly, historical occasions which have changed and enriched the concepts of Powerhood and inter-Power relations coincided with only some of the system-changing epochs, already noted in this study, and were connected with only some of the more concrete causes of dynamic change. Secondly, when into Power relationships which are coming to form a single worldwide system there is introduced a potentially progressive intellectual subprocess, then at least some of the systemic changes in the politics of the Powers have to be categorized as unique and singular events, necessarily not amenable to explanation by the universal propositions of theory—*viz.*, of the theory of dynamics. A serious attempt to push that theory to its limits at last reveals the logical inappropriateness of the theoretical enterprise. History, though history informed by the categories and concepts generated in the attempt to theorize, reasserts itself as the native language of politics, and as the proper mode of explaining—see Chapter 3—systemic change.

This avowal of the limitations of theory may help resolve an awkwardness discernible in our schematizing the more prolonged of the durations significant for the politics of the Powers—i.e., the age, the dispensation, even the period. Except for the ages of Rome and of the Empire in China, we lose sight of Power politics itself at the perspective point of a whole age or dispensation. Theory also loses its grip; for, *pace* Spengler and Toynbee, the twentieth century has not yet the "language" for a cogent *theory* of civilizations and civilizational change—these are still topics for history written in plain English. Yet we were bound to refer to them in the dynamic theory of Power politics, because the material, social and intellectual characters of civilizations provide the matrices that differentiate systems of Powers from each other.

The theory of statics, on the other hand, may be thought to escape the fate of the theory of dynamics by virtue of its dealing—in some, at least, of the quite limited areas in which we have allowed it to have application—with processes brief enough to be unaffected by the evolution of fundamental ideas about the nature of Power politics. Such evolution is, on the whole, so gradually divulged as not to change the terms of power-political transactions in less than a generation or so. Furthermore, some parts of the theory of statics (e.g., Riker's Size Principle, so far as it is valid) concern universal and pervasive political phenomena—in this case, coalition formation—that conceptual change could not affect. But if the occurrence of a revolutionary change in the nature and function of Powerhood such as that adumbrated above, pp. 285–286, is conceivable, its explanation would call for the construction of entirely new families of models in the field of statics. For example, further imputations (see Chapter 10, pp. 213–218) would be needed to take account of the responses that could be made by the administrators of denationalized aspects of Powerhood. The latter, too, should be represented in an *n*-Power model as the $n + i^{th}$ agent or "player." For example, strategic models such as ours of Chapter 6, pp. 129 *et seq.*, based on the notion of a capitulation point, might be modified so as to represent an inter-Power conflict in which the instruments of coercion are not armed forces but, for example, currency reserves expended to cause devaluation by a rival; access to much better markets; influence with an electorally important national minority. Rulers for the time being of a polity under threat of such coercion might decide to capitulate without actually fighting, to the extent of agreeing to partial secession, or to partial or total abrogation of sovereignty, or to permanent partition. Such models might be formally little different from economic ones for duopolistic or oligopolistic competition, though the measure of evaluation employed in them would remain, not a utile, but the political evaluation indicated by the choice of capitulation point.

The question thus arises again, whether the extreme abstractness of all such models does not so narrow the *range* of situations for which they might be preferred as explanation (even though it may well increase their power to explain such rare situations as they do manage to apply to) that the entire enterprise of model building for power-political theory is exposed as trivial. It would be imprudent to discount the possibility of future inventions in logic and mathematics that might provide nontrivial solutions to problems now apparently insoluble, in the way that the invention of game theory itself provided unexpected solutions to previously unmanageable problems. Chapter 2 indicated an approach, the formalizing of analysis of transactions conducted in radical uncertainty; uncertainty to which anticipation of conceptual progress in thought about the nature of the transaction itself might very well contribute. Our approach, as the reader may recall, was to take radical uncertainty as the normal state of affairs, and to interpret as variants of it (1) uncertainty about the outcomes of rational free choice amongst known or expected alternatives, (2) statistical uncertainty, and (3) statistical certainty, i.e., very high probability. The implications of that approach seem to argue still further for the historical and against the universal-theoretical mode of inquiry into Power politics. Nevertheless, models of the inter-Power system that embody the approach through radical uncertainty are in principle capable, perhaps surprisingly, of supplying forecasts (as well as—see Chapter 3—retrospective explanations). For example, a model in statics devised during 1956 forecast the mid-60s disarray of Eastern and Western blocs insofar as that has issued from the development of long-range thermonuclear strike forces. Such forecasts, we consider, are not appropriately designated as scientific predictions, since it is not by universal propositions ("general laws") that they are mediated: the findings of power-political theory reviewed in this study include no laws except our modified version of Riker's Size Principle, which was so generalized as to be of little use for prediction or for detailed historical explanation. Yet forecasting of some kind is a necessary condition of any deliberate political action, and an imaginatively conceived model can provide a base, not wholly subjective, for forecasts. Models, of course, are susceptible to "perspective-dissolving surprise" (see Chapter 2 throughout); but that liability can be reduced by historical criticism of one's picture of the current situation and (see Chapter 3, pp. 62–68) by meditation upon the philosophy and the attempted theory, even though unsuccessful, of Powers and their politics.

IV

In the present chapter we have found cause to revise formerly implicit presuppositions concerning (1) the connections between polity and Power, and (2) the possible ways in which Powerhood, though ineradicable from human relations, might be distributed amongst sovereign and interacting polities. Should we consequently revise as well our statement (Chapter 1, p. 4) that those in a position to take "statesmanly action . . . must be in any age much fewer than those taking action in internal politics"? Need one question whether the actions of these few are ". . . often momentous; and . . . always more or less in the dark"?

A world order that, for example, made it convenient to settle much conflict of interest between polities by reference to an international court or tribunal, and that enmeshed Power politics, more than now, in supranational organizations, programs and conventions, would indeed extend the statesman's range of reliable expectation, and dispel some of the dark he must act in—but only some. A world order that had rendered armed force in its most destructive form self-defeating, and that had "denationalized" the policing of lesser acts of violence, would indeed have reduced the momentousness of some of his acts of policy—yet he could still dispose of formidable economic, social and cultural instruments of power-political coercion. In no possible order, above all, would statesmen ever be numerous: not because the ability is scarce, as is supreme logical or artistic talent (cf. the engaging estimate attributed to Harry Truman, that some two million Americans had it in them to be President of the United States) but because the number of available positions cannot be much greater than the number of sovereign polities; for amongst the ruling group in each, only a handful can be assigned the externally-representing and Janus-faced role. Thus even those changes in the world order that embody a demonstrably progressive refining and civilizing of the categories and of the instruments of inter-Power politics can neither dispense with, nor change the character of, the role of "statesmen"—i.e., of the agents whose interactions (which throughout we have conceived of as typically a "conversation") comprise the power-political process. The latter, admittedly, forms only one strand in a more general process—the conduct of inter-Power or international relations (the strand which, incidentally, this study has concentrated upon, neglecting many others equally as important). But, we have contended, it alone of them can never be eliminated from human life. There will always be a few men representing their several societies in the conversation of external politics, and their conduct will retain the characteristics of power-political action, which is always irreversible, decisive, partisan, debatable, ambiguous, ephemeral. The outcome, often unintended, of such action and interaction may be sometimes a great change, though not of the most profound kind, nor at the level where a civilization's thought and outlook are changed—those of its statesmen included. Consider the effects of the fifteenth-century *Devotio Moderna,* a new education provided by the Brethren of the Common Life; or those of the Royal Society; the first on the Northern Renaissance, the Reformation and the Counter-Reformation, the second on the scientific movement: what issued from each was plainly ruled by the same spirit in which respectively the Brethren and the Fellows began their work; statecraft cannot conjure up such power, nor contrive at those depths.

Statecraft, however, has a scope of its own—one in which scientific, scholarly, philosophic or religious movements have shown themselves incapable of implementing even such changes in world order as they themselves have envisaged. Suppose it became possible to render force self-defeating as an instrument of policy, then the required realignment of Powers, the redirection of the other still useable (e.g., economic) instruments, the proposing of any needed formal inter-Power agreements, would all have to be effected by statesmen. Only some part of such tasks, moreover, can be assigned to bureaucracies that work by rule, precedent, convention and established policy; much will always be a matter of *demarche*—the characteristic initiative of external politics, enacted without benefit of established rules.

Consequently the investigation of statecraft must be at basis historical. We have agreed, nevertheless, that quantitative methods can be fruitful—e.g., for discovering the peculiar style, the guiding world picture, the favored strategies and the feeling for *tempo* of the individual statesman and of the nation's corps of diplomats.

At the conclusion of Chapter 12 we suggested in what ways the critic of Power politics might be necessarily committed to the making of evaluations in the objective study of his subject. Though it was decided that his commitment differed from that attributed to the (internal) political scientist, we noticed that these two diverse commitments shared a common ethos: both meant the valuing of personal initiative, of liberty, of creative imagination, of cooperating responsibility; both presupposed these valuables, whatever the psychological origins of their being valued, to be promoted—and in the case of liberty, promoted solely—through the activity of politics, often indeed through political conflict. Neither commitment, it was clear, is idealist or utopian, setting up final forms for politics or ultimate goals for the world-historical process: but both might be characterized as hopes for the subjugating and humanizing of Powerhood, the one in its internal, the other in its external aspect.

In the present chapter we have returned to the idea of the statesman's act, during conversation and negotiation, as free and as potentially creative. The inquirer into Powers and their politics, then, though by no means aspiring to a climax for the power-political process after which it should "wither away," will value most highly, nevertheless, the uncommon political act that begins from a new vision and that does not suppress the interests of one party or another but, by creating in imagination a new possible world for both, enables the former conflict of interests to be transcended.

Index